ALSO BY STEPHEN M. SILVERMAN

BOOKS

*Where There's a Will:
Who Inherited What and Why*

David Lean

*The Fox That Got Away:
The Last Days of the Zanuck Dynasty
at Twentieth Century–Fox*

Public Spectacles

TELEPLAY

*Hot on the Trail:
The Search for Love, Sex, and Romance in the Old West . . .
and Its Legacy in the New*

Dancing on the Ceiling

Stanley Donen and His Movies

Dancing

on the

Ceiling

Stanley Donen and His Movies

Stephen M. Silverman

with an introduction by
Audrey Hepburn

Alfred A. Knopf   New York

1996

This Is a Borzoi Book
Published by Alfred A. Knopf, Inc.

Copyright © 1996 by Stephen M. Silverman
Introduction copyright © 1996 by The Estate of Audrey Hepburn

A portion of the chapter titled "Curtain Call" originally appeared as "A Right Song and Dance" in *The Times Magazine*, December 11, 1993. Reprinted with permission © 1993 Times Newspapers, Ltd., One Pennington Street, London E1 9XN, England.

Owing to limitations of space, all other permissions to reprint from previously published material may be found immediately following the index.

Library of Congress Cataloging-in-Publication Data
Silverman, Stephen M.
    Dancing on the ceiling : Stanley Donen and his movies / Stephen M.
Silverman ; with an introduction by Audrey Hepburn.—1st ed.
        p.   cm.
    Filmography: p.
    Includes bibliographical references and index.
    ISBN 0-679-41412-6
    1. Donen, Stanley.   2. Motion picture producers and directors—
United States—Biography.   I. Title.
PN1998.3.D65S55   1996
791.43'0233'092—dc20
[B]   95-22589
                                                            CIP

Manufactured in the United States of America
First Edition

To Charlene Stolper

Art is the magic whose lonely trick, here and there, keeps the notion going that the human soul is full of wonders.

BEN HECHT

Contents

Introduction

HOW I wish that early in my career someone had warned me, "Now, one day people will be asking you for anecdotes about the films you made."

If only that had been the case, then I might have started keeping a little diary and filling it with personal observations about some of the extraordinary people with whom I've worked and the times we shared.

Most useful of all, especially as I gaze in absolute horror at these blank pieces of paper before me, I could be relying on this sadly nonexistent private journal instead of my own shaky memory.

That minor confession out of the way, I can easily state that no matter how long the passage of time, or how great the physical distance between us, there is one person whose very name makes me smile in total delight whenever I think of him. And that's Stanley Donen.

Stanley has been an important part of my life for more than thirty-five years. I think of Stanley first as a friend and then as "a famous film director." Of course, there are other great, well-known filmmakers, but take my word, there is only one Stanley Donen.

Stanley is a master moviemaker. His knowledge of film is boundless, from his clever camera technique and choreographic grace, to his finely tuned musical ear, to his exquisite taste in color design and story sense. Most important, in my estimation, is that he combines these remarkable professional talents with an extraordinary amount of sensitivity and patience, and, above all else, a *tremendous* sense of humor.

As a director, Stanley has time and again generously provided insecure actors such as myself the reassurance and courage they need to give him their absolute best. I should know. I have had the good fortune to make three pictures with Stanley—*Funny Face, Charade,* and *Two for the Road.*

Only for Stanley would I have jumped into the deep end of a pool without knowing how to swim.

Only for Stanley would I have climbed behind the wheel of a sports car without knowing how to drive.

And only for Stanley would I have shown the nerve to dance with Fred Astaire.

That last feat, accomplished while making *Funny Face,* was some experience, and I'll never forget the morning I was to meet Fred for the first time. We were to begin rehearsals at the studio in Hollywood, and I remember being so shaken that I threw up my breakfast. Stanley, himself having been a dancer, was remarkably encouraging, but on that particular day I was so ready to crumble that no words of comfort from anyone could have sufficed. And Fred, perhaps, was nervous too, over how he was going to get on with me.

Well, unlucky fellow, he had every right to worry, because sure enough, as soon as we started on the rehearsal stage, the worst that could have happened did. I was tripping all over Fred's feet. I could barely walk, let alone dance with him. I'm sure he and Stanley were silently thinking to themselves: My God, what are we going to do with this clumsy girl?

But if they did, they never let me in on it. Fred, always the gentleman, only said, "That's marvelous, but let's try it again." And so we did. (It was a tiny bit better that time.) And again. (Better still, but nowhere up to his standard, I could tell.) And again, until finally, long hours later, under the quiet, ever watchful eye of Stanley and Fred himself, I was dancing with Fred Astaire. *Imagine—dancing with Fred Astaire!*

Another marvelous leading man Stanley introduced me to was Cary Grant, although, I must confess, I very much doubt if I left him with the best first impression. Cary and I had never met before we did *Charade,* so there we all were in Paris, about to have dinner at some terribly smart bistro. As it was early spring, Cary, who always dressed impeccably, was wearing an exquisite light-tan suit. I know I was thrilled to meet him, and I must have been terribly excited, because not ten seconds after we started chatting I made some gesture with my hand and managed to knock an entire bottle of red wine all over poor Cary and his beautiful suit.

He remained cool. I, on the other hand, was horrified. Here we'd only just been introduced! If I somehow could have managed to crawl under the table and escape without ever having to see him again, I happily would have. Instead I attempted my best under the circumstances. I apologized and apologized. Stanley, though I could hardly look at him, diplomatically concealed his acute embarrassment, while Cary, still dripping wine, nonchalantly removed his jacket and pretended, very convincingly, that the stain would simply go away.

Rehearsing for *Funny Face*
(1956): Audrey Hepburn,
Stanley Donen, and, on
piano, the producer,
Roger Edens

But in the back of my mind I wondered, After what I've just done, how could I ever face this man again, let alone make a movie with him?

(Cary solved my situation like the true gallant he was. The next day he sent over a tin of caviar and a card telling me not to worry about the suit or anything. Then, wouldn't you know, in the movie Stanley had me mess up Cary once more, this time by "accidentally" flinging a scoop of ice cream on him.)

Two for the Road happens to contain one of my favorite scenes in all my movies. That business about changing outfits in the car. That's something I've done in real life. Also that incident about sneaking food into the hotel because the dining room's so expensive, only to find out later that the meals would have been included in the price of the stay. That's happened too. As for the picture itself, I must confess to having been uncertain about taking on the role, but it was Stanley who, through sheer persistence, convinced me to accept it. Freddie Raphael had done a brilliant script, perhaps one that was slightly ahead of its time. It was extremely sophisticated, both in its exploration of the various stages of the man's and woman's infatuation with one another and in the way the story played itself out backward and forward in time. I can't help but think that if the movie were to come out today, it might be more successful than it was. But who really knows about these things?

As for Stanley himself, the record speaks for itself. He was a boy wonder at M-G-M. He made *On the Town* when he was only in his twenties, and then he went on to direct so many memorable pictures. He made *Indiscreet* with Cary and Ingrid Bergman, a super movie. And those brilliant musicals, like *Singin' in the Rain*—that one is everybody's favorite, isn't it?—and *Seven Brides for Seven Brothers,* which was tremendously successful. Not bad for a kid.

Professionally, I can tell you, Stanley works not only with the precision of a dancer, which is his training, but with the experienced eye of an artist who knows exactly what he wishes to capture and convey.

Audrey Hepburn and Stanley Donen in the studio-built darkroom where Fred Astaire will declare his love for Hepburn's "funny face"

That's what gives his pictures their special look and feel, and what makes him a master moviemaker.

Not that I mean to make him sound totally serious. Far from it. When you're with Stanley, be prepared to fall on the floor giggling. He himself has the greatest laugh. In Paris while we were making *Funny Face,* we had a running gag, using Anglo-Franco terms in the wrong way. For example, when the light would come on in airplanes and alert us to stop smoking, it would read "*Ne pas fumer.*" That's when we'd all look at each other and say, "It's time to stop fuming."

Once, Stanley, who at the time was still perfecting his French, was photographing Fred and me floating down the stream on the little raft at the end of the picture. Stanley wanted to dress up the scene by having us followed by a flock of swans as the picture faded out—only the swan wrangler, as we called him, was late with his cue. And so, with the camera rolling, a desperately frantic Stanley started yelling at the top of his lungs, "*Les singes! Les singes!*"

What he meant to say was, "*Les cygnes!*" or swans. Instead he was calling out for monkeys.

And that—even without the benefit of a secret little diary—is what I so happily remember when I think about my life and times with Stanley Donen. We worked hard and we laughed hard.

One last "diary" entry, if you will indulge me. Rather early on in *Funny Face,* I got to sing—in my own voice, thank you very much—a tender and wistful song by George and Ira Gershwin, called "How Long Has This Been Going On?" Of course, it had to do with love. In the case of the impressive film legacy of Stanley Donen, which also has a very great deal to do with love, "this" has been going on for fifty years.

Dear Stanley, what I wouldn't give to see it go on another fifty, at least.

AUDREY HEPBURN
Tolochenaz, Switzerland
September 1992

Prelude

WHEN THE magic of movies is discussed—this is before intergalactic space cruisers and cyborgs took to cluttering our consciousness—certain time-tested sequences inevitably pop to mind, moments driven by dynamic screen personalities being shown to the best of their advantage. Consider the pleasures of watching a love-drunk Fred Astaire dancing on the ceiling of his London hotel room, or an equally besotted Gene Kelly determinedly sloshing about the gutter of a rain-soaked California street, or three carefree, hyperglandular sailors, taking in the unbridled joys of a glistening metropolis called New York.

These small but not inconsiderable separate samplings—there are more to follow—share one common human characteristic: Perched behind the camera, peering through its various lenses, loomed one director, Stanley Donen. Quick-witted. High-aspiring. And the unsung background force responsible for changing the face and form of the American movie musical.

What Donen, starting in the early 1940s with sequences he contributed to *Cover Girl* and *Anchors Aweigh,* brought to the slowly stagnating genre was a new and much required level of energy, color, and maturity. Before his efforts, Hollywood studios rendered reliable if clunky backstage musicals, or else syrupy, snail-paced concoctions, recognizable for being fancifully dressed yet hollow at their core. With the arrival of Donen, musicals snapped to and noticeably came of age, integrating in a naturalistic fashion the elements of song, dance, plot, and realistic character motives. Where once waltzed effete noblemen, who found their romance at courtly balls, now tap-danced Average Joes, who fell head over heels—literally—for the girls next door. All the more admirable is that at the time Donen directed his first musicals—*On the Town, Royal Wedding,* and *Singin' in the Rain*—the precocious filmmaker was still in his twenties and considered the boy wonder of the Arthur Freed Unit at Metro-Goldwyn-Mayer. More impressive, perhaps, is that when he started commanding the shots for Rita Hayworth and Gene Kelly behind the camera on *Cover Girl,* Stanley Donen was nineteen.

Neither did the mature Donen, by then an independent producer-director operating out of London, disappoint once he turned his attention to sharp-witted, European-dressed love stories. Think of Cary Grant and Ingrid Bergman, both ravishing looking and shadowed by her Rolls-Royce, strolling along the Thames in *Indiscreet* as they consider the very real ramifications of his very imaginary marriage to another woman. Or the Audrey Hepburn of *Charade,* taking the awkward matter of first-time physical intimacy with Cary Grant directly in hand when she coquettishly inserts her index finger into the cleft of her leading man's chin. Her question to him as the two ride the lift of her Paris hotel: "How do you shave, in there?" Or Hepburn once again, this time somewhere in the south of France in *Two for the Road,* as she and an equally smitten Albert Finney glance curiously at a somber middle-aged couple sitting in a hotel café. "What kind of people sit like that without a word to say to each other?" Finney asks under his breath.

The resounding answer: "Married people."

WHETHER THEY were examining a different perspective on wedded bliss or devising a new way to convey a particular dance movement, Donen pictures continually managed to break established rules. Sometimes, in fact, dialogue proved not to be a necessary component at all. (Movies had, after all, begun as a strictly visual medium; Donen was lucky to have come along when he could at least employ music, and lots of it.) In his robust *Seven Brides for Seven Brothers,* for instance, the great seduction—of the seven virgins, of the filmgoer—was not in spoken odes to love but in the impressive footwork when the strapping Pontipee brothers vigorously outdance the other fellows in town. In another signature Donen musical, in all probability his most personally distinctive, *Funny Face,* the director successfully combined his unerring taste for beauty and music, his ability for maximizing his actors' strengths (an outgrowth of Donen's admiration for a true artist's talents), and his gift for maneuvering the camera in such a way as to involve the viewer, so that the movie's simple Cinderella story was provided its proper sound, lights, and backdrop.

We see this from the outset of one key sequence, when the funny-faced duckling of the piece is magically transformed into the graceful swan. At the fade-in, the only occupants of an otherwise completely abandoned Louvre are two casually occupied foreground figures and the gloriously lit *Winged Victory* back at the top of the stairs. It is this statue, this triumph of white marble, framed center screen, that commands our attention—for reasons that are not yet plainly evident. The two people, Marcel, an assistant, and Dick Avery, a photographer (his lithe silhouette could belong only to Fred Astaire), fiddle with equipment as they set up a fashion shoot. The music builds, dramatic variations on the opening of Beethoven's Fifth. Peering into his viewfinder, Avery shouts to the unseen model poised behind *Winged Victory:* "Jo? Jo? Jo, where are you?"

"Tell me when you're ready," she replies. The lilt in her voice auspiciously indicates that she has a surprise in store.

"I'm ready," he insists. "What are you going to do?"

"Never mind what I'm going to do. Just say 'Go.' "

"All right," he surrenders. *"Go."*

The music plays, the melody to Gershwin's "Funny Face." Audrey Hepburn, as Jo, emerges from behind *Winged Victory,* resplendent in a flowing full-length red Givenchy gown, arms extended so high that it appears she could practically fly down the grand staircase. She looks every bit like an angel herself.

"Holy Moses!" gasps Avery, frantically snapping the shutter. "You look fabulous. Stop!" he commands. *"Stop!"*

Jo keeps coming toward him. "I can't stop," she declares. "Take the picture."

"Stop!" Avery orders.

"I don't want to stop. I like it! Take the picture," Jo pleads. "Take the picture!"

The frame freezes—the music, the girl, the gown, the staircase, the *Winged Victory*—and the moment is captured, safely, artfully, permanently, as only could have been accomplished by one filmmaker.

A dance-school portrait, Columbia, South Carolina, 1933

Part 1

Dancer

Chapter 1

"That Probably Happened"

I T W A S an eight-millimeter Kodak, and I thought it was the most glorious thing," Stanley Donen said of his first movie camera. "I'd hardly ever let it out of my hands." Despite parental warnings that he could conceivably fall from the moving vehicle, the young Donen would "hang out the windows of the family car as my father drove. I'd shoot signs, the roads, trees, anything we would pass," he said. "I adored spending time with that camera beyond anything else I might have been doing as a child."

The portentous hobby was entirely self-taught, as were the lessons that followed in lens adjustments that made faraway objects appear gigantic and, inversely, close-up objects look small. "The camera itself was so primitive," Donen remembered. "In order to make it work, I had to lift a black plate to let in the light. But I loved taking pictures with it, and with my still camera too. I'd shoot whatever I could find. We had a flood once. I was thrilled."

To view his footage, as well as the handful of professional one-reelers that had been purchased at the local toy store, Donen used to sit alone in his bedroom and run the hand-cranked projector his father had presented to him on a birthday. "I eventually graduated to an automatic one," he said with pride, though his viewing method of choice was to free the sprocketed film strip from its mechanical constraints and hold the print directly to the lamp so it could be inspected with the naked eye. This way Donen could study how the frames differed one from the other, shifted from one visual composition to the next, and, when arranged with attention to a sense of order, could form one fluid, continuous scene.

"The first film I ever owned was a Keystone Kops comedy," said Donen. "Cars crashing, fire engines racing, buildings blowing up. I'd take it out of the projector, hold it up to the light, look at it carefully, then put it back and watch it all over again." For an only child like Donen, the camera was a perfect play object, because its viewfinder never required having to be shared. This, consciously or not, is the first lesson every filmmaker must learn. Donen realized it by the age of eight.

"All I knew," said Donen, "was that the camera was like a constant companion. It allowed me to withdraw into myself."

"He was always crazy about his camera," verified the writer-entertainer Kay Thompson, who knew Donen at M-G-M in the early forties, before she worked with him in 1956, on *Funny Face*. "His movie camera, his still camera, any kind of camera, which makes perfect sense when you think about it. The camera is a wonderful friend to a director. If anybody on the set is sassy, or giving other people problems, the director can be totally carefree, because the camera has already settled the argument, and beautifully."

Stanley Donen was born April 13, 1924, into loving and, as he described them, "completely middle-class" circumstances. "I was born in Columbia, South Carolina," he said, as if by identifying the location he was delivering volumes about the nature of his upbringing. Rather than risk interpretation, however, Donen openheartedly volunteered his feelings toward his hometown: "It was sleepy, it was awful, I hated growing up there, and I couldn't wait to get out."

Columbia, which even its admirers would admit is laid-back, was built at a ferry site on the Congaree, a river that rarely contained enough water to wade across. The town functions as the state capital—South Carolina has long maintained a politically conservative bent, a posture Donen would never assume—and provides the backdrop for Woodrow Wilson's boyhood home as well as the forthrightly named First Baptist Church. That latter structure was built in 1856 on what would become Hampton Street, in honor of the local antebellum hero Wade Hampton. Here, on these very premises, members of the first Secession Convention gathered to pave the way for the War Between the States, one of the strongest and most sustaining influences upon the people of the region. To any loyal Columbian, General Sherman, who burned down three-quarters of the town on February 7, 1865, would ever after into eternity be considered the very Devil himself, as would, according to Donen, a few chosen others.

"My family and I were Southerners," said Donen, "really, really Southern, and really, really American. My mother was born in Columbia, South Carolina. My father was born in Augusta, Georgia, which is just over the border. His father died in Beaufort, South Carolina,* and my mother's mother and father—that is, my maternal grandparents—are buried in the same town where they were born, Columbia, South Carolina."

Yet the family was Southern and American with a distinction. The Donens were Jewish.

"My mother's maiden name was Helen Cohen," said Donen, "and my father's name was Mordecai Moses Donen." Because of the softness of the Southern dialect, the surname is properly pronounced "Dah-nen" rather than "Doh-nen," as it may look upon first glance and is most often mispronounced. As for the decidedly un-Southern appellation Mordecai, Helen Donen, Stanley's mother, in her constant efforts to assimilate, forbade the use of the name, even within the enlightened confines of the Donen household.

"So my father was Mordie," explained his son. "It even says that on his gravestone." In a similar vein, the couple's firstborn—and for most of the boy's upbringing, the Donens' only child—was not to have been named Stanley at all, but Isaac, after Mordie's late father. "That would have been the traditional Jewish thing to do," said Stanley, "but Isaac was a name my mother felt I couldn't live with in Columbia, South Carolina. She was probably right. And somehow, my father must've been convinced that Stanley was a close derivative of Isaac, because I was named Stanley."

Stanley Donen's grandfather Isaac was killed in cold blood during a robbery that took place inside his farmhouse in Beaufort when Mordie Donen was four years old, although details surrounding the tragedy would forever remain sketchy. "All I know," Stanley Donen could furnish, "is that my father's father was murdered and his mother, Betty Donen, my grandmother, was raped and ended up in a mental institution. This guy broke into their house, shot my grandfather, and brutally attacked the mother." Mordie, who was the youngest of four children, was sent to live with his grandmother, who raised the boy as if he were a brother to his uncles and aunts, who were, in fact, relatively his age. As was later gleaned by Stanley Donen, though, the grandmother "did not believe in sending the youngsters to school."

As for Donen's mother, Helen Cohen, "She was a very interesting woman, and a very independent one," said her only daughter, Carla, Stanley's younger sister by thirteen years. "Our mother always had her priorities pretty much in order, with no baloney about her. She had just a

* Seventy miles south of Charleston.

down-to-earth intelligence. She was never dazzled by anything or anybody, including movie stars and money."*

Helen hailed from a proud, middle-class family, although plainly "one with no money to speak of," according to her son. Helen's father, Jack (Jacob) Cohen, sold wholesale jewelry to local shops, and both he and Helen's mother, the former Carrie Goldsmith, opposed Helen's selection of the unschooled Mordie as a suitor. In retaliation, the young lovers eloped in 1923, when Helen was eighteen and Mordie twenty-three.

"My memory of my father is entirely of his selling ladies' dresses," said Donen. "What he did before I was born, I don't know." The women's wear chain that employed Mordie Donen was Mangel's, a purveyor of midpriced dresses, whose closest national rival was the Lerner Shops. "My father was the district manager, and there was another store in Asheville, North Carolina, and one in Knoxville, Tennessee. There were five or six of them in all."

The local outlet, which Mordie ran, stood on one of the three small streets that constituted the unceremonious main drag of downtown Columbia, "called—what else?—Main Street," sniped native son Stanley Donen. As newlyweds, the Donens lived at 3920 Park Street, half a mile from Mordie's place of employment, until right before the birth of their son. The later address was 1729 Crestwood Drive, which is where Stanley Donen grew up. "Our house was nice," said Donen, relying upon one of his most commonly used adjectives (another is "sweet," usually in regard to people). "Nothing special, but nice." Summers would be spent at the family beach house on Pawleys Island, about a two-hour drive from Columbia.

The Donens' two-story residence on Crestwood sat on a modest-size city lot, with a large white pine planted out front and a solarium with handmade Moorish tiles attached to the rear. The entire house was done in the Spanish style, with arches over the windows, a red-tiled roof, and a coral-colored, adobe-like facade. Interestingly, it was eerily comparable in design, albeit smaller in size and dissimilar in interior decor, to the residence of the Gene Kelly character in *Singin' in the Rain*. In southern California it would have been called a bungalow, but during the thirties in Columbia, South Carolina, it was considered a fine house in one of the better neighborhoods.

"Not elaborate, but very comfortable," drawled one longtime resident. "There were always a lot of trees, nice yards, and separate garages."

---

* Asked where Stanley Donen got his sense of humor, his sister replied, "From Mars."

Donen's paternal grandparents, Isaac and Betty Donen (c. 1900), and, holding him at eight months, his maternal grandmother, Carrie Goldsmith

Many of the children who grew up in the neighborhood went on to become professionals. "Nearly everyone went to college," said the proud local. "Several became doctors. One became an oral surgeon."

"Stanley was sort of an icon figure on our block," remembered Betty Walker, who, as Betty Koty, lived two doors down from the Donens, at 1719 Crestwood. "He was a very handsome boy and kind of fun, dark and dashing looking. We'd play in the street—kick the can, hide-and-go-seek, games like that. Stanley was older, but he'd join in. He had a cute girl-friend, Yvonne Harvey, then another one, Muff Rowlette, now deceased."

As for school, Donen recalled it as far from being fun and games. "There was a chant I'd hear in the schoolyard, always directed at me," he said. "It pretty much sums up my childhood in Columbia, South Carolina, and I obviously don't like repeating it, because of the way it also offends others."

After some prodding, Donen stonily recited the perennial playground taunt:

> Roses are red,
> Violets are blue,
> I'd rather be a nigger
> Than a goddamned Jew.

"I'm afraid that probably happened," confirmed Betty Walker. "Columbia was a town with a wonderful group of Jewish people. It's just that there weren't too many of them. They were really outnumbered."

"To be Jewish in South Carolina," declared Donen, "was to be con-sidered a freak, to be thought of as contemptible, a devil, and a cheat. Every ugly stereotype ever foisted upon Jews existed there, and I think I know how this prejudice started. When the Jews began coming to the South in large numbers in the 1850s, first from Germany [the original home of the Cohens] and then from Eastern Europe and Russia [home of the Donens], as they got off the boats dressed in rags and looking the way they did, that was the image of Jews that Southerners perceived, and that was the image that stuck. It was not like being a Jew in Los Angeles or New York, where large Jewish communities have long existed and Jews form part of the traditional fabric of life. In Columbia, South Carolina, we were totally isolated because there were so few of us. And as a child, to be so alienated, to be called names every time I turned around, it was hor-rible, just horrible."

Donen's boyhood religious training was negligible, though he would grow up to be conversant with show-business Yiddish. Mordie Donen, on

At the family beach house, Pawleys Island, South Carolina: Helen Donen, née Cohen, with her son, c. 1926

Stanley's father, Mordie Donen, 1925. "The only regret of my entire life," Stanley Donen admitted in 1995, "is that I did not honor my father's wish that I be bar mitzvahed."

the other hand, was a deeply pious man, and Columbia, despite the relatively few number of Jews who lived there, managed to offer two separate congregations.

"We attended the Reform temple," said Donen, "not the Orthodox *shul*." Though the family belonged to the Tree of Life congregation, founded in 1896, worshiping there was sporadic for the boy. "Right before I got to be thirteen," he recalled, "my father very much wanted me to be bar mitzvahed. My mother didn't care, and to be honest, I loathed the whole idea."

To please his father, Donen attended Hebrew lessons, only to "discover, to my surprise, that what they were teaching me were the symbols for things but not their meanings. I was learning to make these noises—*huch, achad, hech*—and not being given the *faintest* idea of what I was talking about. Finally, I went home and said to my mother, 'Really, this is silly. I could be going to the movies.' "

DESPITE DONEN'S insistence that he grew up in a backwater town, Columbia's population in the twenties was more than sixty thousand, large enough to warrant the town's having its own vaudeville house, the Columbia (Al Jolson played there on March 19, 1909, when he was still part of Lew Dockstader's Minstrel Troupe). Neither did the town suffer for a lack of movie houses during Donen's developmental phase. Of the five cinemas located in Columbia—the Palmetto, the Ritz, the Strand, the State, and the Carolina—three were to be found within the limited confines of Main Street.

"Every day after school, I'd drop off my books at my father's store, then go to the movies," said Donen, whose regular afternoon routine coincided with most of the townspeople's either heading toward one of Columbia's numerous fishing holes or taking a nap. There in the cinema, during the Depression thirties, the boy would sit spellbound in the dark in the same manner that subsequent generations of American children would grow up being glued to television sets and computer screens.

"Westerns, comedies, dramas—it didn't matter to me," said Donen. "I loved going to the movies. At home we'd listen to the radio. We'd sit and stare at it." Jack Benny, with his deft comic timing, was an early hero, as were the sundry protagonists on *G-Men, Gangbusters,* and *Amos 'n' Andy,* programs with rock-ribbed narratives and characters to match.

"But what I really did," said Donen, "was go to the movies. I'd go every day, and then my father used to come find me after he'd close up the shop, and he'd take me home by the hand." Donen did not always depart willingly. "One afternoon my father came to get me, but I was watching *Flying Down to Rio,*" he said. "I was nine, and I'd never seen anything like it in my life. I'm not sure I ever have since. It was as if something had exploded inside me."

Containing the flimsiest of plots—will a Copacabana Beach hotel receive its entertainment license in time for its grand opening?—but enough slapstick and aerial photography to capture the attention of any nine-year-old, the black-and-white 1933 RKO musical boasted one remarkable distinction: It marked the first pairing of Fred Astaire and Ginger Rogers, albeit confined to wisecracking, second-banana roles (the actual stars of the picture were a sultry Dolores Del Rio and a heavily mascaraed Gene Raymond). Astaire and Rogers's attention-grabbing first dance together, "The Carioca," in which they floated across the screen as if attached at the forehead in the manner of Siamese twins, created a national sensation and ended up securing both performers separate star contracts at their studio.

What appealed to the preadolescent Donen upon his initial exposure to *Flying Down to Rio* was neither its "aeroplanes" nor its pre–Production

From the title number, *Flying Down to Rio* (1933)

And when he danced, thought Donen, "Everything in this world was perfect."

Code spicy patter, but Fred Astaire's first solo, "Music Makes Me." In the course of the one-minute-twenty-five-second number, the lanky performer artfully monopolized the film frame simply by letting his body respond to the rhythm of the band.

And he tap-danced.

"The basic idea," as interpreted by the film historian John Mueller, who made a formal study of Astaire, "is to suggest that the music has taken possession of Astaire's body—his feet in particular—and is forcing him to execute the blistering routine contrary to his conscious will."

"I was mesmerized," Donen admitted. "I could not stop watching Fred Astaire dance. I went back to the theater every day while the picture was playing. I must've seen it at least twenty times. Fred Astaire was so graceful. It was as if he were connected to the music. He led it and he interpreted it, and he made it look so effortless. He performed as though he were absolutely without gravity." This last observation was a notion that would stick.

In contrast to the oppressive small-town atmosphere choking the boy in Columbia, "when Fred Astaire danced," Donen noticed, "everything in this world was perfect."

Seldom knowing his mother or father to refuse him any request, and seeking entrée of his own into Astaire's rarefied universe, Donen came home from the movie theater one day and announced: " 'I want to be a tap dancer. The only thing I want to be is a tap dancer.' My parents thought I was crazy, but they said okay. After all, it wasn't very common for a Jewish boy to become a tap dancer."

Donen knew music; he had been taking piano lessons at home since the age of four. He also displayed a talent for perfect recall, a gift that would never abandon him. "Stanley is one of those people who can not only remember every lyric to a song," professed the late lyricist Sammy Cahn, who worked with Donen on both of their earliest M-G-M musicals, "but he can sing you the fourth chorus performed by the third lead in the second number of the first act that was cut in Philadelphia before the show came to New York."

"I was very good on the piano by the time I was six," Donen admitted of his musical prowess. "Then I switched. I started playing the clarinet. If fate had been cruel, I would have continued playing the clarinet instead of going on to make movies. Today I could be with the Los Angeles Philharmonic."

"THERE WERE some dancing schools in Columbia, South Carolina," Donen remembered. "They weren't very good, but they were the only ones around. In class there would be eight or ten students. I'd be the only boy. They probably thought I was a sissy, but I didn't care."*

On school holidays, the boy was permitted to sharpen his skills on a more professional level. "My father spent summers at the home office of his company, which was in New York, and I got to go along. It was the worst time of the year to go to New York, given the hot, humid weather, but I loved these trips, because they meant going to the theater."

---

* Betty Walker insisted that in the neighborhood, at least, this was not the case. "If anything," she recalled, "the other kids looked up to him, because he could do something nobody else could. He could dance."

At the boy's insistence, his mother enrolled him in some New York dance schools, of a better caliber than those at home. One of Donen's earliest Manhattan instructors was Ned Wayburn, "a tall, heavy-set man who didn't look like a dancer," Fred Astaire himself remembered. "[He] was a stage director for Klaw and Erlanger, Ziegfeld, and the Shuberts. I looked upon him as a giant." Wayburn had personally taught the eleven-year-old Astaire some buck-and-wing steps in 1910, so by the time Donen enrolled in his class in the 1930s, the tutor had seen better days.

As for Broadway, "I remember every show I saw, and not just the musicals," said Donen. "It was the Depression, and you could buy a ticket for nothing." What stuck in Donen's memory was "something called *Ceiling Zero*, a flying drama," starring Osgood Perkins and written by the World War I navy pilot Frank "Spig" Wead (later played by John Wayne in John Ford's 1957 movie *The Wings of Eagles*), "and a revue with Ethel Waters singing '(We're Having a) Heat Wave.' " The Waters show, *As Thousands Cheer*, in 1933, was written by Moss Hart and Irving Berlin. Each of its sketches and numbers opened with a topical newspaper headline of the day flashing across the width of a curtain backdrop, a device Donen would adapt cinematically in *On the Town*, when he superimposed the hour of day in electric lights right to left across the width of the screen to mark the advancement of the clock.

"There was another show," recalled Donen, "with Fred Allen, *Three's a Crowd*." In it, Allen impersonated Admiral Byrd, recently returned from the South Pole. The biggest laugh came when Allen as Byrd proudly hailed his latest discovery, "five hundred thousand square miles of brand-new snow."

"I loved going to New York, with all that was going on then," said Donen. "Rodgers and Hart. Cole Porter. The Gershwins. There were playwrights. Kaufman and Hart. Hecht and MacArthur.* Sidney Kingsley. This was Broadway. There was Bob Hope. Ethel Merman. The people I used to hear at home on the radio I could actually see on the stage. As much as I loved the movies I loved Broadway."

Compounding the pull of the metropolis was Donen's own deepening sense of displacement in Columbia. Worse, his lofty position in his own household was permanently usurped on August 26, 1937, when Carla was born.

Repeating his childhood mantra, Donen said, "I couldn't wait to get out of Columbia, South Carolina. There were twelve grades, and I only

---

* Donen considered the team's 1928 *The Front Page* "probably the best American play ever written." His choice for second-best was their *Twentieth Century*.

went ten. In those days they used to skip you if you were intelligent, and as it was, I started a year earlier than I was supposed to because I wanted to go to school and my mother lied to the school board and said I was a year older. So by the time I was sixteen I was finished."

Mordie Donen strongly urged his son to enter college, a paternal desire fueled by his own circumstances. "My father had had no schooling whatsoever," said Donen. "I mean, he could read and write, but he was forced to teach himself those things. Much as it broke my father's heart, I didn't care about college. I wanted Broadway and the movies."

In truth, what Stanley Donen wanted was to be in the movies, "only I couldn't contemplate going straight to California from South Carolina. California seemed too far away. At the time, anyway, movies were thought to be a second-rate art form. They were looked upon the way we later looked at television. I mean, Kaufman and Hart didn't write for movies. Thornton Wilder didn't write for movies. Besides, even though I'm sure my parents were apprehensive about my going, I had been to New York several times."

"I think our mother had spent so much time with Stanley in New York when he was a child that the city was no longer foreign to the family," reflected Carla Davis, née Donen, long afterward. "In fact, in some ways I have to believe that our mother must've encouraged Stanley to go to New York."

Chapter 2

"An Open Cattle Call"

ONEN COULD hardly have chosen a more propitious time to try his luck in show business. With Hollywood coming off its glory year—the Motion Picture Academy's ten top nominees for 1939 were *Dark Victory, Goodbye, Mr. Chips, Love Affair, Mr. Smith Goes to Washington, Ninotchka, Of Mice and Men, Stagecoach, The Wizard of Oz, Wuthering Heights,* and the keeper of the crown, *Gone With the Wind*—so, too, was the New York theater experiencing a deservedly high level of accomplishment and prosperity.

Simultaneous to the "young, green hick," as Donen described himself, casting himself as a fifteen-dollar-a-week lodger inside a couple's apartment at 101 West Fifty-fifth Street, Broadway was embracing the Oliviers in *Romeo and Juliet,* Jane Cowl and Peggy Wood in *Old Acquaintance,* Shirley Booth in *My Sister Eileen,* Ingrid Bergman and Burgess Meredith in *Liliom,* Helen Hayes and Maurice Evans in *Twelfth Night,* Helen Craig in *Johnny Belinda,* José Ferrer in *Charley's Aunt,* Elliott Nugent and Gene Tierney in *The Male Animal,* Flora Robson in *Ladies in Retirement* (her American theatrical debut), John Barrymore in *My Dear Children* (his theatrical return), and the Lunts in Robert E. Sherwood's Pulitzer Prize–winning *There Shall Be No Night,* a play that also earned raves for a newcomer named Montgomery Clift. Musically as well, there was much to appreciate, including Ethel Waters in Vernon Duke and John Latouche's *Cabin in the Sky,* Ethel Merman in Cole Porter's *Panama Hattie,* and Victor Moore, William Gaxton, Vera Zorina, and Irene Bordoni in Irving Berlin's *Louisiana Purchase.*

"The Depression was over," said Donen, and although war had broken out in Europe, the battles seemed far enough away not to impede the goals of the young careerist. Scanning the classifieds in *Variety,* Donen spotted "one or two casting notices, both for musicals, that looked interesting." The first inquiry quickly led nowhere, but the second directed him to the crowded stage door of the Ethel Barrymore Theater, on Forty-seventh Street. "It was an open cattle call," Donen remembered. "The ad didn't mention the name of the show or any of the people involved, and I was just one of the many who tried out. They must have liked my thick accent—'cause *Ah steel tahked lak theeus*. It must've made them laugh, because I got the job."

The show turned out to be *Pal Joey,* chief among whose several distinctions was that it served as the supreme, penultimate effort in the prolific but turbulent partnership of the composer Richard Rodgers (1902–1979) and the lyricist Lorenz Hart (1895–1943). Donen was thereby catapulted into an enviable position from which any greenhorn might benefit, especially so ardent a student of the musical form as he was.

"Rodgers and Hart shows of 1935 to 1943 expanded the scope, style, and subject matter for the American musical theater—crossing frontiers into territories which had never before admitted singing and dancing," noted cultural historian Gerald Mast. Known for the bright burst of wit they brought to their shows (their string of stage hits included *The Garrick Gaieties, A Connecticut Yankee, Evergreen, Jumbo, On Your Toes, Babes in Arms, I'd Rather Be Right, I Married an Angel, The Boys from Syracuse, Too Many Girls,* and *Higher and Higher,* while their movie work, although never on an artistic par with their Broadway output, included numbers in *Love Me Tonight, Hallelujah, I'm a Bum, Hollywood Party,* and *Mississippi*)*, the New York songwriters began their creative marriage in 1919. Hart at the time was a twenty-three-year-old Columbia University School of Journalism graduate, while Rodgers was a sixteen-year-old Columbia aspirant seeking early admission from De Witt Clinton High in the Bronx. Their first encounter, in the Hart family's West 119th Street apartment, left Rodgers speechless over his future collaborator's appearance. Unshaven and unkempt, Hart could have passed for a hobo and, at five foot nothing, with a large head and small frame, was, according to Rodgers, "gnomelike." Young, wiry Rodgers, meanwhile, bore an uncanny resemblance to an accountancy student. But that Sunday afternoon on the Upper West Side, the two person-

---

* Among the innumerable song standards to emerge from these shows and films: "Manhattan," "Blue Moon," "Isn't It Romantic?," "With a Song in My Heart," "Ten Cents a Dance," "The Lady Is a Tramp," "I Wish I Were in Love Again," "My Heart Stood Still," "Thou Swell," "My Romance," "My Funny Valentine," "Johnny One Note," "Have You Met Miss Jones?," "This Can't Be Love," "Little Girl Blue," "Falling in Love with Love," "Spring Is Here," "Lover," "Glad to Be Unhappy," "The Most Beautiful Girl in the World," "Where or When," "There's a Small Hotel," "Mountain Greenery," and "Dancing on the Ceiling."

alities clicked. Both Rodgers and Hart discovered they shared an unwavering admiration for Guy Bolton, P. G. Wodehouse, and Jerome Kern, and sought to follow in the footsteps of such accomplished men of the musical stage.

The first Rodgers and Hart song to be published and performed professionally was "Any Old Place with You," and it contained two lines that more or less summed up the whole of its parts:

> I'd go to hell for ya,
> Or Philadelphia!

Despite its overtly unripe quality, the ditty made its way into the show *A Lonely Romeo,* a Broadway vehicle at the Casino Theater that starred and was produced by the comedian Lew Fields. The newcomers and the experienced vaudevillian had been brought together by the same fellow who had introduced Rodgers to Hart, one Phillip Leavitt, a Columbia classmate of Rodgers's brother Mortimer and part of a family who rented a summer house next to Fields's in Far Rockaway. Thanks to "Any Old Place with You," the team of Rodgers and Hart was launched—though five dry years would ensue before it reached solid footing with *The Garrick Gaieties*—and the two extremely dissimilar men would remain partnered for the next twenty-four years, until Hart's final descent into alcohol.*

In assessing the new theatrical ground that Rodgers and Hart broke during their career together, Gerald Mast said, "The show that went furthest and deepest into that territory was *Pal Joey,*" which effectively blew the lid off the Victorian candy box that had been the Broadway musical.

ALTHOUGH the form of the "light opera," as it came to be termed, dated back to Colonial times, the first original musical to debut in America came about entirely by accident, in 1866. A Parisian ballet troupe, scheduled to perform in downtown Manhattan, arrived to discover their venue burned to the ground. William Wheatley, manager of the neighboring Niblo's Garden, at Broadway and Prince Streets, was hastily persuaded by the dancers' enterprising impresario to intersperse musical routines featuring the stranded Parisians with the dramatic scenes of Wheatley's already

---

* As rocky as was Rodgers and Hart's collaboration during the eventual creation of *Pal Joey,* it was to become totally untenable during the development of their next Broadway show, *By Jupiter.* That schism ultimately thrust Rodgers into a new partnership, with Oscar Hammerstein II, and toward a far more grandiose style.

established production of *Faust*. Thanks largely to the skimpy French costumes of the dancers, the dramatic-musical hybrid, which was called *The Black Crook*, caught on, and thus the American musical was officially born. The show ran an unprecedented 475 performances and spawned fifteen separate New York revivals.

From then on, through various refinements, musical comedies adhered to a fairly standard formula, in which a boy met a girl, the boy sang to the girl, and in the end the boy got the girl. (Despite the epochal nature of the Edna Ferber plot and the Greek chorus of racial tension, Jerome Kern and Oscar Hammerstein's 1927 *Show Boat* followed the same predictable moral path; Magnolia's virtue was rewarded, while Julie's lack of it was not.) *Pal Joey* was to break that sugar-encrusted mold and do so with no apologies: The boy met the girl, the boy sang to the girl, and in the end the girl dumped the boy—before her husband found out.

"It was a hard-edged piece of theater," said Donen. "Some performances, we could sense the discomfort of the audience, on matinee days in particular. Theatergoers had never seen characters like this in a musical before. Most people just hated it."

Joey Evans, the antihero of the piece, was born in the October 22, 1938, issue of *The New Yorker*, nearly two years to the day before the start of rehearsals on his musical incarnation. Conceived as a semiliterate letter from Joey, a wayfaring singer in cheap midwestern dives, to his New York musician friend Ted, the captivating piece was the work of the thirty-three-year-old John O'Hara (born Pottsville, Pennsylvania, 1905; died 1970), who almost single-handedly defined the then still fledgling magazine's pithy short-story style. Joey, as his missive reveals, is superficially contrite for his neglect in not having earlier thanked Ted for an opening-night telegram, then he boasts of a couple of local sexual conquests before telegraphing some job prospects.

"Your old pal Joey is doing all right for himself," the correspondent relates, as he returns thirty of the fifty dollars he borrowed from Ted prior to hightailing it to Ohio.

Sixteen months after publication of the original letter, and fourteen "Joey" stories later, the playwright George Oppenheimer expressed interest in optioning stage rights. O'Hara politely declined, but the idea was sparked. O'Hara, in Hollywood to doctor dialogue for a Betty Grable musical, contacted Richard Rodgers in the East with the tantalizing suggestion that he musicalize Joey's exploits. "I got an idea that the pieces, or at least the character and the life in general, could be made into a book show," O'Hara wrote Rodgers, "and I wonder if you and Larry would be interested in working on it with me." It was an astute move on O'Hara's part; Larry Hart, despite his lofty and bankable reputation in the theater, was, like Joey, a denizen of the low life and no stranger to cheap dives. "After our working day was over," said Rodgers, "I would go home to my wife and family." As for where his partner would roam, Rodgers revealed, "My honest answer is, 'I don't know.'" He speculated that Hart would begin one of his familiar binges at Ralph's Bar on Forty-fifth Street, "in the heart of the theater district. I also know that he frequently went to the Luxor Baths to get steamed out. Other than that—what he did, where he went, and with whom—I have no idea." Perhaps Hart's greatest literary gift, his hard-boiled cynicism, was, like his rampant alcoholism, born out of a gnawing discontent with life and a repressed homosexuality. "From the start he had made it clear that he led the life he wanted and was not about to change it for anyone," Rodgers recalled long after his onetime partner's death, "though I knew it bothered him that, as he once told me, his mother was constantly nagging him to 'settle down like Dick and marry a nice girl.'"

As for Rodgers, in direct contrast to the sweetness of his melodies, which made the astringent Hart his perfect foil, he was no Pollyanna. Professional colleagues, especially the choreographer Agnes de Mille, with whom Rodgers would later work on *Oklahoma!, Carousel,* and *Allegro,* found him mercenary, temperamental, and refractory, an unquestionably gifted artist who approached his craft with the emotional detachment of a surgeon. On the occasion of Rodgers's death on December 30, 1979, after a long bout with cancer, de Mille commented pointedly to friends, "He certainly died piecemeal, didn't he?"

If not for Richard Rodgers, however, there may not have been a *Pal Joey.* Serving as the show's driving force, he began shaping the project by personally convincing the producer-director (and, ultimately, the doctor of O'Hara's troubled book) George Abbott to become involved, despite Abbott's being, on first bounce, completely turned off by O'Hara's unseemly cast of characters—beginning with the protagonist.

"IN THE SHOW," said Donen, "I sort of floated through Joey's life, which is strange, because I looked like such a child."

Act I opens with Joey's landing a job in a cheap South Side Chicago joint once its proprietor is properly satisfied that the singer is attracted to neither cocaine nor young boys. "There wasn't one decent character in the

A scene from the Broadway production of *Pal Joey,* 1940. Here Gene Kelly leads a production number. Van Johnson is in the male chorus, to rear, stage right. Donen, a fellow "waiter," leans on the table, stage left.

play except for the girl who briefly fell for Joey," said Richard Rodgers. "Her trouble was simply that she was stupid."

The dumb "mouse"—Joey's term for every woman, unless she's a "lesbo"—on whom Joey puts the make is Linda English, though it is the wealthy, married socialite, Vera Simpson, who motivates the plot by putting the make on Joey. Using her ample financial means, Vera builds him "the right club," Chez Joey, only to see the whole setup collapse when a pair of inadvertently comic blackmailers threatens to expose Vera to her spouse.

Though the show's book took as its source only two stories in the "Joey" canon, "Bow Wow" and "A Bit of Shock," the stage material remained uncommonly faithful to the spirit of O'Hara. At the same time, it managed to be a lively entertainment, relying heavily on Hart's strongest suit, wickedly clever lyrics, particularly in "Bewitched (Bothered and Bewildered)"—to wit, Vera's dreamy lament:

> Couldn't sleep
> And wouldn't sleep
> Until I could sleep where I shouldn't sleep—

Another number, "I Could Write a Book," willfully takes to task Joey's pretentiousness and illiteracy; as the original *New Yorker* stories proved, the selfish son of a bitch could barely write a letter.

Some elevation of tone was accomplished through production numbers set inside the club, such as "That Terrific Rainbow" and "A Great Big Town,"* and some all-around great hoofing, seamlessly tied together in the airtight style of George Abbott. While some found that tireless theater veteran to be as cold as steel, a trait usually chalked up to Abbott's Scandinavian ancestry, Donen perceived him otherwise and considered Abbott the very model of what an exemplary director should be.

"I found him to be a very sweet man," said Donen. "After all, he hired me. But he was extremely gifted and professional, tireless in his dedication to the job, and he carried out his responsibilities with a minimum amount of ego. He was always 'in charge,' yet in spite of his years of experience, he never closed himself off. He loved new people, he saw everything with open eyes, he always remained willing to hear, and he had an ear for humor," though that last attribute may actually say more about Donen than about Abbott.

Abbott's phenomenal career encompassed 125 shows, in which he served as either actor, playwright, producer, or director, if not a simultaneous combination of all. A native of upstate New York, Abbott entered the theater in 1913 at the age of sixteen (before setting off for Harvard), when he appeared in a play called *The Misleading Lady*. By 1925, the year before Rodgers and Hart struck with *The Garrick Gaieties,* Abbott wrote his first Broadway play, a comedy called *The Fall Guy;* the following year he directed for the first time, a murder mystery he cowrote, titled *Broadway*. By 1932, he was producing plays; in 1935, he wrote his first book for a musical, the circus-inspired *Jumbo,* which inaugurated his collaboration with Rodgers and Hart; in 1936, besides cowriting the book, he directed his first musical, Rodgers and Hart's *On Your Toes,* which gave the Broadway musical its first ballet number, "Slaughter on Tenth Avenue," and two years later Abbott took to producing musicals, kicking off with Rodgers and Hart's *The Boys from Syracuse.* Throughout the thirties, forties, fifties,

---

* The stage-framing device also alleviated that most problematic moment in a musical, positioning the character to shift from dialogue to song.

and into the sixties, George Abbott (1887–1995), with his ramrod-straight posture, his piercing blue eyes, his tall, commanding presence, was a Broadway force to be reckoned with, and even as the millennium approached, it appeared that this consummate man of theater would never stop. During the same 1993–94 season that saw Donen return to Broadway to direct what would be an ill-fated musical adaptation of *The Red Shoes,* Abbott, at the age of 106, was involved in rewriting a generally well-received revival of his 1955 *Damn Yankees.*

Recollecting the young Donen, the normally tight-lipped Abbott recalled, more than half a century after their paths initially crossed, "Stanley started out as just one of the boys. I can't say I remember anything special about him when he came in. But he turned out to be bright."

"I'M TOLD Larry Hart was a trial for Dick Rodgers because he never arrived on time, or sometimes wouldn't arrive at all," said Donen. "But he was a very friendly man, very quick-witted, and never at a loss for talent."

In formation, Donen, as chorus boy, bottom center, for *Pal Joey.* Above him, stage right, is Henning Irgens. The two women exchanging dialogue are Janet Irving (with mirror) and Tilda Goetz.

Donen witnessed an example of this "when we tried out in Philadelphia. The song 'Zip' was a great success, only Rodgers and Hart had written only one chorus." The Act II song was performed as a strip-tease by the bespectacled Melba, a journalist with intellectual leanings (played by Jean Castro), as she satirized contemporary personalities of her day.

> Zip! Walter Lippmann wasn't brilliant today.
> Zip! Will Saroyan ever write a great play?
> Zip! I was reading Schopenhauer last night.
> Zip! And I think that Schopenhauer was right.

"The number 'Zip' had nothing to do with *Pal Joey*," Donen elucidated, "but it stopped the show every night. Actually, if it had a primary function, it was because this newspaperwoman was needed to stand out front during a scenery change."

The song's appeal became plainly evident at the very first out-of-town preview, December 16, 1940, at Philadelphia's Forrest Theater. "The next day," said Donen, "Larry Hart came into the theater and everybody wanted more choruses to 'Zip!' only there weren't any, so Hart said, 'Okay.' He sat down in the back of the house and wrote out two or more choruses on a piece of paper."

> Zip! I consider Dalí's paintings passé.
> Zip! Can they make the Metropolitan pay?
> Zip! Hearing rhumba bands will drive me to drink.
> Zip! Mrs. Perkins isn't red, she's just pink. . . .

"One of Rodgers and Hart's favorite actresses, Vivienne Segal, was to be the married woman in the cast," recalled George Abbott. Segal had starred in their *I Married an Angel*, in 1938. June Havoc played Gladys Bumps, one of the two comic blackmailers, and Donen played Albert Doane, who uttered all of one immortal remark: "I'll have the same."

Several lines up on Donen was another member of the ensemble, Van Johnson, a Newport, Rhode Island, native who had gravitated to New York in 1935 as a well-seasoned young veteran of the New England theatrical circuit.

"Stanley and I were chorines together," Johnson said in 1994. Johnson lived in the same apartment building as Donen, as did the aspiring songwriters Hugh Martin and Ralph Blane, who by day were moonlighting as *Pal Joey*'s vocal coaches. "They had already composed this song, 'Buckle

Down, Winsocki,' for this musical about a prep school they were writing," recalled Johnson. "They used to drive the whole building crazy, banging the song on the piano ad nauseam."*

Donen insisted that once he left home, he completely fell out of touch with his parents "for the next sixteen years. Not a word. Don't ask me why. I loved my family, but I guess I was just so happy to be away from Columbia, South Carolina." His sister, Carla, admitting that the thirteen years existing between her and Stanley may have dulled her expertise,† nevertheless had trouble accepting her brother's dramatic claim. Van Johnson, on the other hand, canceled it out completely when he discussed Mordie and Helen's visit to New York to see their son in *Pal Joey*.

"Very lovely, very warm people," was Johnson's description of the Donens, "and very rich." When informed that his last comment contrasted sharply with Donen's own portrayal of his background as "completely middle class," Johnson backed his own assertion by stating, "Sure they were rich. Mrs. Donen was swathed in furs, and they were Jews."

After the performance, the Donens took their son and Johnson out to dinner, "to the Starlight Roof of the Waldorf-Astoria," said Johnson. "Thank God in those days I always wore a necktie to work. Xavier Cugat and his band were playing, and I'll never forget going, because it was the first time in my life I ever ate lobster thermidor. It had real sherry in the sauce."

Explaining why the Donens would have tendered such an invitation, Johnson said, "Because I was the only person in the cast who was nice to Stanley. Everybody else was so mean and used to make fun of his accent. They thought he must have been some kind of hayseed."

One of the worst perpetrators, Donen recalled, "was this other dancer in the chorus. His name was Henning Irgens and he was about forty-five years old and, I would guess, had already been in about fifty shows. And there I was, a first-timer, unbelievably green and a real beanpole. I must've weighed all of one hundred pounds. Besides my accent, I was also awkward. Oh boy, was I awkward."

One afternoon during rehearsals, Irgens sidled up to Donen and inquired, "What are you going to do about makeup? Actors are responsible for their own makeup, you know."

---

* When that prep school musical, ultimately called *Best Foot Forward,* opened on Broadway in 1941, *The New Yorker* interviewed Ralph Blane for its "Talk of the Town" column. The magazine made note of some of Blane's fellow occupants at his West Fifty-fifth Street address: "a resident ocelot, toucan, and South American bugle bird which bugled 'Yankee Doodle.'"

† "You see," said Carla Davis in 1992, "Stanley left home early and I left not at all."

Donen confessed that he hadn't given the matter any thought, "so Henning Irgens asked, 'Would you like me to help?' " Donen responded with a grateful, "Oh, that would be wonderful," and the two repaired to the local five-and-dime, where Irgens instructed the eager lad in his purchase of "professional" pancake makeup and sponge applicator.

"You'll also need a pencil to outline your eyes," came the voice of experience. Donen knowingly pretended to select the best one off the rack.

"Now," said Irgens, "what will you use to take off your makeup?"

"Cold cream, I guess," said Donen, wishing to appear somewhat less ingenuous than he was. "Or water and a washcloth, I suppose, if I'm in a hurry."

"That's fine at the beginning," said Irgens, "but this show's going to be a hit and run a long time, so you shouldn't use either, or else you'll break out in a rash."

Donen saw Irgens's point. "Let me tell you the secret of what the old-timers use," said the well-established dancer. "Orange marmalade."

"Orange marmalade?" repeated Donen.

"You wipe it all over your face," said Irgens, "and it takes off the makeup beautifully."

"I hardly knew how to thank him," said Donen, relating the story, "especially when he offered to accompany me to the grocery store to help me select the same brand that all the great, experienced dancers used."

They did exactly that. "I was *very* particular about my orange marmalade," recalled Donen. "I wanted a jar with the right kind of screw top instead of some ordinary lid I'd have to keep prying open." Donen and Irgens went so far as to test out the tops in the store, to ensure that Donen was indeed picking the right marmalade jar.

Came the first full dress rehearsal, Donen, in makeup, appeared alone onstage with Joey's stupid "mouse," Linda English, played by Leila Ernst. "Abbott, John O'Hara, and Rodgers and Hart were out front," said Donen, reconstructing the scene, "and it was just Leila Ernst and me onstage, with the entire rest of the cast in back of us. In other words, I was stranded. There was no way anybody offstage could have gotten to me to say anything without everybody else hearing every word of it."

A dramatic moment ensued, requiring Donen to do some stage business in the background. This was followed by a musical number involving the entire chorus. "Then," said Donen, "at the perfect moment, when she saw nobody was watching, Leila Ernst did the single greatest thing that ever happened in my entire life. She leaned over and whispered into my

Joey Evans (Kelly) charms "mouse" Linda English (Leila Ernst), with Albert Doane (Donen) at table. In rehearsal, before John O'Hara, George Abbott, and Rodgers and Hart, Ernst had saved the chorus boy's face— literally and figuratively.

ear, 'They're all in on it and are waiting to watch. So when we're finished, whatever you do . . . *don't use the orange marmalade.*' "

THE SEARCH to discover the right heel to play Joey ended when Richard Rodgers and his wife, Dorothy, attended the opening-night performance of the William Saroyan play *The Time of Your Life*. "In the small role of an aspiring entertainer was an especially engaging young man," said Rodgers. "The stage was aglow with life whenever he appeared, and his dancing was superb."

The actor's name was Gene Kelly.

A former children's dance instructor in Pittsburgh, Kelly (born 1912) had made several unsuccessful stabs at breaking onto Broadway, until in 1938, he was cast as part of a male quartet singing backup to a singer from Texas. Her name was Mary Martin, this was her Broadway debut, the show was *Leave It to Me!,* its score was by Cole Porter, and the song was "My Heart Belongs to Daddy." Martin sat atop a steamer trunk in a Siberian train depot, while Kelly and the others sang and swayed behind her in their parkas, as choreographed by Robert Alton, who would go on to choreograph *Pal Joey* and musicals at M-G-M. Kelly himself could choreograph, and was gaining a reputation as a dance director in summer stock. In 1940 he applied to be and was hired as choreographer of a revue for Billy Rose's Diamond Horseshoe. That same year he was also cast in the Saroyan play.

"Gene had this small part," remembered Donen. "He was supposed to be a sort of song-and-dance man in a bar. Then he got the job in *Pal Joey*, and that was a tremendous thing for him."

"Kelly made the original Joey something special, and Joey made Kelly a star," noted Gerald Mast. "The ballet that closes Act I, when Joey's vision of the world becomes the nightclub of his imagination, was the first of Kelly's dream ballets. Even after the trip to M-G-M," the cultural critic noted of Kelly's soon-to-follow film career, which would also quickly manifest itself into a creative collaboration with Donen, "Kelly never completely rinsed off the aroma of Joey."*

"I remember being impressed by Gene as soon as I saw him onstage," Donen once said. "He had a cockiness, a confidence in himself, and a ruthlessness in the way he went about things that, to someone as young and green as myself, I found astonishing. I also found him to be egotistical and very rough." Donen is able to express a range of feelings and still keep his opinions in check, an outgrowth of his Southern upbringing and his later experience at M-G-M, where personal and professional tales were carefully kept within the confines of the kingdom. Completing his description of the perceived pluses and minuses of Kelly, who in the forties and early fifties was capable of serving as both mentor and tormentor to someone in Donen's position, Donen concluded, "And, of course, wildly talented."

"Gene and I did not get to know one another on *Pal Joey*, as most people think," Donen said on a later occasion. "That really came later. After all, he was the star and I was only in the chorus. You can be in a show with someone every day without really knowing him."

GEORGE ABBOTT's finding Donen "bright" resulted in a promotion for the chorus boy, one that came shortly after opening night, which was Christmas, 1940. "I was made 'call boy' of *Pal Joey*," said Donen. "I was

---

* "In comparison to the ethereal Astaire," Mast continued, "Kelly would always seem more common, venal, vulgar, selfish—in short, mortal. He escaped into dream ballets because he was so solidly anchored to the earth below."

making thirty-five dollars a week to start, but then I was raised another five dollars a week to go around the dressing rooms backstage and call out, 'Half hour, Mr. Kelly,' 'Half hour, Miss Segal,' 'Half hour, Miss Havoc.' Then I'd do the same thing at five minutes before curtain."

Now a full-fledged theater professional, Donen was spared the embarrassment of writing his parents for money or, worse, the ignominy of going home in defeat. "When I left Columbia, South Carolina," he said, "I suppose my parents thought I would go to New York and return in a few weeks, the way we did every summer. I never did return."

Of his first salary, he said, "It seemed a lot, comparatively, I mean, because my father was earning seventy-five dollars a week and looking after his wife and two children. And here I was, only needing to take care of myself."

Embracing the entire *Joey* experience, Donen drew a glamorous portrait of New York that resembled the way his later movies romanticized the metropolis: "There are feelings about New York that I have in my system and can't get rid of," he said. "New York used to represent the absolute best of the best, and the movies were always aspiring to reach up to the quality of Hecht and MacArthur, and Kaufman and Hart, and everything New York had to offer. Being on Broadway, living the life I always wanted, working in this show, which turned out to be this great watershed musical, although none of us really knew that while we were in it—all that added up to what was the best time I had in my life, ever. Suddenly I was in New York, and nobody gave a damn if I was a Jew or a Buddhist or anything."

Chapter 3

"I Became Impossible"

D ESPITE LEGEND that the show lacked popular appeal," Richard Rodgers said of *Pal Joey,* which had divided the critics evenly, "it did have a successful eleven-month run, followed by a three-month tour." The *Times*'s Brooks Atkinson's oft-quoted morning-after put-down culminated with the conundrum: "Although *Pal Joey* is expertly done, can you draw sweet water from a foul well?" The answer proved to be yes, although not for another decade; the show's reputation was not firmly secured in the mind of the public and a repentant Atkinson until a celebrated 1952 Broadway revival that starred Harold Lang as Joey and Vivienne Segal reprising her Vera.

"I must've been in the show a good eight or nine months," Donen said, which would have seen him through the first summer. *Joey* vacated the Barrymore Theater September 1, 1941, to take up residence at the Shubert, where it played through October 18.* By then, Donen, having long departed the show, had already climbed another notch on the Broadway ladder.

"One night during *Pal Joey,*" Donen said, "George Abbott approached me backstage and asked, 'Would you like to be in *Best Foot Forward*?' That was going to be his next show, about these young kids in a prep school." The original title was *Young Man's Fancy,* though this was relinquished when a British film was discovered to have the same name. In any case, Abbott would be requiring young cast members, and Donen was a trained natural. "Then I got lucky," said Donen. "The choreographer on *Best Foot Forward*

---

* It moved one final time, on October 21, 1941, to the St. James Theater, where it ran until its closure, November 29, a mere eight days before Pearl Harbor, which would have signaled the end for the appeal of *Joey*'s cynicism in any event.

at that point was someone named John Lonergan." Lonergan had been the uncredited Broadway dance director on Jerome Kern's 1933 *Roberta.* "After roughly a week of rehearsals on *Best Foot Forward,*" said Donen, "Abbott decided that John Lonergan was hopeless and went to Gene, who was still in *Pal Joey,* and asked Gene if he could choreograph *Best Foot Forward* at the same time Gene was also appearing in *Pal Joey.*" The official reason for Lonergan's replacement, according to a press statement released from Abbott's office, was "an eye infection which quickly demands quick hospitalization."

Aside from Lonergan's unsuitability for the assignment, a large part of the reason Abbott tendered the offer was to placate Kelly and keep him in *Joey;* the song-and-dance man had started out making three hundred fifty dollars a week, which made him, in his words, "the lowest-paid star on Broadway," though it was more money than he had ever made before. As the run progressed, Abbott hiked Kelly's weekly salary to five hundred per, but by then the theater man was feeling the heat from others, who were seeking the services of his leading player, namely Hollywood producers. In November of 1941, Kelly was to start working for David O. Selznick in a contract negotiated by his agent, Leland Hayward. Until then, Abbott and Kelly agreed, Kelly's name would go up in lights over the title on *Joey*'s marquee, and he would choreograph *Best Foot Forward.*

"Then," said Donen, "because I had been a dancer in *Pal Joey,* I was the only person Gene was familiar with among the dancers in this new show." Kelly, in his own words, regarded Donen as "energetic and ambitious." As a result, Kelly approached Donen and inquired, "Would you help me?"

"So I became his assistant," said Donen, "and that's how we got to know each other."

IF *Pal Joey* proved unpalatable for some, the innocuous frolic *Best Foot Forward,* which marched into the Ethel Barrymore Theater right behind it, elicited an entirely opposite response. The new show ran for 374 performances, 56 more than *Joey.* Produced by George Abbott and an uncredited Richard Rodgers, who kept his name off the show in order not to grab the spotlight, the presentation embodied the wholesome rah-rah attitude overtaking America as increasingly louder war threats were heard from Europe.

The show was set in an imaginary Pennsylvania preparatory school named Winsocki, and its rousing anthem, Ralph Blane and Hugh Martin's

"Buckle Down, Winsocki"—the very tune Van Johnson complained about in the West Fifty-fifth Street boardinghouse—was quickly adopted as the fight song at real schools. The show's simplistic libretto was by John Cecil Holm, a former actor who had enjoyed some success cowriting a racetrack comedy with George Abbott, *Three Men on a Horse*. His new story line dealt with the farcical complications that ensue when a timid student (Gil Stratton, Jr.) invites a publicity-hungry Hollywood star (Rosemary Lane) to be his prom date. On the advice of her unscrupulous manager, she accepts, and lest the premise seem improbable, it was based on Holm's own experience of asking the actress Betty Compson to his prom at the Perkiomen School, outside Philadelphia. *She* refused.

The dances in *Best Foot Forward,* with their heavy reliance on tap, were never intended to break new ground, and they didn't. (Reviewers all but overlooked the choreography in their notices, save for the *Newark Star-Ledger* critic, who mentioned "tip top terp staging by Gene Kelly.") At the time he staged them, Kelly said: "The jitterbug style of dancing is passé. I think dreamy dancing is more popular right now." Kelly felt that the jitterbug, or any form of "wild dancing," as he termed it, could catch on only "during wartime." Ironically, barely two months after *Best Foot Forward*'s opening night, America, like Europe, would be plunged into battle.

"On the stage," Kelly said of the high road he wished to take with the teen show, "dancing is becoming more artistic and stylized, with plenty of pantomine and a good dash of ballet. The idea is, I believe, to get as much art into dance routines as possible, and still keep the tired businessman happy."

Kelly's choreographic technique was to build a number around the particular talents of the performer, then match the individual movements to the music for maximum effect. That there was a strong athleticism to the Kelly style, in both his own dances and those he devised for others, was inarguable and had as much to do with Kelly's background as a pugilist forced to defend himself in the tough, blue-collar neighborhood of his adolescence—no easy place for a boy who liked to dance—as it did with his own compact physical frame.

Besides assisting Kelly, Donen was surrounded in the *Best Foot Forward* chorus by two female leads destined to make names for themselves. The first was June Allyson, as the pretty coed; the second, Nancy Walker, had the comic-relief role of the homely, sharp-tongued cutup, given such lines as "I'd hang myself, but I got a dentist's appointment on Tuesday." Walker, who'd been sent to the *Best Foot Forward* audition by her father's agent, was

Donen, fourth from left, one of the gaggle of youngsters in *Best Foot Forward* (1941). He also assisted choreographer Gene Kelly. The comely singer is Betty Anne Nyman.

the daughter of the professional acrobat Dewey Barto, of the team of Barto and Mann. "Her father was about two feet tall," said Donen, "and his partner was about seven. Together they were a great act." In fact, Dewey Barto was four feet eleven and George Mann six feet eight. Partners since 1926, they took their low-comedy routine to Earl Carroll's *Vanities*, although it was *Hellzapoppin,* that Broadway burlesque extravaganza, that landed them on the pages of *Life* magazine in 1938. In Act I, they performed the sketch "Maternity War," described as "a grotesque adagio dance," during which the tiny Barto, wearing a man's suit and floppy fedora, climbs one of the long legs of the gigantic Mann, who is outfitted in Baby Snooks drag.

By the time *Best Foot Forward* opened, on October 1, 1941, Donen, too, had concocted a pretty great act for himself. "I got such an inflated head," he admitted, "that they fired me. It was the stage manager who did it, a man named Jerome Whyte, a big redhead. He became head of Rodgers and Hammerstein's company before he died, and I knew him from when he was the stage manager on *Pal Joey*. That was tough, because between Havoc, Segal, and Kelly, he had his hands full to keep the situation from exploding."

Having earned his stripe, Whyte was then assigned, by George Abbott, the formidable chore of keeping in line the rambunctious young-sters on *Best Foot Forward*. Donen, in turn, was appointed Whyte's assistant, and by his own admission, "I became an impossible little shit. Here I was, this young kid, I'd been in this one other show, and I'd been Gene's assis-tant with the choreography, and I was all of seventeen. It's easy to see how I could have become sort of cocky."

Donen's reason for his job termination conflicted with another account of the incident, that he was fired for having stolen away George Abbott's girlfriend, the eighteen-year-old Victoria "Vicky" Schools, who played the third female lead in *Best Foot Forward*. "She'd been a singer with Rudy Vallee on radio since she was thirteen," said Donen, "and she always used to talk about how much she hated Vallee." Schools, in fact, could be very graphic when she described the sexual demands Vallee repeatedly made of her.

Born in Virginia, Schools, who was christened Erlene, had a voice considered reminiscent of the torch singer Libby Holman's, and in a career that was always showing promise, she had sung with Sigmund Romberg. Unfortunately, in show-business circles, Schools was as well known for her pretty looks as she was for her series of personal problems. "I was late getting to the theater," recalled Nancy Walker, "and was racing to get dressed." Sharing the dressing room with Schools, Walker made a quick grab for her costar's perfume bottle and doused herself. She then headed off to make her entrance, only to be halted by the large hand of Jerome Whyte. "Jerry got a whiff of me wearing Vicky's perfume and said, 'Where do you think you're going?' " remembered Walker. "He refused to let me onstage. Vicky's perfume was straight, eighty-proof vodka."

"Vicky *was* crazy," Donen admitted. When her mother came to New York from Virginia, Donen volunteered to make himself scarce rather than let Elmira Schools discover that he and her daughter were cohabiting. (After leaving 101 West Fifty-fifth Street, Donen shared a room with Schools—who was a year older and making more money than he—at the Gorham Hotel, also on Fifty-fifth Street.) "I told her I'd leave, and Vicky said, 'What for?' " said Donen, who pointed out that their living quarters contained only one bed. Schools's solution was that the three share the mattress. "Which is what we did," said Donen. "Vicky, her mother, and me."

"She was *gorgeous*," said Donen's sister, Carla, who distinctly remem-bered her brother bringing Schools home to meet the family in South Carolina. "She was so sweet and so talented. I remember when I heard Walter Winchell report on the radio that she had killed herself, he said she was headed for a career singing with the Metropolitan Opera."

On November 5, 1948, in her apartment at 405 East Fifty-fourth Street, Schools took two painkillers, which became lodged in her throat. The last time Donen had seen her was in California, sometime after he had received his first on-screen credit, which could conceivably have been a year before she died. "She called me at the studio," he remembered, "totally out of the blue, and said, 'I'm here, come on over to my hotel.' She was staying at the Chateau Marmont, and when I got there she opened the door and was standing there stark, raving naked."

Donen's verbal dismissal from *Best Foot Forward,* for whatever reasons, came directly from Jerome Whyte, who left no room for argument. The seventeen-year-old departed the stage door of the Barrymore Theater, devastated.

"I had no idea what to do," said Donen. "I couldn't find another job. There was no other job."

Swallowing his pride and deciding it was prudent to write Abbott, Donen "was very contrite, and in my letter I said I understood why Jerry had fired me, which was the truth."

A few days later Donen received his reply from Abbott. "He was always a man of few words," said Donen. "This time it was a simple note that contained only one line. It said, 'Would you like to be in *Beat the Band?'*—his next show. Remarkable."

"I HAD some dandy failures," George Abbott recalled, "and the worst of these was *Beat the Band.*"

"We were on the road in Boston," said Donen, "and the choreographer this time was this classical Russian dancer, David Lichine, whose wife ran a ballet school. That didn't do a damn bit of good for *Beat the Band,* because he was completely out of his element." Abbott's answer was to turn to Donen. "*You've* got to take over the musical numbers," said the producer.

Beat the Band opened at the Forty-sixth Street Theater on Wednesday, October 14, 1942, and despite Abbott's opinion, Brooks Atkinson was pleasantly amused, particularly by a number composed by a Harvard graduate named Johnny Green, whom the critic likened to a young Irving Berlin (and who, by the end of the decade, would become the head of

M-G-M's music department). The plot devised by Abbott and his fellow bookwriter, George Marion, Jr., dealt with a high-strung bandleader (Jack Whiting) who subleases a Manhattan penthouse, only to find that the owner's orphaned goddaughter (Susan Miller) has unexpectedly arrived from South America to take up residence herself.

David Lichine is credited in the stagebill with a lively boogie-woogie, "Steam on the Beam," and this he managed to parlay into a job choreographing in Hollywood. In the end, two of the show's major production numbers were Donen's, he surmised; he also performed as a principal dancer in the show and executed a solo. *Beat the Band* represented the pinnacle of Donen's Broadway dancing career.

"As time went on and I became involved behind the scenes with putting on a show, like when I was helping Gene," said Donen, "I actually found that more attractive than performing." Donen went so far as to claim, in the late 1970s, to University of Southern California film professor Joseph Andrew Casper, "I never thought I was very good as a performer."

When it came to assessing the prospects of *Beat the Band,* George Abbott proved more perspicacious than Atkinson, as did Donen. The musical lasted only sixty-seven performances, though by that time Donen,

Donen's final stage appearance (far right), in the Broadway chorus of the short-lived *Beat the Band* (1942)

having once again set his sights elsewhere, had already given notice. Besides, the die had been cast, as it had been two shows before.

"It was obvious from the start that Stanley was going to go places," said Van Johnson. "Every minute he wasn't onstage, he'd be standing in the wings, carefully watching Gene, studying every kick and move he would make."

Chapter 4

"I'll Get You to Hollywood"

WHETHER because he envied his older peers or suffered a normal attack of youthful fecklessness, the solitary Donen migrated west, convinced he was prepared to encounter Hollywood. "I'd saved enough money in New York," he reasoned, "and now I wanted to be in the movies."

Van Johnson already had made the transition to screenwork, as had Gene Kelly, whose Selznick contract was about to be sold to Metro, because Selznick, still coasting on the back-to-back successes of *Gone With the Wind* and *Rebecca,* lacked suitable properties for a danceman.

Former 101 West Fifty-fifth Street neighbors Blane and Martin also had put their best feet forward, into the doors of M-G-M. The songwriters had been hired by Roger Edens, the key associate of the producer Arthur Freed, after Edens had heard them sing backup to Judy Garland and Mickey Rooney at New York's Capitol Theater. Once in Hollywood, Blane and Martin informed Freed that their first Broadway property, *Best Foot Forward,* was about to be sold to a rival, considerably less prestigious, studio, Columbia Pictures.

Freed palliated them; with June Allyson already under M-G-M contract, Freed said, the studio was certain to counterbid Columbia for the film rights—which Metro did, for $150,000. What that sum did not include was the extra $25,000 to soothe the considerable pride of Columbia's studio chief, Harry Cohn, or the contractual agreement for Cohn to use the services of an M-G-M star in a musical he was planning, to be called *Cover Girl.*

As the *Best Foot Forward*–Metro deal was being consummated in Hollywood, excited word about it circulated along the ever fermenting Broadway grapevine. Donen, by then appearing in *Beat the Band* but still plugged into his previous show's backstage gossip, took that as his cue to pack his bags.

"I was so anxious to get to California that I bought an airline ticket, only this was 1942, wartime, and military transport took priority," he remembered. "As it was, planes didn't fly directly from New York to Los Angeles. You had to stop, refuel, and take off again. It took forever, but it was still the fastest way."

In Donen's case, he made it on schedule only as far as Chicago. "I got kicked off and my seat was reassigned to a soldier." Questions about a possible next flight were greeted evasively. "I was told I could either wait or not," said Donen. "I waited."

In the same terminal, facing the identical situation, was "a big, powerful-looking Westerner. He had to be about forty." Earl Thiesen was a staff photographer for *Look* magazine, en route to an assignment in California. "I'll never forget his words," said Donen. " 'Stick with me, kid. I'll get you to Hollywood.' "

Despite the wartime exigencies, Thiesen managed to find the last two places on a train, and Donen recalled how he sheepishly disembarked days later when the locomotive pulled into Los Angeles' Union Station. "I arrived with nothing. Nowhere to go, no contacts, no job, no nothing. Just a kid. Reminds me of the little girl in *42nd Street,* showing up with just her tiny suitcase."

Donen was assertive enough to bus himself directly to Culver City, to the secured gates of Metro-Goldwyn-Mayer on Washington Boulevard, although once again his version of the story veers from Van Johnson's. "Stanley called me when he got to Hollywood," said Johnson, already an established contract player.* "He said, 'Can you get me into the commissary?' It was a way to meet people. I did the same thing for Peter Lawford."

Johnson was only too glad to oblige his old friend, whose parents had once treated him to lobster thermidor.

"So Stanley got into the commissary," said Johnson, "and the rest is history. Only, wouldn't you know it, when the son of a bitch got to be a big director, never once did he hire me."

According to Donen, he went directly to the casting office, with the fond hope of being hired: "I knew they were going to make a movie of *Best*

---

* In 1941, a few months after the opening of *Pal Joey,* Warner Bros. put Johnson under a six-month contract, which lapsed. M-G-M picked him up, and in 1943 Johnson achieved stardom in *A Guy Named Joe,* with Irene Dunne and Spencer Tracy.

Foot Forward. Well, I didn't actually know it. I'd heard it. I had no connection to it, and no invitation, but I went to see if I could get into the movie."

Such moxie saw him through the first door, he said. "I told them I was in the show, could I be in the movie? I got an audition—what Van Johnson said is untrue, because I tried out with a group of dancers—and I got a job. Not only did I get a job; I was put under contract."

Donen, recalling the momentous event in his life exactly fifty years after it happened, said, "I got a job at M-G-M!"

FOR SOMEONE as desirous of being in the movies as Donen, M-G-M was the Holy Grail. "It had the reputation of being *the* studio, the major of the majors," he said, and even that sort of hyperbole was stating the case lightly. As Donen correctly noted, "Everyone wanted to work there."

Like Donen, M-G-M had been born in 1924,* its formation realized by the merger of three relatively young independent film companies: the Metro Pictures of Marcus Loew, the Goldwyn Pictures of Samuel Goldwyn (née Goldfish, who was later forced out of the new operation), and the equally eponymic Louis B. Mayer Pictures.

Mayer (1885–1957), once rightly described as "a bullying sentimentalist who loved operetta, Andy Hardy, and the Republican party," whose private art collection consisted of several works by Grandma Moses, remained to preside over the dynamic new production entity, using as his headquarters the former Thomas Ince Studios in Culver City. Donen referred to the facility, with its four thousand employees, its 187 acres spread over six different lots, and its lab, capable of developing 150 million feet of release prints a year, as "a fascinating factory for making movies."†

---

* Donen was precisely thirteen days older.

† Arthur Freed chronicler Hugh Fordin described a typical day's activity at Metro in 1941, a year before Donen's arrival, as follows: "On Stage Eighteen, Greta Garbo and [the former *Pal Joey* stage choreographer] Robert Alton are dancing the 'Chica Chica Rumba' for *Two-Faced Woman;* W. S. Van Dyke was directing William Powell and Myrna Loy in *The Shadow of the Thin Man* on Stage Sixteen; King Vidor was directing Hedy Lamarr, Robert Young, and Charles Coburn in a scene for *H. M. Pulham, Esq.* on Stage Twenty-two; Spencer Tracy and Katharine Hepburn were rehearsing *Woman of the Year* for George Stevens on Stage Three; in their first scene in *Johnny Eager* were Lana Turner and Robert Taylor on Stage Four, Mervyn LeRoy directing; on Stage Ten Walter Pidgeon and Rosalind Russell in *Miss Achilles Heel;* Nelson Eddy and Risë Stevens prerecording *The Chocolate Soldier* on Stage One; Wallace Beery and Marjorie Main on Lot Two in *Steel Cavalry;* Norma Shearer in Rehearsal Hall A taking dancing lessons; Edward G. Robinson taking off in an airplane on Stage Thirty for *Unholy Partners;* on Stage Twelve Johnny Weissmuller swinging tree to tree; and Eleanor Powell rehearsing a tap-dance routine for *I'll Take Manila* in Rehearsal Hall B." Obviously, Clark Gable was busy off the lot that day.

M-G-M's parent company and financial arm, Loew's Incorporated, kept its safe distance from the studio, geographically at least; it remained headquartered in Times Square, at 1540 Broadway, across the street from the smoke-billowing Camel cigarette billboard.

"I was extraordinarily impressed by the size of the studio," Donen remembered. "There were people, trucks, cars, scenery, stars. The place was just teeming with activity. They were making fifty to sixty pictures a year, at the rate of one a week." M-G-M prided itself on employing the strongest talent pool in the business, although not necessarily the highest paid (and certainly not the most artistically independent), because simply to be at M-G-M was considered a filmworker's strongest equity.

"I was in on the tail end of the building of Hollywood," said Donen. "The original pioneers were still in charge, and I ended up working for a lot of them."

In characterizing that fabled if nefarious group, Donen found Mayer, Harry Cohn, Sam Goldwyn, and Jack Warner to be "their own breed, as much concerned with succeeding financially as they were with their own stature."

In several respects, the pioneer spirit that distinguished the early moguls could also be found in Donen, so much so that the invariably perceptive Kay Thompson once concluded, "Stanley should have bought his own studio, the way [television producer] Desi Arnaz did with Desilu, only who knew? Back then we were all so busy being darling."

Like Donen, the early movie moguls were men of incontestable strong will who could never run fast enough from their humble beginnings. Not that Columbia, South Carolina, could be fairly compared to Minsk, Warsaw, or any of the Eastern European shtetls that spawned most of the Hollywood moguls—Donen, after all, may have endured anti-Semitic name calling as child, but he did not face Cossack invasions.

Somehow, however, the relentless drive to succeed was instilled as strongly in sleepy Columbia as it was in Old World backwaters, not that luck, too, need not have factored into the formula for achievement. Similarly, while it would be stretching the point to consider Donen an uneducated immigrant, which was the unvarnished status of the founding fathers of Hollywood, the argument could be made that the reason Donen fell so easily into the system devised by filmdom's nobility was that he had been cut from exactly the same cloth: They were nonreligious Jews; each had developed an unwavering artistic sensibility based on idealizations of a better existence (the moguls achieved theirs by hiring the best arbiters of taste their money could buy, while Donen had been fed intravenously on nearly everything these people put on-screen*); and all were determined to get ahead at any cost, be it through sheer ruthlessness (the moguls' method) or a kind of knowing guilelessness (Donen's).

To get to the *emmis*[†] of the matter, the movies were just something in these men's blood, and this love of the medium was a recognizable trait in their personalities and perhaps their most dominant characteristic. "The great thing about Stanley," said Frederic Raphael, the screenwriter of *Two for the Road*, "and what separates him from the vast majority of film people, besides the fact that he admires talent in others, is that he never thought it was all that big a deal to become a producer or a director. He simply liked the work."

DONEN WAS signed onto the M-G-M payroll for sixty-five dollars a week, a sizable jump from his Broadway starting salaries. His first major purchase was that Los Angeles necessity an automobile—a boxy gray four-door Studebaker, which he picked up secondhand. His first California address, where he would reside for the next several years, was the Beverly House, a tiny red-brick building well situated at the corner of Wilshire and Santa Monica Boulevards.

As for the job, Donen's Culver City arrival proved a circumstance of being in the right place at the right time. "The war was going on," he said, "and the studio was making as many musicals as it could. Since all the men were drafted, M-G-M needed male dancers—and here I showed up, a male dancer who could dance."

In the nine brief years between Donen's being inspired by his first movie musical and his appearing in one, the genre had made tremendous strides, a few of them backward. By 1933, the year of *Flying Down to Rio,* both the Depression and the Hollywood musical were four years old, the latter having been established as practically an exclusive antidote to the former. Familiarity was breeding apathy, and audiences were becoming as sick of musicals as of the Depression.

Obviously, movies did not sing and dance until they could first talk, although opera plots were often adapted for silent pictures—to wit, direc-

---

* Worth noting is that by the time Donen became a director, he was one of the first—if not *the* first—of his generation to have been raised entirely on sound movies. Subsequently in Hollywood, another generation of filmmakers would come to boast that they were weaned on a steady diet of fifties and sixties television. Behind their backs, these people would be termed "vidiots."

† Yiddish for "truth."

tor Erich von Stroheim's 1925 *The Merry Widow*, starring Mae Murray. When sound became a reality in 1927 and full-scale musical productions were launched in 1929, reasons were required for the insertion of songs. The most accommodating approach was to take a cue, if not the full artistic conceit, from the New York stage. Early sound musicals set the dramatic action backstage and shoved the musical numbers out front, before the footlights.

By 1933, audiences had been satiated with the formula, or, in the case of choreographer Busby Berkeley's backstage musicals for Warner Bros. (*42nd Street, Gold Diggers of 1933, Footlight Parade*), left gasping for air. Hoping to reenergize the genre, moviemakers began to integrate songs with fairy-tale-like plots, as was the case with the Ernst Lubitsch pictures from Paramount (*The Smiling Lieutenant, One Hour with You, The Merry Widow*) and the Astaire-Rodgers vehicles at RKO.

As the thirties advanced, so did the movie musical. Backstage devices such as those deployed by Berkeley became dinosaurs, and the fairy tale and the folk musical took over, among them those that starred Shirley Temple at Twentieth Century–Fox, Jeanette MacDonald and Nelson Eddy at M-G-M, and Irene Dunne hither and yon. The war reversed that trend, with farraginous Follies-type musicals returning with a vengeance, usually armed with a military motif. These were fairly easy for the studios to produce and for escape-hungry audiences to digest.

Typical of the M-G-M product of its time, *Best Foot Forward* was noticeably short on plot but long on production values. Shifting the stage show's setting from a prep school to a military academy as a means to bolster its patriotic possibilities, the screen version retained seven of the show's fourteen songs (some performed only instrumentally) and added three by Martin and Blane, as well as two specialty numbers performed by the big-band leader Harry James during an attenuated prom scene.

"Some of the people involved in the show *Best Foot Forward* were involved in the movie," said Donen, "only not Abbott and not Kelly." George Abbott's movie career had always been tentative at best, dating back to the westward talent migration that accompanied the advent of talkies, when Hollywood desperately needed dialogue writers from New York. Abbott's most notable screen credit, until he collaborated with Donen in the late 1950s in adapting *The Pajama Game* and *Damn Yankees*, was as one of the cadre of screenwriters assigned to the 1930 antiwar classic, *All Quiet on the Western Front*.

As for Kelly, he quickly fell into good company in Hollywood. His first assignment, at $750 a week, was with the nineteen-year-old Judy Garland in

Shooting *Best Foot Forward* in Technicolor at M-G-M (1943). Donen is hidden amid fellow cadets during "The Three B's" number, staged in a gymnasium. The three juvenile female leads posing center court are Gloria DeHaven, June Allyson, and Nancy Walker.

For Me and My Gal; he played a third-rate vaudevillian not far removed from his *Joey* persona. The film was produced by Metro's preeminent overseer of musicals, Arthur Freed (1894–1973), who assumed that princely mantle in 1939, when, as the uncredited associate producer, he had been the party most responsible for midwifing the studio's imaginative benchmark production, *The Wizard of Oz.* "I not only brought the property to the studio," the moon-faced Freed was proud to point out, "I cast it."

"Arthur was the spark plug of M-G-M musicals," Donen said with affection. The artistic trait Donen admired most in Freed was that "he was never interested in settling for anything that was run-of-the-mill." That the two spoke a similar language had less to do with the coincidence that they both hailed from the same state—Freed was born in Charleston, though his family soon moved to Seattle—than with the simple fact that each knew and loved music. Freed began in New York as a song plugger, cut his teeth as a lyricist (his first hit was the 1923 "I Cried for You"), and was wooed to

Front and nearly center, Donen hoists Gloria DeHaven in the film's opening song.

Hollywood by M-G-M supervisor of production Irving Thalberg in 1929, just as the studio was beginning to try out its dancing feet.

"There are certain fundamental things that all producers got from Irving," said Freed, who considered Thalberg his ideal. "An honesty in writing. Character more than plot. Irving always said, 'To hell with the plot . . .' But when it came to musicals, Irving was basically for the operetta. He never did understand what we call musical comedy."

Donen portrayed Freed as a delightful if eccentric boss, who would compulsively jangle coins in his pocket and exhibited discomposure when dealing with people face-to-face. Donen remembered, "We would be staging an entire musical sequence for Arthur—dancers, singers, elaborate steps, everything. Then we'd finish and wait for his reaction. And all Arthur would do was look off into the distance and say something like, 'You know, Bing Crosby is going to win the Academy Award this year.' "

The studio officially housed three producers who devoted the better part of their energies to musicals—Freed, Joseph Pasternak, and Jack Cummings—although as Donen and others, including auteurist critics, would attest, "there was only one, Arthur. It was all Arthur. I don't even understand why it was referred to as 'the Arthur Freed Unit,' " said Donen. "There was no unit. There was nothing organized. He just knew who was right for what material, and he kept making films with the same people."

In 1942, at the time of Donen's arrival at M-G-M, Freed was in production with *For Me and My Gal,* with Garland and Kelly, and laying the groundwork for *Best Foot Forward.*

"Freed hired June Allyson and Nancy Walker and a few others from the show," said Donen. Jack Jordan and Kenny Bowers also made the leap from stage to screen. "Gil Stratton, who had been the lead on Broadway, was given a smaller part, and Tommy Dix, this very short kid with a big, booming baritone voice, for some reason was given the lead."

For the role of the tough movie star who graces the prom, Freed hoped to cast Lana Turner, who was forced to withdraw when she became pregnant. Her replacement was the carrot-topped contract player Lucille Ball—the character in the movie is even called Lucille Ball—although no attempt was made to utilize her substantial comic skills, which eight years later would be displayed to their quintessential advantage on television's *I Love Lucy.*

The lone member of the Broadway chorus of *Best Foot Forward* to make it into the movie was Donen, because, as he well knew, "I made it my business to come to Hollywood."

The slightly built eighteen-year-old (he looks twelve), in his blue Winsocki uniform, is visibly evident throughout the picture, though he is invariably relegated to the background, linked to the exceedingly vivacious Gloria DeHaven, who took over Victoria Schools's role. (It was believed by some that Schools was not cast in the picture because word about her drinking had preceded her west.) In the movie's desultory opening number, "Wish I May," Donen hoists DeHaven high into the air, looking more than a little self-conscious.

"What's funny," said Gloria DeHaven in 1994, "is that I have no memory whatsoever of dancing with Stanley. I can sort of picture him as this tall, narrow fellow in the background, and I definitely remember him acting as the assistant choreographer to Chuck Walters when we were making the picture. But dancing with Stanley? I'm drawing a blank."

Donen *was* tall and narrow in the background. Thanks to his eagerness, he also became the assistant to the picture's choreographer, Charles Walters. As for his performance on-screen, Donen's one glorious moment front and center (actually, off to the left of the screen) arrives some fifty minutes into the listless ninety-five-minute movie, when he jitterbugs "The Three B's" with June Allyson.

This time he's a little stiff.

AS PROVED by his promotion during *Pal Joey,* Donen could be amenable if the situation warranted it. On *Best Foot Forward,* Donen, no doubt comparing the film's oafish director, Eddie Buzzell, to the distinguished presence of George Abbott, rightfully saw little reason to be impressed. The same reaction did not apply to Charles Walters, a former Broadway actor, dancer, and choreographer, who had landed on M-G-M's fast track.

Walters (1911–1982), dapper and fastidious, rose to the rank of M-G-M musical director in the forties, sometime between the ascent of Arthur Freed's favorite director, Vincente Minnelli, and that of Donen. "Chuck had a real ingratiating personality," said Gloria DeHaven, "and a wonderful sense of humor. On *Best Foot Forward* he didn't devote much serious time talking to us, because we were such babies, but compared to most choreographers, who were strictly concerned with the sound track and the movement, he was a very loose kind of guy." Walters's eventual directorial style, though considered impersonal and a throwback to that at M-G-M in the thirties, nevertheless prompted critics of film dance to note favorably that he, like Donen, when staging musical numbers, had an effective talent for mixing paired solos with duets in order to achieve a harmonious balance of the sexes and camera shots.

"Chuck Walters rather liked me," Donen said of his work on *Best Foot Forward,* "so I became his assistant on that and some of his other movies afterward." It would generally fall to the assistant to see that the chorus remained in step, while the choreographer would concentrate on the stars or leading dancers. Donen was also appearing in a string of movies that carried him through his first eight months at M-G-M. "Maybe five, six, or seven movies," he said. "Nothing important, but I was always doing something. The place was just grinding out musicals."

This idyllic situation provided the teenager with ample opportunity to lay eyes upon his idol, Fred Astaire, although, Donen recalled, "It's funny, I can't remember the first time I was actually introduced to Fred." Because Chuck Walters worked with Astaire, it is conceivable that the choreographer's eager and ambitious young assistant was lurking somewhere in the vicinity. "The way it worked at the studio," Donen explained, "there were three rehearsal halls, and they were all laid out together, side by side. Halls A and B were big, and in the center was a small one, Hall C. The dressing rooms were directly above the rehearsal halls, also in the same building. This way, if you were making a musical, you'd be working side by side with all the others. It was impossible for the same people not to run into each other, so at least I was able to watch Fred work, even before I knew him."

Astaire had made his first movie for M-G-M in 1933, *Dancing Lady,* with Joan Crawford and Clark Gable, only he made little impression in his supporting role. He then quickly went to RKO for *Flying Down to Rio* and followed with his string of pictures with Ginger Rogers. (When she turned to dramatic roles, Astaire was partnered with others until he played out his 1933 seven-year contract.) For the next half decade he went freelance, until he joined Metro in 1945, only by then, as he was applying the brakes to his own career, Astaire saw the studio stepping on the accelerator on behalf of its newer and younger dancing star, Gene Kelly.

"Gene and I used to pass each other every day in the street at the studio," said Donen. "One day he stopped me and said, 'I've been hired over at Columbia to do a picture called *Cover Girl,* and I've just seen the musical numbers.' " These, judging by Kelly's face, were in trouble; they had been shot in advance, before *Cover Girl* had cast its leading man.

"Part of my deal," Kelly explained to Donen, "is that I'm going to be able to do my own numbers. Would you like to come along, and you and I will do my numbers together?"

Asked in 1994 to recall the same incident, Kelly told magazine interviewer Graham Fuller: "Stanley was a chorus boy in two of my Broadway shows and came out here as a chorus boy for M-G-M. When they fired him, I said, 'Come on down to Columbia and work as my assistant on *Cover Girl.'* He was like a son to me."*

Donen early on learned to overlook the Kelly swipes, both public and private. "I was never fired from M-G-M," he clarified. "What happened was this: Every week the job orders were handed down by the studio casting office, and, suddenly, one week there was no call for dancers. Instead, I was told to report to some set where I was to play an extra. I was shocked. They couldn't do that to me, I decided. I went back to the casting office—me, this young nobody—and told them, 'You can't have

---

* Kelly is twelve years Donen's senior. His account is riddled with errors but serves to demonstrate Kelly's long-standing attempt to diminish Donen's contribution to their collective work.

me do that. I'm a dancer. If you force me to play an extra, that would hurt my ego.' "

Faced with Kelly's offer, Donen went on to explain, "I had a one-year contract with M-G-M, and Columbia borrowed me because M-G-M at that point would have done anything for Gene. Then, suddenly, *Cover Girl* got to be an experience like *Pal Joey*. I'd only been in California less than a year and suddenly I was really swinging. Now I was really in the movies."

From left, producer Joseph Pasternak, the film's director, George Sidney, set designer Jack Martin Smith, and an ever eager young observer conferring on the Hollywood Bowl scene for *Anchors Aweigh* (1945)

Part 2

Apprentice

Chapter 1

"We Were Appalled"

T HE ATMOSPHERE at Columbia was very different from that at
M-G-M," said Donen. "It was more exciting. Not that I had the
same people around that I had at M-G-M, but because Columbia
was so tiny, it was a great place to do everything."

Physically, the studio was more compact than Metro's sprawling estate
in Culver City, which was surrounded by a high wooden fence of forest
green, looking as though it were protecting a midwestern county fair.
Columbia afforded no such niceties. Guardrails of chain link and cinder
block surrounded Columbia's tight, beige-painted cement compound at
the corner of downtown Hollywood's Gower Street and Sunset Boulevard. As for the two studios' opposing power brokers, L. B. Mayer may
have been a paternal dictator, but nobody ever accused Harry Cohn of
being a father figure. Cohn's oversize reputation incited apprehension
even in people who did not work for him, while his staff furtively referred
to the boss as "Harry the Horrible"—until Ben Hecht coined the definitive nickname, "White Fang."

"Cohn was tough," Donen confirmed, "but also very interested in his
films being good, because his films were a true expression of himself. He
was only being tough about what he thought was right. In a sense, he was
the entire show, and you either pleased him or he'd kick you out." Not one
to be intimidated himself, Donen in fact admired the man: "He wasn't
frightened about doing things that were financially risky, and he was completely without personal feelings, which I think is probably good. He may
have sounded gruff, but all in all, he was a good guy."

The composer Arthur Schwartz, whom Cohn selected to produce
Cover Girl, concurred with the deflected criticism of the Columbia chief.
"In spite of everything people have said about Harry Cohn," Schwartz

Harry Cohn, the head of Columbia Pictures, known to many as "White Fang"; to an admiring few—such as an impressionable Donen—as "a good guy"

related to movie historian John Kobal, "he had an instinct for quality. Jack Warner couldn't have had the taste [to make *Cover Girl*], while at Metro they would have overproduced it—too many girls and too many of everything."

Cohn's dictatorial manner allowed for the extensive filming of *Cover Girl*'s dialogue and musical numbers that did not require the services of its leading man—because, still well into production, *Cover Girl* had no leading man. Larry Parks, a Columbia contractee, came under consideration, as did, temporarily, Gene Kelly, although Cohn balked when Schwartz first made the suggestion. Cohn had seen Kelly in *Pal Joey* and was prompted to buy the show's film rights, but he maintained from the start that Kelly was "too short" to play opposite Cohn's star attraction, Rita Hayworth. When, deeper into the filming of *Cover Girl,* Schwartz brought up Kelly's name a second time, Cohn, for no apparent reason, reversed himself and responded, "Thank God."

"*Cover Girl's* director was Charles Vidor," said Donen, "and the choreographer was a guy named Val Raset." The elaborate title number, a Broadway fashion show with models coming to life on the covers of actual women's magazines, was staged by Seymour Felix, who had choreographed *Yankee Doodle Dandy* at Warners.

"When Gene and I got to Columbia," said Donen, "we looked at the footage of what they'd shot and we were appalled." In the finished film, so as to leave no question that Donen and Kelly were not responsible for the lackluster opening number, an imprecise can-can called "The Show Must Go On," the brash newcomers inserted three reaction shots of Kelly in the wings, shaking his head in disapproval. A permanently visible slap in the face, it would not soon be overlooked.

Other numbers completed before the arrival of Kelly and Donen included two plodding gay nineties flashback theatrical pieces—"Sure Thing" and "Poor John"—which seriously impeded plot continuity, and a so-so nightclub number about current war shortages, "Who's Complaining?"

The rayon-thin plot, originally conceived years before as a comedy vehicle for Jean Arthur, concerns the love-versus-career tribulations of Rusty Parker (Hayworth), a dancer in a Brooklyn honky-tonk, who wins a *Vanity* magazine cover-girl contest. Her face is splashed across newsstands, and she leaps from the Brooklyn chorus to a headlined spot on Broadway. The sudden notoriety also yanks her out of the possessive arms of the pouty owner of the honky-tonk, Danny McGuire (Kelly).

"Though its story has the usual backstage background," Karel Reisz said of *Cover Girl* when he reexamined it, as a critic, in the 1950s, "its numbers are staged in the open air and characters dance in it for the sheer joy of dancing and as an expression of mood." Reisz zeroed in on this departure from setting musical numbers on a theatrical stage and considered the change "the transition from the old to the new."

That calculated shift may be credited to Donen and Kelly. The staging in *Cover Girl,* in the sequences they conceived, choreographed, filmed— and in Kelly's case performed—provides the necessary jolts that the contrived, meandering story and the schmaltzy score cried out for. Virginia Van Upp, Cohn's favored screenwriter and eventually one of Hollywood's

Clowning between takes for *Cover Girl*'s "Make Way for Tomorrow" number: from left, choreographer of record Val Raset, Gene Kelly, director Charles Vidor, Rita Hayworth, Phil Silvers, lyricist Sammy Cahn, and actor Ed Brophy

first women producers, conceived most of the screenplay, while the musical sound track bore the impressive imprimatur of two titans of American popular song, Jerome Kern and Ira Gershwin. (Gershwin acknowledged that his deadline-induced lyrics for the film's most hummable song, "Long Ago and Far Away," were far from being on a level with his best work—even if the number did turn out to be the biggest hit of his career.)

The colorful but leaden movie's first powerful zap of energy comes nearly half an hour into the running time, with the breezy anthem "Make Way for Tomorrow," for which E. Y. "Yip" Harburg, who provided the wise rhymes for *The Wizard of Oz*, collaborated with Gershwin. The number begins at Joe's Oyster House in Brooklyn, where Joe serves the usual to Danny, Rusty, and Genius (Phil Silvers,* playing the comic sidekick role that Donald O'Connor would later assume in *Singin' in the Rain*). The trio

---

* Donen: "A sweet and funny man. When, years later, he was playing Sergeant Bilko, a father introduced his son to Phil and said that he was on TV. 'Really?' said the little boy. 'Are you a dog?'"

orders "ersters with their coats on," to see if any are concealing a "poil," the omen that things will look up for them. Tonight, alas, is not the night, and Genius wistfully sighs, "Better luck tomorrow."

"Tomorrow!" exclaim Danny and Rusty. From behind the counter, Joe points a finger at the diner's piano player and declares, "Here we go again." The three pals spin on their counter stools, leap to their feet, and dance backward out of the restaurant, joyfully making their way down the street, to end up at Rusty's apartment building.

Kern furnishes a lively, freewheeling traveling melody, while Harburg and Gershwin, somehow foreseeing Kelly's great moment in *Singin' in the Rain,* provided the trio with the lyrics:

> What if it rains and it pours?
> It only rains out of doors!
> Let every frown disappear
> And you'll find that tomorrow's here!

Several conceptual and visual elements during the three-minute show-stopper will, in fact, come to light in Kelly-Donen efforts to follow: the sense of camaraderie among a threesome (the sailors in *On the Town,* the ex–army buddies in *It's Always Fair Weather,* and the "Good Morning" ménage in *Singin' in the Rain*), an intruding cop on the beat (here he sends Rusty, Danny, and Genius scurrying around a corner, while in *Singin' in the Rain* the patrolman brings the title number to a close), and the use of ordinary objects as musical instruments (the trash-can lids as tap shoes during the "Binge" dance in *It's Always Fair Weather*).

During "Make Way for Tomorrow," every last prop in the trio's path turns into fair game—a bread stick becomes a conductor's baton, fisherman's oars become bass fiddles, a mailbox becomes an Indian tom-tom. In other words, here is the freedom and beauty of this "new" type of musical: The everyday becomes the extraordinary. The routine transforms itself into a realm of dreams. By the time of *Singin' in the Rain,* a rain-drenched lamppost will be not a lamppost at all but a sunny perch from which a singing herald formally declares his love.

Remarking on *Cover Girl*'s steady parade of vibrant images—as well as its unenlightened notions of feminine sexuality—film specialist and academician Jeanine Basinger noted: "No one who saw *Cover Girl* has ever forgotten it. Man and woman, boy and girl, the audience of the 1940s was galvanized by its glamour, color, musical oomph, but most of all by its goddess-like star, Rita Hayworth, quite posibly the definitive sex goddess."

"Rita *was* a giant star at the moment," said Donen. "Of all the women movie stars I've worked with, she was the most cooperative. It wasn't for the best reason, because I think she had a low opinion of herself. At the time, anything you would tell her she would accept."

It was not until years later that Donen ascertained the reason Hayworth was so compliant. "I subsequently read that she had gone through all these horrible things I knew nothing about, such as an incestuous relationship with her father and a physically abusive first marriage." Eduardo Cansino, Rita's father, had her dancing with him professionally in Tijuana nightclubs by the year 1930, when she was twelve, and her first husband, the pimplike Edward Judson, threatened to scar her face with battery acid whenever she mentioned divorce. By that time she was a star, and Harry Cohn was able to intercede.

Of her musical abilities, Donen said, "Rita was intimidated by Gene. First of all, she felt she wasn't a very good dancer, and I agreed with her. She was not a very good dancer. However you want to put it, she was either too tall or Gene was too short, but the two of them did not work well together."

Contrary to Donen's opinion, the two glide majestically, despite some stilted steps, through "Long Ago and Far Away," an effective number set in the honky-tonk after hours. Hayworth's efforts to keep up with Kelly, though evident, are never an intrusion; if anything, they have the reverse effect and enhance her appeal. (Hayworth's singing voice was dubbed by Martha Mears, just as Kelly was provided a vocal assist on his higher notes.) Jeanine Basinger, in evaluating Hayworth's performance, called the star "beautiful, exotic, enviable, desirable ... dancing, whirling, twirling, active, smiling, laughing ... a living breathing talent." Audiences were inclined to agree.

TWO MORE musical interludes were commandeered by Donen and Kelly: "Put Me to the Test," performed by Kelly and Hayworth on the movie's nightclub stage, and a sequence that Donen, at the age of nineteen, directed entirely on his own, something he called "the double-exposure number, where Gene dances with his own image." It became known as the "Alter Ego" number.

The mood piece deposited Kelly into what would become a familiar backdrop, a deserted nighttime street.

"The sequence occurred to me," said Donen, "because two people dancing together is more powerful, precise, and fun than one person

A publicity still for the "Alter Ego" number in *Cover Girl* (1944). In rehearsal, Kelly's "double" was the scene's originator and, ultimately, its director, Stanley Donen.

dancing alone. Then I thought: What would happen if those two people were the same person? So I went to Gene and asked him, 'How'd you like a number where you dance with yourself?' Well, the idea appealed to him on a number of levels."

Charles Vidor, still the director of record,* was presented with the idea by the two upstarts but insisted that it would be technically impossible. Donen challenged Vidor and claimed he knew how it could be accomplished.

"Years later," said Donen, "we simply would have used computers, but back then this was something entirely new. We would have to repeat the camera moves by ourselves, with Gene performing the dance twice to the prerecorded sound track. I knew it could be done by having him hit the same spots the second time as he did the first, which Gene could do, and then we could film it by having the camera hit the same marks both times, which I knew I could do."

Donen's healthy confidence sprang from his repeated childhood experiments with the camera in the backseat of his family's car. But "Charles Vidor had no conception of anything like that," Donen recalled. "He kept saying, 'It won't work.' And I said, 'It'll work.' And Cohn said to Gene, 'Will it work?' And Gene said, 'It'll work.' So Cohn said, 'Then it'll work.' "

Vidor completely washed his hands of the number and its proponents, declaring one final time, "It won't work."

WATCHING *Cover Girl*'s fifty-year-old "Alter Ego" number on the thirty-two-inch video screen in his own home, Donen commented, "The great thing about choreography for the movies is that there are no hard and fast rules about what you can do. Choreography can be anything from an elaborate production number with a crowd of people to something as simple as Fred Astaire sitting in a chair, tapping his fingers. If you think about it, the three greatest examples of screen choreography aren't in musicals at all but in Charlie Chaplin movies: his dancing with the globe, his shaving the customer to the rhythm of the 'Hungarian Rhapsody,' and his bouncing the dinner rolls on the ends of his forks."

In the four-minute "Alter Ego" number, the choreography begins with the recalcitrant Danny burning shoe leather over being jilted by

* Eve Arden, who played the smart, wisecracking *Vanity* magazine editor (shades of Kay Thompson in the later *Funny Face*), recalled Vidor as "the tempestuous Hungarian."

Rusty. Hands shoved firmly into pockets, he rounds the corner and enters a deserted city block, impervious to what he is passing—a brick wall, weathered advertising posters, telephone poles, and a row of brownstones and shopwindows that reflect his angry image in their glass. Unrelenting, he continues wallowing in self-pity, listening to himself, weighing aloud the ramifications of Rusty's not meeting him, of his never seeing her again, of her career outdistancing his.

"Wait a minute, Danny McGuire," he says to himself. "She stood you up and you know it."

Donen interrupts the screening. "Ever refer to yourself by your full name?"

Kelly continues to brood and stomp down the sidewalk. With no hint of warning, there materializes in one of the shopwindows the image of a stationary Kelly, arms crossed confidently against his chest, in stark contrast to the insecure Kelly in nervous motion on the pavement. "Don't be such a hardheaded Irishman," the psychological twin calls out from the window. "If you really love Rusty you'll let her go." But the real person on the street gives the reflection a cold shoulder, leaving the image to leap off the windowpane and meet his match on the pavement—and chase after him. The reflection then hypnotically draws the real person into a dance, placing *two* Kellys before us, engaged in a high-octane dancing duel.

"The precision's amazing," notes Donen.

The number formally begins, accompanied at the outset by a rhapsodic arrangement of "Long Ago and Far Away." Kelly One and Kelly Two can hardly contain themselves as they test each other's endurance in time to the full-bodied rhythm.

"Gene was always in the right place at the right instant," says Donen, "because he always dances to the music."

Arms outstretched, bodies sliding, feet tapping, two Kellys whirl, twirl, leapfrog, one Kelly over the other . . .

"That was a great trick," says Donen, "his jumping over himself."

. . . stomping left foot and right, upstairs and down, climbing the power poles and then letting go, the mortal Kelly executing a dynamic spin as his protoplasmic alter ego pauses, unnoticed, to take a breather . . .

"The inspiration for that last step was the mirror sequence in *Duck Soup*," says Donen, referring to the time that Harpo (or was it Chico?) fools Groucho into thinking he's looking at himself in a nonexistent reflective glass instead of at a prowler in full Groucho regalia.

. . . until the number ends angrily and abruptly, with the imaginary Kelly returning to the safety of a shopwindow and the genuine Kelly debating whether to join him in the haven or continue to dance in the street.

Once the figment of his imagination refuses to obey, a hostile Kelly summarily disposes of him entirely, by heaving a trash can sideways into the immense plate-glass window and, shoulders slumped just as they had been at the outset, silently skulking off.

How was it done? "With chalk marks and wire and tape and counts on the sound track," says Donen. "We used a fixed-head camera for the necessary precision and then synchronized the two dances in the editing room. First we photographed Gene and then we covered the entire set in black felt. Then we marked with chalk where his steps were and we photographed him all over again. The set was the size of a city block. It took forever because every movement had to be duplicated. I'd work with Gene and count, 'One, two, three, four, pan, two, three, four, tilt,' and so on. If you look carefully, you can see a moment where Gene floats slightly. That's because the moves of the camera the second time were not as precise as they should have been."

The musical arranger Saul Chaplin recalled the arduous rehearsal for the number, with Donen playing the alter ego opposite Kelly. A problem arose, according to Chaplin, because Kelly was such a fast dancer that Donen had trouble keeping up. The worst snag involved the slide down the telephone pole. When Kelly reached the ground before his "shadow," the impatient leading man yelled before the crowd of technicians, "Stanley, move your fat ass."

Chapter 2

"He Called the Shots"

A LL TOLD, I spent a year at Columbia," said Donen, who strove to become less the apprentice and more the sorcerer. "So many hours every day, seven days a week, I spent on *Cover Girl,* in the cutting room, in the dubbing theater, putting together the double-exposure number, doing everything that was required. Gene, by this time, was long gone, back to M-G-M."

Late during postproduction, Donen overheard in the editing room that Harry Cohn was prepared to sneak the picture before an audience that night.

"Great," Donen piped up to his colleagues. "Where's it going to be?"

The others greeted his question with a dubious stare. "We don't know," said one.

"Well, I'm going," announced Donen.

"No you're not," replied another.

When Harry Cohn previewed pictures, Donen was informed, he "would take with him in his car only the people he wanted, the director and whomever, and even Cohn's driver didn't know where they were going. Cohn went so far as to arrange the preview with the theater manager himself, over the phone, so not even a secretary would be in on it."

Any studio employee who had the nerve to crash the preview would be fired, if caught.

Donen had the nerve.

"It was the end of the day, and I was sitting in the parking lot, still trying to figure out how I was going to learn where this thing was being held," said Donen. "I mean, the movie was my baby. I'm the one who had worked on it for a year. There was no way I was *not* going to this preview.

Then suddenly I looked up and saw Cohn get into his car with Charles Vidor and the film cutter."

Donen trailed the black limo as far as downtown Pasadena, where he spied the men emerging in front of the Crown Theater. Donen parked on a side street.

"I bought my ticket and went in," he remembered. Sitting high in the balcony, "I watched *Cover Girl.*"

"Make Way for Tomorrow" received heavy applause. Then something awful happened. More fearsome than being detected by Cohn was the sudden audience reaction to the "Alter Ego" number. Uncontrollable laughter in the theater greeted Kelly when he started talking to himself, thus effectively spoiling the mood and the entire sequence that followed. What had been intended to inspire awe was unexpectedly being met by loud, raucous cackles. No number could survive this, and surely Harry Cohn would demand that Donen's ambitious undertaking be cut from the picture.

It was not, although for a time its survival was in serious jeopardy. Days after the preview, feeling he owed Cohn an apology, the Pasadena theater manager rang the studio chief to explain that the picture that preceded *Cover Girl* on the bill was *Flesh and Fantasy,* starring Edward G. Robinson. In it, Robinson spoke to his reflection in a plate-glass window, so the audience was simply responding to the silliness of the coincidence.

Cover Girl, opening in April 1944, was an immense hit. It filled Radio City Music Hall, established Gene Kelly as a star, and proved one of the great morale boosters during the final year of the war. Seeking to revive the flagging spirits of its staff, the British Ministry of Information's film division ran the picture every morning.

Reflecting on his own attitude toward *Cover Girl,* Donen, to whom sentimentality is about as desirable as singing flat, remarked, "At the time we made it, I was enormously proud. I wanted to take all the credit for it. Then, as time went on, I did everything I could to disown it."

PREPARED TO parlay the success of *Cover Girl* into another Hayworth-Kelly vehicle, Harry Cohn ordered into production *Pal Joey,* to be directed by Victor Saville. Envisioning it as a reunion for the stars, Cohn was prepared to sanitize the story line for the censors' sake and to promote its headliners as the new Rogers and Astaire in order to bring in the crowds.

Whether the performers could have survived the comparison will never be known. As it was, Kelly would never be paired with a semipermanent romantic interest as Astaire was; Kelly generally danced solo or with a buddy (more often than not, two buddies). He and Hayworth were perfect for *Pal Joey,* however, and more than likely, Metro knew this. That may account for why, though Cohn had been responsible for turning Gene Kelly into a box office name, M-G-M refused to allow his services to be available to Columbia.*

"My own one-year contract with M-G-M expired," Donen said of 1943 and 1944, the period when he was on loan-out to work on *Cover Girl.* "Columbia then put me under contract to Columbia. It was a one-year contract, with an option to renew for another seven years, one year at a time."

The first twelve months served as Donen's true apprenticeship. "I did a lot of movies for the studio," he said, "so many I can't remember them all, but they were a lot of terrible B pictures. They were the *Beach Party* movies of their time."

Donen's contributions were "a musical number here, a musical number there, a lot of band numbers, and a lot of Ann Miller numbers. I'd do what I could. I'd have to find an idea, which somehow had to be connected to what was going on in the picture, and make it different from real life. There's no secret to coming up with a dance number for a movie, except you have to get up and keep trying. Dancing is a physical act. I don't know of any choreographer who can dream up a dance while sitting in a chair."

Within the first year of his Columbia contract, Donen was rewarded with a meaty assignment. "The studio was going to make a movie called *Tonight and Every Night,* with Rita Hayworth and Janet Blair, and I was going to be the choreographer. The producer-director was Victor Saville."

Saville had started as a screenwriter for British-Gaumont Studios in 1920 and by the 1930s had directed some of the more prominent Metro pictures to come out of England, including *Goodbye, Mr. Chips. Evergreen,* an airy musical vehicle that starred Jessie Matthews, had also been his, and it introduced the lilting Rodgers and Hart number "Dancing on the Ceiling," about an anonymous dream lover who lives on the floor above. The score for Saville's *Tonight and Every Night* would be by Sammy Cahn and Jule Styne, veterans of Tin Pan Alley who had both worked in Hollywood since the late thirties.

---

* A heavily bowdlerized *Pal Joey* made it to the screen in 1957, the year before Harry Cohn died. Directed by George Sidney, it starred Frank Sinatra and Rita Hayworth, demoted to the role of Vera, Joey's older, world-weary benefactress. Kim Novak played the nightclub dancer Linda English.

"*Tonight and Every Night* was about the Windmill Theatre in London," said Donen. "The Windmill had a sign up that said 'We Never Close,' and all through the Blitz it was open every night. In truth, the movie didn't tell the story, because the reason the Windmill Theatre was such a success was that in England at the time a law existed that said you could have naked girls on the stage—provided they didn't move. In other words, if you presented them as art, like in a painting, they could be as naked as you wanted them. So the Windmill put these stark-naked women on the stage, they never moved, and all through the war they were a gigantic smash. Servicemen flocked inside to see them."

In the script, based on the play *Heart of a City* by Lesley Storm, the setting was renamed the Music Box, which, all through the Blitz, stays open so its visitors can behold beautiful girls in beautiful costumes. In another departure from reality, the generous stage of the fictitious Music Box resembled nothing of the tiny platform of the Windmill.

"After all those hideous B pictures I'd been doing, my being the choreographer on *Tonight and Every Night* was a big deal," said Donen. "Rita Hayworth and Janet Blair."

Donen read the script, "which I thought was awful," and headed off to the first production meeting, which took place in the rather grand setting of Victor Saville's offices.

"There I am," said Donen, "nineteen years old and theoretically the choreographer, sitting with the costume designer, the set designer, Maurice Stoloff, who was head of the music department, and we're all sitting there as Victor Saville is holding court. Now, apparently, as he was talking, I didn't realize it, but I was shaking my head, just gently, reacting to everything Victor Saville was saying."

Donen was shaking his head from side to side, as if to accentuate the negative.

"After the meeting, as the others were leaving, Victor Saville said, 'Stanley, could I see you a minute?' "

The producer asked Donen if he was aware of his actions throughout the meeting.

"No," replied Donen. "What are you talking about?"

Saville demonstrated.

"I'm sorry," said Donen.

"Why did you do that?" pressed Saville.

Donen decided to take Saville into his confidence. "I don't think you understand about musical numbers and what needs to be done," said

Donen. "The ideas for the musical numbers you have aren't very good. There are going to have to be a lot of changes made."

Saville made one right on the spot. *Tonight and Every Night* was choreographed by Jack Cole.

"GENE WENT back to M-G-M to do a movie called *Anchors Aweigh*," said Donen, "and he said, 'I want this guy back at M-G-M,' so M-G-M borrowed me back from Columbia to work on Gene's numbers."

In the interim, Donen's Columbia contract, with its yearly options that were to run through 1951, expired and was not renewed, for reasons Donen was not to learn for another forty-two years. The choreographer Val Raset, whose duties Donen had usurped on *Cover Girl,* had slyly made his opinion heard around the Columbia lot and by Harry Cohn himself that Donen was "untalented." The ploy worked; the young comer's contract was canceled. Jump cut to 1985, with Raset out of the blue contacting Donen to ask that the director *please* have Raset's name removed from the Hollywood blacklist on which Donen had him placed.

"I didn't know what the hell he was talking about," said Donen, who tried to assure Raset, to no avail, that he had never done anything of the kind. "I was horrified. Who did he think I was, to hold all of Hollywood in my hands like that? I felt like that drawing of Shaw on the poster for *My Fair Lady,* sitting in the clouds and controlling the strings of Eliza and Henry Higgins."

Raset confessed to his subterfuges in 1943, but now that Donen had been successful in his own right, surely he could see his way to forgiveness. " 'I forgive you,' " replied Donen. "Then he wanted me to see if I could help get him a job on a musical. Never mind that nobody was making musicals anymore."

Actually, Donen felt, Raset had unintentionally done him a tremendous favor, because "when Columbia didn't pick up my contract, M-G-M signed me to a brand-new one, and M-G-M was the greatest studio in the world."*

---

* Spelling out one of the conditions of his M-G-M contract, which began anew in 1944, Donen said: "I stayed at M-G-M twelve years, until 1956. That made me eligible for the M-G-M pension plan, which meant *bupkes* [Yiddish for, loosely, "beans"], because of the way it worked at M-G-M. To be eligible for the pension plan, you had to have had ten years of consistent service, and there was a sliding scale depending upon your age. That's because the plan had been drawn up for Louis B. Mayer, Eddie Mannix, Benny Thau, L. K. Sidney, and all the executives. They were sixty-five, I was still in my teens. Eventually the plan ended and you had to take the money. I think I got ten thousand dollars."

The world, in turn, was being great to M-G-M. The war drove audiences to the movies en masse, and in 1944, the year Donen returned to Culver City, M-G-M earned an all-time revenue peak, $166 million, a record it was to break the following year, with $175 million.

Picking up where he had left off, Donen returned as a more experienced hand, though one with his nose firmly pressed up against the windows of the Freed Unit. At M-G-M he was daily directed to wherever his services were required on the lot, with the preponderance of his assignments being with the Number Two team, the Pasternak Unit.

Joe Pasternak (1901–1991) was a Hungarian émigré who, before coming to Metro, had made Deanna Durbin a star at Universal and resuscitated Marlene Dietrich's career with *Destry Rides Again*. Donen found him to be "a dear man, a nice man. He liked stories that had a certain . . . the only word I can think of is 'sweetness.' His movies reflected his own attitudes and his interest in singing and girls. I don't mean 'girls' in the sense that he was running after girls, but girl singers, like Jane Powell and Deanna Durbin. Personally, I thought his movies were real crap—and he made so many of them."

Anchors Aweigh qualifies on all those counts. The girl, called Susie, is played by the nasal soprano Kathryn Grayson, and the plot is a mess. Hoping to do for Frank Sinatra what he had done for Dietrich, Pasternak cast the thin crooner, whose film career had been floundering at RKO, and top-billed him as a sexually naive choirboy named Clarence. (The inside joke must have been that Sinatra was about as sexually naive as he was a choirboy.) Clarence is on leave in Los Angeles with his navy buddy, the horny and experienced Joseph (although no one calls him "pal Joey"), played by Gene Kelly. Clarence and Joseph meet Susie's orphaned nephew (Dean Stockwell) when the boy runs away to join the navy, and they meet her when they take him home. Susie has one goal, to break into the movies, and she believes her only way in is to meet the musician José Iturbi, who, before this slow-moving pageant grinds to its finale, plays a snippet from Tchaikovsky's First Piano Concerto and *all* of Liszt's Second Hungarian Rhapsody.

Hanging somewhere on this framework is a scene of Susie's singing part time in a downtown Mexican restaurant. On his way to visit her there, Kelly stops to perform a self-conscious Mexican Hat Dance with a beggar child (Sharon McManus in dark makeup). It's the first in a long, long line of efforts at endearing Kelly to children—and therefore to audiences—by having him dance with them.

Nontraditional casting, 1945: Frank Sinatra as a sheep and Gene Kelly as a wolf. The movie they are publicizing is *Anchors Aweigh*.

As related by Kelly biographer Clive Hirschhorn, such cuteness did not come easily. "While Sharon MacManus [*sic*] and Dean Stockwell adored Gene because he made them laugh," Hirschhorn reported, "little Miss MacManus was also required to dance, and this presented certain problems to Stanley Donen, who was once again Gene's assistant on the film, and to whom fell the thankless task of teaching her the routines."

According to Hirschhorn's account, Donen once exhausted three hours in the morning and another four in the afternoon over the child's single step with a jump rope, by which time Donen "did not wish ever again to see another little girl, or a skipping-rope, unless the . . . rope was for . . . hanging the little girl."

In contrast, "Every half hour Gene would pop into the rehearsal room and airily enquire whether Sharon had got the 'rope bit' yet, and Stanley would reply with an icy 'no'—and glower, at which point Gene would call him aside and say, 'Stanley, but the secret is to make her believe you *love* her.' "

Donen reportedly replied, "But I loathe her."

Little Sharon returned the animosity, "so that by the time the scene came to be shot," said Hirschhorn, "she would have done anything for Gene, if only to spite Stanley."

"WE WERE in the middle of shooting when I called up Gene at three in the morning," recalled Donen, who told Kelly he was so excited that he couldn't sleep. "I have a great idea." The nocturnal inspiration had sprung from Donen's memories of animator Max Fleischer's *Out of the Inkwell* series, which would open with a human artist drawing cartoon figures that popped out of the inkwell on his easel.

"It had better be good," growled Kelly. "You woke me up."

"Gene," said Donen. "How'd you like to dance with Mickey Mouse?"

"Mickey Mouse?" repeated Kelly. "Can it be done?"

"Sure," Donen answered. "I know how."

"The M-G-M brass didn't think it could be done," remembered Kelly, who then, according to Donen, took the idea to Pasternak, who brought it to Mayer. The concept was appealing; if a marriage of animation and human live action could be pulled off, it might conceivably benefit the studio. Pasternak advised Donen and Kelly to find out as much as they could about the process but not to work up their hopes about using it in *Anchors Aweigh*. For advice, Donen and Kelly turned to the most famous animator they could think of.

"We met Walt Disney in his tiny office," remembered Donen. Disney was still operating out of his original facility, on Hyperion Boulevard in the Silverlake district, between downtown Los Angeles and Hollywood. "Actually," said Donen, "at this point Gene and I had given the matter some thought. We didn't want Mickey Mouse at all, but Donald Duck. He was a much bigger star at the time."

Disney greeted them cordially. "He could not have been more sweet and welcoming," remembered Donen, "despite his reputation for being an anti-Semite and a terrible right-winger. Then again, Gene's last name was Kelly and mine wasn't Moskowitz. But he was tremendously kind to us, and a true artist. Oh boy, what he contributed to movies! There's a great story about him—there are a lot, I suppose—but the one that I think says it best about him, and about the care he took in what he was doing and the sacrifices he was willing to make in order to survive, took place in the early years. He opened the studio with his brother Roy, and they were always in some kind of trouble with the banks. One day Roy told him that they're going to have to save money, and one way they can do it is to take away Mickey's tail. It would conserve ink, hours of drawing, whatever, but there was no question about it, Mickey would have to lose his tail. So that's what Walt did. He took away Mickey Mouse's tail. Until the economic crisis passed."

Kelly and Donen spelled out their idea to the animator, who listened with interest. "As a matter of fact," Disney responded, "I'm working on something like that right now. Would you like to see the tests?"

Disney personally escorted them into a projection room and ran the few assembled reels from his upcoming *The Three Caballeros,* in which Donald Duck and a parrot named José Carioca sang and danced with live actors in South America. Donen found the scenes technically unsophisticated, with the animated figures merely superimposed against the authentic background. What he wanted to develop was more of an interaction between the drawn characters and their human costars. And, reversing what Disney was showing, Donen wanted to drop a real person—Kelly—into a completely animated environment.

"After Walt Disney showed us these tests," said Donen, "we told him we had this idea for Gene to dance with Mickey Mouse, and told him the little story we had concocted."

In the sequence, Kelly would begin by telling a group of schoolchildren a fairy tale about an oppressive kingdom where singing and dancing is forbidden, until Kelly meets the king—Mickey or Donald—and, through the dance, convinces him to rescind the order.

Disney said, "Let me get this straight. It's an M-G-M picture?"

"Yes," said Kelly.

"And you want Mickey Mouse to be in an M-G-M picture?"

Donen and Kelly confirmed that.

"Well, I'm sorry, boys," responded Disney, "but Mickey Mouse will never be in an M-G-M picture. He works for me."*

"So," said Donen, "we used the M-G-M mouse, Jerry Mouse."

* Actually, in 1934, Disney did provide a Mickey Mouse cartoon sequence, in color, for M-G-M's *Hollywood Party,* starring Jimmy Durante and directed by Richard Boleslawski, Allan Dwan, and Roy Rowland.

* * *

WITH THE HELP of eight M-G-M animators, Donen assembled the sequence over the span of the next year, while Kelly, having spent two months shooting his part, entered the navy. The M-G-M animation department, founded in 1939 and located on Lot Two, was supervised by William Hanna and Joseph Barbera, who would later spin off their own studio and create Yogi Bear and the Flintstones for television.

For the *Anchors Aweigh* number, the first step was to devise a story-board incorporating the eight minutes of narrative with its musical accompaniment, "The Worry Song" by Sammy Fain and Ralph Freed (Arthur's brother). The cameraman, with Donen at his side, photographed Kelly as if Jerry the Mouse had been present on the set. A cardboard cutout of Jerry was used to help block out the scene.

Kelly would "rehearse with this cutout," recalled Joseph Barbera, "then he'd come back and we'd shoot Kelly by himself." Next, they "took that film of Kelly and laboriously traced each and every single frame onto animation paper." The final process was to pick up the mouse "and put him on the same piece of paper, and we photographed them together."

The first time the scene was previewed at the studio, something was amiss—namely, Jerry's shadow, something Gene Kelly had when he danced inside the castle but Jerry did not. "It looked as though he were stuck on glass," said Donen. The sequence went back to the drawing board.

"The studio kept saying, 'Forget it. Let's release the picture without the cartoon,' " said Donen, "but they had so many other pictures going to theaters at the time that it wasn't a problem. I kept working on the one scene."

"The fact that Disney considered the idea feasible helped us," remembered Gene Kelly.* "I get all the credit for this, but it would have been impossible for me to do without Stanley. He worked with the cameramen and called the shots in all these intricate timings and movements."

"The net result," said Joseph Barbera, "at the preview of *Anchors Aweigh* that I went to, blew the audience away."

"In *Anchors Aweigh,*" ventured critic Gerald Mast, "an odd mixture of high art (Kathryn Grayson and José Iturbi) and low entertainment (Kelly and Sinatra), more pieces of the Kelly portrait fit together." Mast found

---

* Kelly said that Disney charitably rang Eddie Mannix, general manager of M-G-M, to confirm that the effort would have its merits.

"Look at me!" exclaims Jerry the Mouse in *Anchors Aweigh*. "I'm dancing!" Nearly a quarter century later, the Barnaby Tucker character in *Hello, Dolly!*, directed by Gene Kelly, spouts the same line. Here, Kelly is supported by Tom and Jerry.

Kelly guilty of a tactical error in his first film, *For Me and My Gal,* by not wearing a uniform; not only did the oversight cost Kelly some wartime sympathy but, felt the cultural observer, "the military uniform fit him both spiritually and physically." Kelly's manner "suggested the buoyant, jaunty American GI of the nineteen-forties, the spirit that won the war, not the one that dodged the draft. It fit him physically because a uniform combines the formal and the casual, the tight and the loose, that Kelly's style and dancing themselves suggest."

Unlike Kelly's screen predecessor Fred Astaire, with his "reed of a body perfectly encased and showcased, hidden and revealed, by top hat and tails," Kelly had, according to Mast, a body that was "a coiled spring, a compact engine of tense muscles, a panther in human form, straining to break its social cages."

Chapter 3

"The Battle of Culver City"

FREDDIE NEY was this dance extra in *Cover Girl*," recalled Donen. "He played the milkman in the 'Make Way for Tomorrow' number." Donen described Ney as a "devout homosexual, with a decided mince," and one day Ney and he "were walking down Hollywood Boulevard together, when this really gruff-looking army sergeant started coming toward us on the other side of the pavement."

The closer the army man came to Donen and Ney, the more plainly visible was the look of contempt in his face, until finally he shouted at them, "Hey, you two, why aren't you in uniform?"

Freddie Ney promptly looked the irritated sergeant up and down. "What?" Ney replied. "With a war going on?"

"Horrible as it may sound," admitted Donen, "World War II was the farthest thing from my mind. I wasn't thinking about who was going to win, or how. In my head, I was in the movies. Then one day this letter arrived."

Donen was instructed to be on the corner of Beverly Drive and Wilshire Boulevard in Beverly Hills at five-thirty in the morning. "I was to bring a suitcase, a razor, a toothbrush, some underwear, because this was *it*. It wasn't like it had been at the beginning of the war. At that point you were mailed your letter, you went for your physical, then you waited a week or two before you'd get your assignment to Fort Bragg, or wherever. But with me, it was to be a physical and then good-bye. I was going to war."

Kelly, who had yet to ship off to the navy, hosted Donen's farewell party on a Metro soundstage the night before. "I was miserable," Donen said. "Five-thirty the next morning, the bus came. I was taken to the induction center in downtown Los Angeles with these other guys, and I had my physical. Then I was told, 'Go in that room over there and lay down.' "

Donen did as instructed, figuring "my going in there had to be part of the examination." He remained alone in the room for approximately an hour. "Then a guy came in, took my blood pressure, and left. All he said was, 'Just wait here.' "

An hour later the procedure was repeated. "I was still lying in my cot, only this time some other guy checked my blood pressure. He also left without saying a word."

Hour three, "I'm still lying there. This time someone else comes in, checks my blood pressure, and says, 'Come with me.' "

Donen handed over his documents, which were quickly returned after first receiving the heavy imprint of a large ink stamp.

Donen took a look: "4-F. REJECTED."

"I had high blood pressure," Donen discovered. "I never knew I had it. My blood pressure was *astronomical.*"

By Donen's calculation, "I was in the service half a day, from five-thirty in the morning until eleven—because by twelve noon I was back at M-G-M. From then on I fought the Battle of Culver City."

ON THE social front, "every Saturday," remembered Van Johnson, "the bunch of us would meet at Gene Kelly's house for franks, beans, and brown bread, and we'd play volleyball."

"They were always playing games, sports of some kind," remembered Kay Thompson, who had been hired to the Freed Unit by Roger Edens for a myriad of reasons, not the least of which was that she would serve as vocal coach for Judy Garland, Lena Horne, and others. "She wasn't so much in charge of teaching people how to sing note for note as she was to help with vocal styling and arrangements," said Gloria DeHaven. Style certainly seemed to be the operative word when it came to Thompson. "She was an idea person," was Van Johnson's description. "Whenever any-one had a problem, they would say, 'Get me Kay Thompson.' When I had to sing for the camera, I thought I'd die of fright, so they sent for Kay. She came in wearing a lynx coat and just sat there and smiled, and I sang to her. That was it. I got over my fright."

"She was a dynamo," said DeHaven. "Wildly talented, wildly flam-boyant, and wildly wild. When she entered a room, she *entered.* She wouldn't walk in, she'd float in, and her arms would rise. She owned every place she walked into. All eyes would turn. She had that kind of command."

Thompson, the daughter of a St. Louis jeweler, started playing the piano at the age of four (the year varies from account to account), and by the time she was fifteen, she had performed Franz Liszt's "Hungarian Fantasy" with the St. Louis Symphony—starting several bars late and tripping over a potted palm upon her exit. "I was a stage-struck kid," she would later tell a *Time* magazine reporter, "and I got out of St. Louis fast." At seventeen, Thompson went to California and landed her first job, as a diving instructor. Shortly afterward she found herself in a more appropriate setting, on the radio, singing with the Mills Brothers and, later, with Fred Waring. She proved so successful on the air that CBS offered Thompson her own show, *Kay Thompson and Company,* costarring Jim Backus, who would later make a name for himself on the television sitcoms *I Married Joan* and *Gilligan's Island.*

"We were an instantaneous flop," Thompson told an interviewer. "After this show I came to a serious decision. I had to be an actress and I had to be alone. So I went to Hollywood, where I was neither."

One of her first M-G-M assignments was to assist the choreographer Robert Alton with the Vincente Minnelli musical *The Harvey Girls,* starring Judy Garland. "I think I fell in love with Judy the second I saw her sitting on that train in the movie, eating the sandwich," said Thompson, who also brought her considerable songwriting talents to bear at the studio. Frequently she would audition her own numbers for Arthur Freed, who would listen and say, "Katie, you sang that great. You are terrific. Now, who can we get to sing it?"

In the decade immediately following Thompson's four-year stint at M-G-M, she headlined in what is still considered the smartest nightclub act to play the supper-club circuit, Kay Thompson and the Williams Brothers (Richard, Robert, Donald, and Andy); she wrote a series of best-sellers based on Eloise, a six-year-old *enfant terrible* who lives at New York's Plaza Hotel; and she costarred in *Funny Face.*

"I think the story of our lives comes through the wonderful people we run into," Thompson said in 1993. "We run into a stranger and, my God, the electricity. Our lives are ruled by this."

* * *

"[STANLEY] and Hugh Martin and Ralph Blane and all that New York gang practically lived at my house," Gene Kelly told an interviewer in 1994. "Sinatra and Judy [Garland] and Comden and Green were steady visitors, and then people from New York started to come. Lenny Bernstein, Oscar Levant, Johnny Green, Roger Edens, and Saul Chaplin would play the piano. It was a musical house."

"Live there?" echoed Donen. "I never lived there. I may have been at Gene's house day and night, but I never lived there."

"Stanley used to curl up on the floor of Gene's house and fall asleep," recalled Betty Comden, who, with her writing partner, Adolph Green, first came to M-G-M in 1947, to rework the book of the warhorse college musical *Good News* for Arthur Freed. "Stanley in those days," said Comden, "used to be quiet all the time."

"He was such a dynamo when he worked on the movies," said Green, picking up where his collaborator had left off, "that he must have been tired. On the set, his thinking was always precise and exact."

"He was just a kid," stressed Comden, "younger than the rest of us, a kind of good-looking, dark, curly-haired Southern boy."

"He had sort of an accent," said Green, "never a thick one, just a trace. And he was a very laconic speaker."

"Oh, I used to *love* Stanley's Southern accent," said Kay Thompson. "I loved it because it suited him so, especially when he first got to California."

"What we did a lot of," said Comden, "was laughing."

"And Stanley was part of this laughing group," said Green.

"We were laughing all the time," confirmed Kay Thompson. "Don't ask me what we were laughing about; we just had fun and wasted a lot of time. We used to drive down to places like Laguna Beach in between meetings at M-G-M, before he got so busy there. That's when Stanley was at his most Southern."

Providing an example of what struck everyone as so humorous, Donen said, "We used to play nasty, mean tricks on Frank Sinatra, because he was always a pain in the neck. He didn't want to work and was very quixotic and quick to anger, so we used to take great pleasure in teasing him."

One such incident took place in the M-G-M commissary, where each day Donen, Sinatra, and Kelly would break for lunch. "The M-G-M commissary had square tables," said Donen, "with blue plastic tops, pushed against the walls, like in a cafeteria. Every table was square, all but one, and that belonged to Gerry Mayer." Gerald Mayer was Louis B.'s brother, in charge of the physical running of the studio.

"So one day," said Donen, "mean bastards that we were, Gene and I said to Frank, 'Wouldn't it be wonderful if we could have a round table? It's so much nicer that way, because then we could sit closer together.' As soon as Frank heard us say that, he said, 'You watch, I'll get us a round table.'"

Donen's chuckle erupted into a roar. "There was no way Frank was going to get us a round table. We knew that. Then, when he was told to forget it, he got into this *huge* argument. He steamed and he fumed and threw fits and said he was going to quit. All this for a round table."

The commissary was the setting for another memorable incident. "It had to be the first day Betty and Adolph had come to the studio," said Donen. "I had known them in New York."*

"It may have been Stanley came to see us when we played at the Vanguard," said Adolph Green, trying to figure out exactly when he and Comden had met Donen.

"Yes, Adolph, but we went out to California to play the Trocadero before we had even written a movie," said Comden.

"Anyway," said Green, "he knew our numbers and our mentality, and we got to be buddies."

"When Betty and Adolph got to M-G-M," Donen resumed, "we were again having lunch in the commissary, at our square table, and this person sat down to talk with us awhile and asked Betty and Adolph how it was going. When he got up and walked away, Betty asked, 'Who was that nice, white-haired old man?'"

It was Louis B. Mayer.

"Stanley had a sense of fun," remembered Adolph Green.

"And of the absurd," chimed in Comden.

"As I told Betty only a few days ago," Donen said in 1991, "what upsets me now is that we didn't know how good we had it back then, what an extraordinary circumstance it was. We just thought of it as going to a job. M-G-M offered this great experience of having others around every day to meet with, discuss with, and argue about what was going on, not

---

* In 1939, Comden, Green, and their friend Judith Tuvim (Hebrew for "holiday," which she changed to Holliday) became part of a newly formed music-and-comedy act called The Revuers, which included a monologist named Al Hammer and a pianist-guitarist, John Frank. Their first professional engagement took place at Max Gordon's Village Vanguard, in New York.

Adolph Green and Betty Comden, "not part of the permanent landscape," c. 1950

only in movies but on every topic. We were a very small group of people who made musicals, like Lerner and Loewe, and Comden and Green. They were not part of the permanent landscape; they'd come out from New York, work on their scripts, finish them, and disappear. But some of us, like Gene and me, André Previn, Vincente [Minnelli], Roger Edens, musicians like Lennie Hayton, Saul Chaplin, Connie [Conrad] Salinger, we were a constant group, and a small one. We all saw one another every day, in the morning, at lunch, in the evening, in the rehearsal hall, day after day. These two people would be on this picture, and these three people would be on that picture. I think the whole atmosphere must've been similar to the experience shared by the Impressionist painters in Paris, of always being together every day in those cafés, talking about their work. That's what it was like for us."

What Donen and his group did not know at the time of this renaissance was that L. B. Mayer's style of studio leadership was slowly going the way of the silent picture. As soon as the war ended, filmmakers and other members of the talent pool began finding freer means of artistic expression than was offered at Metro-Goldwyn-Mayer.

"At M-G-M," Billy Wilder commented in 1992, "they covered everything in white satin sheets." Wilder was referring not only to the sets but to the overriding attitude toward production. One need only compare his hard-edged *Double Indemnity* at Paramount, based on the novel by James M. Cain, to M-G-M's starched and pressed version of the same writer's *The Postman Always Rings Twice*. Such trappings impeded Metro's ability to move with the flow.

American movie attendance reached an all-time peak in 1946, ninety million people per week, yet for the first time since 1933, when the entire industry was in a slump, M-G-M management ran scared. Although the earnings peaks of the previous two years were to be repeated in 1946, profits plummeted in 1947 and '48, due to a triple blow of inflation, a drying up of the European markets, and the simple fact that the war, as did the Depression, drove the masses into the movie theaters as a means of escape. One immediate disturbance in Culver City was that the great autocrat Mayer was constantly arguing with his East Coast superior, Nicholas Schenck, who controlled Loew's Incorporated, which in turn controlled Metro-Goldwyn-Mayer. Concerned, as were people on the lot, that Mayer was spending too much time with his racehorses and too little on the daily demands of the studio, Schenck ordered Mayer to hire a head of production, a position that had essentially been left vacant (or was theoretically occupied by Mayer) since the death of Irving Thalberg, in 1936.

Dore Schary, late of RKO, was hired in 1948—and thus began the precipitous decline of Mayer, and M-G-M.

AFTER THE *Anchors Aweigh* cartoon sequence, "Stanley became part of the A Group," said Sammy Cahn, "not that he ever acted like he was part of the A Group. He was always a very congenial young fella."

While it would be an overstatement to say that Donen acted as the studio's official in-house musical doctor, that, in a general sense, was his position, bolstering numbers for directors and choreographers around

Lot One and occasionally inserting numbers into pictures even when the original script had not called for any. "Arthur Loew, Jr., who was the son of one of the Loews and whose mother was a Zukor, used to say, 'Here at M-G-M, a documentary is a movie with only four songs,' "* Donen recalled.

Given the unnatural emphasis Metro placed on musical numbers, Donen's advisory role had to have been considered pivotal to the studio's operations, whether this required his shooting a quick take on the spur of the moment or conceiving an elaborate production number, for which he would be given more time. These anonymous assists would continue after he started receiving formal director's credit on his own pictures. As he explained, a scene of his or somebody else's might show up in a movie credited with direction by Vincente Minnelli, George Sidney, Charles Walters, or any of the other M-G-M personnel—"which is why," Donen said, puncturing the auteurist theory, "you can never be too sure when you read a movie's credits who really should get credit for what."†

Of his contributions to M-G-M movies starting in 1946, Donen said, "What I did consisted of several steps. First, I had to arrange the idea for a sequence. Then I would have to organize the music so it would go with the idea, choosing a song that would help the scene. Finally, I'd organize the staging to go with the music. That entailed seeing that the number was properly photographed and edited, and its music arranged."

Regarding the actual shooting of the numbers, Donen explained, "There are many problems associated with photographing movement, particularly dance, which is actually a series of very specific movements linked together with music. But the things that are true about dance are, in general, the things that are true about all movement on film. You have to search constantly for a way to make the movement interesting." One of the first rules, according to Donen, is to bear in mind that movement perpendicular to the camera is always diminished, because of a loss of the three dimensions. "Movement away from or toward a camera

---

* Loew, whose life ambition, said Donen, was to have been a stand-up comic, once interrupted production on one of Donen's early pictures and ordered the camera crane holding Donen to be lowered to the ground, because, as Loew announced, "It's time for Stanley to have his milk."

† Perhaps Donen's observation is best illustrated by his own four days' work on *Kismet,* direction credited to Vincente Minnelli. On July 19, 20, 22, and August 8, 1955, Donen, according to production reports, shot the "Night of My Nights" sequence, the only lively number in the otherwise inert movie, and the only scene in the entire enterprise that adequately fits its CinemaScope frame.

doesn't have the same impact that it has to the naked eye," said Donen, "whereas movement across the screen or with a panning camera will give you a heightened sense of speed—only, as you assemble the scene, you might not be looking for speed at that particular moment. It's a long, arduous road, and as you go along you learn what hurts and helps on the screen."

M-G-M kept Donen's dance card so filled that "I worked on pictures I can't even remember. Some I haven't seen since working on them, like *Holiday in Mexico.*" The 1946 Joe Pasternak trifle, directed by George Sidney, introduced a former radio child singing star, Jane Powell. The picture took on a Latin American theme, as did many movies of its era, because access to European exhibition was limited. Donen's contributions to *Holiday in Mexico* included a swinging Xavier Cugat band number, "I Love You Very Much," in which the Barcelona-born rumba-band leader performed with his pet Chihuahua.

"Cugat was nice," was Donen's recollection. "He used to carry this little dog, and he used to marry his singers."

Donen worked again with Cugat and Pasternak on "something called *No Leave, No Love.* Also terrible, and in black and white. It was the first time I ever did an all-out band number, and all I could think was, 'Oh, God, what can I do with this?' " Donen's solution was to "have these big letters built, fifteen feet high, spelling out C-U-G-A-T. Then I put musicians around the letters and lit them up with lights—the letters, not the musicians—until finally all the lights came on after the last letter appeared, and there was Cugie, standing and holding a violin, which he played rather badly but liked to carry around as a prop."

While the sequence hardly rates inclusion in *That's Entertainment!,* it does bear some distinct Donen touches, beginning with a disciplined structure and a camera technique that displays both his control and his feel for a continuity of motion. The Cugat number begins with an adroitly paced montage of South American instruments to set the mood, followed in quick succession by the introduction of Cugat as seen from a dollying high camera, a sweeping pan to the fingers of a pianist, over to the frantic dancing of a singing señorita, and then a one-hundred-eighty-degree wipe to piccolo players. For humor, the camera also follows a highball glass's movements about the dance floor, as it arrives on nightclub patron Keenan Wynn's table, is picked up by the dancing señorita, placed atop her partner's head, and finally drunk by Cugat, who grabs the glass just as the number winds to a close.

Explaining his daily studio routine, Donen said, "I'd work on numbers one at a time. That's all I could cope with, although I might have ended up doing four numbers all together for one picture. I'd finish one and then start the next."

Among the productions—many of them otherwise lackadaisical—that Donen was assigned to spruce up were *This Time for Keeps* (1947), with Esther Williams playing underwater straight woman to Jimmy Durante's clowning (it was Donen's gag to have Williams rescue the drowning Durante); *Big City* (1948), starring Margaret O'Brien as a foundling and Betty Garrett, in her movie debut, as a saloon singer who strips—within the standards of M-G-M house rules—to "You're Gonna See a Lot of Me"; *A Date with Judy* (1948), with Jane Powell and Elizabeth Taylor competing for the attentions of handsome fellow teen Robert Stack (Donen oversaw Wallace Beery, who played Powell's father, learning to rumba from Carmen Miranda, not that Beery ever becomes what one would consider smooth); and the Frank Sinatra flop *The Kissing Bandit* (1948), a film that *New York Herald Tribune* critic Otis L. Guernsey, Jr., called "a Technicolored vacuum."

The Kissing Bandit, for all its abundance of negatives, did contain one significant number, "The Whip Dance," conceived and choreographed by Donen and performed by the stage dancer Sono Osato, an exotic half-Irish-American, half-Japanese beauty, who had appeared in the 1944 Broadway stage musical *On the Town,* by Comden and Green and Leonard Bernstein. Her role was that of Ivy Smith, the subway poster girl "Miss Turnstiles."

Freud would have had a field day with Osato's sequence in *The Kissing Bandit,* for which she brandishes a six-foot-long bullwhip. In order to seduce the coy Sinatra away from Goody Two-shoes Kathryn Grayson, Osato snaps her weapon in time to the song "I Like You." The femme fatale shows little of the dainty characteristics of a typical M-G-M heroine; while Sinatra cowers before her in a kitchen, she cracks her whip around the room, and even extinguishes a flaming candle, macho style, with her fingers.

"My main function was to be sexy and entice Frank," Osato recalled. To master the whip Donen insisted she use, Osato had to take lessons from a cowboy. She drew the line, however, at one stunt Donen asked of her.

"He wanted me to jump to the floor from the top of a six-foot armoire," said Osato.

Hearing the request, Osato told Donen, "You must be crazy. You've been working with Gene Kelly too long."

BEFORE BEING DISCHARGED from the service in the spring of 1946, Gene Kelly had stepped before the cameras just once since the cartoon sequence for *Anchors Aweigh*. In May 1944, he and Fred Astaire filmed two days' work on "The Babbitt and the Bromide," a comedy dance number in Arthur Freed's episodic *Ziegfeld Follies*. "There was no rivalry at all," Freed said at the time. "Each is a genuine admirer of the other. My only problem was their deference for each other. Each was willing to do whatever dance the other wanted."

The result was atypical Astaire and atypical Kelly, so adroitly executed as to make the inevitable comparison between the two virtually impossible, which may have been the general idea.

"When Gene came out of the navy after the war," said Donen, "the studio was in a big hurry for him to do something." As was common for male stars returning to their home studios, however, Kelly discovered that M-G-M had no suitable properties lying in wait for him. Taking what was available, Donen said, "He made a picture called *Living in a Big Way*, produced by Pandro Berman and directed by Gregory La Cava, who was known for his comedies. Gregory La Cava had made *My Man Godfrey*, and *Living in a Big Way* would have Gene in it and Marie McDonald, who was known as 'The Body.' "

A former newspaper cartoonist who broke into pictures by becoming an animation artist, director Gregory La Cava (1892–1952) developed into one of the masters of the screwball comedy, although he somehow lost his way once that genre expired with the war. More than a few critical observers found his movies—which, besides the Depression classic *My Man Godfrey*, included the madcap gems *She Married Her Boss, Stage Door*, and *Unfinished Business*—better in parts than in their wholes. By any assessment, however, by the time La Cava came to M-G-M he was clearly riding on the coattails of his reputation.

"The movie was terrible," Donen said of *Living in a Big Way*. "Here it was, the picture was finished and the director had left, so the studio said, 'We have to do something to make it better. Gene, can you do a couple of musical numbers?' "

Donen and Kelly contrived three sequences to be inserted into the picture: an Astaire-Rogers *hommage*, with Kelly and McDonald dancing to

"It Had to Be You"; "Fido and Me," with Kelly and a terrier; and an elaborate acrobatic ballet at a construction site, featuring that Kelly mainstay, a dance with children.

"Gene does this number with kids," said Donen. "Why? If somebody else had done the picture, he wouldn't have been dancing with kids, but it was done because it was Gene."

Chapter 4

"Same Desires and Ambitions"

WITH M-G-M's permission, in the spring of 1946 Donen exercised a creative stretch by doctoring musical numbers for the stage production of a Broadway-bound revue, *Call Me Mister*. Through sketches and songs, it explored the theme of discharged soldiers and their return to civilian life.

"The show," said Donen, "had a score by Harold Rome, who wrote the music and lyrics, and was produced by Melvyn Douglas—the actor Melvyn Douglas—and Herman Levin, who later produced *My Fair Lady*." *Call Me Mister*'s sketches were by Arnold Auerbach. "The choreographer was John Wray," said Donen, "the son of a character actor who had been in a lot of movies, also named John Wray. The show had some good songs."

One, "South America, Take It Away," made a star of its performer, Betty Garrett, who played a rumba-weary USO canteen hostess. Garrett had previously acted with Orson Welles's Mercury Theater and danced with Martha Graham. The other career to be launched by *Call Me Mister* was that of the comedian Jules Munshin, a leggy, elastic-faced veteran of Catskill resorts and vaudeville. "He was very funny, very sweet, and I used to joke all the time with him," said Donen. "I'd say, 'Julie, don't worry. When I'm running the studios in Hollywood, we'll make all the Jews the leading men and all the Gentiles comics.' Poor Julie, he never lived to see it, but that is the way it turned out."*

Call Me Mister premiered April 18, 1946, and became the surprise success of the season. It opened a full month before the year's anticipated

---

* Donen cited the 1980s and '90s leading men Dustin Hoffman, Richard Dreyfuss, and Paul Newman, and the comedians Steve Martin, Robin Williams, and Jim Carrey. Jules Munshin died in 1970.

hit—a prediction fulfilled—Irving Berlin's *Annie Get Your Gun*. In contrast to the Berlin show, which was a traditional star vehicle for Ethel Merman and featured a book grounded in the banal notion that a woman must kowtow to a man's ego in order to win his heart, *Call Me Mister* was, in the view of the *Herald Tribune* critic Howard Barnes, "a boisterous romp as it takes satirical cognizance of military life, problems of reconversion, Park Avenue, the deep South, and even South American dances."

Employing adjectives that later could have been applied to Donen's musicals, Barnes deemed the Broadway show "fresh, vigorous, and, what was least to have been expected, it has great style."

HIS WORK on the show completed, Donen was contacted by Gene Kelly to help devise a scenario that might duplicate the box office success of *Anchors Aweigh*. "The studio wanted another Kelly-Sinatra picture, only they couldn't find a story," said Donen. Kelly balked at the studio's desire to pair him with Sinatra as two scheming sailors who convert their aircraft carrier into a swinging nightclub. Kelly and Donen decided to write a story of their own, then persuade the studio to let them codirect it. Intending their material for Freed, the duo hashed out a seven-page scenario on the cross-country trip back from New York.

"The little story was nothing to get drunk about," judged Donen of their final effort, "but it was a way for a fellow to get ahead."

"Story synopsis for a motion picture intended for Frank Sinatra and Gene Kelly, written by Gene Kelly and Stanley Donen," it began, under the title *Take Me Out to the Ball Game*. "The story is laid out in the period between 1905 and 1915, when baseball was really coming into its own as the national pastime. Our general set up is this: Kelly is the short stop, Frankie, the second baseman, and Leo Durocher, the first baseman of the greatest double-play combination since 'Tinker to Evans to Chance.'" Durocher was a colorful, much-admired manager for the Brooklyn Dodgers. The writers intended to call their screen teammates O'Brien (Kelly), Ryan (Sinatra), and Shaughnessy (Durocher).

As Kelly informed Arthur Freed, "I've worked out an Irish jig that Sinatra and Durocher will be able to dance and which will carry on the myth of Frankie's terpsichorean ability (and believe me, this will top any of our joint numbers in *Anchors Aweigh*). And, too, I guarantee not a dry seat in the house when the crooner does one of those sentimental Irish ballads."*

---

* No doubt Kelly meant not a dry eye.

Regarding their characters, Sinatra and Kelly were to play lifelong pals—"same town, same school, same desires, and ambitions"—and be not only the greatest baseball field men known to the major leagues but the greatest vaudevillians on the circuit. "Then the club is willed to C. B. Higgins," the story continued. "When Higgins arrives it turns out to be Kathryn Grayson."

Freed purchased the outline for $25,000 and set the radio writer George Wells to flesh out the story and Harry Warren and Ralph Blane to devise a score. The first positive change to Kelly and Donen's basic premise was Freed's replacement of Kathryn Grayson with Judy Garland. This sat well with the principals, until it quickly became evident that Garland could not handle the assignment. The star, who had grown up at M-G-M, had of late been breaking down under the strain of her work and her domestic life with Vincente Minnelli, whom she had married in 1945 (her first marriage, to the orchestra leader David Rose, had lasted from 1941 to 1945, although the couple legally separated in 1943). Volumes have been written about Garland's related emotional problems and substance abuse, as well as her immeasurable talent. Unfortunately, the former overshadowed the latter during this period, and she was withdrawn from *Take Me Out to the Ball Game.* Garland's replacement, Kelly and Donen learned, was to be Esther Williams.

"A mistake," said Donen, who still had his hopes pinned on codirecting the movie with Kelly. "She was extremely nearsighted. She was practically blind. She'd rehearse her scenes wearing her eyeglasses, and everything would be fine, but then, come time to shoot, she'd take off her glasses and she would crash into the set."

The writer and musicians were also swapped. Harry Tugend, who had written radio shows for Fred Allen and movies at Fox for Shirley Temple, was assigned the script, and Betty Comden and Adolph Green would do the lyrics, to music by Roger Edens. Edens, who loomed large in the memories of those who worked with him, was Arthur Freed's right-hand man, and while he was generally billed as the associate producer on Freed pictures, his contributions were such that many believe that a great deal of Freed's esteemed reputation rested squarely on Edens's shoulders.

"He was a darling man," said Kay Thompson of Edens. "Absolute peaches and cream." Roger Edens (1905–1970) was born in Hillsboro, Texas, and arrived in New York when he was in his early twenties. By October 1930, Edens, still "a stripling," as he was described in a later profile, was playing piano in the orchestra pit of the Alvin Theater on Broadway. The show was *Girl Crazy,* with a score by George and Ira Gershwin (it included "I've Got Rhythm"), and the star was Ethel Merman. Opening night proved a grand success, but trouble developed on night two. Merman's onstage accompanist took sick. Edens replaced him.

"The pit band for the show had quite a bunch of guys in it," Edens recalled. "Benny Goodman, both of the Dorseys, the two Teagardens, Glenn Miller, Red Nichols, Gene Krupa, and Joe Venuti. They all went from there to big things."

Likewise Merman and Edens. She was offered a Paramount contract in Hollywood, where she made some movies with Bing Crosby, although her lumbering body movements and brassy personality would never translate well to the screen. Edens followed Merman west to compose specialty material for her, and when his Paramount contract expired in 1935, he joined Metro, where he embellished movies with such contributions as Judy Garland's "Dear Mr. Gable" number, composed for *The Broadway Melody of 1938*. (The reaction the sequence garnered convinced the M-G-M brass to cast Garland in *The Wizard of Oz*, once all hopes for securing Shirley Temple from Twentieth Century–Fox were dashed; in turn, it was the success of *The Wizard of Oz* that helped to launch the Freed Unit.)

According to the writer Leonard Gershe, who collaborated with Edens and Donen on *Funny Face*, "Roger was responsible for the 'class' of the Freed Unit, and the Freed Unit was the Rolls-Royce of Hollywood." As to why Edens seemingly never received the credit he deserved—the names Freed, Donen, Minnelli, Comden, Green, et al. may be familiar to movie buffs, while Edens is not—Gershe explained, "No one was ever quite certain of what Roger did, but whatever he did was quite crucial to the picture."

In his own portrait of Edens, Donen noted that Arthur Freed held his associate producer in such esteem as to be intimidated by him. "Arthur was somehow terrified by Roger, who knew it and used it to get his way with Arthur. All Roger had to do was raise an eyebrow over an element in a scene that Arthur was trying to put in, and it would disappear."

Donen credits Edens with convincing the producer to make the young musical doctor a full-fledged director. "Roger," insisted Donen, "was my biggest promoter."

"Tall and very good looking," was Betty Comden's description of Edens. "With a deep, whiskey voice."

"Southern, polite, adored what he was doing, and loved to play and to drink," summarized Kay Thompson. "Roger was my best friend. He was married to someone, but I only saw her once. She was not around."

Besides their mutual *joie de vivre,* Thompson and Edens also shared the same birthday, November 9. "On that day every year at the studio they were busy making pictures," she remembered. "Roger and I, however, would arrange to be off in the hills somewhere, having lunch." At night there would invariably be a celebration at Thompson's house. "One year Ralph Blane had written this number for Roger, 'Roger de Coverly,' after an English writer, and Judy Garland and Peter Lawford secretly rented these outlandish getups from the studio costume department and performed this number in my living room. And Roger just sat there listening, crying. That was Roger. What he was, he was young to be old."

"And absolutely indispensable to Arthur," Comden elaborated. "He worked on the script, the music, he coached Judy Garland, wrote for her—Roger did it all."

DESPITE Kelly and Donen's determination that Freed should permit them to direct the picture, "Arthur hired Busby Berkeley, because he felt a great affection for him," said Donen. "They'd done a number of pictures together, and Arthur appreciated him." Berkeley (1895–1975, born as the less alliterative William Berkeley Enos) learned to choreograph by staging marching maneuvers during World War I, and his name will forever remain synonymous with the way he used lines of chorus girls to create geometric production numbers in the backstage musicals he choreographed and later directed for Warner Bros., starting in the early thirties. One looks at Berkeley musicals and either gasps or giggles, but it is impossible not to form an opinion of his work.

"My most poignant recollection of Berkeleyana is the 'Lullaby of Broadway' number from *The Gold Diggers of 1935*," the critic Andrew Sarris wrote in 1968. "For years and years I retained the image of a playgirl plunging to her death from a skyscraper ballroom, and then the lingering contemplation of an empty apartment with a hungry kitten waiting to be fed and outside somewhere a chorus singing 'Good night, baby' as if perchance to die was but to dream of a lullaby as a requiem mass." In reexamining this guilty pleasure from his past, Sarris conceded, "*The Gold Diggers of 1935* revisited turned out to be a long prologue, by turns cynical and fatuous, to a very short production number as a show within a show. I had almost begun to doubt my moviegoing memory when suddenly the playgirl plunged to her death and the traveling camera lingered over an empty apartment, and the lullaby engulfed the screen once more as it had once long ago in the darkest days of the Depression. The magic of Busby Berkeley had been miraculously reconfirmed."

Be it a magic memory or a camp relic, Berkeley's oeuvre was the object of an equally astute diagnosis from Billy Wilder, who found good reason to dismiss Berkeley movies out of hand for nothing more than having "looked like they had been shot from the point of view of the electrician on the ceiling."

For Arthur Freed, however, Berkeley exercised a more benign hand. He directed Gene Kelly's first picture, *For Me and My Gal,* as well as three of the Mickey Rooney–Judy Garland backyard musicals, none of which, for better or worse, bore the mark of the groundbreaker Berkeley showed himself to be at Warners. By the late forties, with Garland and Rooney themselves having graduated to better directors, Berkeley hardly seemed prepared to be the one to resuscitate the flagging spirits of the movie musical.

"*Take Me Out to the Ball Game* serves as an indication of changing trends in the musical film—trends that would have little to do with either Berkeley or the Berkeleyesque," said Martin Rubin in his thorough research into the work of the choreographer-director. Concluding that "the numbers in *Take Me Out to the Ball Game* have little relation to Berkeleyesque spectacle," Rubin went on to note that the musical sequences instead are "relatively small-scale affairs that place the major emphasis on comedy, transitions to the narrative, the cleverness of the lyrics, and the personalities and performance skills of the stars, rather than on spectacle and group dynamics."

The reason the Berkeley touch is not evident in *Take Me Out to the Ball Game*'s musical numbers is that Busby Berkeley did not do them. He departed *Ball Game,* which came to mark his final credit as a director, before the picture's completion, leaving, in an almost symbolic passing of the torch, the body of the work to Donen and Kelly.

"Berkeley turned out to be impossible on the picture," said Donen. "He didn't know what he was doing. He couldn't remember anyone's name. He'd been to jail.* He had no talent by then. It was sad."

"Donen and Kelly," reported Rubin, "are frequently credited with having made the movie musical more 'realistic' and 'integrated.' It would perhaps be more accurate to characterize their contribution not in terms of smoothing over the breach between the realistic (narrative) and anti-realistic (spectacle) sides of the genre, but of articulating the tension

---

* On one of several drunken-driving charges. In one widely publicized case during his Warner Bros. heyday, Berkeley had to pay $95,000 to the families of three people he had killed in a car accident. Berkeley was also known to suffer a mother fixation of such magnitude that some of his six marriages barely lasted past their honeymoons.

Busby Berkeley, Warner Bros.'s star choreographer, c. 1933. Said Billy Wilder: "Busby Berkeley shot musical numbers from the point of view of the electrician on the ceiling."

Typical Berkeley, from *Gold Diggers of 1935*

between those sides in a particularly rich, vivid, and sophisticated manner."

In reviewing the Berkeley legacy and comparing it to the Donen-Kelly-Freed approach, Rubin found that the "full exercise of Berkeleyesque spectacle depends on a clear separation of narrative space from performance space, within which the 'impossible' can run rampant. The classic Freed musicals of the fifties, on the other hand, are built on a more variegated and multipartite irruption of narrative space into performance space, and vice versa."

Ironically, when once asked what was his favorite musical sequence in any movie, Berkeley replied without hesitation, "Gene Kelly's Alter Ego dance in *Cover Girl*."

Its creator could not return a similar compliment. "I thought Busby Berkeley was contemptible," said Donen, "his work, not the man. I thought what he did was just stupid, with no feeling toward people. It was everything I didn't want to do at the time. I thought it stunk. Today I can look at it and appreciate it as some sort of miraculous vision that he and no one else had, something that sprang from deep within him. It's remarkable, and a true creation. It's still stupid, but he did it, and nobody else did it as well, even though everybody tried to copy it. What he did sprang entirely out of Busby Berkeley, which is what true art is supposed to do, grow out of an artist's insides."

Donen based this last claim on an essay on modern art by Paul Klee, in which the Swiss abstractionist offers up the comparison between an artist and a tree. "A tree," said Donen, summarizing Klee, "stands on earth in one place, well rooted to the ground, and whatever happens around it is absorbed and comes out through the roots of the tree, up through the trunk, and out onto the crown and the leaves. The tree is not responsible for this happening. It just stays there and gives out what it is fed, and it does this again and again. The artist does the same thing. He's rooted to the earth, and these things come out of him. It's true. It's honest. It isn't something you can fake."

DESPITE Donen and Kelly's casting suggestion, Leo Durocher never made it to the plate. The role of Shaughnessy was rewritten and recast for Jules Munshin, playing first baseman Nat Goldberg. This permitted the song about field play, "O'Brien to Ryan to Goldberg," with a hora complementing O'Brien's Irish jig and Ryan's Scottish fling. Esther Williams executed a quiet dog paddle, to the rhythm of the title song, in the pool of the Sarasota,

Sinatra, Donen, Jules Munshin, and Kelly on location for Metro's *Take Me Out to the Ball Game*: "nothing to get drunk about"

Florida, hotel where her ball team is holed up for spring training; Donen was asked to conceive an additional aquatic number for her, but did not.

As in *Anchors Aweigh,* Kelly's character is that of an oversexed wolf—the team he plays for is the Wolves—and he displays a particular distaste for the businesslike Williams. A sheepish Sinatra, on the other hand, is instantly smitten by her strengths and smarts. The slack is taken up by Betty Garrett, as a sexually aggressive moll who lusts after Sinatra outside the locker room. She nabs him in the bleachers during their number "It's Fate, Baby, It's Fate," which Donen directed entirely on his own. To put a humorous spin on it, Sinatra is panic stricken throughout the sequence, for fear of losing his virginity.

"Frank was quick but hated to rehearse, particularly the book part, saying that if he did a scene more than once, he'd get stale," recalled Betty Garrett. It had been on *Anchors Aweigh* that Sinatra earned the nickname "One-Take Charlie," a tag that would cling throughout his highly uneven film career. Not that it was Sinatra's lack of preparedness that weakened *Take Me Out to the Ball Game.* Even at its scant ninety minutes, the picture assumes the feel of an epic-length musical, on the order of one of those ponderous 1950s and '60s Broadway musical film adaptations, with intermission.

"It's not one we like to talk about," said Betty Comden, as Adolph

Green shrugged in agreement. As could always be expected, there were a few good moments, though variations of these would be improved upon in later pictures. Sinatra and Kelly's opening vaudeville number sets the stage for Donald O'Connor and Gene Kelly's lightning-paced "Fit as a Fiddle" stage duet in *Singin' in the Rain,* and the celebratory interior piece "O'Brien to Ryan to Goldberg," dynamically if stagily choreographed during the team's mealtime, has its adherents, among them Busby Berkeley champion Martin Rubin.

"[I]n 'O'Brien to Ryan to Goldberg,' " the academician observed, "the space in the dining room periodically ceases to function as a realistic dining room and is momentarily transformed into a formal stagelike space. The foreground becomes like a stage apron, and the performances are directed outward, as if to an audience in the orchestra." Remarking on what was a result of Donen's technical finesse, Rubin pointed out, "Then a cut or camera movement restores the narrative context."

Although Donen and Kelly had delivered their seven-page outline to Freed in the spring of 1946, the picture did not go before the cameras until July 28, 1948. Production lasted until October 26. "For all its high spots," critiqued Bosley Crowther in the *New York Times* on April 9, 1949, "the show lacks consistent style and pace, and the stars are forced to clown and grimace much more than becomes their speed. Actually, the plotted humor is conspicuously bush-league stuff. Don't be surprised if you see people getting up for a seventh-inning stretch."

Chapter 5

"See What I Mean?"

WHILE *Take Me Out to the Ball Game* was in its final prepro-
duction phase, Stanley Donen got married. The date was
April 14, 1948, and the bride was Jeanne Coyne, a former
New York dancer who, as a girl in Pittsburgh, had been a pupil of Gene
Kelly's. It was said that she maintained a lifelong infatuation with Kelly.

On Broadway, Coyne had worked with the choreographers Jack Cole
and Robert Alton, and when she came to M-G-M with a lot of the talent
flow from the East, she assisted in the staging of musical numbers for
many of the studio's major musicals.

"She was a sweet and wonderful girl," said Audrey Hepburn, who
worked with Coyne on *Funny Face* (after her divorce from Donen). The
sentiment was echoed by Gwen Verdon, who knew her fellow dancer in
both New York and Hollywood. "You would look over your shoulder in
the soundstage, and Jeanne would always be there," said Verdon. "A beautiful girl, who also knew how to use a camera."

"All of Stanley's wives have been beautiful," said his sister, Carla, in
1994, by which time she was able to have formed an opinion about five
different sisters-in-law, "but I think Jeannie was really the loveliest. There
was something wholesome about her." As to what that "something" could
have been, Carla Davis said, "she was a bit older than Stanley, and *very*
Catholic."*

Strange—if not confusing—as it may sound, after the Donen-Coyne
marriage ended (the couple separated on April 12, 1950, with a divorce
granted May 17, 1951), Coyne eventually became the second wife of her

---

* "My brother has been married to every religion under the sun, except Jewish," Davis
remarked. Marion Marshall, the second Mrs. Donen, was born a Mormon.

97

own former mentor and her ex-husband's former collaborator, Gene Kelly. This occurred in 1960, three years after Kelly's divorce from his first wife, the actress Betsy Blair, whom he had married shortly after he choreographed *Best Foot Forward*.

As Kelly told his biographer Clive Hirschhorn, the relationship between Blair and Kelly and Coyne and Donen seemed nothing if not accident prone. "Jeannie's marriage to Stanley was doomed from the start," said Kelly, "because every time Stanley looked at Jeannie, he saw Betsy, whom he loved, and every time Jeannie looked at Stanley, I guess she saw me. One way [or] another it was all pretty incestuous."

The Kellys remained married until Jeanne's death, from cancer, in 1973.

As for the several other marriages of Donen—to the former Marion Marshall (1952–1959), to Adelle Beatty (1960–1971), to Yvette Mimieux (1972–1982), and to Pamari (Pam) Braden (1990–1994), the writer Peter Stone observed, "Stanley doesn't like being alone." An embroidered pillow on the sofa in Donen's living room reads: "Eat, drink, and re-marry."

"Marriage?" said Stanley Donen. "I must be very good at it. I've done it so often. Actually, the best line on the subject comes from a movie you wouldn't necessarily think of, Alfred Hitchcock's *North by Northwest*. In Ernest Lehman's script, the Eva Marie Saint character says that there's something wrong with men like the Cary Grant character, who says, 'What's wrong with men like me?' And she says, 'They don't believe in marriage.' Then he tells her, 'I've been married twice.' And she says, 'See what I mean?'"

STILL RECOVERING from Arthur Freed's rebuffing his chance to direct his first picture, Donen set about selling the producer on another idea, which Donen felt was surefire: an adaptation of the 1873 Jules Verne novel, *Around the World in Eighty Days*.

"You can't beat its plot for a musical," said Donen, who devoted the better part of 1948 to shaping a scenario and then persuading Freed to proceed on it. Not that this was a completely original idea of Donen's; on Broadway, the exploits of Verne's hero Phileas Fogg had already been set to music by Cole Porter, whose unlikely collaborator, Orson Welles, had been responsible for the book, the direction, and playing Fogg.

Called, simply, *Around the World,* the shapeless extravaganza opened on May 31, 1946, and closed seventy-five performances later. In order to recoup some of its $300,000 investment, which at the time marked a record loss for a show, Welles sold his film rights to the novel to the promoter Michael Todd, who would make a movie of it in 1956, using neither the Porter score nor any of the Welles or Porter material—which Donen had not intended to use, either.

"When the Mike Todd movie came out, my heart broke," said Donen, who never was successful in convincing Freed his idea would work. "It could have been the greatest musical of all time."

Disappointments of this kind traditionally run rampant in the picture business. About the same time Donen was promoting *Around the World in Eighty Days,* George Abbott put M-G-M on notice, saying that his services were available to direct the picture version of one of his shows that the studio owned, *On the Town.* Abbott's offer was declined. Metro-Goldwyn-Mayer, acting on the advice of Arthur Freed, who was acting on the advice of Roger Edens, had decided that *On the Town* would be directed instead by two former Abbott employees.

Producer Arthur Freed bestows the title on Donen and Kelly. Note who wears the viewfinder.

Part 3

Director

Chapter 1

"Shoot It in Griffith Park"

O VER THE East River, a fiery early-morning sun gilds the mortar and brick skyscrapers of midtown Manhattan. The waterway itself is sparsely populated this peaceful dawn, by a green wooden tug that shares its path with two southerly-directed barges. Quick cut to an overhead shot of a pier in Brooklyn, then dissolve to ground level, where a stocky longshoreman in a bright-yellow-and-red hard hat that reflects the sun's rays swings his tin lunch pail in perfect synchronization with his leisurely gait. Pausing beneath an enormous mechanical crane, the figure yawns and stretches before entering the safe confines of this lonely dock in the Brooklyn Navy Yard. Clearly, these are more innocent times.

Uncharacteristically for so burly a specimen, the worker commences to sing, a capella, a lazy lament that he feels as if he's "not out of bed yet." The sun may be warm, his verse reveals, but more comforting would be his blanket and his lady's arms.

His refrain is brief, for the lullaby mood is soon shattered, alarmingly.

An industrial whistle blares, an unseen orchestra strikes a percussion-heavy downbeat, and the celluloid canvas's visual components figuratively explode into pieces to form a spontaneous combustion of perpetual motion set to music. All at once, what had appeared to be a deserted gray battleship is now overflowing with vigorous white-uniformed sailors, racing to claim their stake on land. Serving as their metronome, a facsimile of the electric news readout in Times Square flashes "SIX AM" across the bottom of the frame—the signal that twenty-four hours' shore leave has officially begun.

Filtering their way within the frenzy are three familiar-looking tars—Gene Kelly, Frank Sinatra, Jules Munshin—who snake through the crowd and weather the race to shore. The three gather at the dockside base of the gangplank, face the city sky, reach out their arms, and joyfully declare:

> New York, New York—a wonderful town—
> The Bronx is up but the Battery's down—
> The people ride in a hole in the groun'—
> New York, New York—it's a wonderful town!

"New York, obviously, was the soul of the picture, and Gene and I had to fight to shoot *On the Town* there," said Donen, who, as indicated in a November 18, 1949, memo from Arthur Freed to a studio executive named Sam Tate, "is going to direct *On the Town* for me." (Freed was requesting that Tate furnish Donen with a "nicer office.")

"We wanted the beginning and the ending to be shot in New York," said Donen, "only we didn't get the ending. The last scenes, which are supposed to take place on Coney Island, are clearly soundstage and look terrible. As it was, it was a struggle to get as much of New York as we did."

The mulish M-G-M mind-set against shooting on location had actually taken hold during the birth of sound. "Before the talking picture," said Donen, "films were made everywhere, because the camera could be taken anywhere. Then, when talkies came in, sound became sort of a giant ogre that controlled the making of pictures for a very long time. The studios felt that because of the sound equipment, you could make movies only on a soundstage, because nobody had learned to loop* or record outside. The whole process was a nightmare."

Little advancement had occurred as the studio prepared *On the Town.* "It was only eighteen years after sound had first come in," said Donen, "and the same people were in charge. Douglas Shearer, Norma Shearer's brother and the man who had perfected the Tarzan yell, was still running the sound department, and the studio firmly believed that there was some mysterious magic that could only occur within the padded walls of Culver City. They had such a snobbish attitude about it that M-G-M had built this entire studio in England but never believed that A movies could be produced there. To Metro-Goldwyn-Mayer it was either Culver City or no place."

The most vociferous obstacle, remembered Donen, was the M-G-M production manager, Joe (J.J.) Cohn. "Joe was in charge of estimating budgets and schedules. He's the one who actually coined the expression 'A rock is a rock, a tree is a tree, shoot it in Griffith Park.' "

---

* Dub in sections of the dialogue sound track during postproduction.

Kelly, Sinatra, and Munshin, at the feet of Lady Liberty. In *On the Town* (1949), the fourth star is New York.

Typically, Cohn refused the *On the Town* company permission to shoot in New York, "so it was Arthur Freed who ran interference," said Donen. "Arthur was wonderful at that, provided he was convinced himself. But one of the great things about Arthur was that he was so easily convinced, because he was willing to go to any lengths to get what was needed on film."

Roger Edens paid a preproduction visit to New York from January 2 to January 25, 1949.* While he laid the groundwork for the shoot and

---

* M-G-M visitors from the coast generally stayed at New York's Astor Hotel. Edens's total hotel bill for his twenty-three days, including meals, room service, and the use of a piano, came to a then lavish $1,307.65, not counting the additional $600 he spent on restaurants, taxis, and tips.

tidied up loose business ends, such as renegotiating a music contract with Leonard Bernstein, the composer of the Broadway show on which the picture would be based, memos about the upcoming production traversed the Culver City lot. Interestingly, every bit of correspondence regarding creative and technical aspects of *On the Town* was addressed exclusively to Donen, with not so much as a single reference to the desires or demands of the picture's "codirector" of record, Gene Kelly.

"I've been asked for years how one 'codirects,' " said Donen, "and I have two standard replies. The first is 'With great difficulty.' And the second, which I used to joke about, is 'If you substitute the word 'fight' for 'codirect,' then you have it. It wasn't always like that with Gene, but it gradually came to be that, and eventually it came to be impossible. As for the actual process of 'codirecting,' if you both agree, then one of you is redundant. And if you disagree, there's going to be a battle."

Kelly has invariably been credited with staging and choreographing the performers, while to Donen was left the camera. No one kept track of exactly into whose domain fell what particular responsibility, but clearly theirs was not consistently a fifty-fifty collaboration. Early on, it was Kelly who carried the clout to demand the inclusion of Donen in his studio projects, yet the young overachiever always came through, for Kelly and the studio.

"On the scenes we did for *Take Me Out to the Ball Game*," said Donen, "I'd organized some of the dance movement. I can't say I ever contributed very much to Gene's dancing, at any time, but there were a few occasions that I did have some ideas about actual dance steps. In *Cover Girl*, I changed the order of a number to give it a better construction, and I remember spending four or five hours one night reconstructing it into an entirely new sequence."

What survive so vividly in *On the Town* are its verve and its technical proficiency, especially in the editing and the exciting but never grandstanding camerawork, principally in the opening "New York, New York" number. All this bears the time-proven imprint of Donen. What distinctly detract from *On the Town*, on the other hand, are its self-indulgent dance sequences, a failing that would also mar, and to a much greater extent, some of Kelly's post-Donen solo directorial work (the showy and pretentious *Invitation to the Dance* in 1956 and the shallow, elephantine *Hello, Dolly!* in 1969), because these sequences no longer seemed new, nor did they do anything to advance the plot (*Invitation to the Dance* did not have a plot). Neither by 1949 had the public's thirst for dance yet been satiated by the lengthy dream ballets that first cropped up on Broadway in 1943 with

Agnes de Mille's Act I finale for *Oklahoma!* and on film starting with an influential 1948 British import that took dance to the extreme, *The Red Shoes.*

On the Town was spawned from Paul Cadmus's erotic painting, *The Fleet's In,* of sailors having a good time. The idea was taken up by Jerome Robbins, who was promised by Ballet Theater (later known as American Ballet Theater) that he could choreograph and create an original work on spec. Robbins, born in 1918, had debuted as a dancer in Frederick Loewe's first Broadway musical, *Great Lady,* in 1938. Two years later he joined Ballet Theater as a soloist. Describing what he had in mind to the composer Vincent Persichetti, Robbins was told that what he needed was a jazz score, and the proper person for the job was Leonard Bernstein. Bernstein was at that time poised on the brink of a major breakthrough; on Sunday afternoon, November 14, 1943, the twenty-five-year-old musician stepped in at the last minute for an ailing Bruno Walter and conducted the New York Philharmonic in Carnegie Hall. The next morning Bernstein's triumph was documented in both a front-page story and an editorial in the *New York Times.*

As Bernstein once described Robbins's work, called *Fancy Free,* it was "a brief, wonderful look at twenty-five minutes in the life of three sailors who had twenty-four hours' shore leave in New York and some balletic adventures in a bar—indulging in a certain amount of competition culminating in a fight—and then wound up pals again." (This theme would also serve as the premise for *It's Always Fair Weather,* which Comden and Green would write for the screen with composer André Previn and which Gene Kelly and Donen would codirect as their final collaboration.) As *Fancy Free* was perceived in 1994 by *New York Times* dance critic Anna Kisselgoff, after a performance on its fiftieth anniversary, "Nothing better illustrates the difference between a cliché and a classic in art than this evergreen masterpiece.... Atmosphere is what *Fancy Free* is really about. Bernstein's wonderful score incorporates the jazz and Latin dance rhythms of a still recognizable urban past."

In its first year at the Metropolitan Opera House—its premiere took place April 4, 1944—*Fancy Free* was performed one hundred sixty times. Its successful reception prompted the set designer Oliver Smith to suggest turning the ballet into a full-fledged Broadway musical, an idea that Bernstein and Robbins resisted at first, in favor of attempting something new and more serious. Eventually they relented, and Betty Comden and

Adolph Green, who had yet to write for Broadway, were enlisted to do the lyrics and book.

Initial investors put up $25,000, but the bucks stopped there, owing to the neophyte Broadway reputations of the creative team. Their answer was to bring in a proven talent, and the person they approached was George Abbott, who found Bernstein, Robbins, Comden, and Green "the kind of people I like to work with—eager, emotional, enthusiastic."

With the Abbott imprimatur on the project, Metro-Goldwyn-Mayer put up $250,000, enough to open the show, which was now called *On the Town,* and to secure the film rights. The show held the distinction of being the first theatrical property to be sold to Hollywood in a preproduction deal.

"PEOPLE ARE always asking me why the Leonard Bernstein score was replaced in the movie," said Donen. "What are they asking me for? I was thrilled that I was going to be directing my first movie. Do people think that at that point in my career *I* had any say over who was going to write the music? The Bernstein score isn't in the movie because Arthur didn't want it. He thought Bernstein was off on cloud nine, and Louis B. Mayer hated the material. He thought the Bernstein score was not songs. He wasn't sure what it was, but he thought it was too sophisticated."

"You know the moguls," said Gene Kelly in 1991, making it sound as though there were still some around. "They want hit songs. The moguls heard the score to *On the Town* and they didn't hear any hits."

Whatever the Broadway score offered—and it was labeled everything from longhair ballet music to the bastard offspring of Gershwin, Copland, and Ravel—most of it did not make it into the picture. Besides Charleston, South Carolina, and Seattle, Arthur Freed most proudly hailed from Tin Pan Alley. Similarly, Louis B. Mayer did not hesitate to parade his loathing of "sophisticated" music in front of anyone, as evidenced by the time he informed Cole Porter that he wanted to be able to cry when he heard the song "Rosalie," which he was paying Porter to compose for an Eleanor Powell movie. (Porter had little choice but to comply with the demand.)

Perverse as their decision was to discard the Bernstein score to *On the Town,* the two picturemakers were probably right. Bernstein did not write M-G-M material. (Bernstein's *West Side Story,* far too tragic and ethnic, never would have been an M-G-M musical, while his *Wonderful Town* and *Candide* were not so much as considered for the screen.) There were even those who argued that Bernstein did not belong on Broadway, an opposing faction headed by no less than George Abbott, who, when assembling *On the Town* for the stage, used to compare his young composer's music to Prokofiev's. Abbott did not intend it as a compliment.

"I hate to keep harping on the subject," said another detractor, *Daily News* critic John Chapman, when he reviewed the show upon its opening at the Adelphi Theater on December 28, 1944, "but a musical needs some music to go with its lyrics. Words which make a rhyme and have rhythm do not necessarily make a lyric, nor do thirty-two bars full of notes automatically make a song." Of Bernstein's contribution, said Chapman, "There are ballets, of course. Cripes, what I wouldn't give to see a good old hoofing chorus again."*

The final judgment rested with the public. *On the Town* ran for 463 performances. That made it a hit in its time, but not on the order of the other eventual long runs to open the same season: *Song of Norway* had 860 performances; Harold Arlen and Yip Harburg's *Bloomer Girl,* 654 performances; Sigmund Romberg and Herbert and Dorothy Fields's *Up in Central Park,* 504 performances; and Rogers and Hammerstein's *Carousel,* despite its downbeat book and reviews to match, lasted 890 performances and sparked countless revivals.

In contrast, in some fifty years since its premiere, *On the Town* has never enjoyed a successful major revival. Some of its songs, primarily "Some Other Time" and "Lucky to Be Me," crop up as standards on the cabaret circuit but cannot be considered part of the pop mainstream (*On the Town*'s most recognizable tune, and that's thanks to the movie, is "New York, New York"). All this, for better or worse, makes M-G-M production no. 1453, even with its highly mediocre replacement score by Roger Edens, the *On the Town* of record—although this still does not account for the material's lofty reputation. Other than the fact that it successfully launched the stage careers of Comden and Green, Robbins and Bernstein, what made *On the Town* so captivating was its simple wartime premise: three innocent, oversexed sailors on a one-day leave in the great metropolis. It was this spirit of youth and movement, rooted as it had been in *Fancy Free,* that Kelly and Donen clutched to their mutual bosom and ran with, and that finally appears on the screen.

---

* Reviews broke down as follows: three raves, three favorable, and one mixed, that being Chapman's. Louis Kronenberger of *PM* called Comden and Green's libretto "the best musical comedy book since *Pal Joey.*"

In retrospect, far more regrettable than losing the Bernstein score, which survives somewhat intact on a myriad of recordings, is that the movie *On the Town* discarded the brilliance of Jerome Robbins's classic choreography,* in favor of Gene Kelly's, which, with the passage of time, does looked clichéd.

The fate of the score was said to have been settled early on, when Louis B. Mayer attended a New York stage performance with Eddie Mannix, the general manager of M-G-M, and Sam Katz, considered a top studio field general. The Culver City troika supposedly walked out, complaining that their company had spent so much as a penny in the production, let alone a quarter of a million dollars. One story went that Mayer was particularly distraught over having witnessed an interracial couple dancing together onstage.

"No," said Betty Comden. "Louis B. Mayer never saw the show. Isn't *that* the story?"

"Yes," confirmed Adolph Green.

"Or did he come to see it?" asked Comden.

"Arthur let him see it and he hated it," said Green.

"Arthur hated it?" repeated Comden.

"No," said Green. "Louis B."

"I thought Lillie Messinger came to see it," said Comden, referring to Mayer's trusted literary scout. According to one account, during the summer of 1944 Messinger called Mayer long-distance in the hospital in California; perpetually under a physician's care for one reason or another, Mayer this time was reported to have a broken pelvis. Messinger could not wait to voice her excitement over what was being created, she said, "by people you've never heard of, but will in the future."[†]

"I don't know," said Green. "But Mayer saw it and he hated it."

As Betty Comden assembled the pieces, "Mayer sent Lillie Messinger to buy *Bloomer Girl,* and she came back east and also wanted to buy *On the Town,* which she did. It *was* a preproduction deal, and Mayer hated the

---

* Robbins's first screen assignment was for Twentieth Century–Fox in 1956, choreographing the adaptation of Rodgers and Hammerstein's *The King and I.* Donen served as a consultant to Robbins, at Robbins's request, on "The Small House of Uncle Thomas" ballet, "for about three or four days," Donen recalled. After that, the film's competitive director, Walter Lang, permanently ordered Donen off the set, saying, "Good-bye. You are not welcome here."

[†] Messinger was obviously privy to an early read-through, because the show was not to open until winter. Although Gene Kelly told a Bernstein Archive Oral History interviewer that he saw the show opening night and it was he who called the studio to convince it to buy the property, Metro had owned the show well before then.

show. I didn't know it was because of an interracial couple. Maybe it was. Isn't it wonderful that as far back as that we had blacks and whites onstage working together?"

Nearly all the Bernstein numbers were scrapped: "I Can Cook, Too," "Lucky to Be Me," "Some Other Time," "Do-Do-Re-Do," and "I Get Carried Away." The bittersweet "Lonely Town," which was also discarded, proved a particular bone of contention, with Comden and Green pleading through telegrams to Arthur Freed right up to the starting date of production that the ballad be retained. In a studio press release during shooting, however, Gene Kelly stated, "It's very hard to work a ballad like 'Lonely Town' into a movie musical because it slows down the action tremendously." The statement is ironic, given the number of Kelly ballets that have slowed down movie musicals, including *On the Town*.

"We had signed to do the picture and additional lyrics," said Betty Comden, "and Adolph and I thought we would be doing this with Lenny. Naturally we were in a bind because at the studio they thought the music was too sophisticated." After protracted negotiations, Bernstein was contracted to come to California for "no more than three weeks" starting June 3, 1949, "to compose the New York ballet on Gene Kelly's choreography." The composer's right of first refusal to write new songs for the movie was dropped in exchange for Bernstein's regaining the rights to his stage songs (those not used in the film), as had been the terms of the original purchase agreement.

"Lenny was very generous," said Comden. "He came out and worked on the film and put the ballet music together for Sollie Chaplin."

The creators were well compensated for their troubles. Comden and Green were each paid $42,000 for their screenplay and another $12,000 for their new lyrics. These sums did not include their share of the royalties from the studio's purchase of the original stage rights.*

---

* Other figures regarding *On the Town* included Gene Kelly's twenty-one-week guarantee of $2,000 per week, or $42,000, to codirect and star in the picture. Donen, as codirector working under the terms of an earlier M-G-M contract, was paid $400 per week, or $8,400 for the same twenty-one weeks. Sinatra was in the fourth year of a five-year contract set to expire January 1, 1950; under its existing terms, he was to appear in two pictures per year, and for *On the Town* he received a flat $130,000. Salaries for the remaining principal members of the cast: Jules Munshin, $1,500 a week, for a grand total of $20,250 (the studio counted workdays and would only pay partial weeks); Ann Miller, $1,000 a week, for a total of $16,833; Betty Garrett, $1,750 a week, for a total of $6,250; Vera-Ellen, $750 a week, for a total of $8,875; and the comedienne Alice Pearce, the only transfer from the stage version (as a nose-sniffling mouse), also $750 a week, for a total of $6,250.

The total cost of *On the Town* came to $2,111,250, including the $13,265 spent on 146 feet of film that was shot and subsequently eliminated. This was a dance sequence. It was Bernstein's "Lonely Town" ballet.

THE SCORE was not the only substantive change to *On the Town*. With Kelly playing the main character, Gabey, the insouciance of the stage Gabey had to be thrown out the porthole. "He couldn't be a helpless, naive type," said Betty Comden, "not with Gene playing him." Neither, for that matter, could she and Green retain all their original stage lyrics to the opening song; in deference to the censorship office, New York, New York, was no longer "a helluva town" but a "wonderful" one.

Various M-G-M interoffice memos attest to other matters of concern. These dealt with issues ranging from how much direct sunlight would be available at what times of day and in which areas of New York, to the chances of using the actual name of the American Museum of Natural History in the scene when the sailor Ozzie topples the dinosaur skeleton ("Feeling is that this dignified group will not like the treatment of the museum and will not okay shooting there"). Lucy Schmeeler, the comic plain-Jane role played by Alice Pearce, had to be renamed by a single letter to Shmeeler, after the research department uncovered some real Lucy Schmeelers in the Manhattan phone directory,* and the generic-sounding Yellow Cab Company was to be renamed, of all things, the Loew Cab Company. Strong precaution was given against photographing any part of the Bond Clothiers sign in Times Square, as M-G-M refused to accept any "advertisements" in its movies.

"We had five weeks of rehearsals, in Culver City, and were so excited that by the fourth week we could have shot the entire picture backwards," said Donen. Rehearsals started February 21, 1949, with shooting beginning Monday, March 28. On May 5, the principals and crew left for New York, where they remained until May 23. "We stretched every minute we were allowed on location," said Donen, "and knew every square inch of

* Another name change was that of the anthropologist played in the movie by Ann Miller, to Claire Huddeson. In the Broadway version, Claire's over-the-top surname was de Loon, and she was played by Betty Comden. Brunhilde Esterhazy, the cabdriver played onscreen by Betty Garrett, was simply Hildy onstage, and played by Nancy Walker, establishing how tiny was the circle in which this crowd traveled. On Broadway, Adolph Green played Ozzie, the most comic of the sailors, acted in the film by Jules Munshin. (John Battles, who took over for a newcomer named Kirk Douglas once it was discovered Douglas could not sing, and Cris Alexander completed the sailor trio onstage.) In the film, Vera-Ellen played Ivy Smith, originated on Broadway by Sono Osato.

the city because we had every photograph book of New York that ever existed."

On May 26, the "book" portion of the movie was completed, allowing Kelly to commence rehearsals on the "A Day in New York" ballet, which Bernstein completed during his visit to Los Angeles. The music was recorded June 24, and shooting of this final sequence for the picture wrapped July 2. In the finished film, the ballet effectively sabotaged the whole movie, by repeating in dance all the action that had preceded it. "[C]lumsily inserted," came the knock from *Time*, which otherwise waxed rhapsodic: "*On the Town* brings airy imagination and solid showmanship to the kind of movie that needs it most: the musical. The film avoids such standard cine-musical trappings as hothouse splendor, the lumbering backstage story and the curious notion that the script ought to give performers a pseudo-logical excuse to burst into song [and] dance.... M-G-M has hit upon a bright new idiom for cine-musicals and a bright new directing team that knows how to use it."

Undeniably, the high point of the picture is its stylized musical opening, with its flashes of reality filmed in New York: the sailors on the Brooklyn Bridge and on the Lower East Side, in Little Italy and Chinatown, at the base of the Statue of Liberty, in Central Park, on Wall Street, aboard the Third Avenue el, and on an open-air double-decker bus barreling down Fifth Avenue. "We had trouble with that shot because people kept peeking out of their apartment windows to see Sinatra," said Donen. "It was worse in Rockefeller Center, because we were all set up with the cameras and sound equipment, and we had Gene, Jules, and Frank's voices pumped up to full volume on the playback. If you look carefully at the movie, over the gold statue of Prometheus in the back of the ice-skating rink you can see the crowds staring down at the camera." Police barricades were required to hold back the hordes of the curious. "At the time," Donen said, "Sinatra was as popular as all four Beatles put together."

The shooting schedule was planned down to the last specific detail, owing to the civic demands of crowd control and shooting permits. "We had brought in our own cameraman, Hal Rosson, and our operator from Culver City," said Donen. "It was much more difficult then because so few commercial films were made in New York, and you were forced to hire a New York crew. Hollywood crews were allowed in, but if you did bring them in, you were in trouble."

The first day on location was devoted to the picture's opening and closing shots, in and around the Brooklyn Navy Yard. "I went out to watch it," recalled Betty Comden. "I was pregnant at the time, and the whole thing was thrilling. It was a gorgeous spring day."

"I didn't go out that day," piped up Adolph Green.

"You may have been in Europe," said Comden.

"I was there," said Green.

"In Europe?" asked Comden.

"No," said Green. "I was there when they were shooting the movie."

"But not the first day," said Comden.

"WHEN WE got to New York and checked into the hotel," remembered Donen, "Julie Munshin said to me, 'I have to have a room on the ground floor.' It turned out he was afraid of heights. Afraid? The poor guy was terrified." He had every right to be. Donen planned to shoot the movie's three stars atop some of the city's more illustrious rooftops, including a carefully blueprinted 360-degree vista of the sailors atop Rockefeller Center's RCA Building, nearly seventy stories above Manhattan. After discussion with Rosson, it was decided that a monorail would be built around the terrace's circumference and Rosson would strap himself to the camera, hanging upside down as Kelly, Sinatra, and Munshin gazed off the ledge.

"This is serious," Munshin told Donen. "Whenever I get into an elevator I have to fall down to my hands and knees." The hotel offered no accommodation on the ground floor. "Sure enough," Donen recalled, "when he got into the elevator, Julie went down on his hands and knees."

Donen kept secret a final shot of the three sailors flush against the unguarded, smooth precipice on the top of the Loew's Building over Broadway. "It was the only place in Times Square we could get permission to shoot, because no building owner was going to risk having some actor flying off the top of his building," said the director. Munshin ended up approaching his task with all the fortitude of the Cowardly Lion. "I can't go up there," Munshin announced.

"We coaxed him," remembered Donen. "It took a long time."

"All right," said Munshin. "I'll try to do the take. *But I cannot rehearse it.*" The declaration explains two facts. The first is why, in the rehearsal photographs, Stanley Donen in mufti is standing on top of 1540 Broadway with Gene Kelly and Frank Sinatra in sailor suits; also why, in the finished picture, Munshin is sandwiched between his costars. (Not captured by any camera was the fact that Munshin had a safety rope tied around his waist

Jules Munshin was deathly afraid of heights and would not rehearse. Donen stood in for him on top of the Loew's Building.

and tucked underneath his sailor suit, to provide him with at least a suggestion of security.) On top of the RCA Building in the opening number, Munshin clings noticeably to Kelly and Sinatra's shoulders as he moves about the surface while lip-synching the glories of New York.

"The whole time," said Donen, "the poor man was absolutely frightened out of his wits."

Donen's nightmare was Sinatra. "The beginning and the ending of the picture were to be shot on this boat"—a battleship. "The idea I had for the last shot was for the guys to arrive in a police van, get out, have the girls embrace them, they race back on board, the other sailors come rushing out, and the boat sails out into the harbor. Fade-out."

Donen presented the proposed finale's scenario to the admiral of the Brooklyn Navy Yard, admitting, "I don't know any of this nautical shit," and being assured by the senior naval officer that he would have the full cooperation of the sailor extras the studio was employing, as well as the captain of the ship. This way, the director was guaranteed, the vessel would leave the harbor exactly as he desired.

On location in Brooklyn, to shoot the opening and the (unused) finale. The latter sequence was nearly ruined, in any event, by a no-show Sinatra.

"We picked the day," said Donen, who relied on experts who knew their weather and sea tides, "and we picked the exact minute. One-thirty in the afternoon. We had the crane all prepared in the Brooklyn shipyard, to pick up the box with the camera and the operator, and we rehearsed this very long scene with the actors, at the end of which the men all got on board the ship. This whole time, I'm standing on the crane, literally three hundred feet in the air, and I'm yelling into the bullhorn, 'Okay, it's time to bring everybody in.' "

The actors entered the shot on cue, all except for One-Take Charlie. "An assistant said, 'Frank got tired of waiting,' " remembered Donen. "Frank got hungry and decided he wanted to have lunch at Toots Shor's, in Manhattan. Here we were, in Brooklyn, the cast, the crew, and the ship. And between Manhattan and Brooklyn was this bridge to cross. I knew we couldn't make the shot after lunch. The sun wouldn't hold. It was now or never."

Donen's temper was about to erupt, the scene to be scratched. To his credit, Sinatra could not have timed it better. The crooner's limousine pulled up. "He ran out of the car, and we just barely made the shot," said Donen. "Only thing, we had to cut it out of the movie. The admiral had told me the ship would pull away and sail into the harbor. What he didn't tell me was that it would take fifteen minutes for it to do that."

THE FIRST public preview of *On the Town* was held at the Bay Theater in Pacific Palisades, near Santa Monica, on the evening of September 9, 1949. Arthur Freed had reserved eight seats, and Donen four. Of the 276 responses to the questionnaire cards handed out afterward, 113 viewers found the picture "outstanding," 95 "excellent," 22 "very good," 11 "good," 4 "fair." No one judged it "poor." Betty Garrett elicited the most positive reaction, and to the query, "Would you recommend this picture to your friends?" 222 said yes, as opposed to six negatives. That approval rate was echoed on the East Coast. When the picture opened at New York's Radio City Music Hall as the 1949 Christmas attraction, it broke existing house records. The film also traveled well. In London, the critic Dilys Powell, seeing how it could trigger a new era in musicals, called *On the Town* "the best musical since *42nd Street*."

April 13, 1949, Donen turns twenty-five. On the M-G-M soundstage, Vera-Ellen and Ann Miller cut the cake, Sinatra sings "Happy Birthday," and Betty Garrett stands to the right of One-Take Charlie.

"Every Edens song for the film ('Prehistoric Man,' 'Main Street,' a vapid title tune, and 'You're Awful') is hackwork—the kind of musical garbage that proved the inferiority of Hollywood musicals to Broadway buffs," was Gerald Mast's harsh assessment.* The first number, set in the museum, allows Miller her first tap dance in the picture and finishes with her newfound friend Munshin toppling the dinosaur. This allows the sailors to flee the police and the picture to assume the plot thread of an extenuated Keystone Kops chase (beyond that, there is no plot).

For "Main Street," a softened Kelly, intimidated by the cosmopolitan Ivy, attempts to win her with his small-town tales of Meadowville, Indiana, not knowing she's from the same cow town. "You're Awful" ("Awful good to look at") is Sinatra and Garrett's love duet atop the studio-built replica of the observation deck of the Empire State Building, and it's immediately followed by the "vapid" title tune, performed by the entire cast. It, too, begins aloft on the famous structure, then finishes on the ground below, where it allows the movie's by then slackened pace to regain momentum as the sailors recover from their "shore leave blues." The final portion of the number, in which the six principals come barreling out of the Empire State's elevator and onto the pavement, works like a double dose of "Make Way for Tomorrow," with twice the number of performers but minus the singular sex appeal of Rita Hayworth.

The weak story line is emphasized all the more in the movie's penultimate number, the seven-minute "A Day in New York" ballet, which reiterates the previous action and adds the distraction of professional ballet performers replacing Sinatra, Munshin, Garrett, and Miller to dance with Kelly and Vera-Ellen. The same device was used when Rodgers and Hammerstein's *Oklahoma!* was brought to the screen in 1955, and it was not terribly successful there, either, except to cue the audience that it was time to go for popcorn, before the dream ballet came on.

The daydream begins when Gabey (Kelly) spots a theater poster on a construction fence, "A Day in New York, A Comedy in Three Acts, with Music." "There are several striking things to the ballet," said Joseph Andrew Casper in a monograph on Donen's work: "[the] dance studio correlative in which Ivy engages Gabey in an erotic *pas-de-deux* around a barre, with a canted camera off to the side catching the dancers and their full shadows on the wine backdrop and thereby energizing the frame with the appearance of four people; the red-lettered eleven-thirty p.m. time

* While agreeing with Mast in principle, Betty Comden preferred to say, "The opening number of the picture was great. The rest wasn't."

strip flashing in the frame's upper-left corner to signal Ivy's exit; and the zoom-out to a high-angle overview of Gabey's clutching a poster."

Casper admitted to finding the ballet "redundant" and "ponderous." "Kelly insisted upon this excrescence—after all, the ballet served him well," concluded Casper. "He would commit this sin again in *An American in Paris.*"

The final number, with the sailors hiding from the police in a Coney Island cooch-dance hall and Ivy's pretense about to be exposed when it turns out she's working there too, is "Pearl of the Persian Sea," performed with gusto by Munshin and spotlighting his talent for burlesque. When his Persian skirt slips, the police step in. This indeed being a more innocent time, the boys in blue then escort Gabey, Ozzie, and Chip back to the ship, and so ends their day in New York, as a whole new group of sailors prepare for their twenty-four-hour spree.

DISMISSING the trite accolade that *On the Town* was "groundbreaking," Donen said about the film in 1992, "We did try to make it, in a sense, somewhat more realistic than other musicals. It had a freer form to it, and it had the energy and youthfulness of the sailors in New York. What it also might have had was a certain sock of what I'd consider raw, American energy that other musicals at the time might have lacked. Also, I think it had more musical numbers that came out of situations in the story than was usually the case. What is not true, despite people's saying it all the time, is that *On the Town* was the first picture to be made on location. That's simply not the case. René Clair* had done a lot of musical numbers using exteriors well before *On the Town,* and Fred Astaire did his golf number [in *Damsel in Distress,* 1937] outside. There may not have been musical numbers done in the streets of New York before, but we didn't break any ground."

"It's dated now, of course," Gene Kelly said on the twenty-fifth anniversary of the film, in 1974, "because the techniques gradually became common and the theme of sailors on a spree has been done to

---

* Clair (1898–1981), who for a time was considered the French Ernst Lubitsch (1892–1947), chose to shoot many of his exteriors on the back lot, exemplified by perhaps his best musical, the 1931 *Le Million.* Of Lubitsch musicals of the twenties and thirties, such as *The Love Parade, The Smiling Lieutenant,* and *The Merry Widow,* Billy Wilder, who idolized the filmmaker, said: "Lubitsch had a kind of stylization in getting into a musical number that did not hit you between the eyes, the way it happened in the Busby Berkeley kind of thing." Asked if Donen might have displayed a bit of the Lubitsch touch, Wilder responded, "He's different, but he's very, very good."

death, but in 1949 the idea of believable sailors dancing and singing in the streets of New York—using the city as a set—was new, and it paved the way for musicals like *West Side Story.*"

"I don't keep reviews, letters, nothing," confessed Donen, "but I do wish I had held on to this one note Arthur Freed sent Gene and me while we were making *On the Town,* because at the time, all anybody was talking about was this picture from England, *The Red Shoes,* by Emeric Pressburger and Michael Powell."

Within the confines of the Arthur Freed collection in the main library of the University of Southern California, a carbon copy of the message has survived.

In full, it reads:

Dear Gene & Stanley:

I just ran the cut numbers of *On the Town* and they were the greatest and most inspiring works I have seen since I have been making motion pictures.

Pressburger and Powell can't shine your shoes—red, white, or blue.

Much love from your producer.
Arthur

Chapter 2

"I Thought I'd Die"

A FTER *On the Town,* Arthur Freed was looking for something for me to direct on my own," said Donen. The first solid offer was "an Esther Williams picture, some sort of Hawaiian thing." *Pagan Love Song,* a Tahitian plantation drama, was to be partly shot on location on the Hawaiian island of Kauai. "It was to be my first picture alone," said Donen, "so what was I supposed to do, say no?"

Donen, it developed, was not afforded that luxury. The coolness that existed between the aquatic star and the team of Kelly and Donen during the making of *Take Me Out to the Ball Game* had been exacerbated when Donen later spied Williams driving onto the M-G-M lot in her brand-new Cadillac convertible.

"Jesus Christ," he shouted to her, "they sure pay you a lot for splashing around that swimming pool."

Before production on the "Hawaiian thing" was to begin, Donen was summoned into the head production office, to be greeted by Esther Williams, Arthur Freed, and Dore Schary. Schary spoke for the other two when he informed Donen, "Esther says that she would find it very difficult to work with you. She doesn't think you think she's talented."

"I was nonplussed," Donen recalled. "I was supposed to convince her that I did think she was talented."

Donen did not do the picture.* "Ever since," said Donen, "I've felt I owe my career to Esther Williams."

Freed made good on his promise to find Donen a film of his own, and the fact that the one he ultimately offered was in trouble should serve as an

---

* *Pagan Love Song,* directed by Robert Alton, is considered the lowest point of the Freed film slate.

indication of the level of confidence in which Freed held the new director. "Arthur asked me, 'Would you like to direct *Royal Wedding?*'" Donen said. "I thought I'd die. Would I like to direct Fred Astaire? Oh, brother."

IN 1946, a year after signing his first contract with M-G-M, Astaire retired to race horses and invest in a national chain of dance schools that bore his name. Astaire's self-imposed break with movies ended in 1948, when Gene Kelly broke his ankle while playing ball in his backyard. Kelly's timing was awful; he was on the eve of production of *Easter Parade,* with Judy Garland. Freed asked Astaire to step in, which he did, thus revitalizing his film career, and Kelly joked afterward that breaking his ankle was the worst move he ever made.

The director of *Easter Parade* was to be Garland's husband, Vincente Minnelli. Under advisement from Garland's psychiatrist, though, Minnelli stepped aside, and in an example of the vertical integration that distinguished the Freed Unit, the director was replaced by Donen's former mentor, the choreographer Charles Walters. (Walters had made his directorial debut in 1947, with *Good News.*) The potent combination of Astaire and Garland and the familiar Irving Berlin songs made *Easter Parade* Astaire's most profitable picture for Metro, inducing the studio to pair the stars again as quickly as possible. That vehicle was to be *The Barkleys of Broadway,* produced by Freed, directed by Walters, and written by Comden and Green—only Garland's increasing unreliability made proceeding with it futile, and she was replaced by Ginger Rogers.

In May of 1950, the *Royal Wedding* package seemed the perfect way to reunite Astaire with Garland—and director Walters. "I got the picture in a very odd way," said Donen. "June Allyson was to do *Royal Wedding* with Fred Astaire, and Chuck Walters was to direct it, but then June got pregnant and had to drop out. Arthur replaced her with Judy Garland, but then Chuck Walters said to Arthur, 'I can't do it again. I've just finished *Summer Stock* with her, and the experience nearly killed me.' It had taken them almost a year to shoot *Summer Stock,* and during that whole time Judy just broke Chuck in half."

Besides showing up late, or not at all, Garland was blowing her lines and causing a general panic on the set. To the alarmed producer, Joe Pasternak, Garland's costar, Gene Kelly, was "a saint. Something in his blood makes him generously inclined to a friend who needs another kind of help. Gene said: 'I'll do anything for this girl, Joe. If I have to come here and sit and wait for a year, I'll do it for her.'"

Astaire was never one to tolerate Donen's—or anyone's—
expressions of admiration. Still, it is easy to read the
director's face.

While Kelly may have put on an angelic face for Pasternak, he wasted
no time letting his feelings be known to Metro's head of production, Dore
Schary. As Schary recalled, "Kelly was finding it difficult to work with
Judy. He explained that she was projecting a terrible odor whenever they
had to play scenes face-to-face. The only clue, he told me, was that her
breath smelled like formaldehyde." Finding it hard to accept Kelly's story,
Schary trumped up a reason to talk to Garland so he could get a whiff of
her breath. From a physician he consulted, he learned that the scent Garland was emitting was probably paraldehyde, "a drug used to bring drunk-
ards out of their deep comas or delirium tremens."

When Freed cast Garland in *Royal Wedding,* said Donen, "Chuck
absolutely refused to work with her again and walked off the picture.

Arthur Freed's original choice to direct *Royal Wedding,* Charles Walters (left), with Fred Astaire and Peter Lawford. Walters refused to work with Judy Garland, and Donen got the job.

That's when Arthur called me into his office and asked me about it. Direct Fred Astaire and Judy Garland? I said, 'Okay. I'm on. Very much. Yes.' Then the shit hit the fan."

Charles Walters's warnings proved true. "Judy never saw any of the numbers we had worked up for her," said Donen. The star did go so far as to listen to the arrangements, said Donen, and for a few days during the second week of preproduction she rehearsed her vocals with Saul Chaplin, all of which served as an encouraging sign. The atmosphere of optimism was further buoyed on Friday, June 9, 1950, the end of the third week of preproduction, when the Freed Unit took over the main rehearsal stage and tossed Garland a twenty-eighth-birthday party. Though no one knew it at the time, that occasion formally marked the end of her participation in the film, and of her career at M-G-M.

The following Monday, Garland informed Donen that she could not rehearse during any of the appointed mornings or afternoons, despite its being the last week of rehearsals. "I wouldn't give up," said Donen, "though I was ready to." The new director implored her to rethink her

June 20, 1950, the day after being fired by M-G-M for not reporting to work on *Royal Wedding,* Judy Garland slashed one of her wrists. This family portrait of the star with her four-year-old daughter, Liza, and her husband, Vincente Minnelli, accompanied news of the suicide attempt over the wires.

decision, but she begged back, requesting, in order to alleviate her burden of stress, that she be allowed to work half days only. Freed permitted her the indulgence, although it turned out to be strictly an exercise to see who could win the argument. That entire week, said Donen, "We could not get her to come in. A million excuses. A tooth pulled. Her stomach hurt. Liza was ill."*

Astaire, it was said, seethed privately, though as Donen professed time and again, "It was never Fred's style to complain."

"It wasn't?" said a skeptical Kay Thompson, who was to work with Astaire on *Funny Face.* "It's interesting, isn't it? The mistake millions of people have made, that stars are going to be different than they are. Fred, you expect, is going to be walking in a spring garden, a wonderful man who's going to be so polite. He was none of that."

* Garland and Vincente Minnelli's daughter, Liza, was born in 1946. In 1951, the marriage was over.

As Donen recalled, the standoff with Garland "ended with my saying, 'Arthur, we're going into the recording studio. If she doesn't come in tomorrow, it's going to be a nightmare.' That made Arthur say, 'Well, if she doesn't come in tomorrow, we'll have to do something.' And she didn't come in tomorrow."

On Monday morning, June 19, 1950, Loew's president, Nicholas Schenck, received a wire from Culver City. "For your information," it read, "Judy Garland's contract has been suspended commencing June 17, 1950." On June 20, inside her Beverly Hills home, Garland slashed her wrist with a broken bathroom glass.

"The press started calling me, saying that I'd fired her," remembered Donen. Reporters also asked whether he felt responsible for Judy Garland's suicide attempt. He did not. Further, Donen did not believe, at the time or ever, that the studio was to blame for the personal or professional traumas that plagued the star. "No employee was ever better treated by any company than Judy Garland was by M-G-M," he said. "They waited on her hand and foot as though she were a princess." As for "his" dismissal of Garland: "I didn't have that kind of power. I only found out she had been fired when I was told she was being replaced by Jane Powell."

Royal Wedding, like the film version of *On the Town,* was instigated by Lillie Messinger. Having been hired away from RKO's story department by L. B. Mayer in 1940, Messinger prodded Arthur Freed into buying Alan Jay Lerner and Frederick Loewe's 1947 romantic Broadway musical fantasy, *Brigadoon.* (The studio had already spent $250,000 on a previous small success by the team, the 1945 *The Day Before Spring.* After a pair of false starts, one under Pasternak and another under Freed, nothing ever came of it, while a lifeless *Brigadoon* finally reached the screen in 1954, via Vincente Minnelli.)

With *Brigadoon* a stage smash in New York, Loewe, who was passionate about chemin de fer, rushed headfirst into a sabbatical, while Lerner received an invitation from Freed to spend ten weeks at the studio in order to see if any creative ideas might be sparked. Lerner accepted.

A poet when it came to his early lyrics and librettos, the Choate- and Harvard-educated Lerner (1917–1986) was first and foremost a playboy, as he himself would admit.* Anticipating his two and a half months in California as a paid holiday, Lerner was more than casually disappointed

---

* Coincidentally, his father, Joseph J. Lerner, owned the Lerner Shops, the chain that competed with the dress company for which Mordie Donen had worked.

when, in the course of his third week in Culver City, Freed presented an irresistible offer: Come up with an idea for Fred Astaire. Freed had it in mind to outfit his dapper leading man in a groom's white tie and tails, for a movie to be titled *Niagara Falls.*

In seeking a story line, Lerner recalled, "We began to discuss the days when Fred's partner was his famous sister, Adele." Out of this "came the idea of doing a film about a famous brother-and-sister team engaged to perform in London at the time of the royal wedding." In the final scenario, the brother, once he arrives in London to perform in a show, falls in love with an English dancer, while his libidinous younger sister falls for a handsome peer. In actual fact, Adele Astaire had married Lord Charles Cavendish, leaving her brother to return to New York solo in 1932, a turn of events that marked the beginning of Astaire's upward career spiral.*

In Lerner's plot, both couples marry on the same day in 1947 that Princess Elizabeth wed Prince Philip. On January 12, 1949, Freed formally requested that the title *Royal Wedding* be registered with the Motion Picture Board. "This will be the story that Alan Lerner is developing for Fred Astaire and June Allyson," the producer alerted the studio. "The Niagara Falls atmosphere is being eliminated and the story will concern American entertainers going to London to entertain at the time of the royal wedding." To complement Lerner's first screen libretto, Freed enlisted Burton Lane, who had composed Broadway's whimsical 1947 *Finian's Rainbow.*

Once Lerner's first draft was finished, the story department did its requisite fiddling. Americanisms were removed (or at least suitably altered, from "Call me on opening night" to "Phone me on opening night") and advice was proffered. M-G-M's London office objected to one character name dreamed up by Lerner, Gladys Belcher, for which the substitute Gladys Hawkley was strongly recommended, "because there are probably several Belchers with the first name of Gladys." ("Hawksley" is what it sounds like in the finished film.) On March 4, an internal memo alerted the filmmakers that if they intended to present the anthem "God Save the Queen" at the start of their picture, an alternative opening number must be prepared for countries of the British Isles. "As you know," amplified the researcher, "this composition is used in Great Britain only at the end of a theatrical performance and is primarily used to 'clear the house.' "†

* The screen's most elegant musical star, like its most elegant nonmusical star, Cary Grant, was a product of humble beginnings. Astaire (1899–1987) was born in Omaha, Nebraska, the son of a local brewery worker and his wife, who was determined that her children enter show business.

† For the film's release in the British Empire, the title was changed to *Wedding Bells,* to prevent audiences from thinking it a documentary.

By June, with Donen attached, the picture was ready to roll, with an approved script and a score, even a last-minute comic vaudeville number that Astaire had personally requested and Lerner and Lane devised in the car en route to the studio. Titled "How Can You Believe Me When You Said You Love Me When You Know I've Been a Liar All My Life?," it plays exactly as it sounds.

Dore Schary passed judgment on the script, telling Freed, "I think it's wonderful, but quite long." In fact, the release print clocked in at a brisk ninety-three minutes, though the action does start to flag at the three-quarter point, to be resuscitated only slightly by the bouncy if garish stage production number "I Left My Hat in Haiti." That song, even Burton Lane conceded, "was contrived."

"Light as the tale may have been," ventured Fred Astaire, "it was an excellent pattern for the numbers."

FILMING BEGAN on July 6, 1950. "A few times," Donen admitted, "I tried telling Fred what this meant to me. I mean, to work with him and actually be in a rehearsal hall with him. It all seemed so soon. I was only twenty-six, and Fred Astaire was this monument in my life. It had only been seventeen years since I'd first seen him in *Flying Down to Rio,* which I guess is a reasonable amount of time, but for me it seemed an extraordinary experience. Only, he didn't care to hear about things like that. He didn't want the responsibility of it. He was only interested in rehearsing."

Casting a love interest for Astaire had been a problem from the outset. At one point, Moira Shearer, of *The Red Shoes,* was a serious contender, although, as Astaire finally came to decide, "I know she's wonderful, but what the hell would I do with her?" "Then Arthur got a terrific idea," said Donen. "Sarah Churchill, the daughter of Winston. It *was* a terrific idea. The only problem was, she had zero sex appeal. She ended up throwing a wet blanket on the whole movie."*

Royal Wedding's choreographer, Nick Castle, whose Hollywood work comprised forty pictures, worked with Astaire only this once. "Fred nor-

---

* Freed signed Churchill after seeing her in *The Philadelphia Story* at the Pasadena Playhouse. Despite her father's having been the Prime Minister of England, the actress had to fight for her billing in the film, an indication that there might have been second thoughts about casting her. This is further implied by her pay reduction, with M-G-M originally offering her $1,250 a week with a twelve-week guarantee, as well as transportation from New York to Los Angeles. The figure was later reduced to $1,041.66 a week for ten weeks, with no transportation, and astonishingly, for the final two weeks of filming she provided her services to the movie company for free.

mally worked with Hermes Pan," said Jane Powell, speaking of the choreographer who devised most of Astaire's most famous routines, including "The Carioca." "Fred and Hermes walked alike, talked alike, even looked alike, so Nick's job wasn't easy." Contrary to Astaire's notorious, if exaggerated, reputation that he would practice with his partners until their feet bled, Powell said that she had insufficient rehearsal with Astaire, who was tired of routines he had gone through once before with June Allyson. "I never got to know him very well," she said tactfully. "In person he didn't have the vitality that you would expect from watching him perform."

Granted, Astaire does occasionally appear tired in the picture. This is especially, and dangerously, the case in his first dance, "Every Night at Seven," a stage number that opens with his sitting on a throne looking as dispirited as Jerry the Mouse had in the same position. Powell plays opposite as an appealing and lively chambermaid. Fortunately, Astaire shakes the look of ennui during the two most inspired moments in *Royal Wedding,* his solos to "Sunday Jumps" and "You're All the World to Me."

"The hardest thing to do in a musical is to find a reason for a number to happen," said Donen. "In most instances, people dance for joy. It's much harder to find a reason to dance for lament. But getting to that point for any reason is always a problem. In fact, Gene and I used to laugh. Once we got going, people started sending us scripts, and they would say things like, 'And here he dances out his love for her.' "

For "Sunday Jumps," Astaire dances alone because his partner fails to show up for rehearsal. As was the case in real life, Astaire would not forgo his usual practice, though as Donen explained, "The genesis of this number is, Fred had a solo. He needed something to do when he's alone aboard ship in a gymnasium, so the scenario then became something only Fred Astaire could do—which was dance with a coat tree, a clumsy piece of equipment. He was looking for a partner to dance with, and since there wasn't a person around, he grabbed whatever he could find." The nearly four-minute scene begins when Astaire, peering out the gymnasium door in search of Powell, accidentally rests a hand on the clothes tree. The song "Sunday Jumps" refers to the jitters a workaholic feels on his day of rest (the lyrics were dropped from the picture but survive in a Lerner anthology):

> Sunday is a thing you lie around on
> A day of peace and gathering new reserves
> Sunday's calm routine,
> Tranquil and serene,
> But brother, how it gets on my nerves.

"You're All the World to Me": Fred Astaire dances on the ceiling in *Royal Wedding* (1951). Part of the number's inspiration harked back seventeen years, to Donen's first sighting of the star, in *Flying Down to Rio:* "He performed as though he were without gravity."

"Many Astaire duets include a beautiful and witty transition step, the Astaire double helix," said Astaire expert John Mueller, referring to the star's habit of circling his partner as if stalking prey, before they front off and dance. "In this duet Astaire uses the double helix to begin the dance as he deftly spins his way around the rotating clothes tree and tenderly takes it in his embrace." After a graceful bow to this partner, Astaire discovers it's too heavy to lift, so he decides to engage the gym equipment to build up his body. "Astaire's encounter" with the weights, "though not as exhilaratingly amusing as his dance with the clothes tree, has its screwball surprises—as when he belts the punching bag with a high kick."

In preparation for the film's best-remembered sequence, Fred Astaire's dancing on the ceiling, the studio's music department was informed by memo: "Tom Bowen (Fred Astaire) comes home to his apartment and sees a photograph of his lover, Anne Ashmond (Sarah Churchhill [*sic*]). He sits down and we hear him sing the verse as though we're hearing his thoughts, then we actually see him sing the chorus. This is followed by four instrumental, fast choruses to which Fred Astaire dances a sensational dance routine on the ceiling, over the walls, etc. This routine is absolutely unique and should create quite a sensation."*

"It was an idea of Alan Lerner's," said Donen, a claim repeated by Lerner himself, although Fred Astaire stated it was his. "I found a spot in *Wedding* for my upside-down-on-the-ceiling-and-around-the-walls dance, which I had planned for some time," the star recalled for his memoir, in which he also revealed that the brainchild awakened him at four in the morning. In his own memoir, Lerner said, "One night I dreamed that Fred was dancing up the wall, all across the ceiling, and down the other wall. I mentioned it to Arthur at lunch the following day and lo, in the film Fred danced up one wall, across the ceiling, and down the other wall."

Donen has no trouble establishing the proper mood. The number starts to take shape back at the theater, where, late at night, Astaire, wearing white tie, top hat, and tails, swipes Churchill's photograph from the billboard out front. Returning to his hotel room, he removes his jacket, briefly paces the floor, sinks into an armchair, stubs out his cigarette, and admires the picture—which, in fact, is magnetized and stuck to the shelf of a metal floor lamp. Unbeknownst to the viewers, Astaire is sitting in a steel-reinforced cylindrical chamber approximately twenty feet in diameter, similar to the spinning barrel at Coney Island. Donen's camera was attached at the base of the revolving cylinder, which the crew referred to as "The Squirrel Cage" and Astaire called "The Iron Lung." Donen would rotate full circle along the barrel's circumference as Astaire performed each step of his 360-degree tap dance.

"The room's starting to move now," said Donen, watching the scene, just as Astaire steps out of the chair and trots around it. The leading man next snaps his fingers, slaps the desk, then starts to alight on the sofa across the room before landing on the wall. He switches to the other wall, on the audience's left, only to bounce back to the right wall, and landing higher this time, until he's fully engaged in dancing on the vertical surface. He mixes in a few bounces on the sofa until he reaches the ceiling, where he ambles around the chandelier and continues his leaps. His style is never

* Donen thinks otherwise: "When the picture came out, nobody paid the number much attention. It was the same way with the Jerry the Mouse number with Gene."

acrobatic, like Douglas Fairbanks's, but more startling and unexpected, like a grasshopper's.

"Astaire doesn't inhabit the same physical space as anyone else," said Gerald Mast. "He is not quite mortal, not subject to mortal and physical law."

Lerner's lyrics add to this sensation that the dancer is exploring a new world; mimicking the laundry list of superlatives Cole Porter compiled for "You're the Top," the lyrics to "You're All the World to Me" carbon an itinerary to the world's more romantic destinations:

> You're like Paris
> In April and May.
> You're New York
> On a silvery day.*

"Fred's coat was sewed to the chair and the chair was screwed to the floor," said Donen, explaining the tricks used in the shot. "The draperies were made of wood. There's nothing soft in the shot." There was only one cut during the sequence—while Astaire is at midpoint on the right wall—necessitated by having to change the roll of film. "We rehearsed this for weeks and filmed it in the morning. Because there was nothing to do but shoot it, we were literally through with the entire sequence by lunch."

"ALTHOUGH Burton Lane wrote some spiffy songs and Fred danced in a way that made all superlatives inadequate," was Lerner's verdict, "my contribution left me in such a state of cringe that I could barely straighten up." Astaire expert John Mueller noted with irony that Lerner's "next script was *An American in Paris,* which, unlike *Royal Wedding,* is sentimental and pretentious, and which earned him an Oscar." Donen concurred with Lerner's opinions of the score and Astaire, but held the view: "The story is not interesting. You look at the movie and you just don't care."

The question, though, does remain, would *Royal Wedding* have been any better if Garland had remained to star? (The issue of Allyson is negligible.) Donen, ever the diplomat, does not so much as hint that Jane

---

* Insofar as Burton Lane's melody was concerned, the composer had used it before, in the 1934 Eddie Cantor film *Kid Millions.* That time the song was called "I Want to Be a Minstrel Man" (with lyrics by Harold Damson) and was performed by Harold and Fayard Nicholas. In successfully securing the rights to his old song, Lane claimed he simply told *Kid Millions*'s producer, Sam Goldwyn, "This is the tune I always dreamed would be good for Astaire."

"Sunday Jumps," a reaction to the restlessness one feels on a weekend. The number was conceived, said Donen, to show that Fred Astaire, devoid of a human partner, could dance with anything—even a clumsy coatrack.

Powell was in any respect a disappointment. While she and Astaire clown their way through the "How Could You Believe Me?" vaudeville routine on his home video monitor, Donen's only remark is, "These were Judy Garland's arrangements. We didn't change a note. There wasn't time." Powell, working for the first time for Freed after having been a mainstay of the Pasternak group,* gives her first non–Junior League performance. She appears to be relishing her role and having fun with Astaire, which translates into a refreshing performance. What *is* implausible is the notion of their being brother and sister. Although their towheaded coloring and sprightly builds are similar enough—certainly to a greater extent than would have been the case with Astaire and Garland—plainly, Powell is two or three decades too young to be his sibling.

What Powell does bring is an unexpected tartness and panache to *Royal Wedding,* unhindered by her usual sweetness, even if she does come across a tad too operatic during the love song "Too Late Now." Still, one can only imagine how Garland, a belter in the Broadway tradition, might have over-whelmed the number.[†] The delicacy of its sentiment ("Too late now to for-get your smile"), which Powell conveys to the handsome but wooden Peter Lawford near a back-lot lake in the vintage M-G-M English countryside, is enhanced by the romantic mood of the moment, with Donen's camera tracking the well-dressed lovers as they stroll across a footbridge against a twilight sky. Turn off the volume, and the direction still delivers the mes-sage that Powell and Lawford will live happily ever after.

Garland, then, might only have seemed a fascinating but neurotic intruder, no doubt enhancing the backstage production-number elements of the film, which are seldom lacking in the first place, but also furnishing the book portion of *Royal Wedding* with more of the one ingredient it def-initely did not require, show-business artificiality.

---

* Powell said Pasternak "was more or less assigned to me, and I to him, the way Judy Gar-land was to Arthur Freed." Powell long looked upon Pasternak as a father figure until, she acknowledged in her 1988 memoir, she learned that the producer was spreading lies about her being "the easiest lay in town."

[†] In fairness, on her 1963 television program, a mature Judy Garland delivered a soft ren-dition of the song, accompanied by a single piano, and found every nuance its gentle lyrics con-tained.

Chapter 3

"Who Could Resist?"

Royal Wedding was completed in October 1950, by which time Arthur Freed had only begun to set the wheels in motion for *Singin' in the Rain.* Donen, a contract employee whose annual pay raises depended upon his cumulative yearly output for the studio, was assigned to the producer William H. Wright, who handed him the script of a comedy about a dance student from New Haven who enters a competition in Manhattan. Once she arrives, she is swept off her feet by a fast-talking Broadway talent agent.

"I had such chutzpah," said Donen. "After Will Wright gave me the script I said, 'Elizabeth Taylor would be good.' I barely knew her. She was already a tremendous star."

Taylor by then was eighteen years old and had starred in her first adult role, in the 1950 *Father of the Bride,* for Vincente Minnelli. She also had been loaned to Paramount for *A Place in the Sun,* directed by George Stevens, though that picture, which would turn out to be arguably the best of her entire career, had yet to be released.

"When she was eighteen," said Donen, "Elizabeth Taylor was as beautiful as any woman who'd ever been born." When the issue arose of casting her in the picture, to be called *Love Is Better Than Ever,* Donen and producer Wright engaged in a verbal tennis match inside the producer's office.

"You want her?" said Will Wright. "Then you ask her."

"I don't know her," said Donen. "I'm not going to ask her. *You* ask her."

"I don't know her, either," said Wright. "You ask her."

"I'm not going to ask her," persisted Donen. Instead he sent her the script.

Elizabeth Taylor, 1950

Sara Taylor did not approve of her daughter's romance with Donen, despite the fact that the actress subsequently converted to Judaism.

Elizabeth Taylor responded in person, by walking into Donen's office. "I don't think she had an appointment," he recalled. "Back then, everything at M-G-M was connected—the commissary, the rehearsal studios, the offices. She just came into my little office, which was in the directors' building." Donen said that Taylor asked him to take over responsibility for her career and her personal life. "She was in the middle of a miserable marriage, to Nicky Hilton, which was breaking up at the time, and she was in tears."

As Donen remembered Elizabeth Taylor that afternoon, "Here was this gorgeous damsel in distress saying 'Help me.' Who could resist her? What fool would try?"

Larry Parks, whose star rose in 1946 when he played the title role in Columbia's *The Jolson Story,* portrayed the love interest in *Love Is Better Than Ever,* the glib agent who shows the Taylor character the town. (Off-camera, Parks was married to Betty Garrett, who since *On the Town* had been suffering a lingering personality conflict with Louis B. Mayer over her refusal to sign a long-term Metro contract.) As for Taylor, already her offscreen entanglements were often more riveting than her movies. *Love Is Better Than Ever* was no exception. While the film barely survives, news photos and items of Taylor and Donen from the period do. Hedda Hopper frequently ventured that Taylor would be named corespondent in Donen's eventual divorce from Jeanne Coyne, although that never proved to be the case.

"Elizabeth gave me an absolutely beautiful platinum watch that she had made by Audemars Piguet," said Donen. "It was square and just elegant." Donen was sporting the timepiece the evening he and Taylor dined at the home of her agent, Jules Goldstone. "Jules's eighty-year-old father was there too," remembered Donen, "and Jules said, 'Stanley, show my father the watch Elizabeth gave you.'"

The senior Goldstone took a good look, then handed it back to Donen with the comment: "Very nice."

"Then," said Donen, "he said, 'Elizabeth, that must've cost you a lot of money.'"

"Yes, Mr. Goldstone," answered Taylor.

"Stanley," said the elderly man, "what time is it?"

"It's eight-thirty," replied Donen.

"Hmph," said Goldstone. "It says the same thing on my watch."

* * *

"ELIZABETH'S MOTHER, Sara, did everything in her power to call it off," Donen said of the romance, which he approximated lasted one year. "Her mother hated me in the worst way and did all sorts of nasty things to break us up, including calling Louis B. Mayer, Eddie Mannix, and several other people at the studio." Donen described Sara Taylor as "this very dominating woman, a terrible person. Elizabeth inherited her face and her looks from her father, Francis, but he was a very beaten husband. Sara, I think, at that time certainly was anti-Semitic, despite the fact that Elizabeth subsequently became a Jew."*

Open warfare emerged between the two camps, Stanley and Elizabeth's—and Sara Taylor's. "Howard Hughes was after Elizabeth in a big way," Donen recalled, "and used to send her really expensive presents, like thirty-five-millimeter projectors. Only Elizabeth was with me and not interested in him at all. This made him *and* Sara furious. That's when Sara went to the studio and told Benny Thau, 'Stanley Donen is a communist and a homosexual and should be run out of town.' When that didn't work, Sara got Howard Hughes to call Sheila Graham, who had a gossip column. Typical of him, he told her to meet him at three o'clock in the morning at the corner of Sunset and Camden, because he had a big scoop for her. So, when Sheila Graham gets there, he tells her, 'Stanley Donen is a homosexual and a communist,' and Sheila Graham says, 'That's very interesting, Mr. Hughes.' 'Well,' he said, 'aren't you going to print it?' When Sheila Graham refused, Hughes became absolutely enraged. He tried to get me run out of town himself, except, to M-G-M's credit, they never did anything about it, despite Hughes's influence. They must've known by then that Sara was behind the whole plot."

What is ironic is that one of the running gags throughout *Love Is Better Than Ever* shows the mother of the Elizabeth Taylor character leaving annoying phone messages for her daughter at the Manhattan hotel where she's staying, messages the daughter willfully ignores.

"It ended in a funny way," said Donen of the affair. "After we finished the picture, the studio wanted Elizabeth to do *Ivanhoe*, and she said, 'No, I'm not going to do it.' They asked why, and she said, 'Because you're going to make it in England, and I don't want to be away from Stanley.' I said, 'Elizabeth, you can't be like that. You're a movie star and I'm a director. Are you saying that our relationship is such that it's impossible for you

---

* In 1957, in anticipation of her third marriage, to the producer Mike Todd (born Avrom Hirsch Goldenbogen), Taylor converted to Judaism.

to go to England and make a movie? Why don't you make *Ivanhoe* and then come right back? I'll still be here.' "

Taylor was adamant, saying, "I don't want to be away from you."

"But it's a big movie and a good part," Donen advised her. ("I've always been a rational kind of fellow," he explained.)

Taylor took Donen's advice and left Los Angeles to star in *Ivanhoe*. "I never heard from her again," said Donen. "She got to London, she met Michael Wilding, and they got married. I never got a phone call, a Dear John letter—nothing. That was it. The end."

Actually, it wasn't. "Professionally," Donen said, "I got the biggest shock of my life. I was in the dubbing theater, just finishing the mix to release the picture, and Larry Parks went up to testify before the House Un-American Activities Committee." Parks was targeted in the second round of the Washington witch hunt that began in 1947. That fall, a group of ten filmmakers, who became known as the Hollywood Ten, were subpoenaed before the committee investigating "Communist infiltration of the film industry," where they stood behind their First Amendment rights. Louis B. Mayer himself put in a grand appearance on October 20, testifying that there ought to be a law against Communists being allowed to work in any American industry, only Mayer no sooner finished his impassioned battle cry than the author Ayn Rand was given the stand, where she denounced an M-G-M film, *Song of Russia,* for painting too pretty a picture of her own former homeland.* Dore Schary, a vocal liberal, philosophically supported the Hollywood Ten, but he remained powerless—some would say spineless—to assist them. In April 1948, they were found guilty of contempt of Congress, and each was sentenced to a thousand-dollar fine and a year in prison. After that, blacklisted, they were forced to seek work abroad or, in those rare circumstances when they found employment in Hollywood, to work pseudonymously.

In 1951, there was a fresh wave of accusations. Besides Larry Parks— who, having headlined in the biggest box office success of 1946, was a star witness in more than one respect—those fingered by the committee included the actors Lloyd Bridges and Sterling Hayden, the director Elia Kazan, the writers Isobel Lennart, Clifford Odets, and Budd Schulberg, and more than three hundred others.

---

* As political factions went at M-G-M, Gene Kelly headed up the liberal contingent, while Robert Taylor represented the conservatives. Taylor spoke before the committee on October 22, 1947, and said he looked forward to the day when Hollywood made anti-Communist movies.

"There was no television," said Donen, "but over the radio came the news that Larry Parks today admitted he was a member of the Communist party." Parks was a member from 1941 until 1945, at which time he resigned, having found the party misguided.

"I was still in the dubbing theater," remembered Donen. "We got a call informing us, 'Mr. Mayer said you can stop. The picture is not going to be released. M-G-M cannot release a picture in which the leading man is a member of the Communist party.' This was in spite of the fact that Larry Parks did *exactly* what the committee wanted him to, he named people. But that wasn't enough to satisfy Louis B. Mayer. The picture wasn't released for years."

"I once asked Stanley why he was never investigated during the witch hunt trials," said Frederic Raphael, noting that Donen's "astute" (Raphael's word) political leanings were somewhat left of center, "and he said, 'The only reason I wasn't was because I just didn't make anybody's list.' "

Love Is Better Than Ever was finally thrown into release in 1952. By then, Parks and Betty Garrett, both jobless in Hollywood, had developed a nightclub act and were touring Europe. As for the film, which under any circumstances would have seemed anticlimactic to the director, the best that can still be said for it is that, using stock location footage, Donen adequately captured the pace of Manhattan through the eyes of an impressionable youth, only this was something he had done before, and better, with *On the Town*.

"I saw it recently on television at three in the morning," Donen said about *Love Is Better Than Ever* in 1992. "Forget about it." Of Elizabeth Taylor, his comment was, "I was gaga about her, and she about me. I suppose we thought we'd get married, but now it's something she doesn't like to remember. Neither do I, actually."

Chapter 4

"The Picture Is About Movies"

H OLLYWOOD MOVIES about Hollywood were a byword for disaster," hypothesized an anonymous *London Times Magazine* critic in 1993, for that publication's "Culture Vulture" column. The writer had set his or her sights on an artistic reassessment of *Singin' in the Rain,* the 1952 musical, which critics waved aside upon its initial release,* praised unanimously at the time of a 1975 reissue,† and clearly have felt obliged to reexamine every two decades or so.

"This musical tale of the transition from silent films to sound ought not to have worked," ventured the "Vulture." Detailing the obstacles that lay before and in the wake of the film, the writer continued: "Debbie Reynolds and—more urgently—Donald O'Connor were only to go on to smaller things. Gene Kelly's grin is about as cheering as a nuclear accident, and elsewhere he was the most self-indulgent of directors. But here, his talents had the genius of the young Stanley Donen as a foil." The end result, claimed the scribe, "was a miracle [with] unmatched musical sequences [making] use of every conceivable cinematic location, from a crowded set to an empty soundstage with nothing but lights and a wind machine." In conclusion, the rave cited "one of the most exhilarating camera movements in screen history, when the camera moves back on a crane as Kelly swings his umbrella around and around while singing the title song."

---

* "[I]ts plot, if that's what you'd call it, concerns a silent film star who is linked with a slut-voiced leading lady while wooing a thrushy new thing."—Bosley Crowther, *New York Times,* March 28, 1952

† "The film . . . is extraordinarily exuberant, always youthful, joyously indestructible. . . . [It] has the freshness of a live performance in the theater, which, I suppose, is another way of saying it seems unique."—Vincent Canby, *New York Times,* May 4, 1975

Over the years, Donen has been alternately gratified and concerned by the praise rendered unto his best-known musical. In 1968, he told the filmwriter Kevin Thomas that after a recent viewing he had found the film "very creaky. There are about four good things in it—Donald O'Connor's 'Fit as a Fiddle,' 'Make 'Em Laugh,' Gene's 'Singin' in the Rain,' and one hilarious sequence when they're recording sound for the first time. But there are no characters except for Jean Hagen."

After this quote was recited to him in 1992, Donen said that except for the overly long "Broadway Ballet" number, "I wondered for a time if the picture wasn't paced too fast, if the jokes weren't coming too quickly. I mean, my God, we never gave the audience enough space to breathe."

The larger question remained as well, that if one singular work by an individual is so universally acclaimed—in 1982, a poll in *Cahiers du Cinema* rated *Singin' in the Rain* the second-greatest film of all time—then where could he possibly go from there? "How do you live with that?" wondered Donen. "The danger is that everything else you've done or will do becomes measured next to that. Worse is if something you've done becomes historical, because you could risk thinking that you are a kind of historical figure yourself."

Two givens remain, however, of which Donen stands utterly convinced. "I've timed the picture," he said, "and what's unusual about it, and I think unique to any movie musical, is that more of its screen time is taken up by its singing and dancing numbers than by its book."

His second claim is, "The title of the picture never should have been *Singin' in the Rain*. Look at the picture. It's not about weather. The theme has nothing to do with rain. The picture is about movies. The title should have been *Hollywood*."

WHEN PRODUCTION CHIEF Irving Thalberg hired Arthur Freed to write lyrics for M-G-M in 1929, the studio was trailing a distant fourth in the talking-picture boom. Predictably, by 1928 Warner Bros. had assumed Hollywood's leading box office ranking by virtue of having instituted Vitaphone, the industry's—and the public's—first accepted sound process. Vitaphone allowed recorded music, dialogue, and sound effects to be played back on phonographic discs in sync with the film, even if more often than not the phonograph needle would skip. The studio's watershed picture, though it contained mere snippets of sound, was *The Jazz Singer*, which premiered on October 6 of the previous year.

"Before sound pictures came in," said Donen, considering how the visual element of movies was altered by the transition, "movies had been a stylized art form, like opera. The characters' lack of ability to talk forced the directors to stylize the action. But when talkies happened, the school of thought was to have not just talking but singing and dancing."

Now Hollywood could compete with the legitimate stage in New York, although movie technicians were not yet fully equipped to handle the material cinematically. "Dancing is more interesting on-screen than singing," maintained Donen, "because it involves action, and action is what good movie storytelling is all about. Talking isn't about action, and singing isn't about action. *Moving* is about action, and that is what the movies did and still do best. Look, there has to be a reason why the movie chase has survived since silent days."

Nevertheless, audiences of the late 1920s were captivated by the various yammerings that were taking place at their local bijous. In the year 1928, Warners released only all-talking pictures, save for ten that contained partial dialogue and/or music and sound effects. At Fox, two-thirds of the studio output started to speak, and by 1929 the ante was raised to a full slate of talkies. At Paramount that same year, only seventy percent of its movies featured sound, while at M-G-M, the percentage of talkies was an embarrassingly low forty-five.

The solution in Culver City was to counteract Metro's backward technological status with a talkie that would rival if not surpass the attention-grabbing device of *The Jazz Singer.*

"Jolson's *Jazz Singer* initiated the Star Performer Musical, in which both the film and the show-within-the-film are built around a star," said Gerald Mast. "The alternative Group Performance Musical would be initiated by M-G-M's first musical (also its first sound film), *[The] Broadway Melody* . . . in which 'kids' invest their energy in the musical numbers and the show built around them. In Hollywood musicals, performers perform."*

Although backed by Thalberg's solid dedication, *The Broadway Melody* suffered birth pains every bit as serious as those that greeted the launch of

---

* Wholeheartedly concurring with that last sentiment, Donen noted that the demise of the film musical could be blamed on not only the lack of musical performers but, equally heinous, the cheap trick of substituting one performer for another, such as the use of a stunt double for Jennifer Beals in the 1983 *Flashdance.* "One of the great qualities about musicals," said Donen, "is that the audience is able to look up at the screen and think: Jesus Christ, that's Gene up there on roller skates [in *It's Always Fair Weather*] or: Look, that's Fred Astaire doing that. Once that sensation disappeared, the musical was doomed."

M-G-M's seminal musical, *The Broadway Melody* (1929): "not just talking, but singing and dancing." And heaps of it. No one less than George Gershwin performed at the premiere.

the flickers. With technicians yet to understand the requirements of soundproofing, stages were built to seal out external noise completely. The result was a suffocating hot box that produced fainting spells among the personnel toiling inside. The sound recordists, already deemed the heavies in this foolhardy experiment, were themselves forced into a padded isolation chamber within the soundstage, wherein they kept the recording devices and the very last traces of oxygen.

As one final guarantee that they would be surrounded by relative silence, the makers of *The Broadway Melody* shot their picture at night, when the studio and surrounding Culver City was at its most quiet. This nocturnal work schedule only led to a further tenseness in the atmosphere and an edginess in the personalities. To compound the underlying sense of frustration, Thalberg seemed never satisfied. The picture existed in such an exhausting state of constant flux—as satirized in *Singin' in the Rain*'s own *The Dueling Cavalier,* only *Melody*'s flubs were for real—that the final result was going to be anyone's guess. As insurance, M-G-M backed up its sound version by simultaneously shooting a silent one.

Production began in autumn 1928. By then, *The Broadway Melody* had already experienced a major conceptual change, from part talkie to what would be the movies' first advertised "All Talking! All Singing! All Dancing!" extravaganza. The scenario had also been completely rewritten, the original, by its director Harry Beaumont and the screenwriter Edmund Goulding, having been thrown over in favor of a Norman Houston–James Gleason script. Still in the offing would be several retakes, including an unsuitably static "The Wedding of the Paper Doll" number, reshot in two-strip Technicolor and repopulated with sixty chorines—though the studio had trouble rounding up suitable hoofers. (The overfed substitutes who were hired ended up satisfying neither Mayer's nor Thalberg's idealized vision of beauty.)

On February 1, 1929, the picture reached the screen. For Metro's initial sound release, nothing less would do than a stellar premiere at Grauman's Chinese Theater, hosted by gossip diva Louella Parsons and broadcast over the wireless. The actual premiere of *The Broadway Melody* made the opening of *The Royal Rascal* in *Singin' in the Rain*—also set at Grauman's and hosted by a parody of Parsons—look like dish night at the Fox Peoria. For starters, preceding *The Broadway Melody* on the Chinese stage was George Gershwin, who played *Rhapsody in Blue*.

As for the picture, it proved a sensation, and the public was sold on the backstage musical.* Following the Grauman's engagement, *The Broadway Melody* inaugurated sound systems in the majority of the nation's theaters, where it was the first sound picture from any studio to play the "nabes." The melodramatic story line revolved around a backstage triangle, loosely modeled on the real-life exploits of Vivian and Rosetta Duncan, a vaudeville sister duo—here called "Hank" and Queenie Mahoney (Bessie Love and Anita Page).† Both are wooed by Eddie Kearns (Charles King), a singer-dancer-songwriter who is costarring with them in the latest "Francis Zanfield" production. Among the film's several precedents was that it was the first to interject songs as part of its plot, the first to utilize large soundstages as the backdrops for its numbers, the first to shoot a sequence in color, the first to predub its song numbers, and the first

* The movie also launched an entire series of spin-offs: *The Broadway Melody of 1936, of 1938,* and *of 1940; The Broadway Melody of 1943,* to have starred Eleanor Powell and Gene Kelly, never reached fruition. In 1940, Metro rehashed the essential plot of the first *Melody* for *Two Girls on Broadway,* starring Lana Turner, Joan Blondell, and George Murphy.

† Although Thalberg considered allowing the Duncan Sisters to play themselves, they lost the roles to Love, a star of silents, and Page. As recompense of sorts, M-G-M starred the Duncans in *It's a Great Life* (1929); their winning stage personalities did not translate to the screen.

musical ever to win an Oscar for Best Picture. One final precedent, integral to the picture's success, was that it marked the inaugural Hollywood effort of a songwriting team who had beaten out Fred Fisher and Billy Rose for the job, Arthur Freed and Nacio Herb Brown. The composer Brown (1896–1964) had been a former real estate agent when he first paired with Freed in New York in 1921, and the two came to M-G-M together, for a weekly starting salary of $250 each. After *The Broadway Melody,* to which they had contributed the title song and "You Were Meant for Me," they were immediately assigned to *The Hollywood Revue of 1929,* which featured appearances by every Metro star but Garbo. For that they came up with a song that they had originally presented in a Los Angeles stage show called *The Hollywood Music Box Revue of 1927,* "Singin' in the Rain."

"I had the title for some time before writing the song," Freed recalled. "[Herb] came to me one afternoon with the news that he'd just written a tune for a coloratura soprano." Brown played the melody, replete with classical trills. "All I could think of," claimed Freed, "was that a vamp in the bass and a few minor changes would give it the zip for some lyrics I'd written."*

Nacio Herb Brown remained at M-G-M and continued to compose breezy melodies, while Freed, starting with *Babes in Arms,* starring Judy Garland and Mickey Rooney, in 1939, joined Metro's producing ranks, and it was under the Freed banner that M-G-M turned out what Billy Wilder called "one of the five greatest pictures ever made, *Singin' in the Rain.*"

"GENE AND I went to Arthur, in our usual less than pragmatic way," Donen recalled, "and we said, 'Arthur, we've got a fantastic idea for the way Gene's going to do the number 'Singin' in the Rain.' "

---

* Other primary sources of the score for the film *Singin' in the Rain* were the 1929 film *Lord Byron of Broadway* ("Should I?"); the 1932 stage revue George White's *Music Hall Varieties* ("Fit As a Fiddle"); the 1933 films *Stage Mother* and *Going Hollywood* ("Beautiful Girl" appeared in both and "Temptation" in the latter); the 1934 *Sadie McKee* ("All I Do Is Dream of You"); *The Broadway Melody of 1936* ("You Are My Lucky Star" and "Broadway Rhythm"); the 1936 *San Francisco* ("Would You?"); and the 1939 *Babes in Arms* ("Good Morning"). "Fit As a Fiddle" was written by Freed in collaboration with Al Hoffman and Al Goodhart. "Moses Supposes," inspired by a diction lesson Comden and Green once overheard in the course of working with George Abbott, featured lyrics by them and music by Roger Edens. "Make 'Em Laugh" has alternately been credited to Freed and Brown, Comden and Green and Edens, and Freed and Cole Porter, who wrote the remarkably similar "Be a Clown" for the 1948 Freed musical *The Pirate.*

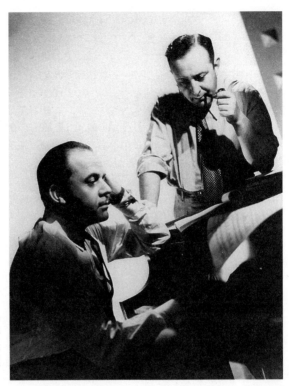

At the keyboard (c. 1930),
Nacio Herb Brown, with a
frequent early collaborator,
the lyricist Arthur Freed

Freed, finding the ever jocular twosome so overly enthusiastic that he girded himself for what obviously would be a setup, soberly replied, "What's that?"

Kelly and Donen responded in tandem: "Gene's going to sing in the rain!" Then they burst out laughing.

At the beginning, not so much as that idea existed. By Christmas of 1950, Donen had finished *Love Is Better Than Ever,* and two weeks later, on January 8, 1951, Kelly wrapped *An American in Paris.* Some versions of the story assert that Freed, having witnessed the success of Irving Berlin's *Easter Parade* and anticipating a similar reception to Gershwin's *An American in Paris,* wished to spotlight his and his frequent collaborator's musical output. Vanity was not beyond being a motivating factor, but more than likely, Freed's decision was largely based on his wishing to seize upon a business opportunity: In 1950, the producer-lyricist had sold M-G-M his songbook for a capital gain of $25,000. The year before, on March 28, 1949, he had been presented with a story outline for a vehicle intended for Ann Miller, titled *Singin' in the Rain.* Its plot was derived from a 1928 silent feature, *Excess Baggage,* written by Francis Marion and based on a 1927

Broadway play by John McGowen. The film starred newcomer Josephine Dunn as a dancer whose marriage to a vaudeville acrobat (William Haines) cannot bear the strain when she becomes a movie star—which sounded remarkably similar to the various versions of *A Star Is Born*. Freed's design for musicalizing *Excess Baggage* dissolved when similar plot elements cropped up in *You're My Everything,* a 1949 Twentieth Century–Fox musical with Dan Dailey and Anne Baxter, set during the advent of talkies. That left Freed with a title, *Singin' in the Rain,* and no plot.

On May 29, 1950, Freed invited Betty Comden and Adolph Green back to Hollywood.

"I rented a house," said Comden in 1992. "We lived in California for three or four months."

"Seven or eight," corrected Green.

"It couldn't have been," said Comden.

"It was," insisted Green.

"That long?"

"Yup."

Before work commenced on what they were told was a picture to be called *Singin' in the Rain,* one issue required resolution. Both writers believed they were operating under a new contract, albeit one by an agent who no longer represented them, through which they had secured the privilege to write the book to a musical *only* if it contained their own lyrics or else those by Irving Berlin, Cole Porter, or Rodgers and Hammerstein. Period.

"Kids," responded Freed, who was familiar with their earlier contract, dated November 1948, "I never heard of such a clause."

After a two-week standoff, their new agent, Irving Lazar, studied the existing document. "Kids," said Lazar, "*anyone* can write lyrics for your picture—Berlin, Porter, R. and H., Freed, Karloff, Lugosi, Johnny Weissmuller—you name it."

Comden and Green began writing *Singin' in the Rain.* "We'd get to the studio every morning at nine," remembered Comden, "just like everybody else. Only we had this bleak little office."

"A cubicle, really," said Green.

"Near the end of the hallway, next to Arthur's office," said Comden. "The Freed Unit was all together."

"Roughly a nine-to-five routine," said Green.

"We used to work a lot of evenings," said Comden.

"We'd leave the studio late in the afternoon," said Green.

"Very often we'd go out," said Comden. "I'd steal a pad of paper. I'd do the writing. For many years Adolph and I would just talk out the script and I'd write it down, then I got used to typing it."*

Roger Edens, sifting through pages of sheet music, played the Brown-Freed songbook for Comden, Green, and Donen on the piano in Freed's office, which was adjacent to his own in the Irving Thalberg Building. "Most of the songs we already knew," was Donen's recollection. "Several possible stories suggested themselves," Comden and Green noted. "For instance, 'The Wedding of the Paper Doll' could well have been the basis for a story about a painted doll who got married."

In a published preface to their screenplay, the writers confirmed, as had Donen, that the songs when they first heard them evoked a feeling of Hollywood in the late twenties, but they go on to say that the initial idea was to have Howard Keel play a minor western hero in silents who sky-rockets to success as a singing cowboy in talkies. "I don't know where that came from," said Donen, who was with the project from the beginning. "The picture was always going to be for Gene, always—never for Howard Keel, never for Van Johnson, which has also been mentioned, and never for anyone else."

Some thought had been given to taking an existing picture and setting it to music. "One idea," said Donen, "was to adapt the Jean Harlow picture *Bombshell,* or else some early talkie. We screened a lot of pictures from that time, literally dozens, but Betty and Adolph said no, they have this other idea." Among the vintage films under consideration were *Merton of the Movies* and *Platinum Blonde,* although inspiration was sought from many sources; a 1950 supply requisition in studio files reveals that Donen was studying 1927 issues of *Vanity Fair.*

The house Comden and Green had taken for the three or four or seven or eight months they were assigned to the project possibly helped to solidify the track they would take. The bargain-priced abode had once belonged to Marie Prevost, a silent-screen star who had successfully made the transition into talkies—only to suffer a severe weight problem that

---

* Asked whether she felt in any way ostracized in the male-dominated domain of M-G-M, Comden said, "I wasn't aware of any difference in the way I was treated. I have spoken to a lot of women writers who did feel differently. For one thing, my partner was a man, which may have had something to do with it. But I also had a sort of cachet that other women did not have. I never felt any prejudice. Usually I was the only woman at a table of guys—Saul Chaplin, Roger and Gene, Stanley. We'd have our lunches together and then head back to work, or else wander around the lot."

eventually killed her career and, after an ill-advised crash diet, her. Furthermore, at the same time Comden and Green and company were searching for ideas for *Singin' in the Rain,* Paramount released Billy Wilder's *Sunset Boulevard,* an acid-etched portrait of a silent star whose fate is tragically sealed by the arrival of talkies. That certainly could have served as an inspiration. Clearly, the creative atmosphere seemed ripe, as did the environment.

After weeks of groping around in the dark, Comden and Green declared, "We decided to kick the nightmarish grip of doom that had settled over us and do something realistic. We would give M-G-M back the money they had paid us thus far, tell them we had failed, and go home."

What existed on paper was what the writers perceived as three false starts. Their protagonist was to be a former vaudevillian, who, after becoming a success in silent pictures, could fall back on a stage career. A splashy Hollywood premiere for a silent picture was to open their tale. Their hero was to give a phony life story to a newspaper interviewer. There was to be another premiere for the same silent picture in New York, and here the hero would meet his love interest, only to lose her and return to Hollywood. Yet from that point on the writers were stumped.

"Writing each picture was not only a challenge," said Adolph Green, "it was like a disaster."

The solution arrived thanks to a close source, Comden's husband, Steven Kyle. After reading the three different openings and laughing out loud, Kyle suggested that nothing be discarded; in fact, he said, the creators would do well to keep the action in Hollywood, blend the three existing ideas, then launch their story from there. The writers considered this their "eureka moment."

"We interviewed everyone at the studio who had survived the birth of talkies," said Donen. "There are no bigger movie buffs in the world than Betty and Adolph, except for maybe me."

The first *Singin' in the Rain* script was dated August 19, 1950, and with a few noteworthy exceptions, it is relatively similar to the finished screen product. Kathy Selden, the young love interest of the protagonist, Donald Lockwood, was originally called Kathy Summers, and the name of the studio was Imperial—in the film it is Monumental—until the M-G-M research department discovered that a film company with that name did exist in 1928 (suggested alternatives were Magno, Mammoth, Big-Art, and Climax Pictures). More important, Freed wanted the pivotal role of Don Lockwood's comic sidekick, Cosmo Brown, to go to the musician Oscar

Levant, who was a friend of Freed's, the resident wit of Freed's parties, the costar of Freed's *The Barkleys of Broadway* and *An American in Paris,* and one of the world's most celebrated hypochondriacs.*

In the initial draft of *Singin' in the Rain,* a sequence called "The Piano-Playing Pioneer" was obviously tailored to Levant's brand of humor. Asked by the studio chief for a musical vehicle in which he pictures himself, Cosmo describes a number that has him cropping up in a Daniel Boone outfit to ward off an Indian raid. He charms his attackers "with a concert selection played on a piano dragged out of a covered wagon."

Other false starts included an elaborately conceived love ballad number (no song was identified, though in a later draft, "Would You?" was suggested), shot against various international locales on the back lot. This was eventually replaced by the simple, bare soundstage wherein Don sings to Kathy, "You Were Meant for Me." "You Are My Lucky Star" was initially thought to be right for the post-premiere party held at the studio chief's house; this was later switched to "All I Do Is Dream of You." Lina's actress sidekick, "Latin spitfire" Zelda Zanders, played in the picture by Rita Moreno, was to have had a song, "Make Hay While the Sun Shines," but in the finished film Zelda/Moreno's scenes are kept to a minimum. The script makes no reference to a ballet, although time was allotted for a "big musical number finale" to take place after the loose ends of the plot were tied together. In addition, the secret of leading lady Lina Lamont—that her hopelessly squeaky voice required the dubbing of another actress—is publicly revealed at the home of the studio chief, not in front of a theater audience, as was later conceived. The picture was also supposed to end comically rather than romantically, closing with the premiere of *Broadway Melody,* a picture that marks the first teaming of Don and Kathy, who by now are Mr. and Mrs. Lockwood. Trailing behind Don and Kathy into the premiere is another married Hollywood couple, Cosmo Brown and Lina Lamont. As the gossip-columnist hostess at the premiere gushes, in Lina's latest film, *Jungle Princess,* the leading lady "doesn't say a word—just grunts!"

Most telling about the first draft of *Singin' in the Rain* is how its centerpiece "Rain" dance was envisioned. It was not to be a solo at all but an ensemble piece—similar in spirit to "Make Way for Tomorrow"—set in

---

* "Do you know what Oscar Levant said to Judy Garland the first time they met and hugged each other?" said Donen. " 'Never before in the history of the world has there been a greater pharmacological embrace.' "

the street after the lead trio leaves a restaurant and intended to feature the combined talents of Cosmo, Kathy, and Don.

"I'LL NEVER forget the day I went into Louis B. Mayer's office and he was sitting there with this girl he insisted I meet," Gene Kelly said in 1991. The teenager was Debbie Reynolds, the 1948 Miss Burbank. After landing on the Metro payroll, she had appeared as boop-boop-a-doop singer Helen Kane in the musical *Three Little Words* and as Jane Powell's younger sister in *Two Weeks With Love,* in which she sang "Aba Daba Honeymoon" with Carleton Carpenter. "Mayer," reported Kelly, "said she was to be my leading lady in *Singin' in the Rain.* That statement hit me like a ton of bricks. He was forcing her on me. What the hell was I going to do with her? She couldn't sing, she couldn't dance, she couldn't act. She was a triple threat."*

In her 1988 autobiography, Reynolds responded in kind. Painting an unflattering portrait of Kelly during the making of the picture, she depicted him as a short-tempered brute, prone to rage. Kelly's singular act of kindness, she allowed, was to explode at Donald O'Connor—calling him "stupid" in front of others—instead of at her, though invariably Kelly's anger was over her inadequacies as a dancer, not O'Connor's. "*Singin' in the Rain* and childbirth were the hardest things I ever had to do in my life," wrote Reynolds. Kelly so broke her spirit that one day she hid under a piano in the rehearsal studio and sobbed to herself, only to be rescued when she looked over and noticed a trouser leg standing beside her. The slender limb belonged to Fred Astaire.

Taking Reynolds by the hand, the cool veteran demonstrated for his audience of one the difficulties of dance and reinforced her self-assurance, at least according to the book. In a conversation that took place in 1993, Reynolds summarily contradicted every comment about Kelly and *Singin' in the Rain* that had appeared in her own memoir.

"Debbie Reynolds was eighteen years old," she said of herself. "I had no experience. I had never danced before that movie. Gene took me under his wing. He was an exacting teacher. I had to learn, and I had to learn fast. Gene's way of working was to push me, and he got, I thought, a performance out of a young, little girl. I was totally with Gene Kelly."

Ernie Flatt was assigned to teach Reynolds tap, and she also worked with Carol Haney and Jeanne Coyne. "My schedule was absolutely gruel-

---

* Whether aware of it or not, Kelly was quoting the script to *Singin' in the Rain,* where the same remark was applied to Lina Lamont.

ing," said Reynolds. "Because I lived in the [San Fernando] Valley with my parents, [I] got up at four in the morning to catch a bus to Hollywood. Then I'd get another bus to Culver City, and a third to the studio. At the end of seven or eight hours of dancing—and Gene would stop in each day to see how I was doing—I'd be so tired that I'd often just sleep in my dressing room rather than take the bus home." (Reynolds temporarily solved the transportation issue when she purchased a second-hand 1932 Chevrolet, which made so much noise that it was forbidden on the lot.)

Of the traumatic incident that sent her crying under the piano, Reynolds shrugged it off in 1993: "I was definitely insecure. Anyone could have made me cry."

As for Donen, she said, "I can't really remember Stanley. He just sort of smiled and would nod at me and say hello. He certainly wouldn't have found anything interesting in me. I was much too young and not his type."

According to Reynolds, "Stanley was on the camera, so I didn't have a lot of close contact with him. Stanley worked a lot lining up all those great shots for our huge dance numbers. Stanley was always with the technical end of it, being Busby Berkeley, because everyone admired Busby Berkeley's camera angles and boom work."*

Supporting Reynolds's casting in the picture, Donen rose immediately to her defense. "I don't know what Gene was talking about," he said. "For starters, that story about Debbie being 'forced' on us, by Louis B. Mayer or anybody, is entirely wrong. We couldn't wait to get her. She had done this musical scene in this movie, 'Aba Daba Honeymoon,' and I thought she was adorable. There was no one else any of us thought of for that part. It wasn't good or big enough for Judy Garland. The only other person who might have been right for us would've been June Allyson, only she was probably doing those pictures with Jimmy Stewart and was too big a star at the moment. But Debbie wasn't 'forced' on us."

The same could not be said for Oscar Levant. Freed remained adamant that he be cast as Cosmo. "The pleading that went on," said Donen. "Betty and Adolph had written the part with Oscar in mind. That's why he's called Cosmo. It's a name that would have fit Oscar. But Gene and I thought the picture would be destroyed if we used Oscar, even if he was Arthur's closest friend in the world and Adolph adored him too. When we went to work on the picture, Gene and I said, 'We're sorry, but this is impossible. It would be a disaster. This is a dancing role.' Oscar

* Berkeley had cameras on the ceiling. Donen had dancing.

Codirectors Kelly and
Donen: "Substitute the
word 'fight' for codirect,
then you have it."

couldn't dance. He was a spastic as a dancer. He was funny and gifted and
wonderful, but Oscar was funereal. His humor was dark, and he was
highly neurotic. Surely he was psychotic. Even Judy wasn't as crazy as
Oscar."

Freed heard none of this. "Look," he told Donen, "Oscar's musical.
Gene's musical. You're musical. So think of something." Donen thought
of Donald O'Connor.

"It's sort of funny the way it got resolved," said Donen, "although it
wasn't funny at the time. By accident, Adolph told Oscar he wasn't in the
picture, thinking that Arthur already had told him." Levant was furious.
Nor was Freed amused. "Arthur had a fit," said Donen, "but said, 'All
right, who do you want?' And I told him Donald O'Connor, except
M-G-M thought Donald O'Connor was a nothing who made these cheap
pictures at Universal."

A deal was struck. Universal agreed to loan O'Connor to M-G-M for
$50,000. "I was in London playing the Palladium," O'Connor told the
writer John Mariani. O'Connor had grown up in a circus and vaudeville
family, which is how he learned his acrobatics, and he had been in movies

since 1938, yet never in an A vehicle. "[A]lthough flattered," he said of the Metro offer, "I said no, because in those days, under the terms of contract, I wouldn't have seen a penny of that fifty thousand. Finally, Universal agreed to give me the money, so I said okay."*

For the role of the "slut-voiced leading lady" with the Brooklyn patois, Nina Foch was tested, but the job went to Jean Hagen, at the urging of the second Mrs. Louis B. Mayer, Lorena. Hagen had already delivered one rich performance on the lot, playing the other woman in the 1949 comedy *Adam's Rib*. Mrs. Mayer's suggestion came in the nick of time; three days into the production of *Singin' in the Rain*, on June 21, 1951, the momentous twenty-seven-year reign of Louis B. Mayer ended at M-G-M. Making good on repeated threats to Schenck that it was going to be either "Dore Schary or me," Mayer furiously walked out of his own studio, never to return—not knowing until it was too late that he had been set up to do this by Schenck and Schary, working in cahoots. Mayer, long unhappy with Schary's encroaching threat to his omnipotence, became completely outraged by Schary's slate of gritty, realistic movies, which included *Battleground* (1949), *The Next Voice You Hear* (1950), and *The Red Badge of Courage* (1951). Neither was Mayer pleased by Schary's Democratic politics. The older demagogue, after calling Schary every profane name in the book, including, according to Schary, "kike," informed Schenck that only one man could run Metro-Goldwyn-Mayer. The head of the corporation backed Schary.

"We'd heard rumblings beforehand," Donen said of the historic power shift (Schary remained in command of M-G-M until he was fired, in 1956). Donen had described his own relationship with Mayer as "I'd nod hello to him and he'd nod back at me," and once Mayer's departure was a fait accompli, "I can't say I was shocked," admitted the director, "but I was surprised. I mean, Louis B. Mayer's name was on the studio. It didn't say Metro-Goldwyn-Schenck."

SINGIN' IN THE RAIN *opens with no sense of time or place, but with the three principals (Gene Kelly, Debbie Reynolds, Donald O'Connor) in yellow slickers and*

---

* O'Connor's total fee came to $90,000. Though originally committed to a ten-week guarantee at $5,000 per week, he ended up spending 108 days on the picture. The entire bill for *Singin' in the Rain* came to $2,540,800, which put the picture $620,996 over budget. This figure included the purchase price of the Freed-Brown songbook, plus a nominal fee for the "new" song they wrote, "Make 'Em Laugh."

*clutching opened umbrellas as the rain pours. They march toward the audience, as if introducing themselves, followed by the titles.**

The story begins in 1927, amid a Hollywood premiere at Grauman's Chinese, as exotic screen personalities of the era are parodied. One, a Nita Naldi–style vamp linked to the arm of a titled European, sports a playful black lacework gown whose plunging back looks like a spider's web.

Donen: "Arthur didn't like twenties costumes. What he wanted were modern, for then, interpretations of twenties costumes, but Gene and I stuck to our guns and went for the real look of the times. There were a lot of strange rules to deal with. Louis B. Mayer hated to see a woman in slacks, so Arthur wouldn't allow us to show a woman in slacks."

Costume designer Walter Plunkett: "I entered the business at the height of the flapper's reign. Many of Jean Hagen's costumes are, nearly as I can remember, duplicates of some I did in all seriousness for Lilyan Tashman. And she was the epitome of chic at the time."

The stars of the evening's movie, Don Lockwood (Kelly) and Lina Lamont (Jean Hagen), send the fans into a frenzy with their arrival. The flashy couple—she is completely tight-lipped—no sooner step out of their limo than they are grabbed by a fatuous gossip columnist,† who insists that Don relate to her radio listeners the story of his

---

* Sets for the production were built starting in April 1951, with a production memo confirming plans to erect the exterior of Grauman's Egyptian. In the finished film, the setting was Grauman's Chinese. Principal photography on *Singin' in the Rain* commenced June 18, 1951, and wrapped August 28. The "Singin' in the Rain" number was shot one month into the schedule, on July 17, with time for retakes allocated on July 18 and 19. The picture's first cut was completed September 6, and the picture was ready for music and sound by October 3. Scoring began October 19, and a first preview was held ten days later, with another on November 9. The negative was delivered for cutting on November 16, and release prints started leaving the M-G-M lab January 11, 1952. On December 2, 1951, the picture, M-G-M release no. 1546, was previewed at the De Anza Theater in Riverside. In the audience survey, Donald O'Connor received the highest approval rating among the cast members ("About time Donald O'Connor received a break," was one comment), and there were excellent notices for Cyd Charisse, in spite of her dance scenes being so brief. An impressive 98.8 percent of the audience said they would recommend the picture to their friends, which the surveyors noted was "the highest rating attained for any picture this organization has previewed." On March 7, 1952, a private screening at M-G-M was held for guests, who included George Cukor, Humphrey Bogart, Ben Hecht, William Hammerstein, Frank Loesser, Groucho Marx, Farley Granger, and Fox musical director Alfred Newman. The Radio City Music Hall premiere in New York took place March 27, 1952, followed by an April 9 premiere at the Hollywood Egyptian Theater, to which Freed had invited Steven Kyle and Betty Comden, Fox director Jean Negulesco, Nacio Herb Brown, Alan Jay Lerner, and Stanley Donen, as part of the Roger Edens party.

† The columnist, called Dora Bailey (in the first script, Dora Beagle), as portrayed by the actress Madge Blake, is such a faithful parody of Louella Parsons—minus the food stains on her gown—that one wonders how Parsons must have reacted. As it was, her unsolicited offer to act in the picture was declined. On November 13, 1950, her agent, Wynn Rocamora, wrote Arthur Freed: "I do think, Arthur, this would make an interesting and colorful spot for Louella; and, she, I know, would be interested in doing this."

career rise. While the radio audience is treated to Don's haughty descriptions of attending the finest music conservatories in the country, the viewer via a flashback montage sees that this two-bit vaudeville hoofer was actually playing cheap dives in such backwater towns as "Oat Meal, Nebraska."

Donen: "It's an unusual way to open a picture. By telling lies."

This spirited sequence, set to "Fit as a Fiddle," properly introduces Don Lockwood, also his childhood pal, fellow performer, and pianist, Cosmo Brown (O'Connor). As their careers continue to spiral downward, Don maintains he has sought but one goal in life, "dignity"—though it is his very lack of it that gains him a job in Hollywood.

Donen: "We shot this early into the picture. Our cameraman for about the first week was John Alton [who had shot the ballet in *An American in Paris*], but the scenes were coming out too dark. We brought in Hal Rosson for the rest of the picture."

Fearless, immodest, and scrambling for screen time, Don catches the eye of the studio chief, R. F. Simpson (Millard Mitchell), and is promoted from stuntman to leading man, opposite solipsistic screen siren Lina Lamont (Jean Hagen).

Donen: "Millard Mitchell was wrong casting. I'm not saying he wasn't good; it's just he's too much of a *shaygets** to play a studio chief. It needed someone Jewish in the role. Today it would be played by Albert Brooks. Only back then, who knew?"

Following the premiere, Don is accosted by fans when Cosmo's jalopy breaks down. Displaying Fairbanksian derring-do, he leaps from the car onto a passing electric streetcar, then into a convertible driven by young Kathy Selden (Debbie Reynolds), who mistakes him for a masher, which, in point of fact, he is.

Donen: "Debbie was adorable in the picture, but she was also a royal pain in the ass. She thought she knew more than Gene and I combined— she knew everything and we knew nothing. For what reason I don't know, but she was very difficult to manage and get to do anything. Nobody else on the picture gave us problems like that. Debbie was very dogmatic, very tough, a real bulldog of a little girl. She used to love the Girl Scouts. She was the leader of her Girl Scout troop, and I guess she was used to bossing people around."

Kathy reveals to Don that she has aspirations of becoming a stage actress in New York; only moments later, she pops out of a cake at the home of the studio chief, as part of the Cocoanut Grove chorus line hired to entertain. The dancers perform a lively Charleston to "All I Do Is Dream of You," while Don chortles—and falls for Kathy's

---

* Gentile male.

physical charms. This infuriates the intolerant Lina, whose distinctly annoying voice, it is by now revealed, has the effect of fingernails on a chalkboard.

Arthur Freed: "She was the composite of a lot of silent stars . . . Anita [Page, who for a time was Mrs. Nacio Herb Brown] was never that bad. Mae Murray was exactly it."

Donen: "I suppose, if we had made the picture earlier, Judy Holliday could have played Lina, but *Born Yesterday* had already made her a tremendous star by then."

During the party, guests tango to a torrid "Temptation," and Cosmo's wisecracks proceed apace. R. F. Simpson displays a novelty, a clip of a talking picture, narrated by a dead ringer for Francis X. Bushman. Most of the guests laugh off the gimmick, while the Nita Naldi character turns to R.F. and proclaims in a thick accent: "It's vulgar." When Don once again tries to get fresh with Kathy, she tosses a pie toward his kisser, only he ducks and its meringue topping hits Lina.

Jean Hagen: "I had an alexandrite ring I'd bought in Mexico, and I told Debbie, 'Listen, get it on the first take or you'll get the cake and ring in your face.' "

Debbie Reynolds: "If I'd flubbed it, Gene would have decked me before Jean would have."

Donen: "We got it in one take. There was also a number we shot that took place right after this scene, a very good one with Gene. He starts out in bed the morning after and does this very athletic dance, to the same song, 'All I Do Is Dream of You.' It had taken several days to work out, and we filmed it, but we ended up having to cut it for time."

Dissolve to three weeks later. Don is still in the dumps over not being able to track down Kathy, who's been sacked from the Grove. To brighten his spirits, Cosmo reminds his pal that it is the actor's mission in life to "Make 'Em Laugh."

Donen: "We were shooting the picture and needed a number for when Donald tries to cheer Gene up. Now, Arthur hadn't written a song in God knows how long, and Gene and I went to him and said, 'Arthur, we've been through your catalog and there's nothing that will work for this spot. Would you consider writing a new song for us?' And Arthur said, 'Herb and I would love to write a new song together. What kind of a song do you want?' 'Well,' we said, 'there was a song that Gene did in *The Pirate* that would fit perfectly, "Be a Clown," ' which of course was by Cole Porter. And Arthur said, 'You want a song like "Be a Clown"? Herb and I will write you a song like "Be a Clown." ' So they certainly did that! Gene and I weren't about to say to Arthur Freed, 'Haven't you gotten a little too close?' And Cole Porter, to the day he died, never said a word to Arthur, because Arthur knew Cole Porter, they had worked together, Arthur

"Debbie was very tough, a real bulldog of a little girl," Donen said of the young Reynolds, here with Kelly, Jean Hagen, and Donald O'Connor (*Singin' in the Rain*).

adored Cole Porter, and Cole Porter was a gentleman. He just never said anything."*

Cosmo's acrobatic number reaches the hilarity level of a Keystone Kops short and employs every self-devised slapstick device imaginable, from Cosmo's leaping into a brick wall to being hurled over a sofa by a headless dummy with whom he grows too fresh.

Donen: "M-G-M had ten buildings full of props, it was bigger than Macy's, and they brought down all this stuff, and one of the props was a dummy. Donald did a double take and started to work with it. So we got all sorts of dummies, some with no arms, some with lipstick and eyes, but finally he chose one without a head."

Donald O'Connor: "The dummy struck me as very funny because it had no head but it had symmetry. And I used something that happened to me back in 1940. I was taking the subway to Brooklyn and was wearing

---

* Irving Berlin, however, once showed the temerity to inquire of Freed how such flagrant "borrowing" came to exist, to which an embarrassed Freed stammered: "The kids and I got together on this."

dark glasses. Suddenly this guy who looks like an ex-fighter sits down next to me. I move away. He moves closer. He moves closer and puts his hand on my knee. Then down to my crotch. So I did a gay voice and said, 'Listen, my boyfriend will beat the shit out of you if you go any further!' That's where I got [the idea for] the bit where I put my hand on the dummy's knee and it smacks me."

Donen: "There was no trick photography. That was all Donald. The only thing we did was make a cut near the end, to get the dummy to move up to speed. But can you imagine Oscar Levant in the role?"

O'Connor: "This number led to such a crescendo that I thought I'd have to commit suicide as a finale. I ad-libbed all sorts of stunts. I'd done the somersault off a wall before in two other pictures. Gene gave me the bit where I scrunch up my face after running into the door. We began to rehearse the number, and I'd get very tired. I was smoking four packs of cigarettes a day then, and getting up those walls was murder. I'd roll around the floor and get carpet burns. They had to bank one wall so I could make it up and then through another wall. My body just had to absorb this tremendous shock. So finally we filmed it straight through, and I went home and I couldn't get out of bed for three days. On my return, Gene comes up to me and asks if I could do it again. 'Sorry,' he says. 'Hal Rosson fogged out the negative by mistake and ruined the footage.'"

On the first day of their new picture together, Lina informs Don that it was she who had Kathy Selden fired from the Cocoanut Grove. During a passionate love scene before the silent movie camera, Don threatens Lina's life, though this does not spoil the take. After the director yells "Cut," R.F. stomps onto the soundstage to declare all production shut down for weeks. The Jazz Singer has proved such a tremendous success that audiences are demanding more talking pictures, and the studio must convert to sound. Furthermore, he anticipates Lockwood and Lamont creating a sensation by starring in a talking picture. "Well," snaps Lina, "of course we talk. Don't ivery-body?"*

Heralding the hatching of the Sound Craze is a breakneck musical montage consisting of "I've Got a Feelin' You're Foolin'," "The Wedding of the Painted Doll," and "Should I?," and culminating in a soft-shoe chorus line rendition of "Beautiful Girl." The elaborate number features a bevy of beautiful chorines and pays homage not only to the early musicals of Busby Berkeley, but to the fashion shows that took place in such forties musicals as Cover Girl.

---

* The Research Department noted that *The Jazz Singer* was not an all-talking picture, but was informed that Arthur Freed and Roger Edens knew this "and didn't care."

Donen: "We are doing Busby Berkeley here, only we're making fun of him."

Kathy is discovered in the "Beautiful Girl" chorus. A delighted Don convinces R.F. to feature her in one of the other pictures, as the younger sister of Zelda Zanders (Rita Moreno). Kathy's being hired, however, must be kept secret from the still-simmering Lina, whose towering ego frightens even R.F.

Taking Kathy on a tour of the lot, Don opens the doors to a bare soundstage, where he shows her some of the tricks of the trade. Admitting "I'm such a ham. I guess I'm not able to say something without the proper setting," Don leads into the song "You Were Meant for Me."

Donen: "Getting into a number so the audience doesn't giggle is the biggest problem in a musical. It's very hard to have people start singing. It's the trickiest moment. Bob Fosse, in his better pictures, wouldn't go near it with a barge pole. In *Cabaret,* he got around the problem completely, by only setting the songs on the stage of the nightclub, although he had one song in a beer garden, but that seemed natural, and the camera wasn't on the boy when the song started. In *Yentl,* Barbra Streisand turned her back to the camera whenever she would start singing. First you would hear her voice and then, eventually, she would move her lips. It's a very difficult moment. Judy Garland, most times, managed to get away with it. She had a very earthy quality to her, and we had seen her singing since her childhood. In the early musicals of Lubitsch and René Clair, they made it clear from the beginning that their characters were going to sing operatically. Gene and I didn't go that far. In 'Moses Supposes,' he and Donald sort of talk themselves into the song. But where it was really sticky was when Gene took Debbie onto the bare soundstage. His turning on the lights and fan helps, but it's still very difficult to make that transition from what we do in life into what we do in a musical number."

Diction teachers are next given the treatment. Lina tests the patience of hers, while Don, with Cosmo's help, deflates the pomposity of his ("Moses Supposes").

Donen: "That number is the best tap number that has ever been done in pictures. Ever. The only other one that comes close is Fred and Eleanor Powell's doing 'Begin the Beguine' in *The Broadway Melody of 1940.* But the one with Donald and Gene is better, for its sheer energy."

Several of the true-life setbacks that befell the makers of The Broadway Melody *are sent up as production begins on Lockwood and Lamont's first talkie,* The Dueling Cavalier. *The microphone fails to pick up Lina's enunciation every time she turns her head. The idea to attach the mike to the bosom of her eighteenth-century French period gown results in the picking up of her heartbeat. Don epitomizes every self-important actor when he asks if he can rephrase his lines. Not only is the scene a verbal gem, it's a visual one; in holding on the arched back and tracking the steps of the agitated director of* The Dueling Cavalier, *Roscoe Dexter (Douglas Fowley), Donen's authoritative camerawork heightens both the comedy and the sense of Dexter's frustration.*

Donen: "Back when we shot the picture, we really hadn't advanced that far ourselves. We were still using discs for the musical playback. We hadn't even gone to tape yet."

R.F. provides the visual punch line to the "wired for sound" sequence by striding onto the set and yanking the cords of the mike, inquiring, "What's this wire doing here? It's dangerous."*

Dissolve to a rainy night in the far outskirts of Hollywood. The Dueling Cavalier *is previewed, disastrously. The picture slips out of sync. Lina's voice, when audible, is affected and awful, as is Don's acting. Yet there is no turning back; the picture is due to open in six weeks. Pipes up Lina, "I liked it."*

Cosmo, Kathy, and Don return to the Lockwood mansion, which a self-pitying Don fears will be placed on the market once The Dueling Cavalier *is released. This is when the "eureka moment" strikes. Cosmo suggests that with a little trimming and reshooting,* The Dueling Cavalier *can be saved—by turning it into a musical. Noting the hour, the three dance a celebratory "Good Morning," reminiscent of "Make Way for Tomorrow." They combine everything from tap to hula.*

Reynolds: "It was eleven at night, and Gene was shouting, 'Dance harder! More energy!' Finally, Stanley gave a signal that it looked all right, and I got up off the floor, only to faint dead away. I was carried to my dressing room, and they called my family doctor. He looked at my feet and saw the blood vessels had burst. 'What are you doing to this girl?' he asked. And Gene said, 'We're making a movie.' "[†]

Gene Kelly: "Fortunately, Debbie was as strong as an ox."

O'Connor: "I got to the set [and after a few steps] Gene shouts at me, 'Stop the clowning, will you?' Later on, he apologized for chewing me out and said, 'Listen, Debbie hasn't been coming along as I had hoped, but I couldn't bawl her out because I didn't want to lose her, so I took it out on you.' I told him, 'That's okay, Gene, I understand. But the next time you do it I'll kick you in the balls.' "

---

* Essays and interviews over the years regarding *Singin' in the Rain* have implied that the characters of R. F. Simpson and Roscoe Dexter were based, respectively, on Arthur Freed and Busby Berkeley. In 1995, French director Bertrand Tavernier recalled Donen's telling him in the sixties, "Douglas Fowley *is* Busby Berkeley, the way he yells on the set."

[†] Reynolds said that the physician prohibited her from returning to the set for three days, but against his orders, she returned "after one day in bed."

Once they've finished expressing their optimism, the trio's spirits sink again: How to overcome Lina's voice? Quips Cosmo, "She can't act. She can't sing, and she can't dance. She's a triple threat." The solution: Have Kathy dub it.

Don sees Kathy back to her boardinghouse, then joyfully, and in love, heads home in the continuing downpour ("Singin' in the Rain").

Kelly: "To help me with this, I thought of the fun children have splashing about in rain puddles and decided to become a kid again during the number. Having decided that, the rest of the choreography was simple. What wasn't so simple was coordinating my umbrella with the beats of the music, and not falling down and breaking every bone in my body."

Donen: "We didn't know it was going to be such a great number. As usual, it took longer to set up than to shoot. It only took a day and a half to shoot. We covered the entire East Side Street on Lot Two with a black tarpaulin and designed, to the music, the puddles in the pavement for where Gene would splash around. The rehearsal took place without the rain, which was piped in with sprinklers. We had to finish at a certain time of day because of a water-pressure problem in Culver City. Actually, the number works because it's so utterly simple. He's dancing because he's happy."*

Don and Cosmo sell R.F. on the idea of musicalizing The Dueling Cavalier, *which Cosmo renames* The Dancing Cavalier *(after discarding the title* The Dueling Mammy*). R.F. reiterates that Kathy's dubbing Lina's voice must be kept secret from Lina and promises that once the picture is launched, Kathy will receive a buildup of her own.*

In the recording studio, Kathy dubs Lina's dialogue as well as her singing voice for the song "Would You?" (In reality, Jean Hagen dubbed her own voice for the speaking part, and Betty Noyes doubled for the singing.)

Donen: "Jean-Luc Godard said that cinema is the truth twenty-four frames a second. I think cinema is lies twenty-four frames a second."

---

* An M-G-M Production Report dated July 17, 1951, provided the following background details regarding the musical's signature number: Kelly was called to the studio at eight, Reynolds at seven, and both were due on the set at nine. Kelly showed up ten minutes late, working until he was dismissed at 6:35. Reynolds, planting the kiss on Kelly and closing the door to the boardinghouse behind her, was finished at 2:30. Jeanne Coyne served as the "dance-in," remaining on the set from 8:45 a.m. until 6:35, the designated time when the Culver City water pressure would drop below forty pounds, a level that would have required additional rigging if the studio wished for shooting to continue. Silent-screen comedian Snub Pollard played one of the pedestrians in the scene and was paid a day-player rate. The actual "doodleeedoo" beginning of the song (a musical vamp written for Kelly by Roger Edens) took place from 10:39 to 11:06 a.m., when, according to the report, "Don leaves Kathy—dolly with him as he walks down street—for start into 'Singin' in the Rain' number."

Kelly and Cyd Charisse during the "Crazy Veil" sequence of *Singin' in the Rain*'s overly long "Broadway Melody" dream sequence. The M-G-M front office fretted over Charisse's skimpy costume.

There is one last "new" scene to be filmed, "The Broadway Ballet," featuring "The Broadway Melody" and "Broadway Rhythm." The thirteen-minute number, originally set to be a simple dream sequence, inflated in length and production values (and budget, to $600,000, nearly eight times its original estimate) after Kelly had done the seventeen-minute Gershwin ballet in An American in Paris. *Its framework concerns a young hayseed who comes to New York to strike his fortune on the stage—it has been suggested that the sequence serves as a bookend to the movie's "Dignity, always dignity" opening fantasy—and he falls for an exotic temptress (Cyd Charisse). This dancing goddess eludes him, however, until he finds her again, only to lose her this second time to a mobster. The piece comes full circle when the Kelly character witnesses the arrival of another hayseed, for that is the cyclical nature of show business and life in a metropolis.**

Donen: "The ballet was always too long. I thought it at the time and still do. Only once did I ever do anything about it. In the sixties, when I

* At one point the ballet was to have included Donald O'Connor, but an October 1951 television appearance on *The Colgate Comedy Hour* precluded his participation.

was living in England, I was a friend of Jules Dassin's. For a while I thought, in addition to directing, maybe I'd become a producer. So one day Julie called me and said, 'I have a great idea for Melina [Mercouri, Dassin's wife]. I want to make a movie about silents to sound. She can play a silent-movie star whose voice is terrible, and when talkies come it's a big problem.' I said, 'Julie, what are you saying? I made that picture.' He said, 'What picture?' I said, '*Singin' in the Rain*.' And Julie said, 'You know, I've never seen it. Could I?' So I took the print and shortened the 'Broadway Melody' sequence, I cut it more than in half and sent it to Julie in Paris, where he lived at the time. It's the only time I've seen the picture that way. And I told Julie, 'Here, you can't make it.' "

The dream portion of the ballet, which was the last segment of Singin' in the Rain *to be filmed, had been worked out by Kelly and Carol Haney, and some consideration had been given to starring Haney as the seductive dancer. The more attractive Charisse won the part, on the advice of Freed.*

Donen: "We needed someone who could stop a man by just sticking up her leg. Cyd was stunning. We stuck a hat on the end of her foot and handed her a cigarette holder, and I had to cue her to exhale the cigarette smoke for when Gene first runs into her, because she couldn't handle the smoke."

Cyd Charisse: "I was never told that Carol Haney was originally meant for my role. She even rehearsed me throughout that whole sequence and never once brought it up."

For the dreamlike "Crazy Veil" portion of the number, a long swath of white china silk was attached to Charisse's skimpy body suit, while, offscreen, airplane propellers blew at her and Kelly.

Charisse: "We spent hours on the stage trying to figure out which way to make those veils go the way they did. It was a question of switching one fan on and another off to change directions, all to a certain beat of the music. And believe me, those fans were strong. It was difficult even to walk against them, much less perform a ballet."

Donen: "Cyd's outfit was a headache, and the front office was going crazy, because it was already so short and the veil pulled it back so far that her pubic hair was showing. Walter Plunkett, the costume designer, would lengthen it a little, but the front office was still worried sick. They lived in such tremendous fear of the censors in those days. Finally, Walter, who was driven nuts by all this himself, came to the set one day. Now, Walter, a very nice man, was very swishy. He was very much like Franklin Pangborn. So this morning he shows up on the set, he's looking very satisfied with himself, and I ask, 'Walter, what's up?' And he said, 'This time we've done it. We finally got the crotch licked.' But that still wasn't the end of it. M-G-M wasn't satisfied yet. So what they had me do was go into the lab and paint in little white lines over her dark pubic hairs. Well, Technicolor prints start to fade, but the white doesn't. What happened was, when the picture was playing in theaters, Cyd's crotch started to light up like neon."

"The Broadway Ballet" ends with Kelly coming in for a close-up above the dancing hordes behind him.

Donen: "We tried the shot two ways, with a crane and with a matte. The crane didn't work, because it wasn't smooth."

The plot takes a twist when Zelda Zanders exposes Don and Kathy's "trick" to Lina, who threatens to sue the studio if the secret of the dubbing is revealed. The premiere of The Dancing Cavalier *is a smash, with the spellbound public devouring the overripe operatics of Don and Lina.*

Donen: "Jeanette MacDonald and Nelson Eddy."

With the response so tumultuous, Lina decides to speak to the public herself for once. Not believing what they hear, the people in the crowd beg the star to sing. Kathy, against her will, is forced to "ghost-voice" for Lina once more, behind the curtain in Grauman's Chinese. Don, Cosmo, and R.F. raise the heavy drape, exposing Lina. Kathy starts to flee, Don stops her, to tell her as the tears well in her eyes, "You Are My Lucky Star."

Reynolds: "I couldn't cry. Nothing sad had ever happened to me. My dog hadn't even died. So they put onions on my cheeks to make tears come out."

The story fades out with Don and Kathy standing before the M-G-M fence with a billboard for Singin' in the Rain, *starring Don Lockwood and Kathy Selden.*

Donen: "The first time Betty and Adolph saw the picture, it was fresh out of the lab and still in black and white. They loved it. That's when we knew we had pulled it off."

Chapter 5

"Kubrick Said It Best"

L OUIS B. MAYER had balls. What he said *went,*" declared the studio's brawny Aphrodite, Esther Williams. "But then I saw the whole studio system come crumbling down before my eyes. The stockholders in New York ousted Mayer and put in Dore Schary, who didn't know what to do with movie stars. He was only interested in feature players, like Nancy Davis."

With the departure of Louis B. Mayer, the comfortable dictatorship that had long defined M-G-M vanished forever. Although possessed of a keen liberal intellect, Dore Schary lacked the grand vision of his predecessor, no matter how clouded Mayer's sight may have become in his final years; this most regal of studio chiefs died in 1957, engaged in a bitter but nonetheless hopeless fight to regain control of his onetime domain.

During his first year of command at M-G-M, Schary shot himself in the foot at least twice. The first illusionary bullet rang out on March 20, 1952, a week before the East Coast premiere of *Singin' in the Rain*. While Hollywood was gearing up for the Academy Awards ceremony to honor its films of the previous year, Schary, seeking to recoup further expenses on the studio's already profitable but pitiful Roman spectacle *Quo Vadis?*, ordered Metro's promotion department to throw its weight behind the period Best Picture nominee. This edict was given despite Schary's personal distaste for the picture, which bore the L. B. Mayer imprimatur, as well as *Quo Vadis?*'s dark-horse status behind the clear-cut front-runners for the Oscar, Paramount's *A Place in the Sun* and Warners' *A Streetcar Named Desire*.

On Oscar night, in an upset victory, the Best Picture award went, not to either of the three, but to M-G-M's *An American in Paris*. Happy as the

Metro executives were with the win, they were ill prepared for it and badly advised on the next step they took.

In addition to *An American in Paris*'s top prize, a special Thalberg Award for Freed, and another honorary statuette to Gene Kelly, "specifically for his brilliant achievements in the art of choreography on film,"* the Vincente Minnelli musical took Oscars for its color costume design, musical scoring, color art and set direction, cinematography, and story and screenplay. To capitalize on the windfall, Schary decided to put the picture back into theaters, where it had already played the previous Christmas, and he did this at the expense of the studio's latest musical, *Singin' in the Rain,* which was yanked in order to accommodate the Oscar winner.

That was shot two.

The subsequent high regard for *Singin' in the Rain* did not begin to take root until the mid to late sixties, when the picture began to crop up at international film festivals, in metropolitan revival houses, and on color television. Between the time of its debut and its later near reverence— Pauline Kael, that often most contrarian of critics, called it "perhaps the most enjoyable of all movie musicals, just about the best Hollywood musical of all time"—*Singin' in the Rain* received only an intermittent nod of approval, albeit from sources far beyond that of the average cineast. Only days before the picture's initial opening, Comden and Green encountered Charlie Chaplin at a party, where he was raving about this new musical comedy that satirized Hollywood's transition to sound. When the proud authors announced that they were fully aware of this movie, Chaplin insisted they couldn't possibly be, the picture hadn't been released yet. Years later in Paris, the writers were sought out by François Truffaut, who personally wished to express his admiration for *Chantons sous la pluie,* which they rightly took to mean their movie.

"Yet at the time the picture opened," asked a bemused Betty Comden in 1992, "where were the critics?" *Singin' in the Rain,* when released, was treated not as *Citizen Kane* but as just another Metro musical, no better than *An American in Paris* (despite the fact that it was), and no worse than *Pagan Love Song* (inconceivable).

"We felt comparatively ignored," said Adolph Green.

"We *were* ignored," said Donen. "What did it get? One nomination, for Jean Hagen, who lost. Not that it's such a big to-do. The year of *Singin'*

---

* At the Oscar ceremony, Donen accepted for Kelly, who was in Europe preparing *Invitation to the Dance.*

in the Rain, the Best Picture went to *The Greatest Show on Earth,* one of the worst movies ever made."

Singin' in the Rain's rank as one of the best movies ever made can be credited to a number of factors, beginning with that most basic: it was built from a strong blueprint. Nor is it weighed down by a sense of sentiment or arty self-importance, as was achingly the case with *An American in Paris.* The playful Comden and Green script spoofs each of its situations and characters (except for the always moving target of Cosmo, who himself is generally busy spoofing others), yet seldom lapses into silliness or, as would have been more damaging in this case, cynicism (when it does weave itself into the scenario, another punch line quickly provides the rebound); the otherwise serviceable Freed-Brown songs, even the cribbed "Make 'Em Laugh," ideally serve a time frame and setting for which they were conceived; and as had not been seen before to such an extent, Donen's choreographic approach to camera movement, which heretofore had wobbly material at its disposal in *On the Town* and a hopelessly constraining story line in *Royal Wedding,* proves a revelation.

"In *Singin' in the Rain,*" perceived Gerald Mast, "the tracking camera mirrors the title song's energetic joy. At that magical moment when Kelly welcomes the rain on his face, already saturated with rapturous song, the camera cranes down and tracks in breathlessly—not Minnelli's camera in terrifying pursuit of a fleeing subject, but Donen's joyful mirror of the performance energy that charges the entire frame."

Regrettably, in the aftermath of *Singin' in the Rain,* except for some long stretches of inspired moments in *Seven Brides for Seven Brothers* and *It's Always Fair Weather,* the material that Metro provided Donen was seldom worthy of these gifts and contributed to his growing desire to leave the studio. To be fair, Donen's other golden musical, *Funny Face,* began as an M-G-M picture, until Audrey Hepburn's participation dictated that the production be moved to Paramount. Curiously, that leap would prove as fortuitous to Donen as the *Pal Joey* call, because it was *Funny Face* that helped propel him out of Metro and into creative independence at the precise moment that a large white flag was being hoisted over Culver City.

WITH THE completion of *Singin' in the Rain,* in November 1951, Gene Kelly departed for Europe to star in a melodrama called *The Devil*

Makes Three and to commence work on his ambitious but misguided personal ballet project, *Invitation to the Dance;* completed in 1952, the film would be severely edited and held up for release by the studio until 1956, whereupon it was greeted with overwhelming critical and commercial apathy.*

With the prints of *Rain* barely dry, Donen was instructed by Arthur Freed to begin a screen adaptation of *Jumbo,* a 1935 Broadway circus musical produced by the showman Billy Rose, featuring a book by Hecht and MacArthur and a score by Rodgers and Hart that had marked their return to Broadway after languishing in Hollywood for three years. The dainty story concerned the attempts of publicity man Claudius B. Bowers (Jimmy Durante) to save a financially ailing circus, though his schemes were merely a platform for a series of specialty acts to fill the cavernous Hippodrome, at the corner of Forty-third and Sixth. George Abbott stepped in to direct—*Jumbo* marked his initial collaboration with Rodgers and Hart—and the highlight of the show was the blue-tinted first-act curtain number, "Little Girl Blue," in which the heroine, played by Gloria Grafton, imagines herself a child again, being entertained by the circus. *Jumbo* (named for the troupe's elephant), one of the most loudly hyped productions of its time, rehearsed for a full six months. It played for five.

For *Jumbo*'s motion picture incarnation, Joseph Harris undertook a screenplay, which then was turned over to Leonard Spiegelgass. The picture was to star the second bananas from *Singin' in the Rain,* Debbie Reynolds and Donald O'Connor, though Freed's first choices had been Judy Garland, now off the Metro payroll, and Frank Sinatra, whose career whims were becoming too unpredictable to guarantee his participation. The whole endeavor came to a crashing halt when O'Connor's contract with Metro lapsed, and the material became lost in an entanglement of restrictions leveled upon it by Billy Rose, who refused to permit changes to its story and score.†

* The plotless film featured a series of three separate thirty-minute "modern classical" ballet segments—the first cut presented four—titled "Circus," "Ring Around the Rosy," and "Sinbad the Sailor." The last was considered the most successful and the most typical Kelly; he danced with a Hanna-Barbera–created Sinbad, although the animation and the technique were neither as charming nor as eye-popping as had been the case in *Anchors Aweigh.* Per Jean-Pierre Coursodon: "The gimmick loses its novelty after a while."

† Joe Pasternak produced an antiseptic *Jumbo* in 1962, directed by Charles Walters and starring Doris Day and Stephen Boyd. The best moments were stolen by Jimmy Durante, Martha Raye, and the pachyderm.

Donen, owing the studio more work, dutifully stepped into another picture.

IF, as Arthur Loew, Jr., had chaffed, at M-G-M a documentary was a movie with only four songs, then what must be said for *Fearless Fagan*? It contained only one.

"What was good about *Fearless Fagan,* and there wasn't much that was," said Donen, "was that it was based on a true story." That story was almost too cute for words: Floyd C. Humeston was a circus trouper who secretly brought his lion, Fagan, with him when he went into the army. That much was true. For the movie, the lion somehow manages to get loose and sets his eyes on a movie star who comes to the base to entertain. Once Fagan sees the star, he develops a romantic attachment to her and, of course, scares the hell out of everybody. He is, after all, a lion.

"What I wanted to do with the picture, but couldn't," said Donen, "was to have the movie star in the story be a really big movie star, like Deborah Kerr. This way it would have seemed more like a dream when the lion falls in love with her."

Instead of Deborah Kerr, the actress is played by Janet Leigh, an M-G-M contract player (and a discovery of Metro shareholder Norma Shearer), who accepted the picture with as much reluctance as Donen. "What gave me a lift," said Leigh in 1992, "was that Stanley was so heavily associated with musicals, and here I was doing a song for him." The routinely staged number was "What Do You Think I Am?" by Hugh Martin and Ralph Blane, a band song lifted from *Best Foot Forward.* Leigh plays Abby Ames, the movie star, who seems to live in a ranch house with Esther Williams's old swimming pool in its backyard. "What impressed me about Stanley," recalled Leigh, "was his attitude. He didn't want to do the film. He knew I didn't, either. So the first day of shooting he said to me, 'Aw, let's just go for it.' It was certainly a lot better than our pouting about it."

Whatever the original intentions, the black-and-white film, with its Eisenhower-era sets and army-post setting, comes off as homespun as a *Boys' Life* story, though it was in fact based on a 1951 journalistic report in *Life.* It bears all the production qualities of a television episode of *General Electric Theater.* "Kubrick really said it best," remarked Donen, referring to *Fearless Fagan* and those early pictures to which he had been assigned as choreographer. "You can never get divorced from a picture."

Given some of the names attached to the production, Donen's aspiration of casting Deborah Kerr was not so far-fetched. *Fagan's* producer was

Edwin H. Knopf (1899–1981), the younger half-brother of the New York publisher Alfred A. Knopf, who maintained a warm and professional relationship with his sibling. Originally an actor, Edwin Knopf turned to producing for the stage—it was he who gave Katharine Hepburn her first professional role, in Baltimore in 1928 (*The Czarina,* with Mary Boland)—before M-G-M hired and appointed him head of the scenario department, based on his taste and his literary ties to New York. Among the films Knopf produced for the studio were the 1944 war movie *Cry Havoc,* the 1949 political drama *Edward, My Son,* and the 1953 musical *Lili.*

The script for *Fearless Fagan* was written by Charles Lederer. Besides being the nephew of Marion Davies, the mistress of publisher William Randolph Hearst, Lederer (1910–1976) had helped adapt the two different screen renderings of Donen's favorite play, the pioneer 1931 *The Front Page* and the towering "coed" 1941 version with Cary Grant and Rosalind Russell, *His Girl Friday,* directed at machine-gun pace by Howard Hawks.

"Charlie's humor was in the situation. He never specialized in one-liners," said the writer Luther Davis, who collaborated with Lederer on the book for the 1953 stage musical *Kismet,* "although he was responsible for the best joke we wrote for *Kismet* and were never allowed to put into the show. The evil wazir shouts: 'Search the harem for the monster! Search every cran and nooky!' "

Lederer spent his early years at San Simeon and graduated from Stanford at the age of seventeen. Through his friendship with Alexander Woollcott, he maintained a link to the Algonquin Round Table, and he frequently wrote with Ben Hecht. Like the clever prodigy he was, Lederer made the most of his connections.

"Howard Hughes refused to give Charlie and Ben a new screenwriting assignment at RKO unless they paid back the fee they received for a script that was never made," remembered Luther Davis. "Charlie got his aunt Marion to wire Hughes: 'Howard, is it true that you're going to give back to the American taxpayers all the money they paid you for that big flying boat that never flew? If so it'll be a big story in all of WR's papers.' Hughes got the message, and Charlie and Ben got the job."

Davis also painted Lederer as "a dangerous man to cross. For some reason he got mad at the M-G-M producer Sam Zimbalist, and when Sam and his wife were away skiing over Christmas, Charlie put an ad in the paper: 'Will Buy Used Xmas Trees After Xmas, Will Pay One to Ten Dollars Depending on Size, Leave on Lawn at'—and he gave Sam's Bel Air address—'Tagged with Your Name and Address to Which to Send the Money.' "

On *Fearless Fagan* (1952),
Donen learned that for a
lion to be properly trained,
he had to develop an erotic
interest in his trainer. This
gave way to many a joke on
the set.

The Zimbalists, said Davis, "came home to a forest on their lawn and in their pool, and a lot of angry telephone calls from irate people who wanted their money."

The best screwball gag in *Fearless Fagan* comes after the lion breaks free and invades the home of some rubes, played by Ellen Corby and John Call. When the couple is interrogated by the authorities searching for the missing feline, throughout the questioning the husband sounds as though his mouth is full of mush, leaving his wife to interpret everything he says.

Among the obstacles to filming the picture were the temperaments of two of the participants, the real-life Floyd and the real-life Fagan. Humeston was to double for Carleton Carpenter, who played the draftee, renamed Floyd Hilsten for the movie, in the long shots, "but then," said the actor, "he refused to work with his own lion." Humeston departed, though a few brief shots of him survive in the finished print. As for Fagan, he was released from his contract too, to be replaced by a newer model. "The second one was so young," said Carpenter, "that his mane had to be added, like a toupee. A lot of times it went askew."

Carpenter's dialogue—the leading man affects a running patter every time he is in close proximity to his pet—had to be dubbed in after the picture wrapped. "As we shot," Carpenter explained, "everyone was always yelling at the lion from off-camera, waving chickens, aiming guns at him. It was terrifying. Then every time I got up and walked away, he'd sink his teeth into me."

As for what lasting effect the picture had on him, Carpenter said, "I had scars on my buns for months."

Chapter 6

"Two Warring Camps"

O N MAY 20, 1952, Donen married for a second time; his bride was the Fox starlet Marion Marshall. He was twenty-eight; she was six years younger. Typically for a Beverly Hills marital union, there was a multitude of interconnections. The Donens wed at the home of Marshall's agent, Jules Goldstone, who had also represented Elizabeth Taylor. Marshall had been the companion of the director Howard Hawks, whose wife, the model Nancy "Slim" Hawks, had left Hawks for the agent-producer Leland Hayward, who had been Gene Kelly's agent. Hayward divorced his previous wife, the actress Margaret Sullavan, to marry "Slim." Marion Marshall gave up her career when she married Donen, and they had two sons, Peter, born in 1953, and Joshua, born in 1955.

"Stanley's a very good father, and he loves his sons," professed Pam Donen, Stanley's fifth wife, "but the only thing is, Stanley prefers his children once they're all grown up." Stanley and Marion Donen divorced in 1959, by which time Donen was already living in England and keeping company with Lady Adelle Beatty. Marion Marshall, in 1963, married the actor Robert Wagner, during the period between his two marriages to Natalie Wood; Robert and Marion Wagner divorced in 1971.

Give a Girl a Break, Donen's first musical after *Singin' in the Rain,* relied far less on production values—and, wisely, little if at all on its feeble script—than on Donen's technical ingenuity and the choreographic inventiveness of Bob Fosse, with whom Donen got along, and Gower Champion, with whom he clashed.

"Bob was as good a musical performer as ever lived," said Donen, who first saw Fosse (1927–1987) at a 1952 talent show in New York;

Donen for a time considered him as a replacement for Donald O'Connor in *Jumbo,* going so far as to run a screen test. "He had more charm than anybody when he played innocent and shy, though he loved playing the other type," said Donen. Fosse grew up worshiping at the feet of Fred Astaire, though it was Gene Kelly's career he wished to emulate, even if, as he admitted privately, he found Kelly's dancing technique comparable to that of a truck driver.* Fosse started young, playing seedy dives; the role he was playing when he was tapped by M-G-M talent scouts was Joey Evans in a northeastern summer stock production of *Pal Joey;* and the scene Fosse enacted in his screen test for Donen was the same one Kelly performed on Broadway in William Saroyan's *The Time of Your Life,* the bit that landed Kelly *Pal Joey.*

Self-deprecating to the point of self-torture, Fosse by the 1970s would become a prodigious stage and film choreographer (*Cabaret, All That Jazz*), yet he was always the first to question his own talent. This was especially true of his attitude toward his work at M-G-M, where in 1952 he was signed to a seven-year contract. Granted, it was hardly a notable start to a career, owing to Fosse's slight, balding image on-screen (the same could be said for Astaire, but in that case other factors were at work), the fading fortunes of the studio, and the public's expanding disinterest in musicals. Except for his playing the lead in the forgotten *The Many Loves of Dobie Gillis,* Fosse was to get his biggest break at M-G-M with *Give a Girl a Break.*

Despite his handsome looks and Ipana smile, Gower Champion (1919–1980) fared only slightly better at the studio. Like Fosse an Illinois native, Champion had danced, from the time he was fifteen, in Los Angeles, where he studied with a dance instructor named Ernest Belcher. After World War II, he formed a partnership with Marge Belcher, Ernest's daughter, who was the Disney animators' model for the figure of Snow White. In 1947, Marge Belcher (by now Marge Bell) and Gower Champion married, having appeared in their first M-G-M musical the year before, *Till the Clouds Roll By,* a limp biography of Jerome Kern. After that, the couple served as little more than an adornment in movies, as was evidenced by their thankless roles as Frank and Ellie in the 1950 version of *Show Boat.* In the sixties, Champion became known as the iron-willed Broadway director of such smashes as *Bye Bye Birdie* and *Hello, Dolly!,* yet even at the outset of his career, Champion showed signs of becoming a martinet (on *Give a Girl a Break,* this would lead to problems with Donen).

* "All Kelly knows is acrobatics and two or three steps."

The Champions: Gower and Marge. Their style conflicted with Donen's and Fosse's—offscreen and on.

The little-seen *Give a Girl a Break* (1953): Kurt Kasznar, Gower Champion, Bob Fosse, Debbie Reynolds, and Lurene Tuttle

Michael Stewart, who wrote the books for *Birdie* and *Dolly!,* once referred to Champion as the "Presbyterian Hitler," while, closer to home, Marge Champion said of her husband's neurotic preparation technique, "His *mother* couldn't come to the rehearsal hall. If he could have eliminated me, he would have been happy." The Champions divorced in 1973.

Give a Girl a Break was produced by Jack Cummings, who joined Arthur Freed and Joseph Pasternak to constitute Metro's musical triumvirate. As Schary perceived the "tall, lean" Cummings, his talents "fell somewhere between Joe's and Arthur's." Cummings, born in 1900, began producing at Metro in 1934, though in nearly twenty years his only noteworthy picture was a not entirely satisfying adaptation of Cole Porter's Broadway musical *Kiss Me, Kate* (directed by George Sidney in 1953, with Bob Fosse notable during a dance version of "From This Moment On"). Comparing Cummings to his confreres, Schary admired Freed's taste and considered him "not a lovable man but a hell of a producer." Pasternak he found "lovable but not as gifted as Freed." Cummings, however, "had taken on the burden of proving he was more than L. B. Mayer's nephew."* Such a detriment, Schary remembered, "made him sensitive and quick to resort to truculence."

Donen simply found Cummings lazy. "After *Give a Girl a Break,* Jack produced *Seven Brides for Seven Brothers* and was always trying to ruin it." By way of illustration, Donen recounted an interview he had given Stephen Farber for the *Los Angeles Times* Sunday "Calendar" section. "It was about 1985," said Donen. "By then, I hadn't seen Jack for at least thirty years and thought he was dead for about three." Farber inquired after the differences between the producers at M-G-M, and this brought the conversation around to Cummings's involvement on *Seven Brides.*

"Jack Cummings insisted upon ruining the script," said Donen. "We'd had this very good script by Albert Hackett and Frances Goodrich, but then Jack put on Dorothy Kingsley, who could barely write, and all the crap she kept putting into the script I had to keep taking out. But worse than that, all he kept saying every day was, 'We have to have a dream ballet in the picture,' because at that moment that was the vogue in movies, and every day I would have to say, 'This is not that kind of picture.' I had to fight him terribly about getting a score written, because he wanted me to use 'authentic old cowboy songs.' I wasted weeks trying to find some that fit, until I finally told him, 'Look, Jack, this is hopeless. We need to get an original score.' But the biggest fight of all was in getting real dancers to play the parts of the brothers. Jack said, 'You can't do that. First of all, you can't have a bunch of faggots'—that's precisely what he said—'flitting across the screen. They're not going to look like real backwoodsmen, and everybody will end up calling the picture *Seven Brides for Seven Sissies.*' "

Donen and Cummings also butted heads over Donen's desire to hire Michael Kidd as choreographer. Donen held firm, "because I knew Michael Kidd's style was exactly necessary for this kind of Americana."

Eventually, Donen said, he won these fights. "Then, when I was making the picture, Jack wasn't there. He was married to Jerome Kern's daughter, but he had this mistress in Mexico, and he was down there the whole time we were in production. We never saw him."

In summation, Donen told Farber that Jack Cummings's singular contribution to *Seven Brides for Seven Brothers* "was simply to make it more difficult."

---

* Cummings was the only son of Mayer's beloved sister, Ida, and her ne'er-do-well husband, Louis Komiensky—the name was anglicized to Cummings. With so many relatives of L.B.'s on the payroll, wags used to joke that M-G-M stood for "Mayer's *Ganze Mishpocheh*"— Yiddish for "entire family."

A few Sundays later, under Farber's byline, the gist of what Donen had to say appeared in the *Los Angeles Times.* "Monday morning," said Donen, "the phone rang at my house, and a man's voice said, 'Stanley?' I said, 'Yes?' "

The voice on the other end announced, "It's Jack."

"Jack who?" asked Donen.

"Jack Cummings."

"Jesus Christ, Jack," said Donen. "How are you?"

Cummings, dispensing with the formalities, ordered Donen to "call up the paper and deny everything you said."

"Now, Jack," said Donen. "You know I can't do that."

"Why not?" Cummings demanded.

"Because you and I both know it's all true."

Cummings smashed down the phone.

"That's the last time I talked to him," said Donen.*

Give a Girl a Break (1953) was originally intended as a combined showcase for Fred Astaire, Gene Kelly, Judy Garland, and Ann Miller, none of whom ultimately came within breathing distance of it. The realized version is decidedly minor league, although at a cost of $1,755,198,† it hardly could have qualified as a B picture. Donen, in retrospect, considered the film "puny," not that he was enthusiastic about directing it in the first place.

"Jack Cummings said, 'I've got this story about these girls who try out for a show,' and I'm sorry to say I got into the project early." The film is short on length (eighty-two minutes), short on plot, and short on virtues, though among them are some clever executions of a bouncy Burton Lane–Ira Gershwin score (their only collaboration) and the golden opportunity to watch a young Bob Fosse dance.

The tired story line revolves around the search for the lead of a new Broadway musical once its headstrong star walks out over a dispute with the director (Gower Champion). Deciding to break in a newcomer, the director cannot decide among three final competitors, played by Debbie Reynolds, Marge Champion, and Helen Wood. Each is the recipient of separate backstage support from, respectively, the eager stage manager (Fosse), the director, and the show's inadvertently comic lyricist (Kurt Kasznar).

* Cummings died in 1989.

† Among the budgetary items: a miscellaneous bill for $29.17 for the fifteen hours of labor required to "repair toupee Bob Fossie [*sic*]."

"The joke of the picture was: notice how the Kurt Kasznar character agrees with everyone?" said Donen. "You'd ask him, 'Hey, have you seen such and such new movie?' and he'd say, 'I saw it. I loved it,' and then you'd say, 'Really? I didn't think it was so good,' and he would say, 'Oh, it's not very good.' Well, that's Jule Styne."

It was while making *Give a Girl a Break* at M-G-M that Donen was able to introduce Fosse to Fred Astaire during a lunch break. Astaire was making *The Band Wagon,* and a tongue-tied Fosse spied his unmistakable silhouette approaching in the studio street. He also noticed the way Astaire skipped over and kicked aside a loose nail in his path. Rather than join Donen for lunch, Fosse spent the next hour in the alleyway beside the soundstage, perfecting his imitation of Astaire's gait and toe movement as he had just witnessed it.

In addition to Gershwin and Lane, every writing credit on the picture carried some sort of pedigree: a story by Vera Caspary, a romantic crime novelist responsible for *Laura* and *A Letter to Three Wives,* and a script from Albert Hackett and Frances Goodrich, the husband-and-wife team who wrote *The Thin Man, It's a Wonderful Life,** and *Father of the Bride.*

"The picture turned into an unfortunate experience," said Donen, "because it divided into two warring camps, with Bob Fosse and me on one side, Debbie Reynolds and Marge and Gower Champion on the other. Marge was the troublemaker. She thought Bob was an interloper, and she used to start things up."

One account credited Marge with standing beside the camera and instructing her husband to "outleap" Fosse, a feat he was never able to do.

Without elaborating upon what issues were at stake between the two camps some forty years before, in 1993 Debbie Reynolds admitted, "Stanley and I had our moments of difficulty on *Give a Girl a Break,* but it wasn't a great film and it wasn't a great script. For me it was a different experience from working with him on *Singin' in the Rain,* because this time he was the director, so naturally we worked closer."

Hinting at a palpable chill between them, Reynolds said, "He and Bobby Fosse were good friends, but I was closer to Marge and Gower Champion. Stanley and I never became friends, because he picked who he wanted to hang out with, and that's who he hung out with."

The film officially credits its choreography to two sources, Donen and Champion, though as Donen pointed out, "The number 'It Happens

* Donen, while an admirer of Frank Capra, whom he considered "the talkies' first stylist," was never a fan of this film. "It's sentimental."

Ev'ry Time' is horrible, and I had nothing to do with it." It is a balletic pas de deux, performed by the Champions in the square manner of Arthur and Kathryn Murray.

"Bobby created the numbers we were in together," said Debbie Reynolds, "and Gower came up with the numbers I did with Gower. I think they wanted to do the best they could to save the picture, because they really weren't that happy about the script. Bobby and Gower were both great choreographers. You can't compare them. One had one style, and one had another. It's like saying, Is Fred Astaire better than Gene Kelly, or is Gene Kelly better than Fred Astaire? The answer is no, they're each great different talents, and Stanley allowed them [Fosse and Champion] to be totally creative. Stanley just operated the camera, because Stanley didn't dance."

When informed that Donen began in the chorus of *Pal Joey,* Reynolds cleared her throat in a theatrical manner and specified, "I'll stand by my original statement. I never saw Stanley dance, and I wouldn't have known he was a dancer. He didn't contribute in that fashion. I think there were enough people to do that, and Stanley was smart enough to know that his talent was stronger in other areas—script, continuity, camera, editing. To Stanley's credit, he could step back and allow these great talents like Bobby and Gower to do their work."

There are three standout numbers in *Give a Girl a Break.* The first is the jaunty "Nothing Is Impossible," set on the naked stage—dressed only by the rehearsal piano—and meant to inspire the blustery Leo (Kasznar) to conquer his anxieties over coming up with an entirely new score in three weeks. Taking their cues from their own idealistic motto, the reed-thin Champion (Ted) and Fosse (Bob) dance impossible steps all around Leo, including, at one point, locking fingers and turning themselves into human pretzels. Leo, by contrast a human marshmallow, meanwhile tries to get in on the act, but is simply left holding his own hands. Later in the song, Kasznar does do the impossible—he defies gravity by bending forward almost to the point of touching his nose to the floor.

"He was wired," Donen divulged, "but I pulled a couple of other tricks on him too. First of all, I had Kurt's shoes nailed to the floor. Then, to get him to bend over at the right second, without Kurt's knowing it I had the stagehands rig a sandbag over him and had the rope measured to drop so it fell just inches above his head. He almost had a heart attack, but it got him to move."

Fosse sweet-talks Debbie Reynolds with a number set on the Brooklyn Heights riverfront (that they are actually on a soundstage is obvious),

"In Our United State." Reminiscent of the Andy Hardyesque virtues pro-mulgated in "Main Street" in *On the Town,* the delightful respite permits Fosse some awestruck small-boy-in-the-big-town swooning and some neat trickery with a hat—which he tears at, somersaults into, and allows to survive him on the surface of the water once he winds up the number by falling into the river.

By far the most innovative number in the film, at least from the stand-point of Donen's visual chicanery, is "Give a Girl a Break." Although it is a dream sequence—Fosse imagines himself in a big production number with Reynolds—it is, contrary to the norm, not a prosaic ballet but a light, invigorating showstopper, played on a skyscraper-roof stage set. Fosse and Reynolds leap among balloons that magically inflate before them, while colorful streamers and confetti float *up.* Though technically com-plex, the concept put a simple new spin on a love-drunk man's ability to dance on the ceiling or laugh at rain clouds. As seen in the picture, it is marvelous for its small scale as well as for the zest of its performance.

"The special effects were accomplished by shooting in reverse," said Donen. "Because he's so in love, everything he touches is as filled with emotion as he is. That's why the balloons blow up. But in fact, the way it was shot was to have Debbie and Bob do the entire number backward, so they are really popping the balloons with pins, which you don't see. The sound track plays forward, but they are dancing backward, if that makes any sense." Why it works is because it's nonsensical; it was definitely an ambitious undertaking for such a small amount of screen time. (The Reynolds-Fosse duet is the first of three during the number, which goes on to spotlight the two other "girls.") As a production report noted, the elaborate idea threw an additional $25,266 onto the budget: "The com-pany has lost a day-and-a-half on the Balloon Number. This was due mostly to the effects . . . which took as much as fifty percent of each day in replacing and resetting the balloons."

"True, the picture was nowhere near Academy Award nomination, but it wasn't this bad," said Ira Gershwin in regard to M-G-M's denying the picture a New York opening and national reviews. Others shared the studio's opinion.

"On leaving the studio projection room after seeing a rough cut of the film," said Gershwin, "my wife asked me if I owned any stock in the film company." Gershwin did, one hundred shares, which he had pur-chased the previous year, and this he reported to his wife, Leonore.

Her response: "Sell it."

Chapter 7

"Whatever You Want, Michael"

S TANLEY WAS one of the first people I met when I came to Holly-wood," said the choreographer Michael Kidd in 1992. To prove how small a world it was, forty-eight years before, in 1944, Kidd, then twenty-five, danced as one of the leads in the Robbins-Bernstein *Fancy Free*. By the next year, Kidd was a Broadway choreographer, and by 1947, a Broadway name, thanks to his work on *Finian's Rainbow*. By the 1950s, Michael Kidd was the reigning Broadway choreographer; if, earlier, Agnes de Mille had given the theatrical dance world its grace, and Jerome Robbins gave it its vital integration of movement meshed with the book, then Michael Kidd injected Broadway with a shot of adrenaline. In his signature 1950 *Guys and Dolls*, the choreographer's energetic positioning of the characters, whether they were scrutinizing the *Racing Form* amid the bustle of Times Square or anxiously rolling the dice inside the deepest recesses of the New York steampipe system, was every bit as instrumental in conveying the Runyonesque quality of the piece as was the street-poet babble of the protagonists and the colorful brilliance of the Frank Loesser score.

"In choreography," explained Kidd, traces of his Brooklyn and City College origins still evident in his voice, "ordinary movements from real life are taken and extended, so they become dance movements, yet the relation to reality must always be there." In creating a dance or, for that matter, any routine, he said, "It's important for me to know who the characters are and what their function is in the script. From there I must be able to illustrate either their activities, their emotions, or their changes in mood by the way they dance, all the while keeping the dance footed in reality and yet making the movements sort of odd and eccentric. This way what they do doesn't look as ordinary as just having a person come in, pull up a chair, and sit down."

As for the Donen connection, said Kidd, "In those days the theater community in New York was very small—it's probably smaller now. Everybody knew everybody. When I came out to Hollywood, I met Stanley through Saul Chaplin, whom I had met in New York." Chaplin, a Tin Pan Alley composer and musical arranger, seemed to travel a similar Hollywood route as Donen's; Chaplin was at Columbia for *Cover Girl* and at M-G-M for the musicals that followed.

Kidd's first job at Metro-Goldwyn-Mayer was to choreograph *The Band Wagon,* to be produced by Freed and directed by Vincente Minnelli. Kidd's contract called for twenty weeks at the studio, which astounded him, given the customary five weeks a choreographer was generally allotted on Broadway.

Fretting over the ramifications of what four times that amount of time might possibly entail, the still-novice movie choreographer* turned to Donen and asked, "What am I going to do for twenty weeks?"

"For three weeks," replied Donen, "you're going to mull."

"What do you mean, 'mull'?"

"First, you're going to have meetings and you're going to plan the musical numbers," said Donen. "Right now they don't exist. They're not in the script, are they?"

"No," said Kidd. "The script doesn't say anything about the staging."

"See? You're going to work on that, and it's going to take you three weeks to a month just to mull. Then you're going to start rehearsing with a small group, a nucleus of people, laying out the numbers."

As Kidd began to absorb the information, Donen laid out the scenario. "Next, you're going to have to audition and hire dancers. That'll take four weeks. Then you're going to start rehearsing them. Then you must start prerecording the numbers. That'll take two weeks. And then they're going to start shooting the picture, and while they're shooting, you're going to be rehearsing the other numbers. If you add all that up, you'll see that's how you're going to spend your twenty weeks."

According to Kidd, "It turned out I was there for twenty-six weeks. Stanley was dead right."

STEPHEN VINCENT BENÉT based his circa-1940 short story "The Sobbin' Women" on Plutarch's "Rape of the Sabine Women," shifting the set-

---

* Kidd's only previous film work had been on *Where's Charley?* for Warner Bros. in 1952. It was based on Frank Loesser's 1948 Broadway musical adaptation of the durable English farce *Charley's Aunt.*

ting of the tale from ancient Rome to the Tennessee Valley. Once Benét's protagonist, Milly, a servant girl hired by the parents of seven sons, has married and become pregnant by the eldest boy, she plants the idea in the minds of her six brothers-in-law to find women to assist her on the farm.

"Why don't you marry 'em first and ask them afterwards?" she harmlessly suggests.

With thoughts of spinning the yarn into a Broadway musical, the story was optioned by a theatrical production company that included the director-librettist Joshua Logan, though the material sat for five years. When the option lapsed, M-G-M purchased "The Sobbin' Women" for $40,000 and assigned it to Jack Cummings, who chose Donen. The director immediately started mapping out ambitious designs for the film, deciding to shoot on location and commission a score by Johnny Mercer and Harold Arlen.

"I told the studio not to get nervous," said Donen, "but I was going to need a year to shoot the picture, because we were covering events in our story that required all four seasons."

Both the studio and Johnny Mercer forced compromises upon Donen, one fiscal and the other creative. As M-G-M profits continued to shrink—averaging $5.5 million per year from 1948 to 1955—Metro continued to pare budgets to the bone. After dispatching scouting expeditions to Sun Valley, Idaho, and checking the snow depths at the closer sites of Crestline, Arrowhead, Idyllwild, Big Bear, and Chilao, Metro allowed only five days' location shooting at Tioga Pass and Twin Lakes. At one juncture, the studio inquired whether Walt Disney would provide footage from his nature films *Beaver Valley* and *Bear Country,* but when Disney demanded screen credit, Metro withdrew its request.

In regard to the score, Donen remembered, "Johnny Mercer told me he wouldn't work with Harold Arlen. Johnny said, 'He's too picky about the words that go with his music.'" As a result, "Gene de Paul did the music," said Donen, "and the score suffered."

Despite Donen's complaints of Jack Cummings's obstruction, the finished film reflects a clear distillation of the short story, presented cogently in the form of a three-act play. The action has been shifted to the Oregon Territory, 1850. In Act I, Adam Pontipee (Howard Keel) meets Milly (Jane Powell), an orphaned cook in town. He sweeps her off her feet, marries her, and takes her to his isolated mountain farmhouse, where she discovers he's shacked up with his six orphaned brothers. Act II: Milly civilizes the mountain men so they are presentable to the girls back in town. The boys wow them with their good looks, their manners, and their muscular dancing prowess. Act III: Now romantically frustrated, the boys kidnap the girls, a brutish act that Milly blames on Adam. An avalanche blocks the route between the town and the Pontipee farm—a disaster triggered by the noise made by the Pontipee brothers' rifles—and this ensures that the girls won't be rescued until the spring thaw. There's a resolution before curtain, with the girls falling for the boys, Milly having a baby, and the fretful fathers of the girls, unsure which one might have produced the child, making sure that the girls are hitched, en masse. Adam's wounded male pride is soothed by the arrival of his new daughter, so all ends happily.

"Not to put too fine a point on it," the novelist Francine Prose offered in 1991, "*Seven Brides for Seven Brothers* is, it seems to me now, one of the most repulsive movies about men and women that has ever been made." She brands it as nothing less than a musical about rape. Prose's argument, though not entirely incorrect, is presented with such vehemence that one feels forced to take the opposing view, for fear of being lumped with the same parochial school of thought that blames idealized fifties television sitcoms such as *Father Knows Best* and *The Donna Reed Show* as a primary cause for dysfunctional families in the nineties.

"Partly," Prose allowed, the charms of *Seven Brides,* which she loved as a child when she saw it at Radio City Music Hall, were to be found in its "pastels, the pretty dancers, and frilly dresses." But then she goes on: "What's chilling about *Seven Brides for Seven Brothers* is its innocence, its fifties naïveté, its unexamined goodheartedness: what an insidious, sinister piece of fluff it has come to seem over time." Besides *Seven Brides,* Prose cited the "almost unimaginably vile" *Gigi,* "another colorful, much-loved musical which from the perspective of age appears to have been about the molestation of preadolescent girls."

"I HAD just done *Can-Can* and come back from New York, and I was tired," said Michael Kidd. "Doing a show is an endless period of great tension and no sleep. I just wanted rest." Kidd had by this time relocated to California, where Donen and Chaplin approached him to choreograph their by now scripted and scored project.

"I don't want to talk about a movie," Kidd replied. "I'm too tired."

Donen refused to be deterred. "But, Michael," he said, "Johnny Mercer wrote the lyrics. Why don't you just listen to the songs?" Kidd, being familiar with the creative team that tried unsuccessfully to get *The Sobbin' Women* musical off the ground in New York, did not relent. "But Stanley could be quite persuasive," said Kidd, "and Johnny Mercer is one of my all-time favorites, he and Frank Loesser, because I love how they both captured the idiomatic use of speech in songs."

After listening to *The Sobbin' Women** score and reading the script, which Donen also happened to provide, the resistant Kidd delivered his verdict to the director: "I love the songs, but it's obvious to me, as it would be to anyone, that you're not going to have anybody dance in this picture."

Donen was not completely sure he understood Kidd's reaction. "Who's going to dance?" Kidd asked. "You have these seven crude ruffians. They're illiterate, ill-mannered, rude, they live out in the woods, they're cut off from the rest of the world, they fight, they brawl, they have no upbringing, no schooling. You can't expect any of them to get up and dance; it would be ridiculous. The audience will laugh you right out of the theater."

Finally, because of his admiration for the score and the fact that "I love staging songs in terms of the scene, and these have a wonderful narrative content to each of them," Kidd agreed to do the picture, "with the understanding that I'll stage the songs as *scenes*. There is to be no dancing in the movie."

Donen replied, "Whatever you want, Michael. You do whatever you think is right."

To ensure that there was to be no misunderstanding between them, Kidd repeated his proviso. "It's very clear, right?" asked the choreographer. "Because I really can't see dancing in this picture, in addition to which, I really don't have the energy to make a dancing picture."

Kidd signed the contract and began mulling, when Donen called to say they were to meet in Jack Cummings's office. "During the course of the discussion," Kidd recalled, "Stanley said to me, 'Well, now that we have you on the picture, we have to figure some way to have dancing in it.'"

"Stanley," piped up Kidd, "I made it very clear that these people *cannot* dance. They live in a house with horseshit on the floor, cows and pigs coming in and out of the place, they're crude slobs. And now you tell me you want dancing?"

"Okay," said Donen, "not dancing. But someplace, perhaps when they come into town, during the big gathering between the townsfolk and the seven brothers, maybe right there, *some*thing could happen. They could get up and do a do-si-do or something."

---

* The title was not to be changed until October 7, 1953, after filming had begun. It was the lyricist Howard Dietz, who also headed publicity at Metro, who came up with the title *Seven Brides for Seven Brothers*.

"Do-si-do?" wailed Kidd. "Don't say that, Stanley. Do-si-do is folk dancing. Nobody wants to see folk dancing. It is not theatrical. Square dancing is participatory dancing. It's only fun for those who are doing it."

"Okay," demurred Donen. "Don't do a do-si-do. But something has to happen there. Something musical."

AS HE STEWED, Kidd said, he "did what I usually do. I looked at the script and asked myself, what's the situation? We have these seven fellows living out of town, isolated from everybody, especially girls, and they're of the age where they want girlfriends. They come to town, where there are seven attractive girls who are already committed to seven respectable local boys; maybe I can involve some kind of a number where these seven crude people try to win over these seven girls from their clean-cut boyfriends."

Despite Cummings's fear of "faggots," Donen prevailed in the hiring of seasoned dance performers, not male starlets, save for one. "Six of the seven boys were good dancers, in one way or another," said Kidd. "Three were outstanding, among the best dancers dancing in Hollywood at that time, people like Tommy Rall, Matt Mattox, and Jacques D'Amboise, who later became one of the stars of the New York City Ballet. We also had Marc Platt, who had been with the Ballet Russe, Russ Tamblyn, who wasn't a dancer but was a trained gymnast and had great spirit, and one fellow who was under contract to the studio, Jeff Richards. He was a very nice guy, very attractive, very clean, but he was not a musical performer at all, only the studio said we had to use him."

Preproduction proceeded. Kidd now mulled in high gear. "In those days you could do something that you can't do now, because of the time pressures," he said. "I called in a propman, a little fellow named Aaron, and said, 'Aaron, they're going to build a barn in this town someplace. Go down to the lumberyard and bring me anything you can find—wooden planks, sawhorses, pickaxes—anything that would be lying around a place like that.'"

An hour later, a deliveryman from Scenery arrived on the soundstage, asked for Kidd, "and dumped a lumberyardful of stuff they wanted to get rid of, every type of lumber you could think of."

Kidd started to walk around, collecting props off the floor and gradually devising ideas for what could be done during the course of a number. "The whole time," he said, "I wouldn't let Stanley watch. I said, 'I don't want anybody around, because I have no idea if what I'm doing makes sense. You have to stay away until I think I have something to show.'"

According to Donen, "Michael wouldn't let anybody see what he was concocting. Then one day the door to the rehearsal studio was open a little, so I looked in, and what did I see? A do-si-do."

"FINALLY," said Kidd, "I let Stanley in and walked him through the number, using only three people."

The "Barn Raising" episode, as Kidd envisioned it, "would start with a little bit of square dancing, and basically it would be a competition showing these Pontipee brothers trying to win these girls away from their boyfriends."

"We'll start here," Kidd demonstrated, "then the three boys will cut in, take three girls away, then two more boys will cut in and take three more girls away, and so forth. Eventually it will reach a point of anger and competition."

Miming a prop on the bare floor of the soundstage, Kidd told Donen, "And here, maybe, you have a water well, because during this competition, at some point one of them can jump on the well spinner, the part attached to the bucket and holding the rope, and you can do a kind of logrolling on the spinner. Of course, we'll have to wire the dancer."

"No problem," assured Donen. "We'll get a harness. Great idea."

"With that sort of agreement," said Kidd, "I went right ahead and laid out the entire number with the cast. Luckily, Stanley had the imagination to understand what I was talking about. Many directors wouldn't have had the slightest idea, because they're not trained dancers. There'd be no point in telling them anything." In that regard, said Kidd, "from my point of view, I'd rather work with Stanley than Vincente Minnelli.* Vincente was a difficult person to communicate with. He was not very articulate, he

---

* As the fair-haired boy of the Freed Unit, Minnelli was generally handed the projects and budgets of his desire. Donen, on the other hand, was relegated to the category of the brash young kid; he himself has admitted for the record that Joseph Pasternak held him in higher esteem than did Freed. Insofar as the two directors' particular styles are concerned, auteurists tend to slobber over Minnelli, though the consensus among cineasts, if not directors, of all stripes is that Donen is the undisputed master of the movie musical. (For some reason, a loud critical chorus seems to have risen to attack Minnelli and Freed's once lauded original-musical swan song, the 1958 *Gigi,* as precious, effetist nonsense.) Analysts of the musical genre, on the other hand, often express a distinct preference for Donen's bold, no-nonsense style of direction over Minnelli's Impressionist visual palette and Expressionist character motivations. Regarding camera technique, Donen proves his agility with his frequent horizontal tracking and crane shots, as opposed to Minnelli's constipated motion of tracking forward or back. Besides choreographers, such as Michael Kidd, performers are also well served by Donen, who allows his camera to keep up with them at live performance speeds.

Seven Brides for Seven Brothers's boisterous "Barn Raising." Michael Kidd to Donen: "Don't say do-si-do."

would leave sentences unfinished. He had a great love of the visual aspects of moviemaking—he was originally a set designer, and people used to complain all the time, 'He shoots the scenery'—but Vincente was not one to engage in collaborative work." While choreographing *The Band Wagon,* said Kidd, "If I came up to him with an idea, Vincente would say, 'Just a minute, just a minute, just a minute. Let me think about it.' He wouldn't engage in conversation about it. I don't mean to detract from Vincente Minnelli's creativity in any way. Vincente was very artistic. But when it came to a dance number, his thinking and mine were not always the same."

In contrast, Kidd appreciated Donen's process of give-and-take. "Vincente would not welcome disagreement or reveal what was on his mind, whereas Stanley would always say what he was thinking, and was very clear and methodical. Vincente may have had an idea of what he wanted—he kept artbooks and cutouts from magazines as examples of what visuals he had in mind—but when it came to talking, Vincente kept pretty much to himself. Stanley, though, would say, 'Should we try it this

Six of the prospective brides, singing "Spring! Spring! Spring!" Donen had envisioned a far more ambitious number.

way, or *this* way? Because, I think, if we try it this way, it's much clearer, don't you think?' "

WHEN THE DAY approached to film "Barn Raising," Kidd recalled, "Stanley took enormous pains with it. He said, 'Michael, it's a wonderful number, and I'm going to break my neck to shoot it as cleanly and as excitingly as I possibly can, so that no nuance of the number is lost.' And he did. Far beyond my expectations."

To give the sequence energy, Donen said, "We put the dancers on small, thin planks, accentuating the danger of the situation. The angle of the camera was raised too, to show the athletic prowess of the boys to better advantage."

Kidd stood on the sidelines and studied Donen's technique. "He shoots so that the intent of the characters, their inner workings, are very clear. At one point the seven people are huddled in the middle of a group going all around them. Stanley came in tight on the seven and then pulled back—we had no zoom lenses then, it was all done with big booms—

and he shot it. He would make suggestions: 'If possible, if you do the following you can get a better transition from here to there,' and so forth. I have to say, he did it with loving care. It took us three weeks to rehearse and prepare the number, and three or four days to shoot. What emerged is a number that has gotten me a tremendous amount of attention, and the irony is still that it was something I had no intention of doing."*

DONEN ALSO pressed Kidd into service for what the director described as "this lament that the fellows sing, 'I'm a Lonesome Polecat.' They're lying in the bunkhouse at night." Kidd felt "the song had a wonderful beat to it," but averred, "I don't think there's much we can do having them lying in a bunkhouse. It's kind of limiting."

"What else would you like to do?" asked Donen.

Kidd believed that, given such a beat, "maybe if they were out in the woods, they could still convey this same longing, because they feel an emptiness, being cut off from the girls." He suggested accentuating the beat by presenting the brothers cutting wood in time to the music. Kidd demonstrated by singing for Donen, "I'm . . . *boom!* . . . just a lonesome polecat . . . *boom!*" Perhaps, too, Kidd said, on the "*boom!*"s the brothers might hammer some pickaxes into tree stumps. "At the same time they're doing this movement, maybe their thoughts could be not on the job they're doing but off in the distance, on the girls. Their eyes must never meet one another's."

Donen's verbal reaction, according to Kidd, was, "Fine. Good. Do it that way." Kidd had one more suggestion, a minute point but essential. Because the song was a dreamy lament, the thoughts of the boys should not be interrupted, therefore Donen should not allow for a single cut throughout the course of "Lonesome Polecat." The director would have to shoot it in one take.

"We can at least try it that way," said Donen, who warned Kidd, "Ordinarily you'd never do it. We'd cover ourselves with several different shots."

* "High impact per se is not Mr. Kidd's style," perceived Anna Kisselgoff in the *New York Times* on March 18, 1994, as she examined a Lincoln Center retrospective of Kidd's cinematic work. "His use of energy boasts the virtue of subtlety." The dance critic similarly pointed out: "The Kidd touch [with its] warm human insight . . . was always recognizable [and] epitomized by a lovesick male clan going courting with an acrobatic challenge dance in *Seven Brides for Seven Brothers*."

"It was about a five-minute number,"* said Kidd. "We started shooting it, and two minutes in, somebody made a mistake." Donen yelled, "Cut," and the take began again. "Three minutes later," said Kidd, "somebody else goofed." Another take. This time, "Camera movement was off," cried the operator. "I'm sorry." "Cut," said Donen. "Back to the beginning."

"By lunchtime," said Kidd, "we were getting calls from the front office, which used to keep tabs on what was happening on the sound-stages, down to the last second. Stanley came over and told me, 'They're complaining. They say we've been shooting all morning and haven't got a shot yet.' " Kidd saw his grand scheme for a single take about to evaporate into the smog over Culver City. "What do you want to do?" he asked Donen, whose answer was to break for lunch. "Afterward," the director told Kidd, "we'll try it twice more. If we don't get it by then, we'll have to slice the scene up into shots."

"First take after lunch," said Kidd, "we got it, and that's the take that's in the movie. It may seem esoteric, an unnecessary effort, even, but I think it has a subliminal effect on the mood of the number."

FOR ALL the praise Donen has received over the years for cracking the vast frontier of CinemaScope—*Seven Brides for Seven Brothers* was Metro's early foray into the process—the director was averse to it. "CinemaScope was clumsy, with an odd, too exaggerated shape," he said. "What we called the Academy aperture, which was square, was a beautiful shape for movies."†

In the early fifties, CinemaScope was Fox chief Darryl Zanuck's great wide hope for combating small-screen television. Through the use of an anamorphic lens, movie cameras squeezed the image during shooting, and a projector unsqueezed it for exhibition. CinemaScope allowed movies to expand their width doubly.

"I never thought it was a good idea," said Donen. "It was too wide and too low, like Japanese theaters. The only thing that made Cinema-Scope effective was that back then you used to have balconies in movie theaters. If you sat in the back row of the orchestra, you used to have what was called 'balcony cutoff,' which meant you could see only so high on the screen. Therefore, the idea of making the screen wider worked beautifully in theaters with a balcony."

* Three minutes, ten seconds.
† The Academy Standard aspect ratio, established in 1906, was 1.33:1. CinemaScope's was 2.35:1.

As had been the case with sound, as well as with Technicolor in the forties, M-G-M was tentative in adopting any new process. Zanuck initiated CinemaScope with *The Robe* in the fall of 1953, and the profitable result was that the Fox biblical spectacle was to anamorphic lenses what Warners' *The Jazz Singer* had earlier been to Vitaphone. Hoping to emulate such success, M-G-M put into production four wide-screen pictures, *Knights of the Round Table*, Mervyn LeRoy's remake of the musical *Rose Marie*, *Seven Brides*, and *Brigadoon*.

"There were three great remarks attributed to CinemaScope," said Donen. "When Darryl Zanuck was running some test of it, he called in [the screenwriter] Nunnally Johnson and said, 'I want you to see this new process you'll be writing for.' After Nunnally saw it, he said, 'Well, what do you want me to do—put the paper in the typewriter sideways?' When it was shown to George Stevens, he said, 'I think it's wonderful for commencement photographs.' Then Art Buchwald saw *The Robe*. Asked what he thought of it, he said, 'I thought it was longer than it was wide.' "

"It was a pain," Michael Kidd remembered of CinemaScope. "I had to stage the dances one way, then turn around, stage them again, and squeeze them."

"Fox's idea was to dupe their pictures down, to show in those theaters that weren't equipped with CinemaScope," said Donen. "M-G-M wouldn't hear of it. M-G-M wanted all their prints pristine and wouldn't allow their movies to be shown as dupes." Faced with such a technical mandate, "when we made *Seven Brides*," said Donen, "we essentially had to make two movies, one in CinemaScope and one without it. I had to shoot and cut everything twice—restage scenes, put in a different set of marks, light it differently, loop it. We had two cutting rooms going, and it cost the studio another $500,000, which was a lot for then."

When it came to staging for CinemaScope, Donen said, "It was okay for some scenes, where you had seven or fourteen people in a wide shot, but when you had only one character or two, it was hopeless." The prime example of such futility was Jane Powell's first solo, "Wonderful, Wonderful Day," which shows off a painted meadow to its worst advantage.

"The backdrops always hurt the picture," said Donen, "less when it came out than now, because then people were used to seeing pictures shot in studios. But it breaks my heart to look at the picture. I was also denied the chance to stage 'Spring, Spring, Spring' the way I wanted. I saw it as a huge number, as impressive as 'Barn Raising.' I wanted to show stop action of a chicken coming out of an egg, fish spawning, snow melting and coming down the mountainside, something very surrealistic. The three days we ended up spending on the number did not even come close to what I wanted."

"The studio was pouring all this money into *Brigadoon* and felt it couldn't afford to do two musical extravaganzas at once,"* recalled Jane Powell. *Rose Marie* was allowed the luxury of going on location in the Canadian woods at the same time *Seven Brides* went into production, and the remake proved a disaster, artistically and commercially, not that the Jeanette MacDonald–Nelson Eddy original was ever anything to sing about. "And of course," said Powell, "*Seven Brides* was a big hit, a real sleeper, and *Brigadoon* seemed to disappear."

"The studio didn't want to distribute *Seven Brides for Seven Brothers*," said Michael Kidd, as another example of the muddled thinking pervading the Schary regime. "They thought it was a B musical. Suddenly, though, the distributors started calling and saying, 'Hey, people are crazy about this movie.' The studio found it had a hit on its hands and started a whole new advertising campaign and reopened it all over."

Seven Brides turned into one of the year's top money earners and won an Oscar for Best Score, but, sexual politics aside, as well as, for a completely different reason, "Barn Dance," some of it does have trouble standing the test of time. Donen was right: the obvious employment of false backdrops and the use of doubles in the establishing location long shots hamper the picture; even the Act III avalanche looks distractingly second-unit,† especially when one remembers how superbly M-G-M technicians pulled off disaster sequences in 1936 and '37—the earthquake in *San Francisco* and the descent of the locusts in *The Good Earth*. But that is no reason to sidestep it or, less understandable, let *Seven Brides for Seven Brothers* disappear, in any form. The flat version, which Donen shot and which was seldom used in theaters or, as would have made sense, for television screenings and videocassette, has been steadily disintegrating in the vault, and in 1993, a source in the Turner Library, which in 1986 acquired all M-G-M titles, said that the already damaged negative was deteriorating quickly and there were no plans to restore it.

On a more positive note, when London's Museum of the Moving Image opened in 1988, it presented as part of its permanent collection a display devoted to Hollywood's passion for wide screen in the fifties and

---

* Another bargain device Donen had to tolerate was the use of Ansco color, a cheaper and less lustrous process than Technicolor.

† In fact, Donen himself shot the avalanche, employing miniatures. He has also noticed the sequence showing up in other, subsequent pictures.

sixties. The exhibit featured one continually running film clip and one clip only: the "Barn Raising" dance from *Seven Brides for Seven Brothers.*

It was here, before a passing parade of spectators with their eyes glued to the oversize screen, that Michael Kidd's "wonderfully prancy" choreography (according to the original *Time* review) and Donen's direction, which "leaves the picture looking as though it just happened" (*Time* again) survived, beautifully intact.

Chapter 8

"I Would Have Run from That Picture"

W HEN YOU look at *Funny Face*," instructed Kay Thompson, "the person I want you to see is Roger Edens. That movie really is Roger." Asked about the Edens-Donen collaboration that preceded *Funny Face*, the purported story of Sigmund Romberg called *Deep in My Heart*, Thompson replied obliquely, "Oh, that. I don't know. I think it was some kind of another life."

When it came to musical biographies, Metro had perfected its recipe for whitewash as well as had Warner Bros., which, in the forties especially, had become the official home to the genre, just as it had been to the pulp-style gangster film in the thirties. In Warners' *Night and Day*, for instance, directed in 1946 by that jack-of-all-genres* Michael Curtiz, Cary Grant portrayed Cole Porter as a glamorous workaholic whose devotion to the next stage hit hampered his marriage to his attention-starved socialite wife; in reality, Linda and Cole Porter lived a hot-and-cold-running marriage of convenience. Not that the Porter biopic should be singled out for criticism. It was simply born out of the success of the previous summer's *Rhapsody in Blue*, directed by Irving Rapper. Despite the portentous if obvious title, the picture depicted George Gershwin, played by a wooden Robert Alda, not as the vainglorious, complex prodigy he was, but as a vague shadow who happened to have great music tumble out of him before he collapsed and died young.

In the 1980s, Martin Scorsese made noises about bringing the true Gershwin story to the screen, though the hindrances he would encounter were the same ones Hollywood faced in the forties and fifties—that is, how to get around a composer's or his survivors' iron grip on music rights.

---

* From *Casablanca* to *White Christmas*.

This best of all explains Hollywood's long infatuation with fatuous musical biographies, in which these giant men of music live for decades, produce hit after hit, yet the only conflict they must surmount involves that of a distant stepniece. Witness Warners' *Yankee Doodle Dandy* (Michael Curtiz, 1942), a much loved musical, that owed as much to the life of George M. Cohan as it did to that of George Washington Carver. Fox's 1952 *Stars and Stripes Forever* (Henry Koster) skirted its subject entirely, not because John Philip Sousa housed any skeletons in his closet but, one must presume, because his life was so dull. The scenario focused instead on some secondary horn player in the Sousa band, played by a handsome young Robert Wagner, who, to lend weepy drama to the tale, loses a leg in battle.

Surprisingly, Metro's *Deep in My Heart,* produced by Roger Edens as his first effort in that capacity, and directed by Donen, takes a similar roundabout course in dealing with Sigmund Romberg, the Viennese émigré credited with turning his homeland's operettas into a populist American theatrical form. The film follows the same sketchy biographical formula that comprised Metro's lavishly dressed but substantively naked composers series, in which the life of the musician at hand was used merely as an atrophied skeleton on which to hang theatrical musical numbers culled from the composer's formidable war chest. In 1946, Jerome Kern (as morosely played by Robert Walker) received this treatment in *Till the Clouds Roll By;* in 1948, *Words and Music* did the same for Richard Rodgers and Lorenz Hart (Tom Drake and Mickey Rooney), telling of their Broadway and London successes until Hart dies as a result of unrequited love for a nightclub singer (played by Betty Garrett); in 1950, *Three Little Words,* about Bert Kalmar and Harry Ruby (Fred Astaire and Red Skelton), at least made some attempt to integrate musical numbers into their everyday lives, possibly because this team's output hardly rivaled that of Kern or Rodgers and Hart.

It was Arthur Freed who produced *Till the Clouds Roll By* and *Words and Music* (Jack Cummings was responsible for *Three Little Words*), and certainly Romberg had a history at M-G-M. Between 1935 and 1940, the studio made the most of his operettas—as well as those by Victor Herbert and Rudolf Friml—by tossing out their silly books but retaining their waltzes and marches for Jeanette MacDonald and Nelson Eddy, combining New World screen prose with idealized Old World romance. The results were the box office successes *Naughty Marietta* (1935), *Rose Marie* (1936), *Maytime* (1937), *Sweethearts* (1939), and *New Moon* (1940), all in the pre-Freed era and all bearing the unmistakable heavy mark of Mayer, not the later sophisticated, freewheeling artistic stamp of Freed.

"Louis B. Mayer loved Arthur Freed, for whatever reasons," said Donen, "maybe because Arthur loved Louis B. Mayer." As Donen also frequently noted, "Arthur was always interested in something new, even if he seldom knew how to go about getting it." In the case of *Deep in My Heart,* he must have tried reaching for it by turning the project over to Edens.

The movie began under Freed, who, wanting to give his second in command a chance of his own, assigned the property to Edens, largely because composer biographies were a secured success. "I don't think Roger had any more affinity for Sigmund Romberg than I," admitted Donen, "and I would have run from that picture like crazy except for Roger. I told him I would direct anything for him."

In 1951, when the project was still carrying Freed's imprimatur, it was announced that *The Romberg Story,* as it was called, would be based on a script by Joseph Fields and directed by Charles Walters. Kurt Kasznar was mentioned as the lead, though Donen had no recollection of such casting and no regret over who eventually ended up in the role. Romberg, ironically, died that very year, leaving Freed to consider a new direction for the endeavor. That is how it landed with Edens. "I think a lot of it had to do with Roger's love for that singer," said Kay Thompson, referring to the Wagnerian soprano Helen Traubel, a star with the Metropolitan Opera.

As Thompson was too kind to point out, love can be blind. Traubel was cast as Anna Mueller, a landsman of Romberg's who runs a Second Avenue café and shares equal screen time with the main character. Yet more bewildering than having so immobile a personality as Traubel on-camera is how a man with Edens's reputation for taste could settle for scenarist Leonard Spiegelgass's hoary script:

ROMBERG: "Do you find it strange that a Viennese should
   write love songs for America?"

DOROTHY (Merle Oberon): "Love is love, whether it's in *Mittel
   Europa* or in America."

ROMBERG: ". . . When a woman is right, who can be righter?"

AS GLEANED from the film, Romberg, who banged out stage hits commissioned by the Brothers Shubert from the teens to the forties, was, like his younger contemporary Cole Porter, exclusively devoted to his art; only, unlike the sybaritic tunesmith from Peru, Indiana, the Viennese was completely asexual. For female companionship he relied on a mother figure (Traubel) and a sister substitute, in the form of the real-life librettist-lyricist Dorothy Donnelly (Merle Oberon, elegant but lifeless). Late in life, "Rommy," as he is affectionately called, even by his male colleagues, falls for a gorgeous blonde, simply because she is a gorgeous blonde, and the less interest she displays in him, the more actively he pursues her. (The blonde is Doe Avedon, the by then former first wife of the photographer Richard Avedon.) Once their mouse-and-cat game ends and they marry, she contentedly lives in the shadow of his "important" work.

As for Romberg, he is played with such unnerving chipperness by José Ferrer, who was deemed musical by both Donen and Edens, as to set the viewer's teeth on edge. The actor, still fresh from his Best Actor Oscar for *Cyrano de Bergerac* and another nomination for *Moulin Rouge,* "was the hottest thing going at the time," said an appreciative Donen. "Roger and I thought we'd burst when we got him."

The picture was a hit in its time. All twenty-eight Metro soundstages were simultaneously employed for it during production, and the talent roll included Howard Keel, Tony Martin, Vic Damone, and Jane Powell. Rosemary Clooney, on loan-out from Paramount, sang "Mr. and Mrs." as a stage duet with Ferrer, who was her offscreen husband. With a Romberg number cropping up in the picture at an average of every eight minutes, it could hardly be said that the composer's output was given short shrift, though his place in American musical history was never afforded any perspective beyond the highly exorbitant claim that his songs "taught America how to love." Of the sixteen numbers in *Deep in My Heart,* Donen thinks there are three good ones. There are actually four, but the last is simply a curiosity, thanks to Ferrer. By far the sexiest—in the picture or perhaps in any film of its time—is a number from *The Desert Song,* performed by Cyd Charisse and James Mitchell, "an Agnes de Mille–type dancer," said Charisse. "The number was laid out by Gene Loring, the choreographer, Jimmy, and myself, with Roger at the piano. It was a very sensuous piece, which we were able to get away with because we were dancing it. In those days, even with the Breen Office so strict, you could get away with an awful lot, such as the way you dressed, so long as you were dancing." Mitchell, in his body-tight leotard, and Charisse, in her skirt that parts clear to the waist, all but simulate coitus.

Gene Kelly performs for the first and only time on-screen with his younger (and less photogenic) brother Fred, a specialty rapid ragtime number called "I Love to Go Swimmin' with Wimmen." The two tap dancers share a strong family resemblance, and the number was said to

Wagnerian soprano Helen Traubel and a toothy, oddly cast José Ferrer, as Sigmund Romberg, in Donen's and Roger Edens's uncharacteristically conventional *Deep in My Heart* (1954)

reflect their vaudeville numbers from the thirties. It is done as a gay nineties bathing beauty routine, with the line of chorines stripping the Kellys of their boaters and pin-striped suits, down to their bathing knickers, so together they can take an athletic plunge into the stage-set ocean.

Ann Miller Charlestons and black bottoms against a John Held–like roaring twenties set, to the song "It," based on romantic novelist Elinor Glyn's notion of what every girl should have. Miller has it in spades, backed up by a raccoon-coat-sporting collegiate chorus.

The one number that is integrated into the story, aside from some treacly arias courtesy of Traubel—toward the end she shamelessly sings "Auf Wiedersehen" to the dying Oberon*—is a tour de force for Ferrer and Edens, who arranged the musical collage. It is called "Jazzadoo" and is a condensed preview of the (fictitious) show Romberg is writing. Ferrer performs it inside his rented resort cabin in the mountains, and his audi-

---

* Thus thrusting Romberg into a new partnership, with Oscar Hammerstein II, and toward a far less operatic and more popular style.

ence consists of his producer, his lyricist and his arranger, and his new girlfriend and her disapproving mother. No theatrical trick is overlooked, with the number incorporating everything from Donald O'Connor–style leaping—in this case, out the window of the cabin—to Jolson's "Mammy"-style singing, replete with blackface. Ferrer is hypnotic, moving too breathlessly to be assessed adequately, and Donen sets him up by not setting him up at all, letting him perform for the camera front and center.

All in all, it is one of the most curious moments ever captured on film.

Chapter 9

"It Was Over"

I T W A S an unusual picture, a dark picture," said Betty Comden, referring to the 1955 *It's Always Fair Weather*, a CinemaScope musical satire
of Madison Avenue, television, fifties American values, and long-
term friendships—an element that also unexpectedly and immeasurably
tempered the atmosphere behind the scenes.

"We were there for the end of it," said Adolph Green.

"We usually weren't around for the shooting of any of our pictures,
because we would be off-salary by then," explained Comden. "We'd keep
in touch by mail."

It's Always Fair Weather—even its title carried an edge, as if friendship
were not meant to withstand the dark clouds that so well shaded *Singin' in
the Rain*—began as an idea for a stage sequel to *On the Town*. Originally it
was to be a look into the lives of the three sailors ten years later.

"One day we casually mentioned this to Gene," said Comden, "who
insisted we turn it into a—"

"He grabbed us by the collars," said Green.

"He was very insistent, and we relented," said Betty Comden. "We're
very proud of the picture."

I T W A S not only the three sailors who had changed since *On the Town;* so
had the parties responsible for its movie success. Besides their ongoing
film work, Comden and Green became well-established Broadway librett-
tists and doctors—performing a rescue mission on no less than *Peter Pan,*
which starred Mary Martin. The motion picture career of Jules Munshin,
on the other hand, shrank to some comic supporting roles, while Frank
Sinatra's had received a considerable boost once Harry Cohn was per-

suaded to cast him in Fred Zinnemann's adaptation of the James Jones wartime novel *From Here to Eternity.* "I forget if at the time of *It's Always Fair Weather* Frank was up or down," said Donen. "He was up and down so many times, it was hard to keep track." Donen had successfully gone solo, and his two Kelly-less efforts for the studio immediately prior to *It's Always Fair Weather* resulted in one smash, *Seven Brides for Seven Brothers,* and one solid hit, *Deep in My Heart.* Kelly's career, though, was ebbing; *Brigadoon,* emasculated by its papier-mâché-and-paint backdrops, combined with director Minnelli's illiteracy with CinemaScope, returned only a modest profit; Kelly's two war dramas, *The Devil Makes Three* and *Crest of the Wave* (titled *Seagulls over Sorrento* in England), quickly disappeared from distribution; and M-G-M had no idea what to make of or to do with his *Invitation to the Dance.*

"*It's Always Fair Weather* marked the end of the Arthur Freed–Gene Kelly road that began in 1942," recorded Gerald Mast. "The Oscar for the ballet of *An American in Paris* went to Kelly's head instead of to his feet. No one could talk to him—and even his pal, Stanley Donen, stopped."

"I didn't want to do the picture," said Donen—a sentiment he had expressed on several previous occasions, "but I said I'd do it and I did it." As he told Freed's biographer Hugh Fordin, "I didn't really want to co-direct another picture with Kelly at that point. We didn't get on very well and, for that matter, Gene didn't get on very well with anybody."

"It was made when the era of musicals was over, at least at M-G-M," said Adolph Green.

"It *was* over," said Betty Comden. "I don't think Gene was quite the star he was. He wasn't that popular anymore, and neither were musicals."

Neither was M-G-M, not with its stockholders, anyway; within a year, Dore Schary would be replaced in the top spot by the producer Sol Siegel, whose own regime would be short-lived. The studio once known for its lush production values now faced uncharacteristic austerity cuts, and these were reflected in its movies—in their costumes, their sets, their orchestral sounds, their general style. Arthur Freed took the downswing as Arthur Freed would, by focusing his attention elsewhere, in this case on his orchid collection at home. This left others accountable for the changes in budgets, protocol, and other matters as they affected the studio and the Freed Unit.

"The way it was in the beginning," said Betty Comden, "when we'd write, we'd do sections of the picture and then take them in to Arthur to read. As time went by, and Dore Schary was in charge—"

"Very much," interjected Green.

"It wasn't Arthur who had the final word anymore," said Comden.

"Arthur was answerable to Dore Schary the way he hadn't been with Louis B.," said Green.

"Well, Louis B. and Arthur had been old friends," Comden said.

"Dore Schary was not a very civilized man," insisted Green.

"It was a new role for Arthur," said Comden, shifting the subject, "answering to someone."

Comden and Green wrote the book and lyrics to *It's Always Fair Weather,* with André Previn composing and arranging the music.* Their story begins with three army buddies in 1945. When peace is declared—right after the first number—the pals share one final drink in New York before resuming their civilian lives and pledging to meet again ten years to the day at the same bar. The plot of *Fair Weather* essentially follows what happens to them in the course of their one-day reunion spree in New York, yet rather than carefree Gabey, Chip, and Ozzie, *Fair Weather*'s Doug, Ted, and Angelo (Angie) reveal a sour if more realistic picture of how people's lives can turn out.

Kelly plays Ted, who fancied himself becoming Adlai Stevenson after the war. But the ten years have turned him into Joey Evans, a two-bit gambler and fight manager. Dan Dailey plays Doug—in his head, Pablo Picasso; in reality, an ulcerous, dipsomaniacal ad exec out of Chicago. Michael Kidd plays Angie, whose sights were set on becoming James Beard. Instead he evolves into the Chef Boyardee of his own hamburger joint in Schenectady, albeit one pretentiously called The Cordon Bleu.

Dan Dailey and Cyd Charisse work for the same advertising firm, which handles the live television program *Midnight with Madeline,* a combination variety program, amateur hour, and *This Is Your Life.* Madeline, so sweet on the outside that she could have sent Lenny Bruce into insulin shock, is a total bitch. Always seeking a ratings-generating gimmick, Madeline (Dolores Gray) intends to reunite Ted, Doug, and Angie live on

---

* Filming began August 23, 1954, and finished January 15, 1955. During this same time, Frank Sinatra was on another M-G-M soundstage, shooting *High Society,* produced by and costarring Bing Crosby and directed by Charles Walters. One day Adolph Green suggested to Previn that they offer Sinatra one of the ballads they'd written for *It's Always Fair Weather,* for him to record as a single. When they got to the *High Society* stage, however, the only performer they found was Sidney Blackmer, a Shakespearean who was playing the Grace Kelly character's father. Rather than retreat, Green suggested to Previn that they ask Blackmer if he'd be interested in recording their song.

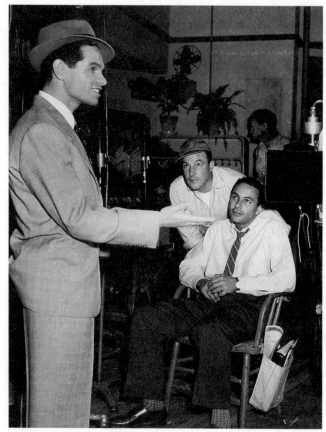

Michael Kidd, whose solo "Jack and the Space Giants" never
made it to release, on the set of *It's Always Fair Weather* (1955),
Donen's and Kelly's final collaboration

the air, not knowing that the former buddies had lunched together earlier
that day and immediately concluded: (a) they no longer had anything in
common, and (b) they hated each other.

The situation becomes neatly interwoven when Ted (Kelly) takes a
shine to Charisse, which leaves him in tow until showtime, while Angie
(Kidd), starstruck over Madeline, stalls his return to his wife, Connie, and
their children in Schenectady.

Charisse, backed by a troupe of hormonally active prizefighters in
training, performs a number in a gym, "Baby, You Knock Me Out!" a
musicalization of the moment in a play or movie when the intellectual
heroine (à la *Pal Joey*'s Melba, the journalist) lets down her hair, removes
her eyeglasses, and reveals herself for the sexy creature she "really" is.

Charisse, whose character spouts Shakespeare, cannot let down her hair, as she is constrained by a fifties bob. In lieu of slipping off eyeglasses, she unfastens her skirt and reveals her legs. They are breathtaking in Cinema-Scope.

"She was always beautiful," said Gwen Verdon, who knew Charisse from their childhood dancing classes, which they attended with Marge Belcher (later Champion). "I was about seven and Cyd was eight or nine, about a year or two older than the rest of us, and she was gorgeous to look at," remembered Verdon. "She had blue-black hair that was cut straight, Dutch-boy style, and she had on this black page outfit, which means that it was solid down the front and back, with a tie—not like the tutu the rest of us all had to wear. And she didn't have matching bloomers like we did, either. Her underwear was pink."

Verdon claimed that the entire class was "in awe of her beauty and appalled by her underwear." Charisse was also a better dancer than Verdon, Belcher, or the others, said Verdon, so she soon graduated to another school. "Cyd's name back then, by the way, wasn't Cyd Charisse," Verdon volunteered. "It was Rose Finklestein."

Contrary to Verdon's claim, a check of several record books confirms that Cyd Charisse's original name was Tula Ellice Finklea, a fact in black and white that Verdon nonetheless refuses to accept.

"I'm sure it's Rose Finklestein," reiterated Verdon. "Try asking should you ever meet her."

In *It's Always Fair Weather,* Charisse was finally permitted to perform book portions for Donen, as opposed to the isolated dance routines to which she was normally confined, though she was frequently a better dancer than actress. After the dance number in the gym, however, her character softens and she is much pleasanter to watch in the straight scenes.

As for her relationship with Donen, which she described in 1993, Charisse found his direction "easy to follow, distinct, and simplified. Stanley was one of the few directors I worked for who could tell you exactly what he wanted. Some were full of their own problems and inhibitions, or could only give me something like, 'Let's have a good one, honey,' and that would be the extent of it. Stanley would come over, tell what he wanted, and then, usually, we'd have a laugh."

"I try to stand back from telling actors a lot," said Donen. "People like to discover things for themselves. With most actors, a raised eyebrow or a slow response to what they've just done is enough to send them into a tailspin. Actors tend to be sensitive by nature and can pick up what a director wants. A few of them, of course, wish to be told. Some want to be bludgeoned. But the majority don't want to hear too much."

THOUGH IT IS Kelly who hogs the screen time, the picture is all but stolen by Dan Dailey, thanks to a patter number—"Situation-wise"—set during a party thrown by his windbag employer. The Dailey character, in a martini-driven stupor (the drinking was instigated by his career frustrations), lampoons Madison Avenue jargon and the people who speak it:*

> Situation-wise
> Saturation-wise
> Competition-wise
> Sales resistance-wise
> Television-wise
> Meathead-wise
> Fatso-wise
> Wise-wise

While Michael Kidd remained circumspect about his codirector and costar Gene Kelly, he considered Dan Dailey, who had been a musical semistar at Fox, "a very gifted performer who never got his just respect. He was a good hoofer and a good actor. I use the word 'hoofer' because he wasn't an all-around dancer, but he was a good song-and-dance man. I think he was very frustrated that he was never given the opportunities to do the things he really could do.† In that era, it was Gene Kelly who became the big star, not Dan, and Dan was a much better actor than Gene Kelly. You never for a moment felt any sincerity in Gene Kelly, in anything he did. When he played an emotional scene, it was feigned emotion. It wasn't real emotion."

"Early in the movie," recalled Donen, referring to the first number with Kelly, Kidd, and Dailey, "March! March!," set against a battlefield background (and shot in Hollywood's Bronson Canyon Quarry), "Gene said to Michael, 'You just slump against this army tank here.' Michael said,

---

* In the script to their 1960 *The Apartment,* Billy Wilder and I. A. L. Diamond do the same, lingo-wise.

† In his 1991 memoir, André Previn told of Dailey's showing up to a press screening of *It's Always Fair Weather* dressed in women's clothing. "That is absolutely one hundred percent not true," said Donen. "He'd never do such a thing. That would have ended his career. Now, he was drunk a lot, but he never showed up in a dress."

Farewell to an era: Michael Kidd, Cyd Charisse, Gene Kelly, Dan Dailey, 1955

'I don't know if I can do that, it's so hard.' Gene shouted, *'Just do it.'* So Michael said, 'Well, can I fluff it up a little?' "

"They had a lot of trouble at the beginning of the picture," said Betty Comden, "so Adolph and I came out and they ran the first few reels for us."

"The atmosphere from day one was very tense," said Donen, "and nobody was speaking to anybody."

According to Betty Comden, the tension was due to some required restructuring of the material. "A lot of decisions had to be made with the routines," she said, "to reorganize them, to get them to work."

"They took out a number Michael Kidd was in," said Green, referring to the dancer's ten-minute solo, "Jack and the Space Giants," in which the Kidd character dances with *children.* It was Kelly who insisted that the song be cut, without benefit of a public preview, because, according to Kelly, "It didn't come across." Donen disagreed, saying, "It was good enough to stay in the picture," an opinion shared by André Previn, who credited the number's excision to what he termed "intramovie jealousy."

"A number with Cyd and Gene was also cut," said Comden.

"The lovers didn't get to have a duet," said Green, shrugging. "Who ever heard of a musical where the lovers don't sing a duet?"

"It was a song called 'Love Is Nothing but a Racket,' " said Comden. Records show that it was filmed, though not at the tempo at which it was conceived. Kelly decided it should be not a ballad but a showpiece. After it was rearranged, staged, and shot, the number was cut.

The climax of the film takes place during Madeline's program, when mobsters come to kill the Kelly character after he has knocked out his own fighter, whom they had paid to throw an upcoming bout. It's at this point that: (a) Donen's CinemaScope compositions are shown to their best advantage, with TV monitors and an in-studio audience decorating the wide interior landscape; and (b) the former army buddies realize their devotion to one another, join forces, and assist their former comrade in arms in thwarting the goons.

"This was the big scene Gene was talking about throughout the shooting, ad nauseam," said Donen. "It's all we heard about for ten weeks, until we were all sick of hearing about it." Kelly kept waxing platitudinous about the scene, and how it symbolized the outpouring of love and devotion that the other two men felt for his character, Ted. When it came time to set up the scene, Kelly was again espousing lofty homilies about motives and meanings. Kidd asked him what he should say when he looks over and finds that one of the mobsters has clobbered his beloved friend. "And Gene," said Donen, "told Michael, 'You look at me and you say, "Ted!" ' "

After all that buildup, Kidd was to be allowed but a single short expletive to convey his love?

Kidd asked Kelly, "Can I spell it?"

"MANY TIMES I thought of quitting, and I almost did," said Donen. "Codirecting, as I've said, is a nightmare. Co-anything is a nightmare— cowriting, for instance. But codirecting is worse, because when you co-direct, you're doing it in front of a crowd of people, so you have to find a way to accommodate the situation. It's very unpleasant and very difficult. To work with somebody, particularly somebody who is so concerned with his image, was impossible. But I said I'd do it, so I did it, only it was a nightmare, from beginning to end."

When it ended, it ended. Donen never worked with Gene Kelly again. For that matter, but for other reasons, neither did he again work with or for Arthur Freed, M-G-M, or Comden and Green. As for the relationship with Kelly, he said in 1992, "I'm grateful to him, but I paid back the debt, ten times over. And he got his money's worth out of me."

It's Always Fair Weather received positive reviews in New York—"an adult and witty musical," said the *Herald Tribune*—but did little business, especially on the West Coast, where Comden and Green personally complained to Dore Schary about his lax attention to its distribution. Kelly actually blamed the picture itself, though in a nebulous manner. "We blew it," he said in 1991.

Donen credited audience disinterest to the movie's satirical approach, quoting the Goldwynism "Satire is comedy where no one laughs." The picture's lack of public appeal sent out an alarm that, perhaps, the musical was dying, or as M-G-M publicity director Howard Dietz wrote to Arthur Freed: "When a picture is as good as *It's Always Fair Weather*, you have cause for great worry, as you say to yourself, 'What can I make that will satisfy them?' If you make corn they call it corn and don't go, and if you make non-corn, they call it satire and maybe don't go also. I guess you just have to produce *White Christmas* in various shades—*Red Christmas, Green Christmas,* and right down through the spectrum."

THOUGH IT WAS an original musical, *It's Always Fair Weather* employed a device that would show up in later screen adaptations of Broadway smashes (*My Fair Lady* being a prime example): holding after the finale of a number long enough for the audience to applaud.* Distracting as this is, there are two numbers in *It's Always Fair Weather* that remain among Donen's favorites. One is Kelly's solo on roller skates—"I Like Myself"— before an appreciative crowd that cheers him on. "Singin' in the Rain" it isn't, and the bleached-out look of the New York street set is emphasized by its CinemaScope canvas, but it does capture the star-performer bravura that the best of the M-G-M movie musicals aimed for. Interesting, too, is that its lyrics speak of self-appreciation and reform; perhaps the Joey Evans heel was at last meant to be laid to rest.

The second number was "I Shouldn't Have Come," a parody of personal impressions during a reunion, set to "The Blue Danube" waltz. In

---

* The Previn-Comden-Green score is largely undistinguished, though "Time for Parting," a melancholy lament sung by an offscreen choir as the friends disperse one final time smacks strongly of the Bernstein-Comden-Green "Some Other Time," the stage finale to *On the Town*.

staging these strange interludes for the camera, Donen divides the screen into a triptych, with each buddy delivering a separate soliloquy lamenting his decision to show up and meet his former pals, and divulging what he thinks of them today. The number is set in what is meant to be the most chic restaurant in New York and was no doubt a scene with which many a person could identify, for who in a lifetime has not at some point been similarly and as uncomfortably trapped in an unwanted reunion with an intimate from his or her past?

On Tuesday evening, November 12, 1991, Betty Comden, Adolph Green and his wife, the actress Phyllis Newman, Gene Kelly and his wife, Patricia, and Stanley and Pam Donen met for dinner at the restaurant Spago in West Hollywood. As Donen would note afterward, the gathering marked the first time he and Kelly broke bread together since the making of *It's Always Fair Weather,* more than thirty-five years before. The reunion followed a salute at the Academy of Motion Picture Arts and Sciences headquarters that commemorated the fifty-year partnership of Comden and Green. During the tribute, which included speeches, songs, and film clips, Donen told the audience that the collaboration of Comden and Green had already outlasted that of any number of other famous unions: "Gilbert and Sullivan, Hecht and MacArthur, Kaufman and Hart, Rodgers and Hart, Rodgers and Hammerstein, Lerner and Loewe—even Laurel and Hardy." Kelly addressed the crowd too, saying, "I would go anywhere in the world to talk about Betty and Adolph." Of his former collaborator, Kelly, without so much as being asked, offered, "Stanley needed me to grow up with. He came to me when he was a boy of twelve, maybe sixteen. I always wanted to be an actor-choreographer. I needed Stanley in back of the camera." The film clip portion of the evening began with the opening to *On the Town,* and when the three sailors leaped off the ship and sang "New York, New York," the primarily young audience burst into tumultuous applause, and Kelly, though slowed by age, spun around in his seat and shook Donen's hand. Afterward, it was Kelly who extended the dinner invitation.

At Spago, some insight was revealed into the group dynamic as it probably existed over the previous forty-five years. The much discussed Kelly anger had raised its face back at the Academy, just as the tribute was about to begin. Some Kelly fans, clutching posters and lobby cards from his movies, requested his autograph. "I'm late," he barked at them, loud and ferocious enough to send chills through the bones of bystanders. "L-A-T-E," he spelled out with machine-gun rapidity, "late, late, late, late, late, late, late, late, *late, late, late!*"

The stunned bystanders stepped aside.

Dinner conversation at Spago began with discussion of a few desultory topics, most of them musical. Donen said that he had an idea to take one movie producer's turkeys and assemble a compilation he wanted to call *That's Entertainment?* Kelly, however, soon demanded to be the center of attention. Speaking softly at first, the star said that during the course of the evening, when the concluding scene to *Singin' in the Rain* was shown at the Academy, he realized that his former collaborator Donen was not only a "genius" but an "inspired" one. Explaining that the backstage mock-up of Grauman's Chinese Theater forced a tight squeeze on himself, Debbie Reynolds, Jean Hagen, Donald O'Connor, Millard Mitchell, and King Donovan, who played the studio press agent, Kelly said, "Stanley had to make it an unusually tight shot in this narrow little space. And then—remember, Stanley?—the press agent farted."

It was then that all heads at the table turned to Kelly.

"Who did *what?*" asked Phyllis Newman, biting her lip.

"The press agent," repeated Kelly. "He farted."

"Did he?" said Adolph Green.

"Yeah, sure," replied Kelly. "He farted. Oh, it was a big one."

Betty Comden put down her drink. "Oh, really?" she said.

"The poor son of a bitch was embarrassed something awful," explained Kelly.

"This is in the picture?" wondered Adolph Green.

"The fart isn't in the picture," said Kelly. "He farted when we were shooting the scene in the tiny space."

"Oh," said Green. "I see."

"It was at that moment that I recognized Stanley's inspired genius," said Kelly. "Because when the press agent farted, Stanley didn't so much as blink an eye. He just said to the cameraman, 'Keep rolling.' "

Breaking the cautious silence that overcame him from the moment Kelly chose to tell the story, Donen commented offhandedly, "Now that you mention it, Gene, that does sound vaguely familiar."

Chapter 10

"Heaven!"

T HEY CALL it Stanley Donen's *Funny Face*," remarked the film's writer, Leonard Gershe. "I don't know why. It's not the way it was when Hitchcock worked on a picture. Then you knew why it was called a Hitchcock picture."

Not that the scenarist was attempting to diminish Donen's contribution, Gershe said. "He did an excellent job with what he did, but all those touches with the Paris fashion scenes were Roger Edens's. Roger said, 'I want her photographed on the steps of the Louvre, now I want her here, I want her there.'"

Richard Avedon remembered that particular decision as more of a group effort engineered by Gershe, Donen, and himself.

"And those wonderful moments when the frames change color," said Gershe, "that was Dick Avedon. Yes, Stanley brought it to the screen, and I don't want anything taken away from Stanley, but I don't want anything taken away from the other people, either."

Still, whether the director existed as a conduit or the driving force, nothing better defines the Donen style than *Funny Face;* it is elegant, it is alive, it has flow, it has color, it has song and dance, it also has a tidy little ending. Yet even if one wishes to downplay the picture, or simply view it in purely cynical terms (as the coincidental right marriage of material to the director's métier), or else label it a May-December romance that strains to shield the age difference between its lovers by never mentioning it at all (Pauline Kael's gripe), or even blow it off as another silly fifties fantasy about how high fashion might change a drab girl's life (the argument of the anti–Audrey Hepburn/Doris Day/et al. brigade), *Funny Face* manages to lift the spirit. Credit for that success unquestionably goes to Donen and to the film's producer, Roger Edens, for it was he who not only saw the

216

Defining the Donen style: an inviting setting, human joy, color galore, and Audrey Hepburn

Avedon, Astaire, Roger Edens, Donen, before the company moved to Paris

casting possibilities inherent in Gershe's Cinderella story but recognized the opportunity to utilize the Gershwin score, and Paris, and Donen.

"I did *Funny Face* because of Roger," said the director, who was thirty and standing well on his own two feet by the time the movie's wheels started turning. Repeating his early film-career refrain, Donen added, "I would have done anything for Roger." While M-G-M still had both men under contract, their separate clout and the studio's faltering fortunes allowed them to start stretching their muscles elsewhere, artistically and administratively. (The apathetic box office that had greeted *It's Always Fair Weather* was not pinned on Donen.)

Creatively, Edens and Donen shared similar tastes—a standard that Edens had set for Arthur Freed and the unit—but taking the Donen-Edens collaboration to a business level once the two men had secured the services of Audrey Hepburn, it was Donen who wound up being the key link to the chain of events that led to *Funny Face*'s being made, in what was to become a sort of three-card-monte game involving M-G-M, Warner Bros., and Paramount.

* * *

"IT STARTED in England," Leonard Gershe said of his original idea. "I was very young, and I went to do some lyrics for a revue that had music by Richard Addinsell. He was a movie composer and a very good one." (Addinsell had scored *The Passionate Friends,* a picture director David Lean unwillingly inherited when the producer J. Arthur Rank yanked first-time director Ronald Neame off it.) "Addinsell and I wanted to write something together," said Gershe. In attempting to conjure a story line, Gershe remembered the reaction he had received from the writer Clemence Dane—"Winifred was her real name," said Gershe, "Clemence Dane her nom de plume"—when he started telling her about his close friends the photographer Richard Avedon and his wife (since 1944), the model Doe Avedon, the former Dorcas Nowell.

Describing the couple, Gershe said, "Doe really did not want to be a model. Dick pushed her into that. As a result, she was never really a great model, like Suzy Parker, because she was self-conscious about what she was doing. Doe was always much too logical to go into fantasies of being the girl on the beach or any other sort of pose, but in those days, when we were kids around New York, she was the hottest thing going. She was unbelievably beautiful, to the point that I remember an opening of a show. Dick and Doe went darting up the aisle of the theater afterward, and a woman came running after them and said to Doe, 'My name is Irene Selznick. I hope you know that no one was looking at the show tonight, everyone was looking at you. Who are you?'"

Selznick, the daughter of L. B. Mayer and the first wife of David O. Selznick, arranged for her husband to screen-test Doe, though, as Gershe said, "She wasn't interested. It was Dick who wanted all this for her, who wanted her in magazines, to be photographed. He was no fool. When they came back from their honeymoon, Dick had something like three thousand pictures of her. I said, 'What a honeymoon.'"

Once Clemence Dane heard Gershe's tales of the Avedons, her reaction was, "What a glorious idea for a musical—the fashion world, a fashion photographer, and a model who doesn't want to be a model. Why don't you write it?" Gershe did and called it *Wedding Day*. It concerned a photographer, a model who does not want to be a model, and a bossy women's fashion-magazine editor who bows to the photographer's idea to photograph this involuntary novice—whom he ends up marrying by the Act I curtain.

"By this time it was already a couple of years after the war," said Gershe, "and I had to come back to America. I couldn't afford to stay in

England, and Richard Addinsell wasn't particularly interested in coming to America. We split up, and then *Wedding Day* came to the attention of Vernon Duke and Ogden Nash." The two wrote a score for Gershe's book, and the entire package was optioned by the producer Clinton Wilder. "He wanted me to talk to Robert Alton, who was a choreographer and director, to see if he would want to do it," said Gershe. Alton at the time was already working in California, and Gershe traveled west to meet him. "Robert Alton liked the piece very much," remembered Gershe, "and he said he was interested in directing it on the stage, *if* Kay Thompson would play the fashion editor."

AFTER FOUR YEARS of teaching the lot how to sing, Thompson's stint as music coach at M-G-M was set to end in 1947. The year before, Sam Goldwyn borrowed her at his studio to assist on a Danny Kaye musical, *The Kid from Brooklyn.* "I was in that picture for about ten minutes," said Thompson. "Sam had wanted me, I can't imagine why, to come and do the music for what was needed—for Vera-Ellen, for instance—and I went because I just wanted to be around Sam."

Asked to describe the mogul, Thompson confided, "He was very odd, and the whole experience was weird." She said both she and Goldwyn would be standing on the set, only neither one knew what the picture was about. "Finally," said Thompson, "Sam said, 'Do you want to play a milkmaid?' I thought: If ever there was anybody who was a milkmaid, it certainly isn't me." Thompson did play the milkmaid in *The Kid from Brooklyn,* however. "I thought: This man is so sweet to ask, so I said yes, and that was the end of that."

Back at M-G-M, said Thompson, as her contract was drawing to a close, life was not easy. "I had had a headache for two years, I was getting a divorce,* and I thought: I've got to get out of this place. Everything was saying, You're going someplace else."

One of those places was Robert Alton's office at Metro. As Thompson described the conversation, "My contract was up on the seventeenth of May, so Bob and I had a talk, and he said, 'Katie, what are you going to do when you leave here?' I said, 'I don't know, Bob. I suppose I could always sing in a saloon.' "

Alton suggested that she assemble an act.

"What's an act?" Thompson answered.

* From CBS radio producer Bill Spier.

Alton knew that a group of singers, the Williams Brothers, were available and invited Thompson to his house to discuss developing some sort of revue, with these four fellows as her backup group.

"I drove my car across a golf course," said Thompson. "Bob's house back then was right next door to Hitchcock's."

Parking in the front drive, Thompson hopped out and rang Alton's door.

"Where do you think you've been?" snapped Alton, answering the bell with mock anger. "You're five minutes late."

"I'm Eloise," Thompson replied in a little girl's voice. "I'm six."

"Well, I'm Nicholas Aubrey Carstairs, and I'm three and a half," replied Alton. "Get in here and let's dance."

"That started it," said Thompson. Her inner child, Eloise, had lingered in this grown woman's soul for years, but on Alton's doorstep that day, the tot was given a voice for the first time. "She was just waiting to speak to someone who understood her," said Thompson. "Bob was most imaginative and wonderfully creative."

The act opened at Ciro's on October 16, 1947, and a nightclub legend was launched. "Dressed in one of her twenty-five sleek slack-suits, comedienne Kay Thompson stepped into the spotlight, looking like a caricature of the neurotic, world-weary woman of the twenties," *Time* reported. "Bouncing about behind her were four young, mobile-faced Williams brothers, who served as a kind of combination *corps de ballet* and hot choir. Anything went: patter, pantomime, or pratfalls, and *Pauvre Suzette,* a song about a young woman with a Restoration bosom." The magazine credited Thompson and company with wowing the crowds—which included Irving Berlin and nearly every other influential New York and Hollywood name—with their shades of Beatrice Lillie, Agnes de Mille, Noël Coward, and the mime Angna Enters.

"The act was such a big surprise," said Thompson, who ended up touring the country with it well into the next decade. "It was all a matter of going someplace else." So, too, did Eloise go elsewhere, appearing in a bound volume written by Thompson in 1955, though much of that enfant terrible's earlier development took place as part of the backstage banter with the Williams Brothers. "The boys loved talking to Eloise, and they gave themselves names too," remembered Thompson. "Andy was Junior and Melvin, the good and the bad. One helped his mother. The other smoked marijuana."

Per Robert Alton's instructions, Leonard Gershe tracked down Kay Thompson and presented his musical script to her.

"Kay Thompson read *Wedding Day*," said Gershe, "and she would have absolutely nothing to do with it. That was the end of the whole thing."

DISSOLVE TO approximately two years later. "I met a man named Roger Edens, a producer at M-G-M," said Gershe. "He was associated with Arthur Freed but was looking for things of his own." Edens read *Wedding Day* and took to its story and characters (Rick Avery and Jo Lowell, later changed to Dick Avery and Jo Stockton). Edens, though, was not interested in the Ogden Nash–Vernon Duke score and proposed shifting the wedding before intermission to the end of the show. "Roger," said Gershe, "also figured out that the songs from *Funny Face,* plus one that wasn't from *Funny Face,* fit very well into this and could be enhanced with some specialty material."

Funny Face, about a chase for a missing bracelet,* was a 1927 George and Ira Gershwin stage musical that had starred Broadway's preeminent song-and dance team, Fred and Adele Astaire (the Gershwin brothers had previously written the 1924 *Lady, Be Good* for them). The show's songs included the title number, "Let's Kiss and Make Up," "'S Wonderful," and "He Loves and She Loves," which replaced the languid "How Long Has This Been Going On?" (The show also contained the Gershwins' specialty number "The Babbitt and the Bromide," which Gene Kelly and Fred Astaire performed in Arthur Freed's 1946 *Ziegfeld Follies.*) From the Gershwins' 1926 *Oh, Kay!* Edens plucked the rousing "Clap Yo' Hands."

"I rewrote *Wedding Day* according to the specifications that Roger felt would be more suitable to the screen," said Gershe. "We changed the title to *Funny Face,* and then Stanley came in on it."

"It was the story of the ugly duckling who became the beautiful swan," said Donen, who appreciated that he could pinpoint the exact place in the script when the dramatic transformation took place, and as a director he could make the moment a visual stunner.

It would be set inside the Louvre, with his heroine descending the staircase in front of the *Winged Victory.*

"I DON'T KNOW why," said Richard Avedon, tracing his involvement in *Funny Face,* "but as a birthday present, Marlene Dietrich had my horoscope

---

* Robert Benchley, the original book writer, was replaced out of town by Gerard Smith and Fred Thompson (no relation to Kay).

cast by Carroll Righter, and he said that on a certain week I would be receiving information from overseas that would necessitate a change in my life." At the precise time Righter had indicated, Avedon was vacationing in Jamaica. A telegram reached him, via his New York photography studio, that had been sent from Culver City by Roger Edens and Stanley Donen. "The message," said Avedon, "asked if I would consider working on a movie in which Fred Astaire would be playing someone based on me."

Agreeing to such a request, Avedon realized, "would involve many changes, including moving to Hollywood for a while, which was just as the horoscope said." Aside from being impressed by Righter's foresight, Avedon said his overall reaction was: "To be thirty-three years old and have Fred Astaire playing me? I was thrilled. When I was a child, I always wanted to grow up and become Fred Astaire. I wasn't alone in that, right?"*

Astaire claimed that he first learned about the picture at a cocktail party in the home of Clifton Webb. He was set to star as an inebriated father in a period comedy for Paramount, *Papa's Delicate Condition* (Jackie Gleason eventually made the picture, in 1963), when Roger Edens approached and asked, "What are you doing?" Whatever it was, Edens told Astaire, he should get it postponed; he and Stanley Donen could offer him something better.

For the role of the timid model, said Gershe, "it was Roger's idea to cast Carol Haney, who had a big hit in New York doing the 'Steam Heat' number in *The Pajama Game*." Describing her as "a pixieish, funny-looking girl, who really would have been awfully hard to believe as a model," Gershe said, "it came to the point that M-G-M was going to shelve the whole thing because Carol Haney wasn't big enough to build a picture around."

Before such a decision was handed down, as indicated by M-G-M records of the time, the name of Cyd Charisse cropped up and the dancer was considered. "If that's true," Charisse said in 1993, "I was certainly never made aware of it, but I would have loved to have done the picture."

Then Gershe happened upon "an interview in a movie magazine about Audrey Hepburn, and it said that she had been in musicals in London before she had ever done any screenwork." The publication had caught up with the star when she and Jean Simmons were attending the London movie premiere of *Guys and Dolls,* and quoted Hepburn as saying, "I'd love to do a musical one day."

---

* Gershe said that the character Dick Avery was based not on Avedon's "biography" but on his "aura."

Role model: Photographer Richard Avedon served as the basis for writer Leonard Gershe's protagonist Dick Avery (played by Fred Astaire). Even so, Paramount ordered Avedon off the set.

Avedon judged Astaire's agility with the camera equipment "convincing." The star with his director on the New York set of the studio lot, preparing the scene in which Astaire will first encounter Hepburn in a Greenwich Village bookstore

"I went to Roger with this," remembered Gershe, "and said, 'She may not be Judy Garland and she may not be Ethel Merman, but she's obviously musical, and she'd like to do one.' " Edens told Donen, and they both snapped at the bait. "In those days," said Gershe, "Audrey Hepburn was *the* hottest thing in the business."

As the thinking man's Marilyn Monroe, which had as much to say about her lack of bosom as about her nonthreatening appeal to both sexes, Audrey Hepburn in the 1950s essentially owned Hollywood, Broadway, and the fashion pages of magazines. According to Leonard Gershe, "Marlene Dietrich once said, 'A woman looks good either in or out of clothes, not both'—she being the exception, of course. Audrey would have been perfect for us, because she was the first actress who actually did appear on the cover of *Harper's Bazaar.* Audrey looked radiant in clothes. I'm not sure what she would have looked like without clothes, but she had that pencil-thin linear look of a model. That was a first for Hollywood. Before we did *Funny Face,* whenever a movie with a fashion background was made, the model would always be someone like Rita Hayworth, some voluptuous, sexy, gorgeous creature of Hollywood, not of the fashion world. But the truth is, magazine editors like Carmel Snow or Diana Vreeland never would have put Rita Hayworth on a cover of *Vogue* or *Harper's Bazaar.*"

By 1951, after playing some bits in English films, the Belgian-born gamine with a cigarette-thin waist and a distinctive voice lodged somewhere deep inside her esophagus overtook Broadway as Colette's personal choice to play *Gigi.* Paramount Pictures quickly beckoned, and William Wyler and Gregory Peck agreed to hire her as the runaway princess in the romantic comedy *Roman Holiday.* The role not only permanently typecast Hepburn as Cinderella but won her the 1953 Oscar for Best Actress. She followed, before *Funny Face,* which was her first musical, with Billy Wilder's *Sabrina,* King Vidor's *War and Peace,* and, on Broadway again, Giraudoux's *Ondine.*

"There still hasn't been anybody who made quite the impact that she did," said Leonard Gershe in 1992. "Everybody wanted her, and she was booked forever." Undeterred, Edens and Donen made an appointment with Hepburn's agent, Kurt Frings. The two described their movie and said, "We must have an answer right away."

"She's at the Raphaël in Paris," Frings told Donen and Edens. "Send her a copy of the script and send one to me."

They did just as instructed, only Hepburn's copy of the script had not so much as landed in Paris when Kurt Frings rang Roger Edens to tender

"The great moment," said Donen, "when the ugly duckling becomes the beautiful swan."

his reaction. Donen vaguely remembered the agent's thinking it "not good."

"Not good?" exclaimed Gershe. "Kurt Frings *hated* it. He kept saying how embarrassed he was that he had told Roger and Stanley to send it to Audrey, because he couldn't stand it."

"I read it in Paris," remembered Hepburn, "and I fell in love with it. It was a charming story, plus I knew that I would get to dance with Fred Astaire." Told that her opinion conflicted with that of her then agent's and, in fact, caused him to have to eat crow when he contacted Donen and Edens with her acceptance, Hepburn, who managed to be well protected during her career, replied, "Well, you see, these are things I never knew anything about."

DURING the period Leonard Gershe was still conceiving of his story as a stage musical, the role model for his magazine editor was Vivienne Segal, Gene Kelly's costar in *Pal Joey,* "because," said the writer, "I was crazy about Vivienne Segal, also her timing." As he began to research the world of fashion journalism, however, a young editor at *Harper's Bazaar,* Didi Dixon, set him on a different course. "She worked with the editor in chief, Diana Vreeland," said Gershe, "and Didi would feed me expressions and things that Vreeland said, words like 'bizzazz.' "

Bizzazz? As Gershe explained, "The word 'pizzazz' actually came from *Funny Face.* It was 'bizzazz' in the picture. I did not invent that word. Diana Vreeland invented it, and the movie popularized it. For want of a better word, she would look at a layout and say, 'No, no, no, it has no biz-zazz.' And I used the word in the picture. Somebody a couple of years later made a mistake and spelled it 'pizzazz,' which is much better. The hardness of the *p* makes it more effective. Vreeland and I once talked about that, and she said, 'Yes, I wish I had said 'pizzazz.' "

By the time Gershe finished creating the fictitious character of the editor Maggie Prescott as a carbon image of Diana Vreeland, not even Vivienne Segal could have played her. "Kay Thompson was perfect," said Gershe, "only I didn't know her then. I only knew Kay Thompson from hearing her on the radio."

As an example of how Vreeland served as his muse, he cited the opening number in the finished picture, "Think Pink!" in which the gray-clad Prescott commands her minions to editorialize on the nation's vital need to wear pink—clothes, hats, and lipstick. "Diana Vreeland did speak that way," Gershe said. "She'd announce, 'I want the entire country in pink!' Or, 'Pink is the navy blue of India.' "

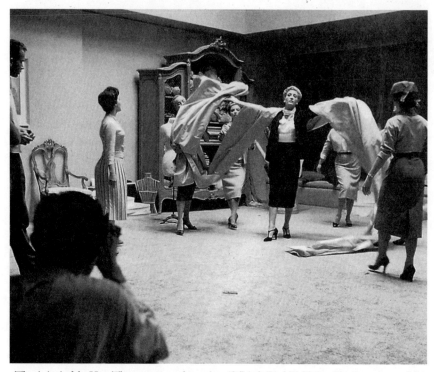

The inimitable Kay Thompson, rehearsing "Think Pink!" *Funny Face* (1957) would have been a stage show years earlier if only she had said yes.

"I don't like to say it," offered Kay Thompson, "but I knew Vreeland before we started the picture." The legendary fashion doyenne of *Bazaar* and, later, *Vogue,* was credited with knowing more about style than more or less anyone on earth (but fatally to her career, she knew or cared very little about journalism or publishing economics, or about dealing with anyone's ego other than her own). "I didn't do *her,*" Thompson said of her portrayal in the film, "I just did that kind of woman. She wouldn't have known quite what we were doing. She'd have no idea we were doing a characterization. She was in fashion and concerned with how people should look, models and that. It was an entirely different world."

STANLEY DONEN and Roger Edens may have wanted the 1927 Gershwin songs to *Funny Face* and the 1926 song from *Oh, Kay!,* but the Gershwin music catalog was controlled by Warner Bros., and the company did not look kindly upon leasing out its assets, especially to rival studios. This

situation marked one of several occasions during the course of preproduction when it would look as though *Funny Face* would be, as Donen said,
"dead in the water."

The lifeline this time was a letter the director received in the mail from
a source who had rescued him before. "I hadn't heard from George
Abbott in years," said Donen. More than likely, he speculated, the last time
had been 1942, during *Beat the Band.* "One did not get to be intimate
friends with George Abbott," said Donen, "at least I didn't, not then. So
out of the blue a letter arrives—not even airmail, but by regular mail.
George Abbott did not put airmail stamps on letters."

Typically, too, Abbott's message was succinct. "It said, 'Dear Stanley,
We're going to make a movie of *The Pajama Game*. Would you like to direct
it? Sincerely, George Abbott.' I swear, that was the entire letter. I picked up
the phone, called him in New York, and said, 'Yes.' "

Fortuitously, *The Pajama Game* would be made by Warner Bros. This
provided Donen with some bargaining leverage, although as a contract
employee of M-G-M, as was Roger Edens, he would have to let his studio
act as his intermediary, once the terms had been dictated by Donen
through his agent. As Donen recalled, "I said to Roger, 'Here's the deal.
I'm going to go to Warner Bros. to make *The Pajama Game,* but what I'll do
is, I'll get my agent to make an agreement that says Warner Bros. can have
my services *if* M-G-M gets the rights to use *Funny Face.*' "

Edens was agreeable, as was, after some convincing, Warners. "So
now," said Donen, "we've got the script, we've got the songs, we've got
Audrey, and Roger and I went to Metro and said, 'Great news—Audrey
Hepburn wants to do the picture.' Slight problem: Paramount had Audrey
under exclusive contract and wouldn't let her out. The picture was dead in
the water again. Roger and I didn't want to make it with anyone else."

While the project lay dormant, "Roger and I got an idea," said Donen.
"We'd go back to M-G-M and say, 'Look, you're paying Roger, you're paying Stanley, you've put up the money for development,* you've got the
score. If we can't bring Mohammed to the mountain, we'll bring the mountain to Mohammed. Will you sell us and the picture to Paramount?' "

M-G-M, according to Donen, replied, "For the right dough, yes."

"Negotiations went on for months," said Fred Astaire, who at the
time was also under contract to Paramount, though he was not in the same
demand as Hepburn (he would take second billing to her). "I was repeatedly told that there was no way to put the deal across. However, I knew

* By this stage, approximately $300,000.

In conference, Hepburn, Avedon, Donen, Astaire. On far left, in the shadows, is Marion Marshall, the then Mrs. Donen.

that Audrey wanted to make the picture and that sooner or later they would all come around—because Audrey is a lady who gets her way."

"Miss Hepburn was all shrewd businesswoman till the deal was signed," recalled a negotiations-weary Roger Edens, "a long-drawn-out process, believe me."

At the start of the summer of 1956—Edens had first read Gershe's *Wedding Day* in autumn 1954—*Funny Face* was ready to start shooting, at Paramount's Hollywood studios on Melrose and then in Paris.

"By the time we made all the deals," said Donen, "it had cost a million dollars—and that was before a single foot of the film was even shot."

THE CONCEPT of assigning an expert still photographer to a film was not new and, as Avedon pointed out, something of a commonplace among established directors during the fifties. "It was a period in which the idea of a visual consultant had been created because a photographer named Eliot Elisofon was brought out to help John Huston with *Moulin Rouge*," said Avedon, who would serve *Funny Face* in the same capacity. "Fashion photography and photography in general was more inventive at that moment than was Hollywood." This first became evident "just after World War II," said Avedon. "The great name at that point was the colorist Hoynigen-Heune, and he went out to work with George Cukor. For the opening sequences of *A Star Is Born* he was right at Cukor's side, so the idea of photographers working with directors had some tradition."

In describing his own working relationship with Donen,* Avedon put his finger on the director's single most noticeable trait. "Stanley has the greatest laugh in the world," said Avedon. "We worked and laughed, we laughed and worked. We'd spend afternoon after afternoon on the lanai, as they called it, of his house. Stanley is very visually minded, and he, Leonard, and I went over what would make good pictures for the fashion montage—the train, the flower market. I somehow don't remember the barge and Audrey's catching the fish being my idea, but we all just threw in possible ideas for photographs."

So much time was devoted to breaking down how the technical end of the picture would be executed that Avedon began to worry that other elements of the picture were being overlooked at his expense, such as the actors. "I finally said to Stanley, 'But when are you going to direct Fred and Audrey?' And he said, 'Direct Fred and Audrey? Dick, they know what to do.'"

For the fashion sequence in which Astaire shoots the Givenchy-outfitted Hepburn against famous Paris landmarks, Donen and Avedon decided to freeze-frame the shot in the film, to show how the scene would appear in a fashion magazine, complete with color separations. "If you froze a motion picture frame in those days," said Avedon, "the grain would be enormous, so we couldn't go to that large a frame in thirty-five millimeter." The solution, said Avedon, "was that we took my actual eight-by-ten camera, attached it to the movie camera, and shot through a mirror, so I would take the picture with my camera at the exact same moment it was happening on film. In the lab they could locate the same frame, insert mine, and therefore have a much better quality image."

Donen and Avedon were surprised to find the Paramount technicians uncooperative to several of their requests, although the company had its reasons. "The studio had just brought out VistaVision," said Avedon, referring

---

* Avedon estimated that he worked with Donen in Hollywood for approximately three months, during which time he and his (second) wife, Evelyn, rented the house that Marilyn Monroe had lived in during her marriage to Joe DiMaggio. Tour buses would go by, he recalled, "and every morning Evelyn and I would be in bed and hear, 'That's the bedroom of Marilyn Monroe and Joe DiMaggio.'"

The choice was between a yellow light in the darkroom or a red one. Reality would have dictated yellow. Donen selected red—"it photographs better."

to Paramount's answer to Fox's CinemaScope,* "and the great pride was that it was sharp from the furthest left of the screen to the furthest right."

"Only I didn't care about that," said Donen, "because I wanted certain scenes in the picture to have a soft, smoky focus, to look like some of Dick's fashion shoots."

"This was the opposite of what Paramount had spent a fortune to achieve," said Avedon, who, with Donen, concurred that his fashion-magazine look should remain, in spite of the studio protestations. "I said,

---

* VistaVision, born in 1954, utilized a special camera in which the 35 mm film ran horizontally (as opposed to vertically), resulting in the exposure of twice the normal size of a 35 mm frame. Despite its technical superiority, the expensive process fell out of favor by 1960.

'It's no big deal, Stanley. We'll take a silk stocking, or tissue paper, or cellophane, take a plate of glass and spray it, put it over the lens, and see what it looks like.' So Stanley just got out a sixteen-millimeter camera, and he and I went out like two amateurs, sticking things in front of the lens to see what they'd look like."

"Stanley was having problems with someone at the studio," said Kay Thompson, remembering the argument as having to do with the look of the picture.

"It was Barney Balaban, the president of Paramount," said Donen. "He kept looking at the rushes and telling me to fix the picture or else I'd be fired."

"They made it a little uncomfortable," said Thompson. "I don't know the details, because I didn't stick around to find out. Roger Edens and I had a similar rule: If you hear a voice that's a little bit too loud, go the other way."

"The big issue," said Avedon, "was Audrey's dance in the café in Paris, which was shot in Hollywood. The style of a lot of my photography at the time had lights flaring into the lens, and that's what Stanley and I wanted for the café." *Funny Face*'s cinematographer, Ray June, was an experienced M-G-M cameraman, whose highly regarded career encompassed his shooting *The Great Ziegfeld* in 1936. June's expertise extended as far back to his working a hand-cranked camera for the Signal Corps during World War I. "In Hollywood," said Avedon, "he was famous for having kept Jeanette MacDonald in the business an extra twenty years, because he was capable of making things look so beautiful."

June's history did little to impress the Paramount execs. "Every time the rushes from this café scene were shown at the studio," remembered Avedon, "they would call him upstairs and say, 'It's your ass if there's one more foot of these flaring lights in this footage.'" According to Avedon, "Ray June died at the end of the film, and I think it's because they killed him."

In its war to have the picture turn out looking its way, Paramount arranged for Avedon to be prohibited from exerting any of his influence on the *Funny Face* soundstages by order of the unions. "They banned me from setting the lights, because I wasn't the lighting director, and I was told I could no longer speak to Stanley." Rather than surrender, said Avedon, Donen and he "worked out a system using my necktie. First I'd swing it over to the direction of the light in question. I'd look at Stanley, Stanley'd look at me. Then, if I opened the knot in my tie, it meant that he should widen the aperture of the light. If I tightened my tie, it meant to narrow the spotlight and move it to the left, so it would flare, but not too

Professional model Dovima lent another dose of fashion-realm reality to *Funny Face*.

much. You know the smoke in the scene? Well, I was working my tie and found that I was losing consciousness. The last thing I remember seeing were all the grips who were working the beeswax blowers coming at me and smoking me out."

"AUDREY WAS supposed to make Billy's picture in Paris, *Love in the Afternoon,* only he was running overtime with *The Spirit of St. Louis,*" remembered Leonard Gershe. "That was lucky for us, because while Billy was finishing *Spirit of St. Louis,* Audrey was free to do our picture."

"Audrey who?" said Billy Wilder, in whose Beverly Hills office Gershe was standing when he made the pronouncement.

"Hepburn," Gershe answered.

"Oh," said Wilder, "because if it was Audrey my wife, she would be available to make a picture anytime."

Donen, Avedon, Gershe, and Thompson all used the same words— "professional" and "very hardworking"—to describe Hepburn, who was twenty-seven at the time of *Funny Face* (Astaire, thirty years her senior, recoiled when a critic referred to *Funny Face* as offering "something old, something new"). "Fred would assure Audrey that she was a wonderful dance partner, and she would assure him that he was not too old for her," Donen wrote in a remembrance of Hepburn for *Vogue* magazine, after she had died of cancer on January 20, 1993. "What held it together was that both thought the other was near perfection."

"Audrey was very serious," said Kay Thompson. "There was no coziness, no demanding to speak to Stanley on the side, no secret conversations, no anything like that." Donen said that the nervousness Hepburn claimed over working with Astaire was never evident, and he found her properly trained as a dancer to withstand any instructions he, Astaire, or the choreographer Eugene Loring would demand.

"Gene Loring was very soft-spoken," said Hepburn, "he wasn't a slave driver. I was so used at that point to having had Russian dance instructors yelling at me."

"Audrey Hepburn had undergone a little dance training," said Astaire expert John Mueller, referring to Hepburn's ballet classes and fledgling career as a professional dancer, "and that may be worse than none at all." Mueller found that in the Hepburn-Astaire duet "He Loves and She Loves," the slender young star "keeps trying to project as a lyric dancer, and the results are awkward and sometimes embarrassing." (Astaire and Hepburn also dance the title song together, in a red-lit photo lab, as well as a portion of the "Bonjour, Paris!" number, and the finale, to "'S Wonderful.")

Donen does not buy Mueller's case. "Audrey was skillful, and her training helped speed her understanding of what to do." Where Hepburn did hesitate was over a costume decision upon which Donen was immovable. "It was her only dance number in the picture without Fred Astaire, and it was important that you saw her movements," he said.

"It was a minidrama," corroborated Hepburn. "Remember the scene in the nightclub? I'm dressed in a black sweater, black pants, black moccasins, and when we were getting the outfit together, Stanley wanted me to wear white socks. I did not want to wear white socks. Having had my ballet training, I thought the line should be all black, that it would make a better silhouette. Only, Stanley wanted white because it was something he'd learned from Fred Astaire, because that way you would see his feet. Well, that's great if they're Fred Astaire's feet. I was miserable."

"She had tears in her eyes," said Donen.

"I don't remember being quite that emotional about it," said Hepburn, "but Stanley obviously understood how much I cared about how I looked, because I am rather complex. Finally, we did it his way and it looked great, and I wrote him a note about it. But what I was not to tell Stanley until years later was that there was something he did not realize at the time about why I was so upset. You see, as a little girl I had a terrible complex about my big feet—I wear size eight and a half—and I'd grown up with ballerinas who were little things. I was always too tall, and if I wore white socks, people were going to see what big feet I had, compared to the girls I always admired with pretty little feet and pretty shoulders and a bosom and everything I didn't have."

"The poor thing was doing something monumental in a hurry," said Kay Thompson. "Fortunately, the songs were perfect for her. That one with the hat? Heaven!"

"To me," said Donen, "Ella Fitzgerald has the most tranquilizing singing voice on earth, and Audrey has the most tranquilizing speaking one." And her singing voice? "Soft, gentle, but dear."

Hepburn's first number, "How Long Has This Been Going On?" is set in the Greenwich Village bookstore where Jo Stockton works. After Maggie and her models, with Dick Avery, have invaded the premises for a fashion shoot, the hat remains as a remnant and a reminder of the excitement the fashion people caused, also of the kiss Avery planted on her, which awakens a romantic spark within.

"Stanley had Audrey pretend something from the very start of the picture," said Thompson. "He had her do a whole thing of young-girl attitudes toward Fred, so she felt, like so many of those actresses, that she was really half in love with him from the beginning. She would get him his orange juice, like a little girl. Only he was something else."

"Fred never said anything," said Donen, "but it was *clear* that he hated doing the 'Clap Yo' Hands' number with Kay, and she was very uncomfortable. I think the reason is—because he would never express it—he liked women to be extremely feminine, like Ginger, girls who were very floaty, and he thought of Kay Thompson as someone he didn't want to be close to. He knew she had an amazing talent; he just didn't want to be near it."

Hepburn said that white socks were fine—provided they were on the feet of Fred Astaire. She and Donen fought over the fashion touch. She lost, but denied his claim that she cried.

"I could have shot Fred," said Kay Thompson, "but didn't. Fred had no feeling at all. I had known him long before, in New York, before he even went to Hollywood, or I. He was on a radio show in New York and I was on it and he was dancing on the radio, if you can imagine it. Well, why not?"

Thompson depicted Astaire as terminally crotchety on the set of *Funny Face*. "I never considered myself Ginger," she said, explaining that the atmosphere had been friendly at the outset. "People would say, 'Hello,' 'Good morning,' then Stanley would say something, and all Fred would say was, 'Where do you want us to go, Stanley?' Finally, we all got together and knew how to act with each other, because Fred didn't quite know what he was doing. Well, he knew everything was a fight; not a real fight, but this nagging demand of 'What do you want me to do?' or 'What is he doing over there?' 'What is she doing over there?' So what Audrey and I did, separately, without saying a word to each other, was go up the stairs and wait for somebody to call us."

Eventually, said Thompson, "Stanley got the message, because he kept saying, 'Oh, Fred, you're my idol.' And he found out Fred wasn't really his idol. They adored each other, but it was always this business of Fred's demanding out loud, 'What are you doing?' "

Thompson said the situation worsened once the company moved to France.* "Fred was impatient," she said. "He was Fred Astaire, and he wanted to be great in front of Audrey, I guess. Those scenes at Chantilly, of Fred and Audrey crossing the water on a little raft—Fred stopped her four or five times right in the middle of the scene and said, 'What are you doing?' "

"It had rained forever," was Hepburn's tight-lipped remembrance, "and we had to dance in the mud. I ruined several pair of my white satin pumps."

---

* With the company on location in Paris, Art Buchwald turned his column over to Kay Thompson for a day. She penned her contribution in the manner of Eloise:

> My name is Kay.
> I live at a hotel in Paris.
> If you want to get me on the telephone
> Simply ask for Kay,
> And the operator will say "Qui?"
> And you will say, "No, Kay."

Eventually, the column promised, if the caller to the hotel was persistent enough, he would be connected to Eva Marie Saint. "She lives there too."

As Thompson cared to reveal, "After Fred had yelled at Audrey a couple of times and she was in that white dress and her shoes were blackened from the mud and she was smiling and they were supposed to be in love, finally the scene was over. The three of us got into the car that we all had to get into, because we were all staying at the same hotel—that way no one could ever say, 'I'm leaving,' because you couldn't, you had to wait for the others and ride back in silence with your grievances—and we got back to our rooms. I called her and said, 'Audrey, no matter what you do, remember the camera is on you, and whatever he says is unimportant. Don't listen. Do you understand what I'm saying?' Her answer was the greatest line during the whole picture."

Thompson, a gifted mimic, re-created Hepburn's response in that famous proper little whisper. Said Hepburn: "Yes, well, it is a bit of a strain."

"Heaven!" said Thompson. "Is that heaven?"

"STANLEY NEVER YELLED at anybody," said Thompson, "except at Fred, sort of, at the end. Fred was irritating. On 'Clap Yo' Hands,' it started with me on the piano, which didn't play, of course, and you never knew what you were going to do quickly, so when Stanley said to me, 'Okay, Katie, you go to the piano'—and Fred came in and he had been late getting his goatee on and he was irritated, hating the people in makeup, this most disconsolate person. And I went to the piano, and I'm *da-diddle-la-dum*-ing, and Stanley said, 'Okay, roll 'em,' and I'm playing the piano, and about eight bars into it, Fred said, 'Stanley? Come over here.' Stanley said, 'Okay, stop the camera.' And Fred said to him, 'What is she doing on the piano?' Now, there was no reason to ask that. It was obvious. What business was it of his?"

Thompson said that once that skirmish was resolved, "we went back again, and again it was, 'Stanley? What is she doing?' And finally Stanley said, 'She's doing what I asked her to do.' "

The point at which Thompson said she could have reached for her revolver occurred at the finale to "Clap Yo' Hands," "when Fred finally yelled at *me*. This was after we'd gotten up the stairs in the scene. We sang, 'Come along and join the jubileeeeeeeee.' Stanley was doing what he could to get through it and not pamper Fred, and I turned around and Stanley said, 'Cut. Print. That's it.' That's when Fred grabbed me out of the blue and said, 'Where did you learn balance?' "

Despite Kay Thompson's declaration that Astaire was chronically cranky because "he wanted to be great in front of Audrey," Donen disagrees. "He wanted to be great for himself," says the director.

Thompson said she did not reply. "It wasn't worth the time. He was just somebody who was frightened."

"EVERY STORY they tell about Fred is true," said Richard Avedon, "the discipline, the graciousness. We were all in awe of him. He was very easy. At the very end of the film he gave me a pair of shoes he bought on the Champs-Élysées, a pair of suede moccasins. Imagine actually being given a pair of shoes by Fred Astaire?" Not that Avedon ever donned the gift: "In those days," he said, "only Fred Astaire could have gotten away with wearing suede moccasins. I just put them on the mantelpiece for years. I never wore them. They were actually too big."

"The most emotional moment I ever had as a picturemaker," said Donen, "was the morning we laid out Fred's sequence of the 'Bonjour, Paris!' number. It was a Sunday, we were on the Champs-Élysées, I was directing Fred Astaire, and we had to have extras dressed as policemen to keep away the crowds. God, we didn't know what would happen. We used crumpled-up cigarette packages as Fred's marks, and then I hit the play-back and Fred started singing that song. I thought, 'This is it. In my entire life, this is all I ever wanted to do.' "

The split second when Astaire exits the taxi, catches a glimpse of the Arc de Triomphe over his shoulder, then tips his hat, casually slips a hand in his trouser pocket, and begins to stroll the boulevard, absolutely sums up the Astaire style, just as the whole of *Funny Face* sums up Donen's. Blithe. Seamless. Effortless *looking*.

"A delightfully balmy romance," was Bosley Crowther's summation. "The outdoor, romantic settings have the qualities of Boucher and Fragonard paintings," praised Kate Cameron, the mainstream (and pseudonymous) reviewer for New York's *Daily News*. "The movie reaches its height of beauty and invention when Astaire photographs Miss Hepburn in various Paris settings," William K. Zinsser said in the *Herald Tribune*. "He snaps her carefree at the flower market, elegant at the Opera, exuberant at the *Winged Victory*, tomboyish on a Seine barge, misty-eyed in a wedding dress outside an old country chapel. . . . *Funny Face* is that rare thing on screen—a polished musical. It is also great fun."*

"Fred taught me a step," said Avedon, "because I said I can't let this experience be over without my learning something. He taught me the most wonderful Fred Astaire–like step, with an umbrella. It was a complete throwaway; it was almost invisible. It was in the way he walked. As he moved along, he bounced the umbrella on the floor to the beat and then he grabbed it. It was effortless and invisible. As a matter of fact, a few years later I was photographing Gene Kelly and told him that Fred Astaire had taught me this trick with an umbrella. And Kelly said, 'Oh, I'll teach you one,' and he did, and the two tricks with an umbrella in some way define the difference between Fred Astaire and Gene Kelly, and, in my view, demonstrate who is the greater of the artists. With Gene Kelly, he threw the umbrella way up into the air, then he moved to catch it, very slowly, grabbing it behind his back.

"It was a big, grandstand play, about nothing."

---

* Among the carping from some French and British critics was a general disfavor regarding the film's choice of a villain, a Sartre-esque philosopher whose convictions are less strong than his desire to put the make on the Hepburn character. Funny as their seriousness seems, in light of the carefree nature of the musical, Donen still noted of the drubbing, "I was accused, along with the film, of being anti-intellectual."

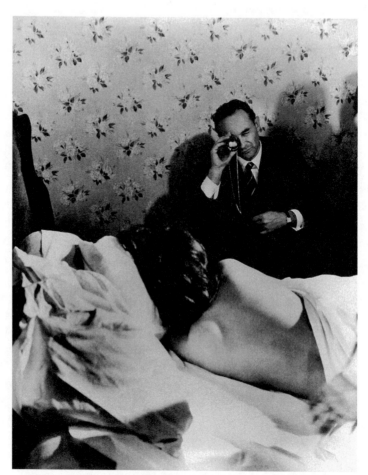

Producer's prerogative, focusing on Sophia Loren, for *Arabesque*

Part 4
Producer

Chapter 1

"Better than Jeanette MacDonald"

HOLLYWOOD," George Abbott once observed, "is jealous of Broadway because it is better, and Broadway is jealous of Hollywood because it is richer."

"So George Abbott came out to Hollywood," remembered Donen, who was loaned to Warner Bros. for a period of twenty-six weeks, at a fee of $110,000. "At that point," said the film director, "I was not on familiar terms with him. I only knew him from the three shows we'd done together. I still called him Mr. Abbott."

Asked in 1992 if he could recall the reason he contacted Donen to direct the movie version of *The Pajama Game*, George Abbott replied: "I had some knowledge about the camera, but he knew more."

The Pajama Game was born as a Broadway musical when Abbott's stage manager, Bobby Griffith, and Griffith's assistant, Hal Prince, presented the producer with a 1953 novel by Richard Bissell, *Seven-and-a-Half Cents,* about a wage dispute at an Iowa pajama factory.* In its planning stage, Abbott wanted Frank Loesser to do the score, Abe Burrows the book, and Jerome Robbins the choreography. All three declined. Robbins, who was expanding his purview from choreographing to directing, ended up sharing codirector credit with Abbott and suggested a first-time stage choreographer, Bob Fosse, for the dance sequences. Abbott approved the hire, provided Robbins would oversee Fosse's work. Frank Loesser made his contribution as well, acting as a musical godfather and mentoring the show's young songwriters, Richard Adler and Jerry Ross (the show's star, John Raitt, claimed that Loesser wrote at least two of the show's numbers,

---

* On August 12, 1955, the Federal Minimum Wage Bill increased the hourly worker's rate from seventy-five cents to a dollar. This law took effect early in 1956.

"A New Town Is a Blue Town" and "There Once Was a Man," while rumor has long had it that Loesser also came up with the main musical strain of the show's pop-hit ballad, "Hey There"). Novelist Bissell, a former factory superintendent in Dubuque, cowrote the book with Abbott, who described his collaborator as "a Harvard man and one of the smartest fellows you ever saw, but for reasons best known to himself he likes to play the part of a hick and a midwestern eccentric." It was Abbott who came up with the title of the show, also the romantic subplot involving the insanely jealous foreman (Hinesie, played by Eddie Foy, Jr.) and the ditzy, flirtatious bookkeeper (Gladys, played by Carol Haney). The main story involved the arrival of a new plant managerial supervisor (Sid) and how he falls for the head of the union's grievance committee (Babe). His timing for both events could not be worse, for the workers are threatening to prepare a wage strike.

Given the novice status of the producing and writing teams—save for Abbott—the show, which opened at the St. James Theater on May 13, 1954, was a surprise smash, and Adler and Ross became to blue-collar factories what Rodgers and Hammerstein had been to Oklahoma cornfields. (Ross died of a bronchial ailment in 1955, at the age of twenty-nine, shortly after the opening of their next and only other show, *Damn Yankees*.) *The Pajama Game* ran for 1,063 performances on Broadway and then proved an enormous success on the road, to the extent that Jack L. Warner alerted one of its producers, Hal Prince, to his concern that the show's 1957 summer bookings, which would run concurrent to the movie's premiere, would adversely affect the movie's box office. Prince responded by assuring Warner that the high visibility of the show could only help the cumulative box office.

"On the movie," said Donen, "I was the director and George Abbott was the producer." Describing their work routine and his new relationship with Abbott, who was then seventy years old, Donen said, "His days were wonderful. First thing in the morning, he'd play two sets of tennis, then he'd come to the studio in Burbank and sit with us in the rehearsal hall for an hour. He'd have lunch with us, then he'd leave."

During those sixty minutes together in the rehearsal room, Donen would turn to Abbott and ask, "How did you stage this in the theater?"

Abbott's response was invariably the same: "Doesn't matter. Do it any way you want."

"I might do it any way I want," Donen would reply, "but you might as well show me the way you did it in New York."

"Well, if you want me to, I will."

"It went on like this for three or four days," recalled Donen, who thought that Abbott's stance, no matter how noble, was something of a waste of time. "George Abbott was a strange man," said Donen. "Finally, I went to him and said, 'Look, I've codirected before. It doesn't mean anything to me. If it will make you feel at ease about talking to me, I'll put your name on as codirector. This way I can get from you whatever you have to offer."

Abbott's reply was long in coming: "I don't know. Let me think about it."

After tennis the next day, Abbott returned to the soundstage. He told Donen, "I've thought a great deal about what you said. You can put my name on as codirector *if* you let me put yours on with mine as coproducer."

Coproducing would mean that Donen, sharing fifty-fifty with Abbott, would be responsible for control of the picture, its casting (which was completed), its financing (which was in place), its promotion (a procedure Donen normally eschewed), and ancillary sales (the rights were sold off shortly after the first run). Donen agreed to Abbott's terms.

"He did that," said Donen, "and we went on exactly as we had before. He'd play tennis, come watch on the set for an hour, then watch the rushes, then go home. It was the antithesis of codirecting with Gene. I wouldn't mind codirecting with George Abbott again."

ACCORDING TO studio records, Warner Bros. wanted Frank Sinatra, but George Abbott's first choice for the film's leading man was Marlon Brando, despite the Method actor's having received mixed grades for his performance as Sky Masterson in Joseph L. Mankiewicz's overly stylized and talky 1955 movie version of *Guys and Dolls*. Bing Crosby was the third consideration, but his price—$200,000 against five percent of the gross for him alone, then another twenty-five percent of the gross for his company in exchange for its investment of between $150,000 and $250,000 of the eventual $2.6 million budget—was ultimately judged as being too high.*

---

* In addition to Donen's directorial fee of $110,000, costs on *The Pajama Game* included $100,000 to George Abbott, $250,000 to its star Doris Day, $75,000 to its authors for the stage rights, $25,000 to its choreographer, Bob Fosse, $25,000 to John Raitt, and $30,000 to Carol Haney. Donen and Raitt shot a day and a half in Dubuque with a Chicago crew—bits of it appear in the opening credits sequence—while the only other locations were one week of filming the "Once a Year Day" picnic in Los Angeles's Hollenbeck and Griffith Parks. Donen and Bob Fosse worked with the eighty dancers the entire week.

Because the popularity of musicals was on the wane, *The Pajama Game* was going to be stitched together as parsimoniously as possible; two initial financial concessions were the deployment of monaural instead of stereophonic sound, and the use of a normal screen size instead of CinemaScope. John Raitt, who after some nail-biting wound up re-creating the role he had played onstage, recalled the movie's cast as having to work at such a breakneck pace under Donen "that I never had the chance to sit in the canvas chair that had my name on it." The story circulated on the set, said Raitt, "that Donen was promised a thousand dollars for every day we came in under schedule, and Jack Warner, that SOB, had us work until six p.m. Christmas Eve, although we didn't do anything but sit around and sing Christmas carols."* Donen said, "The picture was made in something like just under six weeks, because the studio didn't care if it was made or not. So I told George Abbott that I'd shoot it as cheaply as possible, which meant shooting it quickly." Production was completed February 6, 1957.

To land the role of Sid, Raitt was screen-tested in the East, with the footage then shown in California to Doris Day, who would play Babe, the role originated in New York by Janis Paige. By this time Abbott was also making noises about Stephen Douglass, who had opened on Broadway as Joe Hardy in Adler and Ross's—and Abbott's—newest musical, *Damn Yankees*. Jack L. Warner received five heartfelt letters of support from fans of Douglass's; all bore different names, but three were written in the exact same handwriting, while the other two shared a New Jersey postmark.

Once Doris Day viewed Raitt's screen test, Jack Warner was wired by an underling: PUTTING IT MILDLY NOT KEEN ANYONE. SHE TALKED DONEN ASKED ANY CHANCE DEAN MARTIN OR EVEN GORDON MACRAE. After some discussion, it was arranged that Raitt be flown to California and film a test with the star herself—which, obviously, the Broadway baritone passed.

"To get the movie," said Raitt, whose first and only film was *The Pajama Game,* "I had to turn down *Bells Are Ringing* on Broadway, but I wanted a shot at being in the movies. I'd heard one of my main competitors was Howard Keel, because he had just done *Calamity Jane* with Doris, but George Abbott told me to sit tight, he was going to push for me." Part of the reason Keel did not get the nod may have had to do with the lead-

---

* Donen described Warner as "a vulgar, nasty, selfish, loud vulgarian. He used to preside over his private dining room and boast of his private chef. It was in this same dining room that Warner said to his daughter's husband, Milton Sperling, 'You've set the son-in-law business back fifty years.' "

John Raitt, Doris Day, and a "factory worker," before the alfresco picnic number in
The Pajama Game (1957). George Abbott originally wanted Marlon Brando for the
Raitt role; Bing Crosby wanted it for himself. Day inquired whether Dean Martin was
available.

ing man's having tried at the outset to have Donen replaced on *Seven Brides
for Seven Brothers* by his *Kiss Me, Kate* director, George Sidney.

The Pajama Game is a virtual transplant of the Broadway version,
except for Day's star role and the deletion of four of the show's fifteen
songs, two of which had been used during scenery changes; another, "A
New Town Is a Blue Town," sung by Raitt, "I just found boring," said
Donen. It had to do with the life that Raitt's character left behind in
Chicago. A new number, "A Better Word than Love," was written and
timed (it lasted three minutes), but discarded.

Eddie Foy, Jr., gives a performance he always gives in movies, that of
a lovable blowhard, and with his vaudeville training, he is in complete control of his situations. The same assuredness was characteristic of the
rotund but graceful Reta Shaw, who plays one of Foy's foils, the secretary
Mabel. Their duet, "I'll Never Be Jealous Again," is a charmer in the
purest theatrical sense and generated applause during the movie's first run.

The film gave Carol Haney her best stab at screen fame. Arthur Freed
had released the dancer–choreographer's assistant from her M-G-M contract when George Abbott offered her the *Pajama Game* stage role of

Gladys the bookkeeper, and she brought down the house every night with Bob Fosse's Chaplinesque dance for her, "Steam Heat." (Her understudy Shirley MacLaine went on for Haney at the performance seen by the producer Hal Wallis, and that is how MacLaine's screen career was launched.) As Leonard Gershe had said, Carol Haney was pixieish and had a funny face; the morning after *The Pajama Game* opened on Broadway, the critic John Chapman noted: "Miss Haney looks like a tall but awkward Audrey Hepburn." Given how broadly Haney delivers her lines and the way she mugs in the film, however, the resemblance most assuredly stopped there.

AS EARLY as October 5, 1955, Jack Warner told Abbott that the contents of the show added up to a full hour of music and between seventy and eighty minutes of book. "This would, of course, mean an overlong picture," said Warner. Once Donen came in, he not only effected further cuts in the script but employed dissolves to keep the stagy action moving. Monologues, such as the factory owner's hard-times speech at the picnic, are sparsely dispensed, all for the betterment of the film. The final result is a swiftly paced 101-minute condensation of the two-act original that compromises none of the show's freshness or spark; if only the dialogue, especially in the love scenes, were not so corny, and better thought had been given to Day's and Raitt's then trendy fifties buzz cuts. Not even Brando could have survived those.

The ingratiating score is what keeps the movie working best. "The Pajama Game" is played inside the Sleeptite Pajama Factory and under the movie's opening credits, led by Eddie Foy's Hinesie, before he sees to it that his workers are "Racing with the Clock." Midway through the first shift, Babe and Sid meet, and the women tease Babe over her evident attraction to the handsome new superintendent. She responds by assuring them that "I'm Not at All in Love," though she doth protest too much. Hinesie, who is engaged to Gladys and cannot tolerate her so much as looking at another man, is convinced she has fallen for Sid, leaving it to Mabel to expose his rage as meaningless and woo him back into calm ("I'll Never Be Jealous Again"). Sid's own attraction to Babe is overwhelming. While composing a business memo into the Dictaphone, he finds his mind wandering and his voice on the machine accompanying him as he sings "Hey There." The company picnic moves the action out of the factory and allows the workers to vent their jubilation on this "Once-a-Year Day." Sid and Babe own up to their mutual infatuations, and their relationship deepens at Babe's house, where Sid informs her that he has no interest in making "Small Talk." Ever wary of the nature of romance, Babe annotates, in the bluegrassy "There Once Was a Man," that no male can be trusted when it comes to matters of love—a prophecy that is soon fulfilled. The two opposing sides that Sid and Babe represent at the plant succeed in pulling them apart. Gladys and some of the boys help spur company morale with a dance at a workers' rally, "Steam Heat," while Sid seduces Gladys into letting him peek at the company's books, which is his best effort to thwart the strike. Gladys leads him on a merry chase to "Hernando's Hideaway," unaware that the two are being followed by a knife-wielding Hinesie. In the happy wrap-up, the workers receive the hourly "Seven-and-a-Half Cents" they demanded, and the couples end up properly mated and matched in their pajamas.

Despite such ingenuousness, "it was a good fifties movie," was John Raitt's appraisal, "certainly better than Jeanette MacDonald and Nelson Eddy." Much of the credit for that goes to Doris Day, who at this juncture had shaken off the sugar coating of her early musical performances and not yet assumed the impenetrability of her later manufactured movie roles, those Rock Hudson comedies that forever brand her in most movie-goers' minds as an innocuous heroine. In truth, Doris Day seldom received the acclaim she deserved. As an actress she projected conviction and range. As a singer in movies she had few peers and was capable of establishing standards with her own distinctive renditions. Her comedic timing was impeccable, whether physical or verbal. She was attractive in a way that could be both naughty and nice. Unfairly, it was the latter quality that overwhelmed the former, got pinned on her, and ultimately denied her serious acceptance as a leading actress. Probably it was a matter of the times; the fifties did not offer seriousness on too many levels. In another era, perhaps, Doris Day would have competed for the same roles that went to Barbara Stanwyck, Rosalind Russell, Jean Arthur, and Irene Dunne. Talk about versatility. In place of outstanding Doris Day vehicles, however, audiences were able to enjoy her in flashes of brilliance in movies that ran from mediocre to very good. She herself, perversely, took to denigrating her more serious roles, in Hitchcock's *The Man Who Knew Too Much,* the melodrama *Julie* (a rotten movie but highly watchable because she plays against darkness so interestingly), and probably her best performance (certainly producer Joe Pasternak's best movie), *Love Me or Leave Me,* in which she portrayed the singer Ruth Etting—and subtly played the part close to the bone.

In looking at Doris Day and being fully aware of her strengths and weaknesses, Donen has called her *Pajama Game* performance "energetic, lively, lovable. I remember the track to 'There Once Was a Man.' It was remarkable, unlike anything she's ever done, and the best thing she's ever done." No one else, he thought, could have given *The Pajama Game* what Doris Day brought to it. "Janis Paige was very different in the role on the stage," he said. "She was like a woman made of steel. I liked her, but probably in the film she would have appeared so tough that you would never have found her vulnerable."

As for her view of the endeavor, Day considered the making of *The Pajama Game* an "arduous" experience. "I was the only one in the cast who had not played it on Broadway, and I had to fit into a polished company that had been together two years," she complained in a 1975 memoir that otherwise completely overlooked the picture.

Being the only outsider, "Doris didn't quite get into the camaraderie we all had," said John Raitt. "She had just gone through a nervous breakdown and was well into Christian Science."

"She felt out of it," said Donen. "It had nothing to do with the picture. At the time, she was in love with Willie Mays and used to cry a lot in her dressing room."

"WHEN WE did the second picture," said Donen, "I said to George, 'Should we do it just as we did before?' He said, 'Okay.' It was very nice."

Damn Yankees sought to duplicate the smash Broadway status of *The Pajama Game* by employing the same behind-the-scenes talent, plus a new name. Novelist Douglas Wallop, whose 1954 novel, *The Year the Yankees Lost the Pennant,* served as the basis for the book, acted as coauthor with George Abbott, with some help from Richard Bissell. But it was the minuses and not the pluses that in this case altered the end product. Frank Loesser this time did not assist Adler and Ross, to the detriment of the score, and Jerome Robbins did not oversee Fosse, who no longer required supervision. The story relied on the legend that had launched the American musical theater, Faust, only in this instance the Devil strikes a bargain with an armchair fan of the losing baseball team, the Washington Senators. Like any good loyalist to the game, this fellow will do anything to defeat the unbeatable New York Yankees.

The premise was irresistible. Another virtue of the show was that the Devil shot off some witty one-liners. There were also some fine numbers, including the hummable hymn "(You've Gotta Have) Heart," the bouncy "Shoeless Joe from Hannibal, Mo," and, to Donen's mind, two Fosse-choreographed dance duets, "Two Lost Souls" and the mambo "Who's

Bob Fosse's exuberant choreography for *The Pajama Game*'s "Once-a-Year Day," with Los Angeles's Hollenbeck and Griffith Parks doubling for bucolic Dubuque

Got the Pain?" Even so, the show was not in the same league as *The Pajama Game,* and neither is its film version.*

"The decor of the film is surprisingly flat in comparison to the dynamically deep space of *Pajama Game*'s tree-filled park and machine-filled factory, the camera and the choreography surprisingly inert," said Gerald Mast, who speculated that the money package for the two film musicals may have been running out.[†] Certainly Fosse's movie choreography in *The Pajama Game* outshines *Damn Yankees'* stagy staging by a mile, as is especially evident in the "Shoeless Joe" number, which, except for a finale that provides close-ups of the players, looks transplanted directly from the footlights.

"I don't think it looks like a movie," said Gwen Verdon, who plays *Damn Yankees'* seductress, Lola. "I think it looks like a stage show, which is not good. And I'm sure Stanley, who had done great movies, did not want to shoot it that way, but he did it out of deference to George Abbott."

---

* *Damn Yankees*—the title was Abbott's idea—opened at the 46th Street Theater on May 5, 1955, and ran for 1,019 performances.

[†] One concession Donen and Abbott were forced to accept was not having their cinematographer of choice, Harry Stradling, shoot *Damn Yankees.* Warners had previously assigned him to another, favored picture, *Auntie Mame,* with Rosalind Russell.

As a director "on stage," said Verdon, "George Abbott was great. He'd say, 'Oh, that's fine. Just get up and say the words. Say them fast and let's get out of here.' "

For the movie, said Verdon, "I think Stanley really got that first number to work ['Six Months Out of Every Year'] with that split screen. He was able to establish the opening look of the movie that way, because it was such a boring number. As a matter of fact, the whole movie, when I look at it, looks like something out of the thirties. There's one scene, just before the two sisters come walking down the street, when Jean Stapleton says, 'We've just come from our ballet lessons'— well, right before you see them, a car goes around the corner, and I kept saying, 'What is that antique car doing in the movie?' Because it looked like something from the twenties or something. I don't remember cars looking like that in the fifties."

"Except for Tab Hunter," said Ray Walston, who played the devilish dealmaker of the story (and Lola's employer), Mr. Applegate, "we were the same cast from Broadway down to the last chorus gypsy." Hunter, a Warners contractee, was given the lead role of Joe Hardy, whom Applegate turns into the star player for the Senators.

"He wasn't very good," bellowed George Abbott.

"Not very good?" repeated a flabbergasted Donen. "It was George Abbott who fought to have Tab Hunter in the picture! When we found out, Hal Prince and I nearly fainted." Asked to assess Hunter's performance, Donen quoted, "He couldn't sing, he couldn't dance, he couldn't act. He was a triple threat."

"We needed a name," said Abbott.

"I did five shows with George Abbott," said Ray Walston, who knew the veteran producer-director as someone whose authority was never to be questioned, "and I witnessed something on the picture that I'd never seen happen to George Abbott before. He went up to Tab Hunter and gave him some bit of dialogue he wanted Tab to say."

The line was the exclamation "Hot dog!"

"What?" said Hunter, reacting to Abbott's instruction.

"I want you to say 'Hot dog!' " Abbott reiterated.

"I won't say that," replied Hunter. "How about if you let me say 'Jesus Christ!'?"

In defense of Hunter, Gwen Verdon said, "Tab would always tell George Abbott, who himself was always trying to tell Tab what to do, 'Well, it doesn't feel natural to me.' I don't know what George Abbott wanted from Tab, but whatever it was, Tab did not agree."

"No one ever answered George Abbott back before," reported Ray Walston. "Finally, he just told Tab, 'Oh, do what you want.' "

BY THE TIME of *Damn Yankees,* Bob Fosse and Gwen Verdon were an item (they were married in 1960), and the show made her a Broadway star. "Miss Verdon is, I believe, some sort of mobile designed by a man without a conscience," raved Walter Kerr in the *Herald Tribune.* "As she prances mockingly through a seduction scene, flipping a black glove over her shoulder as her hips go into mysterious but extremely interesting action, beating the floor idiotically with whatever clothing she has removed, coiling all over a locker-room bench while batting absurd eyelashes at her terrified victim, she is simply and insanely inspired." Verdon's Lola is very much a fifties Kewpie doll—by the midsixties, writers and performers would gradually become more sensitive to such stereotypical portrayals—and in the movie, the role is essentially played as Verdon delivered it onstage. "*Damn Yankees* was the first movie I ever did with a large speaking part," the actress said in 1992. "I had minuscule parts and dance parts in pictures before that, so Stanley was very gentle with me, because he felt I didn't know what I was doing. Which was true: I didn't. The only scene that came out with me performing well is what I call the 'ladder' scene, before the big rally for Joe Hardy in the theater. There's a ladder in the shot, with Tab on one side and me on the other. By then, I finally understood what Bob and Stanley wanted me to do for the movie."*

In terms of how Fosse and Donen collaborated in helping Verdon block out the action for Lola, she said that a lot of ongoing conversations took place. "Many times Bob would say things to me, but I'm sure Stanley would say things to Bob, who would say things to me." As it was, Verdon recalled, "the movie was made under really terrible circumstances."

A musicians' strike was under way, Donen remembered, meaning that rather than have fully prepared orchestrations for the cast to work with, the entire playback consisted of a "click track," with the actors having to lip-sync to a beat instead of a full orchestral accompaniment. This led to a general sense of anxiety.

"The directors were set to walk out next," said Verdon, "which meant all the floor men, assistant directors, everybody who was part of that union." The only solution was to charge full speed ahead. "We made the

---

* Stripped of her theatrical affectation, Lola informs Joe, "I'm just a blond hussy who's organized a fan club . . . without instructions from Applegate."

whole movie in either twenty-eight or twenty-nine days," said Verdon, "which was unheard of."*

To make time, Donen filmed while Abbott rehearsed Hunter, who lacked the experience the rest of the cast had with the material. Abbott also played a more active role than he had on the previous film, with Walston observing continuous conversations between the codirectors. "The first scene we shot," said Walston, "was the Devil's first appearance, when he meets 'old' Joe. The house was built on the back lot at Warners, which looked like a little neighborhood town. The atmosphere was wonderful, and the wind was blowing a little bit."

Applegate pops out of a shrub and makes himself known to the "old" Joe Boyd (Robert Shafer), before Applegate transforms him into virile young Joe Hardy (Tab Hunter).

"Who are you?" says old Joe.

"A man who agrees with you," Applegate answers.

"Cut!" yelled Donen.

"Cut?" called out Abbott. "Why? The atmosphere's perfect."

"The scene's not scheduled now," explained Donen. "We'll do it on the soundstage."

"Oh, pshaw," said Abbott.†

DONEN'S SPLIT SCREEN speeds up the material at some points, but not often enough. He helped stylize the opening credits by writing music department head Ray Heindorf: "I am so bored with main titles being 'caught' that I would much prefer just having some lively sound played for the title footage." The movie begins with the roar of baseball fans cheering.

Verdon said Donen and Fosse had strong disagreements over how to shoot "Who's Got the Pain?" which Fosse himself performed with Verdon. It is a stage piece done in an auditorium during the rally to honor Joe Hardy. "Bob wanted it black, with a real vaudeville spotlight, and Stanley said, 'It'll look like the black hole of Calcutta.' I remember thinking: These two are friends? They sure don't sound like friends. But Bob got his 'black hole of Calcutta,' and it looked fine."

---

* Production actually lasted for forty-three days, forty of which were at the Burbank studio, with one day for location shooting at Griffith Stadium in Washington, D.C. (two travel days were allocated). Rehearsals began April 14, 1958, and lasted two weeks. Prerecording occurred from April 28 to May 2, and production began May 5.

† Asked at the age of 106 if he was proud of his many accomplishments, George Abbott responded, "I don't flatter myself."

"It's not easy to get Stanley upset," said Walston, "although one day Stanley had devised some moves with the camera boom, and after three or four takes, the operator kept missing what Stanley wanted. Stanley finally went to the guy to see what was wrong, and the operator said, 'It's too difficult.' When we came back after lunch, there was a new operator. It was clear you didn't mess with Stanley Donen."

To introduce Verdon into the picture at an earlier point than that in which she appeared on Broadway, Donen inserted a scene of Applegate speaking to her on the phone. "That did not exist onstage," said Verdon. "I didn't appear until I sang 'A Little Brains, a Little Talent.' But Stanley said, 'She's got to be on before that.' " When Applegate rings up Lola, she's in bed, reclining. For her entrance, Donen thought it imperative that she look perfect. "Stanley did not think short hair was sexy," said Verdon, "so we shot that scene in the bed with me wearing a wig with all this long red hair, curls, and black lace, sort of Ann-Margret-ish. Honestly, I just looked like a man in drag." The scene was reshot, to feature Verdon with her own closely cropped hairdo. "I mean, even Stanley had to admit that long hair doesn't go over unless it's pulled back, ballet style," said Verdon.

When Lola offends Applegate by admitting she's in love with Joe, he transforms her into an ancient crone. "In the theater," said Verdon, "I would fall offstage in one half, so my feet were always onstage. Then dressers would quickly shove a mask on me with all that straggly gray hair, and I'd be back onstage in ten seconds. In the film, I had to report to makeup at about five-thirty in the morning, and they'd spend two to three hours on my face and hands."

As a point of interest, said Verdon, the old witch's mask she wore in the stage version "was modeled on Agnes Moorehead, because we have almost the same profile. So if you think about it, the star of *Damn Yankees* was Agnes Moorehead."

Damn Yankees opened in September of 1958. "We did some sneak previews in California," said Gwen Verdon, "not where people had buttons to push but where they filled out cards. I went to one and took my nephew, who grew up to be a president of a bank." Newspaper reviews were kind but not truly enthusiastic, with a lot of blame for the film's shortcomings laid upon Tab Hunter.

"In New York," said Verdon, "the picture opened at the Roxy. They got me up on the marquee outside the theater, and I posed there for pho-

Damn Yankees's star lineup: Donen, Tab Hunter, Gwen Verdon, George Abbott. The veteran theater man argued constantly with Hunter, who did not hesitate to argue back.

tographers. I'd played the Roxy before, onstage, with Jack Cole. We did weekends, five shows a day, Jack Cole and His Dancers."

"The Roxy was smaller than Radio City Music Hall," said Donen, whose pictures usually premiered at the larger venue. "The Roxy was gaudier, brassier. It was Ethel Merman. Radio City was first class, the Roxy was second. Radio City was *Life* magazine, the Roxy *Look*."

Like the original Hollywood musical, the Roxy was facing its demise. The cathedral of the motion picture was razed in 1960, to make way for a parking garage annexed to a Woolworth's. The original musical fared little better as the decade progressed, from ill-conceived Julie Andrews vehicles in the late sixties, such as *Star!* and *Darling Lili,* to wretched musical renderings of such classic thirties films as *Goodbye, Mr. Chips* and *Lost Horizon.*

One safe musical direction that Hollywood musicals took—for a time, at least—was to adapt Broadway hits and inflate them (Robert Wise's *West Side Story,* George Cukor's *My Fair Lady,* Wise's *The Sound of Music,* Sir Carol Reed's *Oliver!,* William Wyler's *Funny Girl,* Norman Jewison's *Fiddler on the Roof,* each from a director known for his earlier solid dramas), although these were mostly static affairs rather than what *The Pajama Game* was, a joyous exercise.

Jean-Luc Godard spoke well for the beleaguered genre when he wrote, as a critic: "Donen is surely the master of the musical. *The Pajama Game* exists to prove it." This auteurist chieftain of the French New Wave was admittedly seduced by the light political frosting on the airy love story set inside the pajama plant—" 'she' is the trade-union delegate in a pajama factory of which 'he' is a management executive"—while he was completely smitten by its cinematic approach: "It is the first left-wing operetta, quite skillfully filmed, for Donen sticks to the Broadway conventions but pushes them to their utmost limits, which results in a rather eccentric and totally unrestrained work." In particular favor with Godard was the film's exterior-shot picnic sequence. "Once-a-Year Day," choreographed by Bob Fosse, "with its marvelous, frenzied tempo, surpasses anything of the kind that has been done, notably, good as it is, *Seven Brides for Seven Brothers.* But this time Donen has not hesitated in going too far . . . juggling with red lipstick, blue jeans, green grass, yellow flags, white skirts, to compose a wild and ravishing kaleidoscope."

Donen considered *The Pajama Game* and *Damn Yankees* "fun movies, but there's not much I could contribute to them, beyond photographing them." This is why, after these two convivial collaborations with George Abbott, Donen got out of musicals altogether, save for a fleeting return in 1970, with the elusive *The Little Prince,* and again, eight years later, for a short spoof of Busby Berkeley in *Movie Movie.* In spite of such a career stance, Donen for years remained on studio short lists of bankable directors practically every time a Broadway-musical property was sold to Hollywood, which became increasingly the case as the decades wore on, until the film musical literally croaked its last after some poorly guided, expensive turkeys that no one wished to see—*Paint Your Wagon, Hello, Dolly!, Man of La Mancha,* even Bob Fosse's initial foray into film directing, a moribund adaptation of his stage hit *Sweet Charity.* These releases completely lost sight of the small charms that were once the hallmark of the Freed Unit.

"Dick Zanuck begged me to direct *The Sound of Music,* and *Hello, Dolly!,* too," said Donen. "But when I was reading the script to *The Sound of Music* and got to the point where they were yodeling with a goatherd, I said, 'This isn't for me.' "

As for the tireless Dr. Pangloss of the American musical himself, Arthur Freed caught what direction the new wind was blowing, and he set about retiring.* His final project, aborted in 1970, when M-G-M manage-

---

* Freed's last musical was a tepid adaptation of *Bells Are Ringing,* directed by Vincente Minnelli in 1960.

ment was changing so often that no one knew who was in charge, was a musical biography of Irving Berlin, to have been called *Say It with Music.*

Whatever was to be said was left forever unsung. Arthur Freed died in 1973.

There did happen to be two stage properties that Donen would have liked to adapt to the screen, only they were two that were never offered to him: Lerner and Loewe's 1956 *My Fair Lady* and their 1960 *Camelot.* Both musicals showcased to near perfection (in the case of *My Fair Lady,* to absolute perfection) the advancements *Pal Joey* originally brought to Broadway in 1940. *My Fair Lady* was based on George Bernard Shaw's 1913 play *Pygmalion,* while Camelot took as its source the Arthurian legend, focusing on the birth of chivalry and the romantic ménage à trois of King Arthur, Queen Guinevere, and Sir Lancelot. Both shows contained literate plots, vibrant lyrics, and drop-dead music (*Camelot*'s only drawback was an unwieldy book), and both ended up as disappointing movies.

"*My Fair Lady,* the show, touched me so," said Donen. "To take a human being and turn her into another human being by teaching her to speak differently. It's so rich in feeling, it makes you feel good, and oh, God, the musical numbers on the stage were wonderful. I thought they just stunk in the movie."

George Cukor's gorgeously gowned 1964 film version, with Rex Harrison re-creating his Henry Higgins of the stage and Audrey Hepburn playing Eliza Doolittle, was a veritable stuffing and mounting of the show. "The only thing that saves the picture," said Donen, "is Rex's performance, one of the great performances ever, and there it is, preserved. But it's not a good movie."*

When it was first announced that Warner Bros. had bought the film rights, Donen wrote Alan Jay Lerner and Jack Warner, offering his services. Though he had worked with both before, Donen ended up never hearing from either, "not even as a courtesy."

As for *Camelot,* exquisitely orchestrated by Alfred Newman, breathtakingly dressed by John Truscott, acted with intelligent sexuality by Vanessa Redgrave (as Guinevere, opposite Richard Harris as a camp Arthur and Franco Nero as a punch-drunk Lancelot), and lugubriously filmed by Joshua Logan, Donen said in 1992, "I'd still love to film it—and get it right."

---

* Asked whom he would have cast as Eliza Doolittle—the stage original, Julie Andrews, or his own frequent star, Audrey Hepburn, who, with a singing voice dubbed by Marni Nixon, did end up starring in the film—Donen chivalrously replied: "The choice would not have been left to me. As it was, Jack Warner didn't get the cast he wanted. He wanted Cary [Grant] to be Higgins, only Cary refused."

Chapter 2

"Cary Grant Wants You"

W HEN I first came to Hollywood in 1942," said Donen, "Cary Grant had already been a star for close to ten years." Grant, né Archibald Leach and late of Bristol, England, as well as the lifeguard station at Coney Island, New York, got his big break in 1933, when Mae West cast the charismatic twenty-nine-year-old opposite her in *She Done Him Wrong*. In the gay-nineties period comedy, the curvaceous grand mistress of the innuendo tossed Grant what was to become her trademark line, "Why don't you come up 'n' see me?"

By the late 1930s, Cary Grant was a screen trademark all to himself.*

"I always thought of Cary not only as a wonderful-looking man and a movie star," said Donen, "but as someone who also gave some great performances. In *His Girl Friday*, there's never been a better performance than Cary's. In *The Philadelphia Story*, everybody talks about Jimmy Stewart. Didn't he win an Oscar for it?† But in fact, if you look at the picture, it's Cary's."

In 1957, while still under contract to M-G-M, Donen received a phone call out of the blue. "The message was: 'Cary Grant wants you to direct a movie and would like to meet you,' " Donen remembered. "I was thrilled. I'd never met him." Typically, Donen was at a loss to explain why, saying only, "He selected me for whatever reasons."

The two met and discussed a property Grant was interested in doing, "but I didn't like the script he gave me," said Donen. "I didn't really want to do the movie. My first reaction was to say no." The film, written by

---

* Katharine Hepburn, who starred with Grant in *Bringing Up Baby, Holiday,* and *The Philadelphia Story,* said in the course of a private conversation in 1992 that she personally preferred Grant's "fleshy, baby-faced" early stage, as he looked with Mae West, over his appearance during the lean, dapper phase that followed.

† He did.

Julius Epstein, was based on a 1944 Broadway play, *Kiss Them for Me,* by a recent graduate of Yale named Luther Davis. Davis had based his three acts on a 1943 novel by Frederic Wakeman, titled *Shore Leave.*

"I was very familiar with the property," said Donen, "because Judy Holliday was my girlfriend for a while, and she was in the show in New York." The play marked Comden and Green's former partner's Broadway debut, as Alice, the "innocent" hooker with a heart of gold. "When it was a novel," said Donen, "it was very hard-hitting and very profound about the moment, because it was written during the war. It was about how the civilian population, mostly the businessmen and industrialists, were trying to make money from the war and how they didn't realize the horrors that the military personnel were going through. The book really was good. The play was mediocre, but Judy Holliday won the Tony for her performance in it, which is the reason she was cast in *Born Yesterday.*"

"The play was not a great triumph," said its writer, Luther Davis, "but it was what it was." Part of the show's lack of appeal, noted Davis, was that the war suddenly ended and, with it, people's attitudes about it. "Mostly what the show had," said Davis, "was Judy Holliday's entrance into the world. She played a little girl who thought sex was clean. Then who does Stanley Donen cast in the movie but Jayne Mansfield, who could make a spoon dirty."

Mansfield, who displayed a more potent knack for publicity than for talent, was the Twentieth Century–Fox executives' weapon to keep Marilyn Monroe in line. The only snag was that Mansfield, measuring in at an overamplified 41–18–35, never attracted a movie audience. *Kiss Them for Me,* her fourth picture, would mark her final major-studio Hollywood release; after its completion, Fox farmed her out to its European branch until her contract expired.

"The movie was cast," said Donen, referring to the time when he and Grant first shook hands. "When I found out it was to be Jayne Mansfield in the part Judy was so adorable in, I was horrified."

"What sort of a supine director would allow Jayne Mansfield to be cast in his picture?" asked Luther Davis. "And Cary Grant was all wrong too. It was supposed to be a young man, twenty-three. On Broadway it was played by Richard Widmark, and even he was starting to get too old for the part. But Cary Grant was fifty-three."

"Cary appealed to me to do it," said Donen, "and I found it impossible to refuse. That's how it started."

* * *

THE PLAY *Kiss Them for Me* had been sent to Warner Bros., where a reader noted: "Seems to me this is not nearly as solid a story as *Mr. Roberts.*" In 1950, RKO took a look, considered the play as "a possible Mitchum-Russell vehicle," but never took any action. Columbia showed little enthusiasm when the property was submitted there, which is how it finally ended up at Fox. In August of 1956, the studio, still shaking from the self-imposed departure of its founder, Darryl F. Zanuck, was not keen on the project, although its producer, Jerry Wald, believed "there is great movie material" in the original Wakeman novel.

Julius Epstein, a writer on *Casablanca,* was hired to adapt the play, and made himself heard about his personal dislike of the title *Kiss Them for Me,* which sounded like a "trivial, tittering little title for a tittering little musical comedy." Wald, meanwhile, concentrated on finding a director. His wish list, as approved by the studio, consisted of Charles Vidor (who had directed *Cover Girl*), Donen, Rouben Mamoulian, Walter Lang, Moss Hart, Leo McCarey, Hank Potter, George Cukor, and John Ford.

On March 20, 1957, Donen was hired.

"Part of my deal," said Donen, "was that my contract from Metro be bought out. It still had a year or two to go." Jerry Wald negotiated the buyout, and Donen was out. Donen found Wald, who was said to be the role model for Hollywood ruthlessness personified, Sammy Glick, "exactly as Budd Schulberg depicted him in the novel [*What Makes Sammy Run?*]."

As for Grant, "That's a book in itself. I found him extremely simple to work with, very cooperative with others. He had this reputation for being very tightfisted. To me he was very generous. He gave me a lot of gifts, and I gave him a watch. After he died I found out that he had it written in his will to have it given back to me."

Mostly, said Donen, "Cary was easy and friendly, and he loved English music hall humor." Grant would typically amuse Donen with tales of Alfred Hitchcock. "For instance," Donen remembered Grant's telling him, "Hitchcock loved corny things. He would come into his office every morning and ask his secretary, 'Alaskan beer today?' And she'd say, 'Yes, sir.' Alaskan beer was Nome ale—no mail. Then Hitchcock made up a game that Cary and I would carry on further, playing with the names of the people on the set. For example, the leading lady was named Dolly Shot. The cameraman was named Otto Focus. Some of them were quite funny, actually. The writers were called The Daileys. The heavy was called Mike Shadow. That was Hitchcock's, and Cary loved playing games like that."

4

"Not only a wonderful-looking man and a movie star, but someone who also gave some great performances," Donen said of Cary Grant. They made four pictures together. Their first, *Kiss Them for Me* (1957), was the weakest.

Donen recalled that he and Grant "used to talk endlessly—which I will not talk about—about his personal life, his love affairs, and his marriages and divorces. Altogether, he and I made four pictures. Two of them were good, one is better than the other, but two are mediocre." Donen was referring, in descending order of quality, to *Charade, Indiscreet, The Grass Is Greener,* and *Kiss Them for Me,* a cacophonous exercise that he and most others consider the nadir of his collaboration with Grant. Even so, one incident during its making bears retelling, as reported by Ray Walston, who costarred in the picture.

Grant, the assistant director, and some other members of the cast—Walston, Larry Blyden, Nathaniel Frey, and Harry Carey, Jr.—decided to play a practical joke on Donen during the final scene. "We were in a PBY taking off from the wharf and flying over the breakwater," related Walston. "You were to see us taking off, then Donen would cut to Suzy Parker, waving good-bye to us. We got the pilot to take the plane out, get it up to speed, and then, once we got over the stone breakwater, to take it down immediately."

When that occurred, Donen turned to the assistant director and asked, "What happened?"

"I believe it went down, sir," said the AD.

"Get a man over there," ordered Donen. *"Quick!"*

The fellow came back and told Donen, "It crashed and sank."

"Were the actors in it when it sank?" asked Donen.

"Yes, sir."

"Are they dead?" asked Donen.

"I'm afraid so, sir."

"At that point," said Walston, "Stanley looked at his watch and said, 'Lunch!' "

"IN THE MIDDLE of doing *Kiss Them for Me,*" said Donen, who was now known as a free agent in Hollywood, "Norman Krasna, whom I knew, sent me a screenplay he had written that was later made with Yves Montand and Marilyn Monroe, *Let's Make Love.* At that time it was called *The Billionaire.* I read it and said, 'Not for me.' " (George Cukor eventually filmed *Let's Make Love,* in 1960.) Krasna, raised in the same Kaufman-and-Hart, Hecht-and-MacArthur tradition that Donen had been spoon-fed, wrote comedic plays and scripts, with his specialty involving cases of mistaken identity. A perfect example was the 1953 *Kind Sir,* one of the great theatrical calamities of its time.

Model-turned-actress Suzy Parker, Grant's love interest in *Kiss Them for Me*. Beautiful, yes, but on-screen she failed to ignite the necessary sparks.

As the show prepared for Broadway, Charles Boyer and Mary Martin starred, and Joshua Logan directed, only the veteran theater man* was deep in the midst of undergoing electroshock therapy for a nervous breakdown. His fatigue prevented him from pulling the show together in time for its opening, and it failed, miserably, despite the high hopes that had been pinned on it. When Krasna first gave Logan the script, the playwright said the only two actors right for it would be Alfred Lunt and Lynn Fontanne—a joke, because they were too old. Fearing the play would therefore be impossible to cast, "I was amazed," said Logan upon reading *Kind Sir,* "at the way Norman could take a small misunderstanding, a white lie, and turn it into a full-length, funny, and even romantic play." Logan's summary of the plot: "A distinguished man, to keep out of the matrimonial trap, tells any woman *before he gets involved with her* that he is already married." Logan hired Charles Boyer as the diplomat and Mary Martin as the

* By 1953, Logan had directed and/or cowritten *Annie Get Your Gun, Mister Roberts, South Pacific,* and *Picnic.*

accomplished actress who dazzles him—and then pulls a similar stunt herself, faking an affair with another man as a means to get even.

Kind Sir opened on Broadway at the Alvin Theater on November 4, 1953, with a million-dollar advance, reportedly the highest ever for a non-musical. But the reviewers held their collective noses. "My idea of pairing Mary Martin and Charles Boyer in a light romantic comedy backfired," admitted Logan. "The public came to see a combination *South Pacific, Algiers,* and *Mayerling.* With their appetites set for a juicy steak dinner, they had been served fish."

After rejecting *The Billionaire* screenplay, "I told Norman his story about this guy who lies was an absolute knockout of a plot," said Donen, who was in turn informed by the playwright, "Well, it's deader than a doornail in Hollywood. I've tried everywhere, and nobody will touch it. If you want it, it's yours."

"It was a disaster," said Donen. "The critics ripped it apart. But I told Norman I couldn't take it for free, but if he'd work with me a couple of weeks to see if we could come up with a treatment, I'd see what I could do."

"No movie company bid for the rights," recalled Logan, "so when, years later, Norman Krasna offered to buy them for himself for ten thousand dollars, a ridiculously low figure, everyone involved with the show—Mary, Charles, and myself—accepted Norman's offer."

Donen and Krasna worked in tandem for approximately two weeks, during Donen's after hours on *Kiss Them for Me.* "Once we had the treatment," said Donen, "I took it to Cary and said, 'I want to make this picture with you,' and he read it and said okay, just like that. He wasn't like the actors you often hear about. If I sent him a treatment or a script, he'd read it that day and I'd have his answer that very day or the next morning. He had no staff, he had no nothing, just himself, and in general, if you look at the career, he made good choices, all the way, of what he was going to be in. Anyway, Cary read this treatment of Norman's and mine and said he'd do it—*if* I could get Ingrid."

Cary Grant and Ingrid Bergman had set off sparks before, in 1946, when Hitchcock paired them in the romantic thriller *Notorious.* The two stars had met in 1939, at the home of David and Irene Selznick. The producer had brought the statuesque Swedish beauty to Hollywood to be paired with Leslie Howard in a remake of *Intermezzo,* in which she had already starred in Sweden.

By the time she appeared in *Notorious,* Bergman had captivated Hollywood and the public with *Dr. Jekyll and Mr. Hyde, Casablanca, For Whom the Bell Tolls, Gaslight,* and *Saratoga Trunk.* "Cary Grant," she once recalled, "I only went out with once, when I was in New York, and we met Howard Hughes." The aviation mogul was a friend of the actor's. In *Notorious,* which was written by Ben Hecht, Grant played an FBI agent sent to test the loyalty of Bergman, who portrayed the daughter of a convicted Nazi spy and the wife of the villain, played by Claude Rains. In the course of assisting Grant in framing Rains, Bergman engaged her leading man in a screen embrace that lasted a good five times longer than the censorship board normally allowed.

"A kiss could last six seconds," said Bergman. Under Hitchcock's eye, she and Grant cleverly prolonged the act in a perfectly legal way. "We just kissed each other and talked, leaned away, and kissed each other again. Then the telephone came between us, then we moved to the other side of the telephone. So it was a kiss that opened and closed."

If *Notorious* served as a high point in her career, Bergman's extramarital relationship with Italian director Roberto Rossellini in 1949 marked the low ebb. Bergman became persona non grata in Hollywood—in all of America—when she abandoned her husband since 1937, the dentist Dr. Peter Lindstrom, and their daughter, Pia, for Rossellini, whose child she was carrying. Bergman was labeled "a free-love cultist" on the floor of the United States Senate, and the equally hypocritical Hollywood power brokers refused her services until 1956, when she starred in and won a Best Actress Oscar for *Anastasia,* which had been filmed in England. At the time of her victory, Bergman was living in Paris—there were rumors of a rift with Rossellini—and starring in the French stage version of Robert Anderson's *Tea and Sympathy.* Accepting the Oscar for her in Hollywood was Cary Grant.

Grant's instructing Donen to go get Ingrid Bergman at this point was nearly the same as producer Will Wright's telling him to fetch Elizabeth Taylor six years earlier. "That's impossible," Donen replied to Grant. "She's in Italy with Rossellini and doesn't make American movies."

Grant stood firm. No Ingrid, no Cary.

"So here's what I did," said Donen. "We were still shooting *Kiss Them for Me.* The studio didn't know what I was up to, but I called her in Rome. I don't remember how I tracked down her phone number, but I called her and said, 'I'd like to make a movie with you and I'd like to come talk to you about it; could I come this weekend?' She said, 'Yeah, sure,' so I walked off the Fox soundstage that Friday night, I went straight to the airport, flew to New York, switched to another plane to Rome, and got to Rome midday Saturday, Los Angeles time."

To Donen's surprise, "Ingrid met me at the Rome airport. She was an incredible woman. I got off the plane, and she was just standing there. I walked over and said, 'Hello, I'm Stanley Donen.' And she said, 'I've come to take you to your hotel.' "

The two climbed inside "Ingrid's mini-Fiat. The two of us could barely get into the car," recalled Donen, "and she drove and said, 'Would you like to go to your hotel and change, or would you like to come right away to my apartment and tell me about the movie, because I know you must go right back.' I told her it would be wonderful to go right to her apartment, so I could give her the script."

Donen remembered the Bergman-Rossellini apartment as "huge, two floors, it went on and on, with kids running around, and maids." The two repaired to Bergman's room and she closed the door so they could talk quietly. It was she who initiated the conversation. "I want to put you at ease," said Bergman. "I'm going to do the picture."

"Incredible," said Donen. "She said yes before I could even explain what we wanted to do."

Bergman substantiated her acceptance by explaining to Donen, "First of all, I've read an article about you that was very recently published in *Cahiers du Cinema,* and they said you were very gifted." The piece she was probably referring to, by Claude de Givray, was a rave for *It's Always Fair Weather.* "I then spoke to my friend Art Cohn,"* Bergman continued, "and he said you were wonderful. And Cary, obviously, wants to work with you. That's enough for me. Only, please, if you'd be kind enough to tell me, what is the picture about?"

CARY GRANT AND Donen formed their own production company, Grandon, named for the two of them. "Forming a production company is nothing," said Donen. "Just find a movie and agree to make it." A financing and distribution deal was set up at Warners. The title *Kind Sir,* which carried the stigma of the Broadway flop and was not particularly enticing in any event, needed to be changed. Jack Warner suggested calling the picture *Irresistible.* Grant and Donen preferred *Indiscreet,* but Jack Warner was yet to be entirely sold, and the title had been used before, in 1931, for a Leo McCarey ten-reeler. The Motion Picture Association of America received from the studio three other titles for registration, and accepted *Better than Married* and *As Good as Married* but rejected *Mister and Mistress.*

---

* Cohn, a former newspaperman turned screenwriter, lived in Rome. Among his credits was *Stromboli.* When Cohn was killed in the same 1958 accident that claimed the life of producer Mike Todd, writer Harry Kurnitz envisioned the headline: "MIKE TODD KILLED IN PLANE CRASH. Additional death by Art Cohn."

Ingrid Bergman and Grant, with Donen, during the making of *Indiscreet*

Grant and Donen then proposed *They're Not Married,* but, as Jack Warner memoed them, "with Ingrid Bergmann [*sic*] in the picture, it would be extremely dangerous to use the word 'married.' " On November 13, 1957, five days before the start of principal photography, the title was set, *Indiscreet.*

Shooting took place at Elstree Studios outside London through February 6, 1958, with the company taking a short break for the holidays. Bergman sent a letter to Burbank to thank Jack Warner for his flowers on the first day of shooting, and Donen wrote and invited him to "come visit" (Warner did, by Christmas, and he viewed the rushes, en route to the casinos in the south of France). Grant, prompted by a visit to the set by the Duke and Duchess of Windsor, wrote the studio chief and said, "The Duke sends his regards—Love, Cary. As a matter of fact, *all* the Dukes send their regards." Grant, or rather the production, bought a brand-new twenty-three-thousand-dollar 1958 Silver Wraith Rolls-Royce, the first one off the line, with left-hand (American-style) drive, and placed its cost on the $1.5 million budget of the picture. (Grant's salary was $25,000 a week for twelve weeks, while Donen, for tax reasons, requested that his salary be reduced to $25,000 plus, according to a deal memo, "full weekly living allowances.") The car was sold to Grant after the filming, as a used car.*

Off-camera, Ingrid Bergman was indeed facing the dissolution of her marriage to Rossellini, and the inexorable press was smoothly kept at bay by a protective Grant. "The press was waiting at Heathrow for a statement," recalled Bergman. "I'd ruined my career by marrying Roberto Rossellini, they said, and now I was going to ruin it again by leaving Roberto Rossellini?" Arriving inside the transit lounge for the press conference, Bergman was relieved to find Grant waiting for her. As the actress remembered, "He shouted across the heads of the journalists, 'Ingrid, wait until you hear my problems!' That broke the ice. Everybody burst into laughter."

Bergman considered *Indiscreet* "a light comedy," in which she played "a famous, wealthy actress," Anna Kalman. She is also a loner, though not exactly by choice. Grant, Bergman said, "was an American diplomat protecting his bachelor status by pretending he was already married. I found out and asked how dare he make love to me when he wasn't even a married man! It ended happily ever after."

In spite of the compact nature of the script and the company—there were only eight major speaking roles—the production rendered the usual industrial-strength headaches. Asian flu felled some of the crew, including Donen, and some quick juggling was called for when the Australian actress Margaret Johnston took issue with her director one too many times. She was replaced with Phyllis Calvert. Donen had another standoff on the picture, this one involving the esteemed cinematographer Freddie Young, though Young was not shown the door. "Freddie Young was a very difficult man," said Donen. "I'm very precise about what I want in a picture, down to the last edge, as I'm sure most directors are." Donen had set up a long shot, left the set for a break, then returned to find that Young had undone the shot, removing Donen's desired view of the ceiling in the process. "Freddie," he complained, "we have to start all over again and relight."

"No, we don't need the ceiling," Donen said was Young's reply.

"From there we just went at it. I decided then I'd never go near this man again."

---

* Another major expense item was Ingrid Bergman's wardrobe. It broke down as follows: 646,500 francs and 39,000 lire, plus another 1,642,500 francs to Christian Dior. Donen personally supervised her selection of clothes in Paris.

*   *   *

DONEN EXERCISED his own bit of Hitchcockery in *Indiscreet,* though in a highly Donenesque fashion. After the use of his split-screen triptych in *It's Always Fair Weather,* the diptych Donen uses in *Indiscreet* might have seemed anticlimactic, except that on one half of the screen Cary Grant was shown in bed in Paris, talking on the telephone to Ingrid Bergman, in her own bed in London, on the other half of the screen. The two looked to be cozying up to each other while sharing the same mattress, unheard of at the time in movies, even among married couples. At one point he even seems to paw her. The trick was doubly successful, as a visual tease and as a skirting around the censors. It is also genuinely funny.

Despite the stage-bound nature of Krasna's script, which a bemused Josh Logan found to differ from the stage version by only a few altered lines, Donen manages to convey the sensation of being in London, making full use of the few locations actually employed in the course of the production, which also cost a lot less than it looks or implies; at one point Grant offers to buy Bergman a yacht, and given the lush trappings and

"How dare he make love to me and not be a married man!" announces Bergman, summing up the plot and theme of *Indiscreet* (1958). The elegant romantic comedy recast Donen as something more than a director of lively musicals.

lifestyle of the protagonists, there is no reason to scoff at the plausibility of such a gift. For this lighthearted love story is an escapist delight, arguably what all movies should be and, from this point on, what they tended to be in Donen's work. Donen's signature song-and-dance music on the playback track was replaced, starting with *Indiscreet,* by the well-dressed backdrop populated by well-dressed—and well-behaved—European-style protagonists. With no grandstanding or voyeuristic stopping to gawk at the scenery caught by the camera, the Grant and Bergman characters breezily carry on their affair amid the splendors of the Crush Bar of the Royal Opera House at Covent Garden, beside Cleopatra's Needle and the stone lion statues along the Embankment, and inside the Scala Theater, the Leicester Art Galleries, and the Garrick Club. Bergman's elegant Buckingham Palace Gate flat is decorated with Picassos—at least two dozen of his drawings—a Dufy, a Rouault, and a John Piper. (The flat was an Elstree set, but the artwork was authentic.) Equally enviable was the delightfully irreverent dance performed by Grant, a Scottish reel, which he executes to impress Bergman (shot in a studio recreation of Sir Christopher Wren's Painted Hall in the Palace of Greenwich). Only Cary Grant could get away with such a display, and only Cary Grant could make an observer not feel jealous. That was the actor's *true* gift: He made every man want to be Cary Grant, without making them hate him for their failure to do so. If nothing else, *Indiscreet* successfully reflects Bergman's—and Donen's—appreciation of this fact of nature. The grandeur of the relatively modest picture is that Bergman behaves as Grant's peer, which, inarguably, she is. Donen's role is to provide them the freedom to act upon their natural impulses. It was a successful marriage for all three.

"*Indiscreet,*" said *Time,* "is a conventional comedy of what Hollywood supposes to be upper-class manners, but it is flicked off in the high old style of hilarity that U.S. moviemakers seem to have forgotten in recent years. Director Donen deserves a cash-register-ringing cheer."

"The picture," said Donen, allowing it no more and no less than he thought it deserved, given that he never truly did extricate it from its stagy origins, "was sort of sweet."

Chapter 3

"The Son of a Bitch"

S TARTING WITH *Indiscreet,* Donen was no longer tethered to a Hollywood home base. "It got to the point," he said, "that I hated living in studios." Donen saw the daily routine at a movie factory as involving his "getting up in the dark around five, going to the studio for fourteen hours, and then going home in the dark, six days a week. Studios had no streets, no shops, no newspapers, no life, as if the real world did not exist. Politics, economy, sickness—everything the movies are about— did not exist inside studio walls. It was as close to being in prison as you could get, and I lived roughly my first fifteen years in Hollywood entirely inside studio walls. It was enough."

Donen's solution, starting in 1958, was to uproot himself and move to London, where he set up his own offices, complete with fully equipped screening rooms. "When we shot *Indiscreet* in London," he said, "I decided I liked it and decided to stay. This was in the years right before the city gained the reputation of 'Swinging London.' Most of the people who were already there ahead of me were running away from the blacklist— Carl Foreman, Joe Losey, Michael Wilson. Julie Dassin was in Paris. Stanley Kubrick came over to England to make *Lolita,* which was an odd place to make *Lolita,* but that's how I got to know him. I loved London. I ended up staying seventeen years."

Another part of the attraction was Donen's new romantic interest, Adelle Beatty—actually, Lady Adelle Beatty, whose title had come from her second marriage, to Lord Earl Beatty. Husband number one was the socially prominent Los Angeles attorney William O'Connor, whom she met while working as a hostess at the Don the Beachcomber restaurant in Santa Monica.

The attractive blue-eyed blonde was born Adelle Dillingham, in Ard-more, Oklahoma, and had been a model at Neiman Marcus in Dallas after her graduation, in 1940, from the University of Oklahoma. Between hus-bands she had been linked romantically with Senator John Kennedy, Frank Sinatra, and Aly Kahn.

"I'll say this for Adelle," said Donen as he sorted through some fam-ily snapshots several years after their bitter divorce and only a few years after her death, "she was beautiful. Crazy but beautiful." She and Donen had one son, Mark, born in 1962, two years after the couple married. "I wanted to bring up Mark in his father's faith and spoke to an Orthodox rabbi about it," Adelle Donen told one interviewer. Her son Timothy, by her first marriage, was Catholic, her daughter, Diana, by Lord Beatty, was Anglican ("We called her Lady Di," remembered the writer Peter Stone), and Adelle herself was Protestant. "When I filled him in on the roster of religions under one roof," she said, "he laughed and suggested I forget about it." Despite the ecumenical sentiment of her statement, several observers recalled Adelle, paradoxically, as anti-Semitic.

"A meticulous hostess, Adelle looks up guests in *Who's Who* before a party," was one of several admiring statistics about the third Mrs. Donen to appear in a lengthy 1967 *Life* magazine profile, headlined "Beautiful Pacesetter of the London Whirl." The Donens resided on London's "Mil-lionaires' Row," Hyde Park Gardens, near the home of Princess Margaret and Lord Snowdon and within walking distance of Stanley's suite of offices in Marble Arch before he relocated to a fashionable alley behind Mr. Chow's restaurant in Knightsbridge.

"It was magnificent," Peter Stone said of the Donen home. "Stanley and Adelle had about four apartments connected together on property owned by the crown on the 'North Shore' of Hyde Park. They also had a country estate in Querns.* The joke around London at the time was that at four o'clock, everybody goes over to the Donens' to watch the chang-ing of the servants."

"I mix my guests the way I mix furniture," Adelle told *Life*. "Mies van der Rohe with Louis XV." Next to a portrait in the magazine of a bespec-tacled Adelle, the caption read: "This is Adelle between parties—the med-itative, self-assured woman who cherishes her moments of solitude."

"She was very much a socialite," remembered Deborah Kerr, who made *The Grass Is Greener* with Donen in 1960 and who, with her husband,

* Fourteenth century, in the Chiltern foothills, to the west of London.

the writer Peter Viertel, used to see the Donens frequently. "She was a great beauty," Kerr added, "also very keen on royalty." Nearly everyone who had any contact with the Donens during this period was left with a distinct recollection of Adelle's looks. "God," gasped Audrey Hepburn, "she was beautiful." *Life* described her as "the outward personification of the international jet set. Her honey-blond hair and large, blue eyes have attracted a multitude of men."

"Adelle *was* unbelievably beautiful, and a bit crazy,"* said Frederic Raphael. "My wife and I were once having a party in our apartment, seventy or eighty chic people, when Stanley and Adelle walked in. She was wearing a Mondrian-like dress, and all she had to do was stand in the doorway and the entire party went dead silent."

"Of all of them," said Donen, "the only messy divorce I had was with Adelle." At issue was money, but in the end that became moot, because in violation of English law, Adelle's attorneys leaked details of the divorce proceedings to the press, in this instance the New York gossip columnist Suzy. "It will be a rough and dirty case," the social chronicler reported in her New York *Daily News* column of January 21, 1971, two years after the Donens had separated. Less than a month later, a humbled Suzy was forced to report: "The Adelle Donen vs. Stanley Donen divorce case, expected to be one of those sizzling scandals that light up gossip for weeks, petered out after a week and a half in the London courts."

A mutual divorce was granted. Adelle remained in London after the breakup, and died, of cardiac arrest, in April of 1990. According to Donen's sister, Carla, "Adelle was eaten up by 'grandiosity,' if such a disease exists. Even if it doesn't, that's what killed her."

"WHEN I first left California to go live in London," said Donen, "I made a deal, in Los Angeles, with Columbia Pictures." Like several of the other studios during this period, Columbia was existing in a state of flux. Harry Cohn had died in 1957 while still in the driver's seat, and at Fox, the studio was experiencing a shakedown after its founder, Darryl F. Zanuck, relinquished his position, to pursue independent productions starring his mistresses in Europe. In Burbank, Jack Warner was feuding with his sole surviving brother, Harry, while in Culver City, M-G-M's downward spiral accelerated. In a development in Washington, D.C., that made itself felt in Hollywood, alterations in the federal tax laws and the strength of the dol-

---

* Friends remember Adelle Donen as a highly vocal proponent of Jungian analysis.

lar made it advantageous for American movie artists to work abroad. This attractive situation, which Zanuck seized, as did Donen, left the majority of the studios to function merely as funding and distribution bases, operations that could be run from their New York headquarters. Thus did Hollywood enter its initial period of decline as a moviemaking capital.

"There was confusion as to who was head of Columbia," said Donen insofar as this international scenario affected him. "Abe Schneider was the man in charge, and I made a deal with him to do three pictures, and then I went off to London. This was 1958, and Mike Frankovich was at that point in charge of the London branch of Columbia Pictures."

Donen proceeded to make two pictures for Columbia, both (under)written by Harry Kurnitz and both (over)acted by Yul Brynner— *Once More, With Feeling* and *Surprise Package*. The first was based on Kurnitz's own play about a tyrannical orchestra conductor (Brynner) and his mistress (Kay Kendell in her last performance, and a terrific one); she decides that in order to leave him and marry someone respectable, she must wed and then divorce the tyrant—which on the surface sounds like the sort of plot that would attract Donen. Yet it was, in Bosley Crowther's words, "forced and funless," not a Donen specialty. In *Surprise Package*, based on a novel by Art Buchwald, Brynner played an American hood exiled to a Greek island, where he attempts to get back in the chips by relieving the local king of his crown. The king was played by Noël Coward, and the surprise package was Mitzi Gaynor. Enough said, although Coward did jot in his customarily candid diary: "Stanley Donen is really an excellent director, gentle, thorough, and patient. There is much less tension working with him than with Carol [Reed, with whom Coward had made *Our Man in Havana*]. Actually, I'm enjoying it very much."*

Too little of this enjoyment was transferred to the audience. Told at a preview that he had stolen the picture, Noël Coward replied, "My dear, it was petty larceny."

"After *Surprise Package* I had three other properties I liked a great deal," said Donen, "and I told the studio I'd like to make them. One was a magazine article that became *Charade*, the other was *A Man for All Seasons*, and the last was *A Patch of Blue*." In obtaining the rights to Robert Bolt's play about Sir Thomas More, Donen made a personal deal with Bolt to write two more movies, "and this was before he had written any screenplays,"

---

* Donen remembered Coward as "very nice, hysterically funny. He went to the opening of Lionel Bart's musical *Blitz*, and afterward Noël said, 'It was longer and louder than the original.'"

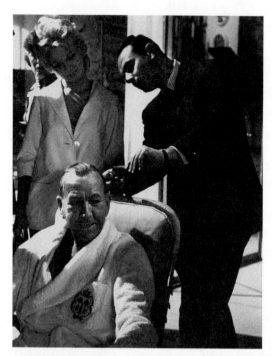

Grooming the master, Noël Coward, on *Surprise Package*

With leading man—twice—Yul Brynner; unfortunately, *Once More, With Feeling* and *Surprise Package* (both 1960) failed to live up to expectations. The former is still notable, however, for the performance—her very last—of Kay Kendall.

said Donen, who had secured the services of a genuine comer. Immediately after his London West End success with *A Man for All Seasons,* Bolt was engaged by the producer Sam Spiegel to redraft a script that displeased Spiegel's director David Lean, *Lawrence of Arabia.* Bolt won the Oscar for *Lawrence,* as he would eventually do again with *A Man for All Seasons,* albeit not under Donen's direction.

"Right after *Surprise Package,*" said Donen, "I made a deal with Alec Guinness to be in *A Man for All Seasons,* and Alec Guinness at the time was the hottest thing in pictures." Guinness had won the Best Actor Oscar for Lean and Spiegel's earlier collaboration, *The Bridge on the River Kwai;* as the mad Colonel Nicholson, Guinness had been catapulted from British character actor to international movie star.

Donen then married Adelle Beatty and set out on a honeymoon voyage from London to New York. "While we were on the boat," said Donen, "I got a cable from Mike Frankovich, saying, 'We are not going ahead with *A Man for All Seasons* or *A Patch of Blue,*' and subsequently they dropped *Charade.* Then, six or seven years later, the studio did *A Man for All Seasons* with Freddie Zinnemann, and *A Patch of Blue* with Sidney Poitier, and they were huge hits, and I'll never forgive Mike Frankovich, the son of a bitch."

DURING THIS PERIOD, Donen could have used a hit. After the two sluggish Yul Brynner vehicles, the director picked up a bit of speed by regrouping with Cary Grant, although they would not again hit their stride until the picture after.

"When *The Grass Is Greener* came out," Donen said of his 1961 film, which his and Grant's Grandon Productions made for Universal at England's Shepperton Studios, "I outraged one of the English critics. He wrote that I had some nerve trying to pass off Osterly Park Manor as the home of Cary and Deborah Kerr, because everyone who went to see the film would undoubtedly know what they were really looking at."

Donen's counterattack was to write back to the critic. "I said: 'Let me tell you how *The Grass Is Greener* was made. As you know, it was a play about Lord and Lady Rhyall, by Hugh and Margaret Williams. I bought the film rights, and the first thing I did was try to cast it. I went to *Debrett's Peerage* and discovered, to my surprise and horror, that there *was* no Lord and Lady Rhyall. What could I do? I was prepared to abandon the film, because, obviously, there was no honest way to make it. Then, a thought occurred to me. Wait, I said to myself, I know what I'll do. I'll hire actors and have them *pretend* to be Lord and Lady Rhyall. With that in mind, I went to Cary Grant and Deborah Kerr, and now I had a Lord and Lady Rhyall. Then I had to give them a house, which in the play was called Rhyall House. I searched all over England, but discovered there was no such house. It then occurred to me that I might be able to do the same with the house as I had done with the actors.' " Donen continued to rag the critic in the same vein, until he felt sure he had made his point.

And the critic's reply? "He wrote me a really shitty letter," recalled Donen. "He said: 'Once there was a filmmaker named Stanley Donen who used to make pictures the way they used to be made.' "

IF *The Grass Is Greener* has a central critical fault, it is that it rarely shucks its stage boundaries, despite the backdrop of Osterly Park Manor and some London café scenes. The film's situation was current—Lord and Lady Rhyall (Grant and Kerr), in their genteel poverty, open their stately home to admission-wielding tourists; and the love story was plausible, within the circumstances—Lady Rhyall is captivated by one such tourist, a divorced American oilman (Robert Mitchum, to whom Deborah Kerr says, "All the Americans I meet tend to be millionaires, especially the oily ones"); and the cast, God knows, was attractive—even if Mitchum grumbled that his role consisted of little more than having to say "Why?" or "Really?" after one of Grant's breathless monologues. But *The Grass Is Greener* lacks film energy.*

"The picture wasn't that bad," said Deborah Kerr, placing the emphasis on the last word in the sentence in that crisp Deborah Kerr voice, which makes a rapt listener want to give one's all to whatever subject she is discussing, be it England, Siam, or a pot of tea. "And it was a joy to make. Cary I knew. We had made *An Affair to Remember*,† and Bob was always fun, and we had just made *The Sundowners* together. We'd also done [*Heaven Knows,*] *Mr. Allison*. And Stanley and Adelle and my husband and myself used to socialize quite a bit in London, so all in all it was a very jolly time."

Kerr hesitated before bringing up one other point. "Now," she said, "Cary, whom I loved, was very particular about everything, not just the acting . . ."

---

* Noël Coward sang some of his songs for the sound track—"Stately Homes of England," "Secret Heart," and "Mad About the Boy." Upon seeing a rough cut, Coward judged the film as "only fairly good because it is too slow and the color is hideous."
† Also *Dream Wife*, in 1953.

With Deborah Kerr on *The Grass Is Greener* (1960); off-camera she loved to joke with Cary Grant, who did not always appreciate her sense of humor.

Robert Mitchum complained that his role consisted of little more than reacting to what Cary Grant had to say.

"He had these strange whims from time to time," admitted Donen.

". . . but what everyone looked like," amplified Kerr.

"Cary Grant acted like a real old granny over the way *he* looked," carped the cinematographer Christopher Challis. "He was coproducer with Stanley, so he wielded more power than if he'd only been an actor. He could be an annoyance."

"Before we'd shoot a scene," said Kerr, "Cary would ask, 'Is anyone wearing red?' because in that case, they were to be removed from the set. Cary would say, 'The eye always goes to something red.' He wouldn't stand for that."

Challis said that Grant's sessions under a sunlamp "gave him a heavy phony tan and gave us trouble from a color point of view." The cinematographer did concede that Grant "was all right, really, and he had a great sense of timing," but Grant was also demanding. "All the sets had been built by the time Cary got there," said Challis, "only when he arrived, he said he felt they dwarfed him." As coproducer, Grant exercised his right. "They were rebuilt and made smaller," said Challis, "which affected the lighting."

The cinematographer could also recall "a little story of the green velvet smoking jacket that Cary wore in a scene in the billiards room. Several weeks later he had to wear the same jacket in another sequence."

Grant said to the cinematographer, "Look, Chris, I don't know if you're aware of this, but back home in the States I have twice been voted Best-Dressed Man. But if I wear this jacket, they'll think I'm a queen. Can you do anything with a filter?"

"Cary sometimes got these funny fixations," said Donen, "and now and then he got bizarre thoughts about what Deborah was wearing."

"In this one scene I was all dressed up in a white satin dress because I was going into London to see Bob Mitchum," said Kerr. "I had on with it a small diamond necklace, only when Cary saw me, he said, 'You can't have those on. We're playing people who are not that well off.' "

"Cary came to me," said Donen, who remembered the incident as involving a simple strand of pearls, "and he said, 'She can't wear those pearls.' I said, 'Why not?' He said, 'We're not supposed to have money, because people pay two and six to come and see our house.' I said, 'Yeah, but look at your shirt studs. You're wearing pearl-and-emerald studs. You know how it works in these situations, Cary. These families pass these things on from father to son. You have no money, but you have possessions.' "

Kerr essentially made the same argument to her leading man. "Can't I just have the diamond necklace because we've had it in the family?" she asked.

Grant cited the fact that the Rhyalls were so poor that they grew mushrooms in their cellar and sold them at market.

"Cary," said Donen, "you're poor but you have this house, you have these paintings on the walls, these acres. Deborah can have the necklace. Besides, she looks good in it."

"Cary told me, 'You can't wear it, you mustn't,' " said Kerr.

"She took it off," said Donen. "She was a good sport. But then, at the wrap party, because Deborah can be very funny . . ."

"I'd gotten the costume department to make me a necklace of mush-rooms," said Kerr, "and I went swishing up to Cary and said, 'Good morning, darling.' His nose was stuck in his newspaper, and he wasn't quite looking at me when he said 'Good morning, darling' back, but then he looked up and his mouth fell open."

As Deborah Kerr recalled, "Poor Cary didn't think it was the least bit funny."

Chapter 4

"More Violence"

GRIFFITH PARK could no longer double for exteriors, as had been the case when Donen and Kelly did their dance to convince the front office that *On the Town* should be shot in New York. What had been a Hollywood anomaly in 1949 became commonplace over the next dozen years. By that time, film audiences had become too aware, and camera lenses too revealing, for picturemakers not to provide anything but realistic landscapes in their movies. Among the more successful releases of 1963, for example, nearly every one of them, if not all, relied on their locations to fill one of the star roles of the picture: Tony Richardson's *Tom Jones* (England), Martin Ritt's *Hud* (Texas), Terence Young's *Dr. No* (Jamaica), Joseph L. Mankiewicz's *Cleopatra* (Italy and Spain), John Sturges's *The Great Escape* (Germany), and Ralph Nelson's *Lilies of the Field* (the rural South).

As Donen first proved in *On the Town* and, with a greater time budget on his hands, in *Funny Face,* he was no stranger to realistic settings. Moreover, he could bring out the best in a location just as he could with an actor.

In the case of his 1963 *Charade,* which ended up being the greatest box office success of his career, the three stars of the picture are Cary Grant, Audrey Hepburn, and Paris. Interestingly, and perhaps a contributing factor to ticket sales, is that the Paris in *Charade* is not strictly the city that a tourist or a visiting fashion photographer would see, but the Paris of someone, albeit a moneyed someone, who lived there.

With its generous doses of mistaken identity and its playful attitude toward corpses, *Charade* has often been likened to a Hitchcock picture, a comparison that Donen finds offensive. "Who said it was only Hitchcock

During the making of *Charade* (1963), newcomer Walter Matthau informed Donen that he should be playing the Cary Grant role.

who had the right to make mysteries?" queried Donen, who nonetheless appreciated much of Hitchcock's popular yarn, *North By Northwest.* "I liked it until the auction scene," said Donen. "What I admired most about Ernest Lehman's script was its basic story. Cary's character was mistaken by everyone for somebody who didn't exist. It's a marvelous situation. That way, he could never prove he wasn't somebody who wasn't alive."

This may explain Donen's attraction to a plot in which every character lied, except for the female lead—and this virtue in her, in keeping with the twisted, one could say Hitchcockian style of the rest of the piece, was compensated for by casting the actress totally against type. Of the many layers of surprise on display in *Charade,* perhaps none is so big as the soon apparent fact that the picture provides audiences with a very un-Hepburn-like Audrey Hepburn.

Charade began as "a really poor novel," according to its author, Peter Stone. "I wrote what was in fact my first screenplay, and wrote it with Cary

Scenarist Peter Stone (center) based *Charade* on "a really poor novel"—his own.

Grant and Audrey Hepburn in mind, the way a writer always writes with certain people as models." The name Peter Stone chose for his male lead, written for Grant, was Peter.*

Stone sent the script to his agent, Robbie Lantz, who, according to Stone, submitted it to and received a rejection from "every studio in Hollywood."

It was Stone's wife, Mary, who suggested that her disconsolate husband take the script, "fill it out a little," and repackage it as a novel, only Stone rejected her advice. "I had never written a novel," he said, "and I didn't want to write a novel. But then Robbie Lantz said the same thing my wife did."

The book was published as a twenty-five-cent paperback by Fawcett as part of its downscale Gold Medallion series, and its first serial rights were sold to *Redbook*. "*Redbook* had to change the title of the story," Stone explained, "because the magazine in those days had to have 'dog,' 'wife,'

---

* As it turned out, this was merely one of a few aliases the character used.

'Lincoln,' or 'God' on the cover." *Charade* was rechristened "The Unsuspecting Wife."

Once the issue hit the newsstands, said the writer, "I got six movie offers in six weeks, five of them from the same places that had originally rejected it." The lone newcomer to the bidding table, according to Stone, was Donen. "Stanley made the offer for the screenplay, the amount for which I'm not going to divulge, because it was the smallest of the six and I don't want to embarrass him."

Despite the paltry sum, Stone went with Donen. "In weighing my decision," said the writer, "I realized that Stanley was the only *director* who had bid on it. The others were studios and producers. Stanley was also fabulous at getting stars and had worked in the past with Audrey Hepburn and Cary Grant. He also had style and sophistication." There was one final deciding factor, said Stone. "I had just written my first Broadway show, *Kean,* starring Alfred Drake, and it didn't work. I was sort of anxious to get out of the country for a while." As Stone realized, of all the parties who had bid on the property, Donen was the only one who lived in Europe.

On April 1, 1962, Stone met Donen in London, and they began to work on the screenplay, under the auspices of Donen's umbrella deal with Columbia Pictures. "The basic plot remained unchanged," said Stone, referring to the story about a search for the missing $25,000 left by a murdered husband of an unsuspecting wife, "as did some of the characters. Stanley wanted me to put in some things that he thought would work in the movie. The writing took until early summer, when Stanley had to go get the cast—except at that point something odd happened with Columbia."

Donen had submitted *Charade* to the studio with the potent marquee names of Cary Grant and Audrey Hepburn attached. His budget, three million dollars, was on the high side but not disproportionately so when one considered the magnitude of his two stars and the everyday expenses of his particular foreign backdrop.

"I sent Cary the script," said Donen. "He did as he always did, he read it very quickly, and he said no, he didn't like it. He was going to do this picture with Howard Hawks, *Man's Favorite Sport,* even though Howard wasn't finished with the script yet."

"Audrey said she'd do it if Cary did," said Stone, "and when Cary wouldn't do it, Stanley went to Columbia with Natalie Wood and Warren Beatty."

For a Natalie Wood–Warren Beatty picture, Columbia would allocate only $2.2 million. "I told Columbia I couldn't make it in Paris for $2.2 million," said Donen. Columbia said he could make it somewhere else—namely, another studio.

Once Columbia relinquished the script and Donen from his production deal, Stanley Donen Productions set up shop at Universal. "I was in California, at the Beverly Hills Hotel," Donen remembered, "and the phone rang at about midnight and it was Cary. He said, 'Have you cast that picture?' I said no, and he said, 'Well, I'd like to have breakfast with you tomorrow.' He only lived up the street."

Grant and Donen met the next morning. "I read Howard's script last night, and I don't want to do it," said Grant.* "If you still want me, I'll do *Charade*."

"This coincidence," said Stone, "which was lucky for me, was extremely unlucky for Stanley. Columbia hated the coincidence of it and sued Stanley, saying that he knew Cary was going to change his mind. Eventually the case was settled."

Before shooting, Grant requested that Stone make some changes in the script. "I was scared to death," said Stone. "I had never met Cary Grant." The meeting took place in Grant's suite at the Plaza Hotel in New York. "Cary came to the door wearing only a towel," remembered Stone. "He had just gotten out of the shower." Stone said that he and Grant then proceeded to argue for the next three days. The basis for most of the conflict centered upon Grant's advancing age. He would turn fifty-nine during the production of *Charade* (Grant was born in 1904).

"At that age," said Stone, "he thought it unseemly of him to chase the girl. He wanted the girl to chase him." Grant's major bone of contention was a scene in Hepburn's hotel room. Her character, Reggie Lampert, was to vamp Peter, by now called Dyle in the story, into removing his clothes, a touchy situation that he escapes by taking a shower in front of her fully clothed.

"Cary thought it was an absurd scene," said Stone. "He couldn't understand it, he couldn't justify it, he wanted it out. Finally, he wore me down. I said, 'Screw it. Take it out.' That's when Cary said, 'Now, wait a minute,' and I learned my first lesson about Cary Grant, which Stanley later confirmed. There were certain things in pictures that Cary did not want to take respon-

* The film was eventually made with Rock Hudson. It was awful.

One of screenwriter Peter Stone's great throwaway lines (Hepburn to Grant): "How do you shave, in there?"

Reading the trades: makeup man John O'Gorman with Cary Grant. Originally the leading man said no to doing the picture, and he said it several times.

sibility for having done, so if he could claim it was done under protest and then it didn't work, he could say, 'See, I told you so.' "

The scene stayed in the picture.

IN ADDITION to the French capital, filming took place on location in Megève, a picturesque ski resort in the Alps. "We shot the opening there, where Audrey meets Cary," said Donen, "also the last scene in the picture, in what's supposed to be Cary's office. Actually, there was no soundstage available to us there. And it was freezing. We had to shoot the scene in a garage. We moved in the props and the lights from Paris."

Production began in October of 1962 and ran into the following February. Walter Matthau, who had yet to establish himself as a movie leading man, was cast in a small character role as one of the four heavies—the others were George Kennedy, James Coburn, and Ned Glass—who menace the Hepburn character, stalking her at every turn, making attempts on her life, even tossing matches at her while she is trapped in a nightclub phone booth.

"I'd done something like twenty-two movies by the time we made *Charade*," Matthau recalled. "When I started out in movies I only played heavies. When you're not pretty you're either a comedian or a villain, and I wasn't pretty. By the time of *Charade*, I hadn't established any comic personality. I didn't do that until one day when some casting guy saw me smoking a cigar after lunch and asked, 'Can you play comedy?' "

"I hope you got the script all right," Donen said when initially greeting Matthau upon the actor's arrival in Paris.

"I got the script," growled Matthau. "You know what's wrong with it?"

Donen looked at Matthau.

"I should be playing the Cary Grant part."

Donen started to chuckle, until he examined Matthau's face more closely. The actor was not kidding.

"It would have been a much better picture if I had played the role instead of Cary Grant," Matthau was still insisting in 1995. "Cary Grant was too handsome. If you read the script, the role called for someone with small eyes and a bulbous nose, someone who had suffered a lot of the pain of a minority group from the ghetto. Cary Grant didn't show any of that."

Matthau also took issue with his assigned role. "I was to play two different characters in the story, which I thought was a terrible cheat," he said. "I kept asking Stanley about it. I said, 'Isn't the audience going to know? I mean, I'm sort of this light comedy fellow eating yogurt and cottage cheese, and then suddenly I turn out to be the murderer?' He told me not to worry about it."*

Peter Stone remembered Donen arriving on the set every day, no matter the weather or the hour, wearing a suit and tie. "We had a very good time," said Stone, who was kept around throughout production, a rare circumstance for a writer. "Audrey was there, with Mel [Ferrer, her husband]. They'd taken a château outside Paris with a full staff of servants, always with white gloves on. Stanley and Adelle took an apartment, Mary and I had an apartment, and Cary lived at the Raphaël, with Dyan Cannon visiting back and forth. New Year's Eve, we had an enormously elegant affair at Mel and Audrey's, where she served these gigantic Idaho baked potatoes and Cary brought a huge tin of caviar, and we spooned the caviar and sour cream into the potatoes. Strange evening, because, through a series of circumstances, Mary and I were the only ones who remained married."

"I used to break Audrey up a lot, just by saying my lines," said Matthau. "Cary always wanted to know if I could tell him any jokes. He liked to collect them. Audrey I distinctly remember cracking up when I asked her if she was saving her money." Matthau considered his working relationship with Donen "good. Stanley's an appreciative director. I like that. When I'd do a scene, he'd really laugh." Comparing Donen to another director he worked with, Billy Wilder, Matthau said, "Billy showed appreciation in his own way. He would never clap his hands, but he would say, 'You're a very good actor. You're efficient.' He prized efficiency above all else. That's why Marilyn Monroe drove him so crazy on *Some Like It Hot*. She would be hours late showing up to the set. Much as he prized efficiency, though, I did once hear Billy say: 'You know, my Aunt Tipka is very popular, very nice. She always comes early and is never a problem. But she doesn't sell movie tickets.'"

Almost midproduction on *Charade,* shooting came to a grinding halt. As the stalemate escalated between the United States and the Soviet Union over the Cuban missile crisis, reports of it were being monitored over the radio in the studio canteen. The tensions reached such a point

---

* Confirming his worst suspicions, Matthau said that when he finally saw *Charade* in a theater, he was sitting behind a couple of boys and overheard the following exchange: "I know who the murderer is," said the first fellow. "Who?" asked the other. "Walter Matthau." "How do you know?" "He wouldn't be in this picture unless he's the murderer," said the first boy, "because it's such a small part."

that Donen couldn't stand it anymore. "The world is going to blow up at any second," he announced from behind the camera, "and here we are making a dumb movie.

"There's no point in continuing," said Donen. "If we're all going to get blown up, that's it. If we're not, we can always go back to work."

DONEN WAS INFORMED by the studio that the completed version of *Charade,* with its murders, its glib attitude toward the dead husband, and its numerous attempts on Audrey Hepburn's life, was "too violent." The picture opens with Hepburn's husband being tossed off a moving train. The next scene takes place in a chapel where a mourner walks up to the casket and sticks a needle into the corpse to make sure it is dead.

Donen argued with the studio, and the Universal executives decided to open the issue to public debate. *Charade* would be previewed in two different versions, the first with the violent scenes intact, the second with them excised. What also made the studio boys jittery was the climax of the picture, in which George Kennedy, as a one-armed killer, attempts to throw Cary Grant off the roof of the American Embassy.

Stone joined Donen for a drink right before the initial showing, and the two discussed how they were going to convince the studio to keep its hands off their picture.

"Look," said Donen, "they'll hand out preview cards after the show. Let's you and I each fill out five of them."

As scheduled, the audience was polled after the picture, and Donen and Stone stuffed the response box. "When the card asked what was our favorite part of the picture," said Stone, "Stanley and I wrote down, 'When it's violent.' What part did you like least? 'When there's no violence.'"

After the second-night preview, the same scenario unfolded: "What did you like least about the picture? What could be done to improve the picture? 'More violence.'"

"Monday morning," said Stone, "Universal said, 'You're right. The audience loves the violence.'"

Charade opened at Radio City Music Hall on Thursday, December 5, 1963, as the 6,200-seat theater's Christmas picture, the most sought-after booking on the circuit. It had not even been two weeks since the assassination of President Kennedy.

In Megève, in the French Alps, for *Charade*'s opening scenes at the resort; among those surrounding Hepburn during the tea break is the actor George Kennedy (far right).

"The word 'assassinate' was in the picture," said Stone. "At the time, you could not so much as say the word." In the picture, it was used twice.

Grant and Hepburn agreed to redub the two references, replacing the sensitive term with the less offensive "eliminate." Yet a certain stigma lingered.

"Bosley Crowther was still upset," said Peter Stone, "and blamed us for the Kennedy assassination." The picture, wrote the *Times* critic, "has so many grisly touches in it and runs to violence so many times that people bringing their youngsters to see the annual Nativity pageant and the Christmas stage show may blanch in horror when it comes off."

Crowther was not alone in his reaction. Arthur Knight, reviewing *Charade* for the *Saturday Review,* editorialized: "Our films and our television have made us so familiar with murder that we can laugh about it and shrug it away—until murder walks the streets and lurks in police corridors."

Oddly, both Crowther and Knight cited numerous reasons to praise the picture. "There's a lot to be said for it as a fast-moving, urbane entertainment in the comedy-mystery vein," the former admitted, while the latter labeled it "a stylish and amusing melodrama." Judith Crist, then at the height of her influence as the critic for both the New York *Herald Tribune* and television's *Today* show, was unabashed in her appreciation of the "grown-up, tongue-in-cheek romance. . . . It really *is* a Christmas show at Radio City Music Hall." Pauline Kael found *Charade* "probably the best American film of last year—as artificial and enjoyable in its way as *The Big Sleep*," seeing in it, and in John Frankenheimer's *The Manchurian Candidate*, "a freshness and spirit that make them unlike the films of any other country."

"THE PICTURE was a hit," said Donen, "and the studio wanted to follow it up with something similar as quickly as possible."

What it got was *Arabesque*, hardly in the same league as *Charade* but in some respects just as fun and eminently watchable.

"*Arabesque* wasn't Stanley's idea at all," said Christopher Challis. "The script was done for Cary," said Donen, "but he didn't want to be in it. It wasn't a good script and I didn't want to make it, but Gregory Peck and Sophia Loren, whom I loved, wanted to be in it and the studio implored me to make it, because, they said, 'It's ridiculous not to make a film with Peck and Sophia.' They said it would make money, and they were right. It made money. But I wish I hadn't done it."

"I got a call from Stanley," said Peter Stone, who was in California at the time, "and he said he was in London, shooting a picture with Gregory Peck and Sophia Loren, and that the sets were built but the script made no sense."

Donen informed Stone that shooting was to begin in three weeks. As Stone recalled, "He said that if I tricked up the dialogue, he'd trick up the camera angles, and then maybe people wouldn't see that the story made no sense."

Stone did the rewrite, under the pseudonym Pierre Marton (the writers of the first drafts were Julian Mitchell and Stanley Price), "and," said Stone, "Stanley, true to his word, shot it better than he ever shot any picture. Everything was shot as though it were a reflection in a Rolls-Royce headlamp."

Arabesque—which Gregory Peck recalled as being his suggestion for the title—was based on a nondescript 1961 novel by Alex Gordon, called *The Cipher*, which had been the working name of the movie. Its New York professor hero was a thirty-five-year-old schlepper of an archaeologist

On the lam, constantly, Sophia Loren and Gregory Peck in the circuitous *Arabesque* (1966), a brightly colored yet still pale imitation of *Charade*

Gregory Peck: "I was to be an Oxford professor and what Sophia represented didn't make much sense at all, so Stanley's idea was to keep the whole thing comedic." The director, Peck also recalled, "loved filming Sophia's décolletage and rear end."

Visitors to the set, British stage designer Oliver Messel and Claudette Colbert. Charlie Chaplin also dropped in, to ogle Sophia Loren.

manqué named Philip Hoag; in the movie, he becomes a dashing exchange professor at Oxford named David Pollack. While deciphering a code, Hoag/Pollack stumbles onto an attempt on a Middle Eastern politician's wife, and the plot starts gyrating from there. Like *On the Town,* it is little more than an extenuated chase. In Pollack's case, the route has him blazing through the London Zoo, the races at Ascot, and the London M-4. Tagging along for the run is Sophia Loren as Yasmin, a Middle Eastern consort.* No matter how much trouble the two of them encounter, her mountain of hair always seems to stay in place.

"The more the script was rewritten," said Christopher Challis, "the worse it got. Stanley said, 'We have to make it so interesting visually that no one will think about it.' "

The look of the picture, through its camerawork, portends many of the op-art effects that characterize a lot of other crazy sixties movies, such as Joseph Losey's *Modesty Blaise* and the multidirector *Casino Royale,*

---

* In the course of shooting *Arabesque,* Donen introduced Sophia Loren to Charlie Chaplin, who at the time was preparing *A Countess from Hong Kong,* also to star Loren. When the seventy-seven-year-old Chaplin saw his future leading lady, he told Donen, "Ah, to be sixty-five again."

pictures whose mise-en-scènes smack a lot more of psychedelic posters than of a Hollywood tradition of cinema.

"Stanley had a terrific instinct," said Gregory Peck, "like a choreographer, which, of course, he had been. But even in an ordinary dramatic sequence he'd use the body to punctuate what was happening—standing, relaxing, everything, it was all choreographed. If you look at the picture, we were always moving, because Stanley just wanted to keep the ball in the air the entire time, and he used every camera trick you could think of. He also loved filming Sophia's décolletage and her rear end."

Peck confessed he was not always up to meeting the rigorous demands of the picture, be they stunts or comedic delivery. His ongoing excuse off-camera: "But Stanley, there's only one Cary Grant."

CHRISTOPHER CHALLIS'S most sustaining memory of *Arabesque* was of a moment when he and the director were distanced from the rest of the company. "Stanley and I were shooting on the roof of a farm building in the English countryside, toward the end of the picture, and we were waiting for the weather to improve," the cinematographer recalled. "Stanley was producing the picture, and he looked down at the company, which was very large and spread out, and said, 'Look at them, Chris, all those people, eating and drinking at my expense. You know what I'm going to do as my next picture? Something small, just two actors, and we'll shoot and eat our way through France.' "

Challis asked Donen who he thought those actors might be, "and when he said Audrey, I told him that I bet we'd have a unit of at least a hundred eighty people, between her hairdressers, her designer, her dressers, and everybody else attached to her.

"And that's exactly what we did."

Chapter 5

"An Enormous Turn-On"

"A UDREY IN MANY ways had the same effect on me as Fred Astaire," said Donen, as he had been saying since first they met. "I think of them, and my heart and spirit just soar."

If a chemistry existed between star and director, as most clearly there did, others could sense it from afar. In 1991, when Hepburn was honored by the Film Society of Lincoln Center, *Time* magazine movie critic Richard Corliss wrote in the evening's program: "If [Billy] Wilder mined Hepburn's vulnerability,* Stanley Donen saw her glamour. In *Funny Face, Charade,* and *Two for the Road,* he dressed her in smart frocks (courtesy of Hubert de Givenchy), and clever dialogue (courtesy of Leonard Gershe, Peter Stone, and Frederic Raphael). Donen escorted her from girlhood to womanhood, pairing her with Astaire and Cary Grant, Hollywood's top icons of masculine suavity, then got her to tame the angry-young-man generation in the person of broody, brutey Albert Finney."

"I was bloody lucky, let's face it," said Hepburn. "With Stanley, certainly, and with practically all my costars and directors, but with Stanley on a somewhat more personal level. I do know that my private life was not always happy, but with Stanley, I would always be happy on the set. Stanley made me laugh, and that, for me, was an enormous turn-on."

Yet from the point of view of Donen, as he revealed in his *Vogue* magazine memorial tribute to Hepburn, there was a side of the Hepburn personality that he sensed was being withheld from him. "I longed to get closer, to get behind whatever was the invisible, but decidedly present barrier between her and the rest of us," Donen disclosed, "but I never got to

---

* After *Sabrina,* as Billy Wilder liked to say, "Audrey Hepburn and I made *Love in the Afternoon* together."

the deepest part of Audrey." By that, he explained, "I don't mean to imply that I thought she was playing a game with me. But she always kept a little of herself in reserve, which was hers alone, and I couldn't ever find out what it was, let alone share it with her. She was the pot of gold at the end of the rainbow."

LIKE DONEN's allowing Audrey Hepburn to laugh, *Two for the Road* is an audience turn-on. The reasons for this are strange. The film, though lovely to look at, is not about a cheerful or even a contented relationship. "A happy marriage would not have meant a good story," said Donen. Frederic Raphael's story is more painful than it is romantic, yet it contains many romantic moments—Hepburn's soothing Albert Finney's throbbing headache, her squirting him in the hotel bath with the shower nozzle, their nuzzling in the Riviera twilight. Many people consider it one of the most romantic movies ever made. Perhaps that is because the situations and the characters, for whatever reasons, allow the viewer to project his or her own experiences into the overall perception of the movie. Yet however one approaches *Two for the Road,* it stands the test of time as Stanley Donen's best work. It is the picture that film students most request to speak to him about. It is his most personal film and his most passionate. It moves to his rhythm. It reflects his originality. And it is a film that has a lyricism all its own.

Looking at his own picture, Donen delivers an equivocal yet on-target critical assessment. His opinion is colored by the fact that, unlike *Singin' in the Rain, Two for the Road* is not perfect. At times one wonders whether its male character ever understands what it is like to be in love, let alone what he has ever done to be deserving of such a mate.

"It did come out a little one-sided," said Donen. "*Two for the Road* is not meant to be as downbeat as it is. If you read the script, you won't get the same feeling. The husband and the wife are supposed to be equally responsible for the difficulties in the marriage, and the story is supposed to be about what happens to people when they become too familiar with each other's habits, how our little idiosyncrasies eventually irritate us and cause us to drift apart. As I said, it came out a little one-sided, like he's a shit, and he wasn't supposed to be."

The fault may lie in Albert Finney's performance as the architect, Mark Wallace: "Albie doesn't like to play anything charming," said Donen. "He doesn't think he's acting, in spite of the fact that in *Tom Jones* he was completely charming. I don't know, maybe it was me. Maybe I couldn't communicate it to him, because he wanted to be more difficult as that man, and that tipped the movie a little."

THE SCRIPT, originally titled *Four Times Two,* examines four stages in the Mark-Joanna relationship, before they presumably go on to live realistically ever after: first they are students (he originally has eyes for another on Joanna's choir tour, the leader, Jackie, played by Jacqueline Bisset); then they're newlyweds and young parents on holiday (the script never shows Mark and Joanna at home); then half of two traveling couples (the others being Mark's obnoxious former girlfriend, her fussy husband, and their shrill, undisciplined brat); and finally a sullen and mature husband and wife.

"What do you mean, was the couple in the picture based on anybody in particular?" sniffed the film's writer and originating force, Frederic Raphael. "I happen to be married."

Raphael, a Cambridge-educated novelist and screenwriter (born in 1931), and Donen, the American expatriate, met in London in 1964. "I was told about him by another director-producer, with whom I was not getting on," said Raphael. "He was so unbelievably boring, a man named

Albert Finney's ongoing imitation of Humphrey Bogart in *Two for the Road* (1967) was his own idea, as it was that his character should never be charming.

Norman Panama." Panama, formerly a writer, had worked on Danny Kaye and Bob Hope comedies before moving to England. The day-to-day working relationship between Raphael and Panama became so acrimonious, said Raphael, that he ended up telling the director, "You'll probably blacken my name and I'll never work in films again."

"Christ," reflected Raphael, "I wish he had."

Instead Panama informed Raphael of Donen's flattering reaction at a dinner party when he heard the two were collaborating: "You lucky SOB," Donen said to Panama. "Why haven't I got him?"

"You see," said Raphael, "I wrote a film called *Nothing But the Best,** and it was rather good and it was being discussed. Everyone said, 'Isn't it brilliant?' And Stanley Donen, apparently, said, 'No. It is not a brilliant film. It is brilliantly *written.*' Stanley's very odd. He not only likes other people's talents but actually admits it."

Donen rang up Raphael and the two met. It soon became apparent that they should work together, only neither had any ideas. "Maybe I'll find you a book," Donen offered, and the two left it at that. Raphael, accustomed to the glad-handing writers often receive from picturemakers, fully never expected to hear from Donen again.

Cut to Raphael not long after, "driving down to the South of France, as I did a lot in those days, in a fancy car," he recalled. "I was rich then." As Raphael sat behind the wheel, he thought: "Imagine if we overtook ourselves on the road ten years ago. Ten years seemed a long time in those days. Then I said, 'Wait a minute. That's a movie.' "

Raphael first brought the idea to the director John Schlesinger, for whom he had written the 1965 British New Wave film *Darling,* starring Julie Christie. Schlesinger found this road premise "too difficult." The writer's next sounding board was his more recent filmmaking acquaintance; Donen was intrigued, in an encouraging way, Raphael remembered, and replied, "So what do we do now?"

"You do nothing," said Raphael. "You sit here. I'll go away and write it." Raphael also went so far as to suggest that Donen give him money to initiate a first draft. "Stanley was mortified," reported Raphael.

"The last time I did that with a writer," claimed Donen, "I never saw him again."

"That's the risk you take," replied Raphael.

Unsure whether he should make the commitment, Donen tested the waters to see if a box office name would be interested. "He rang Audrey,"

* Directed by Clive Donner in 1964.

said Raphael, "and she said, 'It's a great idea, but it'll never work. I just made a picture called *Paris When It Sizzles,* and it's a lot like that.' " Actually, *Paris When It Sizzles,* directed with a thud by Richard Quine, contained flashback sequences and a goofy premise, about a washed-up screenwriter (William Holden) who works through his various stages of writer's block by fantasizing scenarios starring himself and his secretarial temp (Hepburn). Raphael took offense at the star's reaction to his idea. "People always think one thing is like another," he complained. Nevertheless, Donen and he reached a tentative agreement on moving ahead with the idea.

"I went to Rome and wrote the script, on cards, and arranged it as a montage," said Raphael. He then sent the finished draft—which in its time adjustments came out reading like a mosaic on marriage—to Donen. Awaiting the director's reaction, he frankly expected the worst. "I'm not easily amused by film directors," Raphael admitted, "or anybody, really. Schlesinger and I had big rows on *Darling.* You see, I'm constantly being crossed by very tiresome people."

Raphael did hear from Donen. Over the phone from England, Donen said, as reported by Raphael, "Freddie, it's just the most wonderful script I've ever read in my whole life. I wouldn't change a word. Maybe it's a little long."

Raphael recalled the first draft as being 140 pages, "in those days considered 'generous.' " He said that the incidents in the script were "based mainly on the experiences of my wife and me, but with a certain degree of expansiveness. These are not necessarily things that happened, but what might have happened." Donen learned that Mark's most chronic affliction in the film (besides his surliness), losing his passport, was Raphael's own.

The writer was elated by Donen's reaction. "I'd made movies," said Raphael, "but Stanley Donen was *Hollywood.* He flew my wife and me back to London, put us up, gave us some money, then said, 'Now we've got to go see Audrey in Geneva. I'll fix it, and you've got to come with me.' "

Raphael remembered Hepburn as "gracious, entirely sweet, and unassuming. She loved the script.* She was married to Mel Ferrer, whom she called Melchior. He was a one-hundred-percent pain in the ass, very bor-

---

* Donen said that it took a good deal of convincing on his part to get Hepburn to accept the role. Hollywood had not yet taken a realistic look at marriage, and Hepburn, as would any star, especially one operating from so great a distance from California, was perpetually image conscious. The picture contained an ancient Hollywood taboo: she would have an extramarital affair. Hepburn also fretted over the sporty wardrobe Donen wanted her to wear, which would not allow for her usual Givenchy clothes, "although once she agreed to do the film," Donen said, "she was entirely cooperative" about every preproduction impasse.

Cinematographer Christopher Challis stands over Hepburn and Donen at lunch. He claimed to know from the start that *Two for the Road* would never be a "small" picture.

ing. The whole time we were making *Two for the Road,* he only wanted to talk about this film he hoped to make in Spain, about El Greco."

Two for the Road was shot in one area of the south of France, with the production headquarters established at the Hotel du Golf, in Beauvallon, near Saint-Tropez. "The atmosphere was very festive," said the widow of the actor Claude Dauphin, who played the noisome French patron of Finney's architect. "In those days," said Ruda Dauphin, "everybody still smoked and drank." She explained that the mustache her husband sports in the picture hid a scar incurred during an automobile accident, "when Claude drove away mad and hit a tree after I was dancing in Cannes with Peter Ustinov."

In establishing the look of the film and conveying a sense of movement, Donen and Christopher Challis experimented, successfully, with attaching the camera to car windshields,* for realistic reflections on the

---

* The couple's modes of transportation varied from jet and ferry crossing, to hitchhiking, a vintage racing-green MG drop-top (the car with the engine "donk"), the patron's gray Rolls-Royce, the stifling yellow Ford station wagon belonging to Mark Wallace's former girlfriend and her anal-retentive efficiency-expert husband (played by Eleanor Bron and William Daniels), the Wallaces' red Triumph Herald, and, ultimately, their white Mercedes 230, signaling their "arrival."

glass and a heightened sense of road movement. Henry Mancini provided, not entirely voluntarily, two different musical background scores; the first was discarded. "It was a long-metered melody," said Mancini, "like 'Days of Wine and Roses.' " The second theme was written after Donen pointed Mancini in a straighter direction, toward capturing a sense of "travel and time. It had a moving figure in the counterline. It was unique, it had heart, and it pushed you along rather than letting you sit there, as the first theme did."

Mancini (1924–1994) was a prolific and well-liked Hollywood composer who would remain best known for writing, with Johnny Mercer, "Moon River" for the Blake Edwards picture *Breakfast at Tiffany's*. He composed three scores for Donen: *Charade, Arabesque,* and *Two for the Road.* "Stanley and I met in Hollywood, long before he moved to London, when I was still working at Universal and he was at Metro," Mancini recalled in 1992. He attributed bumping into Donen and Cary Grant "at the only deli in London" as the most likely reason Donen thought to hire him to score *Charade*. "Stanley knew I could write suspenseful music, because I'd done the *Peter Gunn* TV shows, and he knew I'd had some success with Audrey, with *Breakfast at Tiffany's*."* Donen said that he found Mancini the easiest possible composer to work with, "because you show him the movie and that's it. He writes the score." As for Hepburn's influence on his composing, Mancini replied, "John [Mercer] got very poetic when it came to writing for Audrey. There was a scene in *Charade* where the *bateau mouche* sails down the Seine and the [offscreen] chorus comes in. The phrase in the lyric 'sad little serenade' was inspired by Audrey, and I think 'Charade' is the best work John and I ever did together."

The budget for *Two for the Road* was set at five million dollars, on the lavish side for what was essentially a two-character drama. "No one wanted to give us the money," remembered Raphael, "and we couldn't find a leading man. Paul Newman said no. Then Audrey got pregnant." Six months after Newman's refusal, "we got Albert, and Stanley got the money from the last available source, which was Fox."

Albert Finney's film career could have been best described as sporadic before *Two for the Road* (as it also was afterward, before it picked up again with a series of leading character roles in the 1980s). Finney, one

---

* Besides Oscars for Mancini and Mercer, the 1961 film provided Audrey Hepburn with her most identifiable role, as Truman Capote's heroine Holly Golightly. Mancini said that it was thanks to *Funny Face* that he was able to calculate Hepburn's vocal range and thus tailor "Moon River" to her.

of the more handsome leading men to come out of England in the early sixties, belonged to the John Garfield school of dangerous male presence. He burst upon the international film scene in 1963 as the star of Tony Richardson's bawdy and often brilliant *Tom Jones,* though he might have achieved stardom a year earlier had he not backed out of the leading role in David Lean's *Lawrence of Arabia* four days after shooting commenced, for reasons never fully explained by Finney. Lean said the actor did not wish to be tied to an indentured-servant contract handed him by the producer Sam Spiegel, and that in any event Finney was "afraid to become a movie star." After *Tom Jones,* Finney was described as "the next Olivier," a label Olivier himself was prepared to affix to the new leading man. Between his roles in *Tom Jones* and *Two for the Road,* Finney's only movie appearances were in Carl Foreman's *The Victors,* where he was part of an ensemble, and Karel Reisz's little-seen *Night Must Fall.* It has been suggested that during the making of *Two for the Road,* Finney and Hepburn carried on an affair, which significantly contributed to the depth of her performance. It would not have hurt his, either.

Insofar as finding a studio, Donen said that Universal, which had financed and profited from *Charade* and *Arabesque,* had originally said yes to Newman but backed out once it came to believe that audiences would be baffled by the leaps in time frame.

"We made a few cuts in the script, nothing major, and that was it. I never did a second draft," said Raphael, "and the experience from there on was as near to perfection as anyone could have hoped it would be. It was sublime." Raphael said that what ended up on the screen is fairly close to what he envisioned while writing in Rome. "Perhaps I'd like it to be a little less trendy looking, her clothes,"* he said, "but the picture's so honestly acted."

"The role," Donen said of Joanna Wallace, "required a depth of emotion, care, yearning, and maturity that Audrey had never played before. She gave what I think is her best performance."

* Because Audrey Hepburn wearing anything but Givenchy was considered news, the *New York Times* saw fit to print on December 27, 1966, while the picture was in postproduction, that the star's twenty-nine costume changes broke down as follows: "In [Givenchy's] place came Ken Scott, an American who rode out of the Middle West to set up designing in Rome; Paco Rabanne, a Spaniard who works in Paris; Mary Quant, the London Mod designer, and Michele Rosier, the 'vinyl girl,' who designs for the ready-to-wear French house of V de V. Odds and ends were found in London and Paris boutiques.... The not exactly curvaceous Hepburn figure, usually kept under wraps in films, is displayed in Scott swimsuits."

Audrey Hepburn and young Kathy Chelimsky, who played her daughter, Caroline, in the movie. They are on a beach in Saint-Tropez. Hepburn's husband, Mel Ferrer, was also on the scene, and behaving, according to screenwriter Frederic Raphael, like "a one-hundred-percent pain in the ass."

Hepburn with Finney at the outset of the story. The maturation she accomplished in *Two for the Road* was seldom, if ever, evident in her other films.

Raphael, who was nominated for an Academy Award for his screenplay (the prize went to William Rose, for his of-the-moment *Guess Who's Coming to Dinner,* was incredulous that Hepburn did not win an Oscar for the film, which that year went to Katharine Hepburn, also for *Guess Who's Coming to Dinner* (Audrey Hepburn was nominated for *Wait Until Dark* and not *Two for the Road*). Neither the picture nor Donen was nominated; in fact, Donen has never received an Academy Award nomination, in any category. "The year of *Two for the Road,*" he said, "the studio spent a lot of money on *Doctor Dolittle,** and that's where its Oscar budget went." The studio decision had been personally explained to Donen by Fox production chief Richard Zanuck, and he understood and accepted it. Yet if at any juncture in the Donen career an Oscar nomination, if not an outright win, was deserved, it would have been for *Two for the Road.*

WHEN ASKED what popped into his mind at the mention of *Two for the Road,* Stanley Donen recalled two incidents. The first had to do with Hep-

---

* A costly musical flop starring Rex Harrison.

burn's introduction to her leading man. "Albie and Audrey had never met, so I arranged a luncheon in Paris. He was playing in London, in *Black Comedy,* by Peter Shaffer, and he brought along the soundman for a movie he was about to star in and direct himself, called *Charlie Bubbles.* Albie decided that at this lunch he was going to pretend to be a homosexual interior decorator, and he was absolutely brilliant at it. He played with only the slightest trace of effeminate mannerisms, and all through the meal he would say things like, 'We're so excited about making a movie with you.' He was just on the edge. Never once did he say 'I'; it was always 'we.' The entire lunch, Audrey's jaw kept dropping and she'd be looking at me, her eyes growing larger by the minute and she never saying a word, although obviously thinking: How ever am I going to play a love story with this man?"

The second incident occurred in the critical weeks just prior to the New York opening. Donen was already steamed up over the studio's having booked the film into Radio City Music Hall. The decision had been based on Donen's long association with the showplace, only he knew that his new film, though lushly appointed, was too intimate for so overwhelming a venue. "But it was too late," said Donen. "That was Fox. Then the studio made another decision, that the picture was for college kids. Why, I don't know.* The studio flew Freddie Raphael and me to New York, where it had collected the editors of every college newspaper in the United States, for a screening and a sort of press conference. The gathering was huge, maybe a thousand people, and the studio invited Bosley Crowther."

The junket kicked off with the preview, attended by the *Times* critic and the collegians, but not Donen and Raphael. "We had breakfast with everybody the next morning," said Donen, "then assembled for a discussion, on a dais, consisting of Bosley Crowther, Freddie, and me." Donen received the first wave of feedback from the students. "They loathed the picture, hated it. I thought I'd flown across the Atlantic to meet the intelligentsia of the United States that morning. I didn't. Who I met were the future publicists of America, the future toadies. Having been led by Bosley Crowther, these kids proceeded to rip the picture apart, until there was nothing left, of it or me. Then Bosley Crowther got up, walked over and stood right beside me, and said, 'Mr. Donen, I saw your picture last night, and it's just another version of commercial American trash. If you

---

* After the success of *The Graduate,* Hollywood discovered and sought the youth market, which accounted for the majority of ticket sales, a trend that was to continue and eventually overtake the movies.

want to see what's going on in the movies today, you must go down to Greenwich Village and look at Mr. Antonioni's *Blow-Up,* because that is the way movies should be made and the way they are headed.' And he went on to say that 'Mr. Antonioni had the courage, which no one else has had in a commercial film before, to show pubic hair on the screen. You must stop making films for Radio City Music Hall and try to make pictures that reach out to the people.' Bosley Crowther was cheered and applauded by the entire house. So I got up and I said, 'Bosley, if I had known that pubic hair would have gotten me a good review, I would have brought you a bucketful of it. I have seen *Blow-Up,* and while I have nothing to say against it, it does seem to me to be a sort of combination of *Rear Window* and *Funny Face.'* Then I turned to the kids and said, 'First of all, I flew three thousand miles to meet you as equals. I thought you would be intelligent and have decent manners, but you are rude and you don't know what you've just seen, because it is a wonderful picture. It's a picture full of humanity, about marriage and life. And you, Bosley Crowther, you have no manners whatsoever. You have every right, in my opinion, to say anything you want to in the *New York Times.* They pay you for that. But I am here as a guest. You owe me a certain courtesy, and as far as I'm concerned, you are nothing but an impossible son of a bitch.' "

With that, the students burst into a long and deafening round of applause.

Chapter 6

"God's Great Gift"

ONEN RETURNED to England, although the debacle over opening *Two for the Road* was far from finished. He and Fox would continue to rue the studio's decision to book the picture into Radio
City Music Hall, where, as Donen remembered, "it died." Shortly after
closing there, the picture was moved to the Plaza, a playhouse for art and
foreign films within a stone's throw of Bergdorf Goodman, and there *Two
for the Road* enjoyed a respectable New York run.

Whether the lavishness of his "small" road movie was a contributing
factor or not, Donen kept his next film, *Bedazzled*, again for Twentieth
Century–Fox, on a tight budgetary leash. Shot in six weeks in and around
London, it would require only $2.1 million in rentals to achieve break-
even; on its first North American run alone it took in $2.825 million, one
of the few profitable films to be released during what would ultimately be
the last days of the Darryl and Richard Zanuck regime, which fell thanks
to a string of expensive productions—*Doctor Dolittle, Star!, Hello, Dolly!*—
that unsuccessfully tried to milk Fox's 1965 musical cash cow, *The Sound of
Music.*

Bedazzled, essentially an arch, two-character vaudeville revue (complete with the Devil's music, rock and roll) about dabbling in the seven
deadly sins, was as far afield from those mastodons as was imaginable.
Some fans of film, even fans of Donen and especially of *Bedazzled,* have
wondered, rather cheekily, how the same person who made *Singin' in the
Rain* could have gone on and made so offbeat a movie as *Bedazzled.*

The answer is obvious if one is even the least bit familiar with
Donen's background.

Both films grew out of his attitude and training. *Singin' in the Rain,* with
its M-G-M gloss, was a product of his studio lessons under fire; *Bedazzled,*

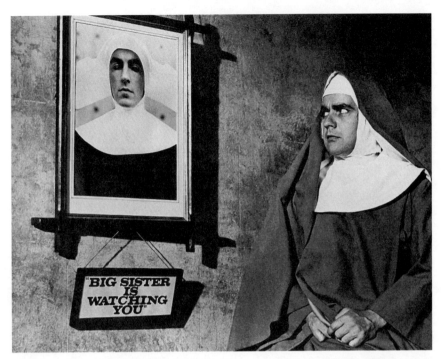

Wishing too hard: Lucifer (Peter Cook, lurking in picture frame) grants the wish of *Bedazzled*'s hero, Stanley Moon (Dudley Moore), that he be completely surrounded by women.

with its theological patina, is a throwback to his even earlier education, the aborted Hebrew lessons and the theatrical and literary tradition Donen witnessed when he attended Broadway shows with his parents. The later picture also happened to reflect the freewheeling spirit of its times, as was especially evident in Donen's adopted hometown of London, where the Beatles had exploded upon the scene only a few years before. Donen, keenly aware of music, was going to be influenced by any new movement in that realm, just as he was by the relaxed camera movements finding popularity in sixties cinema (though he was still working in wide screen, with Panavision).

"*Bedazzled* owes infinitely more of its personal style to Dudley Moore and Peter Cook than to Stanley Donen," wrote Andrew Sarris in his 1968 auteurist overview, *The American Cinema.* As it was, the American spokesman for the auteurist movement was never willing to give Donen his due—to wit: "He was dismissed for a time as Gene Kelly's invisible partner. . . . Donen moved to Warners with *The Pajama Game* and *Damn Yankees,* two transposed Broadway musicals seemingly dominated by

George Abbott's vigorously theatrical pacing. Even when Donen received sole directorial credit, his more notable efforts seemed only marginally personal. *Seven Brides for Seven Brothers,* for example, is stamped (and stomped) with Michael Kidd's muscular choreography; *Funny Face* is graced with Richard Avedon's witty fashion photography.... Where Donen has come closest to projecting a personal style is in *Indiscreet,* a comedy that eventually collapses under Norman Krasna's plot indiscretions, but not before Donen reveals the serious temperament necessary for high comedy. His timing is sharp, and he seems at home with an elegant cast."*

"Andrew Sarris seems to condemn me for trying to work with the best people," replied Donen. "Frankly, I would have thought that that was my job as a director."

"BECAUSE OF my mother," Donen admitted, "I never became religious. I'm an atheist. I don't believe in God. I never did.† I don't think it's possible. He made such a mess of it if there is."

It was the BBC that begat *Bedazzled.* "I was living in London and saw Peter Cook and Dudley Moore on British TV," said Donen. "They had a weekly show, just the two of them, and I thought they were the best things I'd ever seen, so I called them and said, 'You are the best things I've ever seen, and I'd like to make a movie with you.' I'd never seen them in a movie, but it turns out they were in *The Wrong Box."*

The Wrong Box, with a script by Larry Gelbart, was a 1966 farce directed by Bryan Forbes and based on a novel by Robert Louis Stevenson. Two elderly Victorian brothers attempt to wipe each other out in order to receive an inheritance. Cook and Moore were innocent bystanders in supporting roles.

The two television comedians came to see Donen in Hyde Park Gardens, with a movie script they had written. "That script was *Bedazzled,"*

---

* Strangely, Sarris listed Donen in his chapter titled "Expressive Esoterica," explaining: "These are the unsung directors with difficult styles or unfashionable genres or both. Their deeper virtues are often obscured by irritating idiosyncrasies on the surface, but they are redeemed by their seriousness and grace." Among those with whom Donen shares this distinction, besides Allan Dwan, Alexander Mackendrick, Robert Mulligan, Arthur Penn, and Donald Siegel, are the western director Budd Boetticher (whom Sarris listed as missing in Mexico) and such obscurities as André De Toth, Seth Holt, and Edgar G. Ulmer.

† Informed, however, that prints of *Once More, with Feeling* and *Surprise Package* seemed no longer to exist, Donen replied, "Then there *is* a God."

said Donen, "although it was called something else, but it was the Faust story. It was about a guy who got seven wishes from the Devil. It was pretty weak."

"It had been to a number of people before Stanley," remembered Dudley Moore. "But when it got to Stanley, he very much wanted to do it."

"I said, 'It's a great sort of idea for the two of you,' " recalled Donen, " 'but it needs a lot of work. We'll have to throw out what you've got and just use the bare bones.' "

"I was actually doing another film, *Thirty Is a Dangerous Age, Cynthia* [directed by Joseph McGrath], which kept me heavily occupied," said Moore, "so Peter did the screenplay, really, apart from some additions and alterations from me, though we both took credit for the screenplay because we both improvised a great deal."

Donen said that in putting together the script with Cook, "I used as my Bible a book called *Mere Christianity,* by C. S. Lewis." Clive Staples Lewis (1898–1963), having been a don at both Oxford and Cambridge, was "an atheist who late in life converted to Catholicism," said Donen. "He was a great theologian and did a great study of Christianity, not just Catholicism. His is the only book I know of that doesn't point out the differences between religions but the similarities, the places where they all meet and agree. That book was the basis of the whole picture, because I wanted it so that if any Christian saw *Bedazzled,* he could be outraged but he could not fault it."

The trigger point of *Bedazzled* and the theme of the picture, said Donen, "is something I used to be obsessed with, the prospect of selling out. It's about the struggle I had, and which I guess most people have—certainly writers and members of the press have it—about not selling out. Publishers push to sell papers and books, and that may shove writers in a certain direction away from what they want to say. For myself, I was obsessed with not trying to sell out, and wanted to show how important that was to each and every one of us, and in a funny way, that's a very Catholic idea. I mean, the sin of pride, in the Catholic way of thinking, is *the* cardinal sin of all sins. Murder, taking the Lord's name in vain—forget it. Vanity is puny, infidelity is meaningless. But pride, the sin of pride, that's the worst, and that is simply selling out. I was hooked on that. Because of the terror I felt inside about it, the movie meant a great deal to me.

"Some movies, like *Pajama Game* and *Damn Yankees,* they're fun, but I don't feel I contributed a lot to them, because they were what they were.

Donen with Peter Cook, about to shoot the scene where the Devil requests entry to heaven, which looks remarkably like Kew Gardens.

They came to me fully formed. And some movies I felt I had a great deal to do with 'creating,' much as I hate that word. 'Making,' I suppose, is a better word."

Bedazzled begins with a dizzying set of titles created by Maurice Binder, who handled that responsibility for every one of Donen's films since *Indiscreet,* which opened with its pair of falling yellow rose petals. Binder was best known for his title sequences for the James Bond movies. For *Bedazzled,* Binder came up with an amusement fair setting, and Donen shot from a ferociously spinning carousel through a red-filtered lense. "People say there's a lot of red in my pictures," said Donen. "Frankly, I don't see it. Red is a good color, though. People also say there's a lot of water in my pictures."

Perhaps what Binder and Donen—and Cook and Moore—are saying is that life is a spinning carousel, and one must hold on or fall off. As *Bedazzled*'s narrative begins, one of life's losers, Stanley Moon (Dudley Moore) is in the throes of deciding which route to take. Standing in church, addressing God, Stanley says, "Now, you know I believe in you, but could you just give me a little sign?" With that, a darkly bespectacled George Spiggot (Peter Cook) drops a secret latch and peers out from a vestibule.

Stanley wishes to get to know Margaret Spencer (Eleanor Bron, continuing to show the finely restrained hilarity she displayed as Finney's ex in *Two for the Road*). Margaret is the leggy waitress in the Wimpy Bar where Stanley is the sweaty cook. Stanley dreams of Margaret, and as his inner thoughts turn to the term "holy wedlock," he slaps a cheese slice on a greasy grilled burger. With Margaret unwilling to give Stanley a second look, he attempts to hang himself in his miserable little flat. Unfortunately, the exposed plumbing is too weak to support him or the noose.

Enter George Spiggot. Despite his claims and his red-satin-lined cape and matching socks,* Spiggot could not possibly be the Devil, insists Stanley. For one thing, the Devil is not called George Spiggot. "God keeps changing his name too," replies Spiggot. "He used to be the Word."†

If Stanley wishes Margaret Spencer to notice him, Spiggot can arrange it. He produces the standard contract, granting Stanley "seven wishes in accordance with the mystic rules of life. Seven days of the week. Seven deadly sins. Seven seas. Seven brides for seven brothers. Look, if you're not interested, I'm sure there are thousands of others who'd jump at the opportunity." While Stanley follows Spiggot around his headquarters—a red nightclub called the Clubroom and decorated, as Stanley says, "in early Hitler"—Spiggot attends to some everyday duties: placing scratches on phonograph records, cutting collar buttons off new shirts, tearing the last pages out of Agatha Christie novels. Every tacky wish, one through seven, Stanley asks for in his unrelenting quest for Margaret Spencer is met, only to have Spiggot spoil it somehow. There is to be a payoff for the Adversary, however; in a reversal of the Clarence-the-angel character in Capra's *It's a Wonderful Life,* one of the several sources Donen and company are sending up here, Spiggot wishes to return to heaven, whence he was originally dispatched, to sit once again at the knee of God.

"We had a lot of jokes we didn't use in *Bedazzled,*" said Donen. "We used to talk about God's great gift of piles."

"The movie was just a series of sketches," said Dudley Moore, who, as Stanley, gets to end each bad turn of events by blowing a raspberry. Dur-

---

* Ray Walston's rapscallion, Mr. Applegate, wore red socks too, in *Damn Yankees.*

† As for the name Stanley Moon, that was an in-joke. Some years before, John Gielgud provided Dudley Moore a letter of introduction to Noël Coward. It read: "Dear Noël, this is to introduce a very clever young man who is certain to amuse you. His name is Stanley Moon."

ing one sketch, Raquel Welch, as Lillian Lust, attempts to insinuate herself into Stanley's bed. Envy is embodied in a bitchy homosexual (Barry Humphries). Gluttony (Parnell McCarey) is played as a fat slob. Sloth (Howard Goorney) cannot stay awake. Anger (Robert Russell) is the Clubroom's brawny bouncer. Vanity (Alba) is mirror fixated. Avarice (Danielle Noel) is penny pinching. Stanley Moon, like Jules Munshin, is acrophobic—and Spiggot repeatedly places him on heights. "Julie Andrews" is the Devil's magic word. Beelzebub is also not above punning: "Rotten sins I've got working for me," moans George Spiggot. "I suppose it's the wages."

Cook and Moore similarly render their specialty, perfected in their 1961 stage revue *Beyond the Fringe*, sideswiping British "types," such as when Stanley steps into the shoes of a chinless rich husband while his randy wife, Margaret, makes hay with a humpy chap named Randy.

"The movie's got fairly kitsch performances from Peter and myself," said Moore, "and the dialogue was sort of stilted, but in many ways that seemed to help what we were doing. Peter didn't like to have any dialogue that was not necessary or mere filler. He wanted to have bare-boned, economical, witty dialogue. I quite agree, but sometimes he used to insert not any lubrication, so things got a little stilted."

"The picture," said Donen, "never strayed from what religion actually believes to be true. When we finished, I invited a group of ministers and priests to come and see it, and most of them loved it. The picture does sort of poke a finger at religion, but it's their own Gordian knot, which they can't untie, that it pokes a joke at."

One other aspect of the movie's iconoclasm is that it features an unusual pace for a Donen film. It operates at exceptionally low velocity, which gives it not only a studied feel but an unexpected commonality with perhaps the screen's greatest black comedy, Stanley Kubrick's 1964 *Dr. Strangelove*. Making a stylistic (and substantive) leap from Kubrick to Donen in this instance may not be as audacious as it perhaps seems on the surface—at least not as audacious as the two master filmmakers themselves.*

"Viewed from the other side of the Atlantic, Donen's films are part of the renaissance of the British film in the late fifties and sixties," opined

---

* A few years after *Bedazzled,* Kubrick invited Donen to view a scene from a film he was working on, *A Clockwork Orange;* he wanted Donen's permission to have its antihero, played by Malcolm McDowell, sing "Singin' in the Rain" while he is on a raping rampage. "He wanted to make sure I wasn't offended," said Donen. "Why would I be? It didn't affect the movie *Singin' in the Rain.* He said the scene didn't work the way he originally shot it, so he added the song, to show that the guy was very happy."

film scholar Joseph Andrew Casper. "The first half of the springtime, known as 'Free Cinema,' largely comprised the contributions of directors like Lindsay Anderson, Karel Reisz, Tony Richardson, and Jack Clayton, as well as the Angry Young Men school of writers like John Braine, Colin Wilson, Alan Sillitoe, Harold Pinter, Shelagh Delaney, and David Storey. The impact of foreign directors in London—France's Truffaut, Italy's Antonioni, Poland's Polanski, and America's Losey (who had been there since 1964), Kubrick, and Donen—as well as the mod British comedies, were responsible for the second half."

Strong as Casper's argument is, there were dissenters. "Those Hollywood people like Stanley Donen came over to England in the sixties," said Lindsay Anderson in London in 1994 (only a few weeks before a heart attack claimed him at the age of seventy-one while he was on holiday in France), "and seeing what we had done here, they brought with them their intent of making 'serious' films, serious English films. Well, in the end, they didn't, now, did they? They made 'Hollywood' films in England."

Anderson, an unbridled purist, personally knew and very much liked Donen, he said, and he adored *Singin' in the Rain,* "though I can't forgive it for that steal from Cole Porter in that one number." Anderson also fondly recalled his offer to Donen, an invitation that was declined, when Anderson was artistic director of the Royal Court Theatre in Sloane Square. Anderson wanted Donen to direct a musical stage adaptation of the film *Good News,* with a new book by Comden and Green.

"You Americans would say, 'That might have worked,'" said Anderson. "We English would have preferred to say, 'Sounds like a good idea.'"

Bedazzled caught on with American college students, who viewed it and re-viewed it, and howled. It is certainly Donen's quirkiest movie.

"Stanley liked to be in control," Dudley Moore said of his director's technique, "and Peter and I found that a little constricting. We were more used to the slightly more lax atmosphere in a TV studio." Moore was, however, at Donen's allowance, free to compose the *Bedazzled* film score. "My first attempt was very William Walton-ish," said Moore. "Stanley told me to try it again, only on this go I was to make it sound 'more like songs.'" It sounds jazzy.

"At the time it was over," Moore said of the production, "Stanley made me very sad. He said, 'Film disintegrates, you know. This will probably be gone in about twenty years.'"

Donen, in this instance, was wrong.

Chapter 7

"I Know Frank Sinatra"

THERE IS the good Stanley Donen and the bad Stanley Donen," wrote Richard Schickel in *Time* magazine in 1984. "The good one has for thirty-five years directed elegant entertainments like *Singin' in the Rain, Charade, Two for the Road,* and *Movie Movie.* Every once in a while, though, his dark double appears and turns out something like *Staircase* or *Lucky Lady* and, now, *Blame It on Rio.* Inelegant is too mild a word for it; even distasteful doesn't quite cover it. Shall we say disgusting?"

"There are not two Stanley Donens," said Donen in 1992, still remembering Schickel's review. "There's only one, and I stand up for *Blame It on Rio.* I think it's a good picture. I thought I told it like it is, and it's a funny picture, with good dialogue. It is about how men are—some men, not all men. A beautiful girl wants to screw. You have to be pretty powerful to turn her down. And *Lucky Lady,* in spite of the beating I took, is a pretty good picture too. It's nice to look at, nicely shot, the scenes are funny or interesting. Rum-runners on dirty boats. I speak honestly about my movies, and I have no shyness about *Lucky Lady.* There are the pictures I loathe. *Saturn 3* is a piece of shit.* But *Lucky Lady* is not a bad movie, and neither is *Blame It on Rio.*"

---

* A futuristic science fiction story set in outer space, it was released in 1980. After the success of *Star Wars* in 1977, film financiers looked to the galaxies just as twelve years before they had looked to Broadway musicals after the box office returns on *The Sound of Music.* In the case of *Saturn 3,* Donen served as the producer, with the Academy Award–winning set designer of *Star Wars,* John Barry, as director. "A big miserable experience," said Donen, who had to take over the direction when it became evident to him and to the film's backer, Lord Lew Grade, that Barry was in above his head. "I did what I knew was ethical, but what I've suffered as a result of my being ethical was so gigantic that I don't know if I should have done it." The film *is* only a footnote on the Donen career, although one incident about it is worth dredging up: Frederic Raphael was beseeched by Donen to doctor the script and tried to beg off, insisting, "But, Stanley, I have no idea how people talk in outer space." "Yes you do, Freddie," replied Donen. "They talk just like you and me, except through helmets."

* * *

"I DON'T THINK *Staircase* was really my fault," said Donen of the still-born 1969 movie. "The material was superb, both the play and the screenplay. I wanted to make the picture with Paul Scofield, who played it onstage. It was his greatest role. For him it was what *My Fair Lady* was for Rex. It never occurred to me that he would turn me down."

The Royal Shakespeare Company production of Charles Dyer's autobiographical play opened in November of 1966, directed by Peter Hall. Scofield and Patrick Magee played two lovers bound—and unbound—by their relationship, which sparks verbal fireworks. The two men, Charlie and Harry, occupy a flat above their London barbershop in unfashionable Brixton.

Once Donen sent Scofield the screenplay that Dyer had adapted, "I got back one of the longest letters I ever received in my life," said Donen. "It was in longhand, in script about an eighth of an inch high, so tiny you practically had to read it with a magnifying glass. It was long, expansive, lucid, and incredible. In short, which it wasn't, Scofield said, No, I don't want to do it. He felt the part required his having personal contact with the audience. He said, 'I can't act it in front of the camera.' Personally, my feeling was he did not want to play a homosexual on film."

Donen placed an overseas call to Richard Zanuck, who was running Twentieth Century–Fox in Westwood, and explained his predicament: He had an actor's vehicle without the actor he had intended it for. "There must be somebody else," said Zanuck. Perhaps there was, only Donen, mistakenly, tripped on his own sense of humor. Instead of an actor, he threw out the name of a star. Two stars.

"Well," replied Donen, "you could do it with Rex Harrison and Richard Burton."

"Really?" said an impressionable Zanuck.

"Sure," said Donen.

"Send them the script tonight," ordered Zanuck.

"I did," remembered Donen. "Foolishly."

As it turned out, both Harrison and Burton were tickled not only by the challenge of playing against type but by Fox's offer of $1.25 million salary (plus percentage of the gross) to each, in addition to generous living expenses. The two British subjects refused, however, to shoot the film in England, where the fragile story was set. They wished to escape their country's weighty income tax.

Donen feared, rightly, that he would lose the necessary atmosphere he could gain by shooting on location. There was also the Elizabeth Taylor factor. Donen's long ago friend and Burton's very much publicized wife was shooting *The Only Game in Town* for Fox at Paris's Studio Boulogne. To keep both Burtons happy, the very English *Staircase* set up production on the adjoining French soundstage. This hurt both pictures. *Staircase* lost the gritty feel of London; *The Only Game in Town* gained the intrusive visits of Richard Burton—who threatened to punch Elizabeth Taylor's costar, Warren Beatty, for getting too familiar with Mrs. Burton in their love scenes.

Over on the *Staircase* stage, Harrison, already noted for his vanity and temperament, walked off the set one day and returned to his home in Portofino, until Richard Zanuck threatened legal action that would have made the star responsible for expenses incurred in finding a replacement. Harrison returned, said Donen, as if nothing had ever

Camping on *Staircase* (1969): Rex Harrison with his director, then again with his costar, Richard Burton. The press had a field day with the two boastful womanizers playing a gay couple; audiences, however, did not.

happened. With Burton, the problem was not temperament. It was dissipation.

"Richard," said Donen, "would never learn his lines. He only cared if his feet were in the shot, because for some reason he didn't like wearing these carpet slippers we'd given him. Rex was the complete opposite. Rex would rehearse and rehearse. He was an absolute perfectionist, down to the last detail. He wanted fifty takes until he had the last eyelash right. But with Richard we had to keep pinning his lines in front of him, on the pillow, on the ceiling. Then at six o'clock, he would start to drink. After that, you could forget about working with him."

Before the start of one weekend, Donen remembered, "I said, 'Richard, you have your big scene coming up, a monologue. It's one page long, and there's no one else we can cut away to. Richard, you've got to learn your speech.'"

Monday morning, Burton strutted onto the soundstage. "'I've learned it,' he said, very proudly. 'Stanley, do you want to come into my dressing room and hear it?' Which I did. I went into Richard's dressing room and he performed his speech for me. I couldn't believe it. I said, 'Richard, you learned the wrong fucking scene. We shot that weeks ago.'"

Donen admitted to being fond of Burton, and to liking Harrison too, within the confines of anyone's being able to like Rex Harrison.* "Alan Lerner once made the greatest remark about Rex," said Donen. "He said, 'You have to forgive Rex for being difficult. You see, when he wakes up every morning and opens the blinds, he has this terrible shock. He sees that there are other people in the world.'"

Burton, Donen discovered, "was a compulsive talker. He told wonderful stories, but he never shut up. It would get to be three in the morning, and he'd still be talking." Donen would still be listening. "One morning he stopped midsentence and looked me straight in the eye. He looked like he was about to keel over and drop dead. He just froze. It scared me to death."

Burton leaned forward, without ever blinking, and said: "I'm desperate."

---

* "I'd heard all these horrible stories about how difficult Rex was supposed to be," said Audrey Hepburn in 1992. She had starred with him in *My Fair Lady* (1964). "But actually, I didn't hear them until after we'd done the picture. While we were making it, he behaved like a perfect gentleman, to me at least. It's always afterward that I'm told these stories. I was told, for example, that Truman Capote didn't want me at all for *Breakfast at Tiffany's*. He wanted Marilyn Monroe. Thank goodness I didn't know that before we made the picture, or I never would have been able to do it. Perhaps that's why I always enjoyed being around Stanley. He made me feel sheltered."

"I knew *exactly* what he was talking about," said Donen. "His life with Elizabeth. His career as an actor. His drinking. I started to say something to him, but then he said, 'Aw, forget it,' and went right back to his story."

Staircase was a disaster. Critics found it turgid, and it never found an audience. A two-character study lacking the spine of a plot, it never should have been mounted as a major studio production; even an art-house director would have faced enormous obstacles in bringing it to life. Without making a case for it as a piece of filmmaking—"the sets made it look so false," said Donen—he did hit the mark when he said of the film, "It had two bizarre characters who alienated the audience just by having to look at them, but the picture is about humanity. If you have no compassion for the characters, Charlie and Harry, then I'm sorry, you are not a member of the human race."

"I DON'T THINK *The Little Prince* was an absolutely superb movie," said its director, "but it has some good things in it. Bob Fosse's dance as the snake. Gene Wilder as the fox, and some cinematic things that are interesting."

Antoine de Saint-Exupéry's fable has captivated reading audiences since its publication in 1943 (a year before the author was shot down during a wartime mission), and among those caught in its captivating spell have been a slew of theatrical adapters.* Stage versions by various talents have surfaced over the fifty years since the story's introduction, invariably with little success. Moviemakers, reportedly ranging from Orson Welles to Walt Disney, also have been transfixed by its lighter-than-air approach, as were flower children in the sixties. Only, what is so enticing about this fey fairy tale? A pilot, crashing in the Sahara, encounters his lost innocence in the form of a mop-topped little prince from a distant asteroid, and together they journey to find a meaning to life. En route they meet a string of colorful characters, who underscore the lessons. Didn't Frank Baum accomplish the same mission with Dorothy in Oz?

The 1974 movie began taking shape in the sixties, when A. Joseph Tandet, an entertainment attorney, secured the rights to the novel from Saint-Exupéry's widow and Gallimard, the Paris-based publisher. Tandet

* Saint-Ex's two great childhood literary influences were Hans Christian Andersen and Jules Verne. Verne was the author of *Around the World in Eighty Days,* which Donen had tried to adapt as a musical—and which may, in part, explain his attraction to *The Little Prince.*

approached Alan Jay Lerner, who wrote a script, which Tandet forwarded to Lerner's former partner, Fritz Loewe. Loewe had retired after the ordeal of putting together *Camelot,* but he obviously could not resist the material, and thus there developed what would be the final Lerner and Loewe score.

With Lerner's participation, the picture was guaranteed to be made. The librettist was in the midst of a five-picture production deal with Paramount, and his package to date included *Paint Your Wagon* (directed by Joshua Logan, 1969), *On a Clear Day You Can See Forever* (directed by Vincente Minnelli, 1970), and what would be a screen adaptation of his 1969 Broadway musical (with music by André Previn), *Coco,* based on the life of the couturier Chanel and starring Katharine Hepburn, croaking out the songs. *Coco* never dressed for Hollywood, however; after the box office deaths of *Paint Your Wagon, Clear Day,* and *The Little Prince,* Paramount knew that musicals were finished.

"WHEN STANLEY was in preproduction in Tunisia," remembered his sister, "he called me at home and said, 'I want a rabbi.' I said, 'Sure, Stanley, anything you want. What for?' "

"I'm getting married," Donen reported. Furthermore, he wanted to have the ceremony performed in his dreaded Columbia, South Carolina.* (Helen Donen, Stanley and Carla's mother, was still living in Columbia, as were Carla and her husband. Mordie Donen had died in 1959, at the age of fifty-nine.)

"Anything you want, Stanley," repeated Carla.

"Well," said her brother, "aren't you even going to ask who I'm marrying?"

The fourth Mrs. Donen was the actress Yvette Mimieux.

"Stanley, if you want a *chuppa,* we'll get you a *chuppa,*" said Carla Davis, referring to the ceremonial Jewish marriage canopy. The event was held at her home, on November 24, 1972. "It wasn't easy finding a rabbi who would perform a mixed marriage," said Carla. "The one we finally got would have married a hippopotamus to a rhino."

Carla rationalized that her brother's uncharacteristic decision to "come home" to be married, under rabbinical supervision, was born of his desire

---

* Carla Davis is of the opinion that her brother overstates his feelings about his hometown. "He does visit," she said in 1994. "He just does not visit often."

to see that this marriage lasted. "Stanley worshiped Yvette," Carla Davis said in 1994. "He still does. She was a very unique individual. She could not always act on-screen, but she could everywhere else. She was very smart, she knew about art and business. Yvette was terrific. She affected Stanley as no one else ever did or ever will. My brother was madly in love with her."

With sisterly affection, Carla Davis added, "Stanley's only problem is, he keeps thinking that romances will turn out just like they do in the movies."

CASTING the pilot in *The Little Prince* posed a problem. Richard Harris, Jim Dale, Robert Goulet, and Nicol Williamson were auditioned. Gene Hackman was given consideration. Richard Burton offered his services. Richard Kiley, Broadway's *Man of La Mancha,* was hired. Then the studio rang Donen. Frank Sinatra wanted the part.

The official version went that One-Take Charlie had heard the score at the home of his Palm Springs neighbor, Fritz Loewe, had fallen in love

Bob Fosse's final on-screen dancing role, as the snake in *The Little Prince* (1974). The young monarch is Steven Warner. By this time, however, the popularity of the movie musical had waned.

with the songs, and now coveted the role of the pilot. Whatever his motivation, Sinatra pushed Frank Yablans, the studio president, into hiring him for the role, and Yablans pushed Donen, who stood firm against it.

"I know Frank Sinatra," Donen told Yablans. "Frank Sinatra will get to Tunisia, which is where we're going to shoot this picture, and in two days he will not want to work. He'll kill the movie. Frank Sinatra is *not* doing this picture."

War broke out between the Sinatra-Yablans and the Donen camps. Donen said it eventually reached the point "where I wouldn't have been surprised if I had walked out of a building and a big bank safe would have fallen on my head."

Donen won. Richard Kiley played the pilot. Bob Fosse played the snake in the grass. (The choreographer-director, after refusing Donen's repeated requests to do the role, finally relented when his young daughter, Nicole, said she would like to see her father in a movie.) "Bob enjoyed doing *The Little Prince*," said his widow, Gwen Verdon. "It was a very funny number, because out in the middle of the desert Bob does a 'sand' dance. He took the sand out of his pocket and sprinkled it on the ground."*

"Stanley wanted the picture to look different," said Christopher Challis. The production, which was shot on an arid stretch of land more than one hundred miles from the Tunis airport, has an exceedingly gritty look to it, in major contrast to the glossy, elegant style of Donen's other movies. "We had to build an oasis," said Challis, "because Stanley wanted a scene to look lyrical, but when we finished with it, it looked as though it had been shot in a gravel pit."

"The picture," as Donen put it, "was disemboweled." Those wielding the sharpest knives were the critics and Alan Jay Lerner.

"The director, someone named Stanley Donen," Lerner committed to his memoir, "took it upon himself to change every tempo, delete musical phrases at will, and distort the intention of every song." There was more

---

* As Verdon confirmed, there is a scene in Fosse's autobiographical 1979 film *All That Jazz* that was lifted from a real-life incident involving Donen and Fosse. When *The Little Prince* opened, in 1974, Fosse, then in the midst of editing his movie *Lenny* and mounting the Broadway musical *Chicago* (in *All That Jazz*, the properties are called *The Stand-Up* and *New York to L.A.*), was hospitalized to stave off a potential heart attack. Donen was visiting his friend when *The Little Prince* was about to be reviewed on television by Pat Collins (the reviewer in *All That Jazz* was played by Chris Chase), and Fosse suggested that he and Donen turn on the TV and watch. Donen resisted, but Fosse insisted. They heard Collins's devastating review of the picture, and Fosse reacted by having his heart attack.

than the score that was wrong with *The Little Prince*. Its pace, its look, its style, its enervated stars, the lightness of the raw material in constant battle with the heaviness of its Broadway-style score—all conspired to work against the movie.

Audiences stayed away in droves.

Chapter 8

"A Worldly Sophistication"

I F *Blame It on Rio*, as Frederic Raphael once said, was a "victim of Stanley's love affair with Larry Gelbart," then so was its "good" twin, produced seven years before, the delightful pastiche *Movie Movie*. In two separate sections, it faithfully re-created Clifford Odets dramas and Busby Berkeley musicals of the thirties and then affectionately skewered them.

Gelbart, born in 1925, was another writer grounded in the Hecht-MacArthur* school. He had worked for Danny Thomas on radio and Sid Caesar on television, and was famous for a prolific and lightning-quick wit. He had cowritten, with Burt Shevelove, the book to the 1962 Broadway musical *A Funny Thing Happened on the Way to the Forum* (Gelbart uttered the remark that is often incorrectly attributed to other sources: "If Hitler is alive today, I hope he's out of town with a show that's in trouble"), and among his early film scripts was *The Wrong Box*. Yet the property for which Gelbart will most likely be best remembered was his long-running television-series adaptation of the Ring Lardner, Jr., novel and subsequent Robert Altman movie, *M*A*S*H*.

Donen cannot come off sounding objective when speaking about Gelbart. He makes it sound as if the writer were the brother Donen never had, while Gelbart considers Donen "the best friend a writer can have, because he's as generous with his enthusiasm for your work as he is with remedies for it when it does not enthuse him. Even if you're not working with Stanley, he's a great friend to have, because his lively mind can't fail but ignite your own."

Movie Movie, Gelbart claimed, was ignited by the sudden spate of

---

* Gelbart hailed from Hecht's hometown, Chicago.

movies in the 1970s—a good many of them from Mel Brooks—that satirized early Hollywood styles, "either specific movies or certain film genres," said Gelbart. "My feeling was that even the best of them were simply extended sketches, not really well served by having to run for the length of the feature. I thought it was a pity that a movie of this kind couldn't be forty or forty-five minutes long, knowing that there was no such animal as a movie that takes that little time."

From there, said Gelbart, "my mind, which more or less has a mind of its own, said, Why not a *pair* of short movies, a double feature, two pictures back-to-back, using the same actors, similar sets, similar stock shots—movie conventions so popular in the days when the studios cranked out as many films a year as record people turn out music videos today?"

With Gelbart's contract for the first ninety-seven episodes of *M*A*S*H* winding to a close, "I decided it was time to write myself an honorable discharge," he said. He adapted Ben Jonson's *Volpone* for the stage—called *Sly Fox*, it starred George C. Scott—then set about pitching his double-feature idea to Universal. The studio put up the funds for him to start writing.

"After working alone for a while, I decided I needed help," said Gelbart, "so I asked another writer, Sheldon Keller, to collaborate." Together they finished the script, including some sets of lyrics for the original songs in one of the two featurettes. In addition to Odets and Berkeley, their inspiration, said Gelbart, came from certain common elements found in Warner Bros. movies of the thirties: "Poor boy makes good, unknown girl makes good, and love—sacred and profane."

Gelbart returned to the studio with the script, titled *Double Feature*. According to Gelbart, "An executive whose name escapes me, much as his job later escaped him, said the studio was disappointed with the work, that the studio felt this was not the kind of thing that a youngster would walk into Tower Records to buy the sound track. I reminded him that what I had promised the studio was a movie and not a record album."

Gelbart turned to his Broadway producer of *Sly Fox*, Martin Starger, whose partner was the British entertainment mogul Lord Lew Grade; both appreciated the script. Gelbart is not sure whose idea it first was to seek Donen as a director. "My memory is as sharp as it ever was," he said. "It's the past that's getting fuzzy. But Stanley was our first and only choice, because no one knew movies better than Stanley."

The two features, in what was ultimately retitled *Movie Movie*, are *Dynamite Hands*, a black-and-white boxing drama about a young tenement lug who boxes so his kid sister can have a new pair of eyes, and *Baxter's Beauties,* a very poor man's *The Great Ziegfeld,* about an impresario's last spectacle, in color. In between, there is a trailer for an upcoming aviation drama à la *Wings,* and beforehand, introducing the package, in an unbilled cameo, is George Burns, who explains the idea and how it harks back to the days when "the boy always got the girl, crime never paid, and the only four-letter word in a movie house was 'exit.' " From there, the pace achieves the same breathless velocity as it did in *Singin' in the Rain.* The film's most effective gimmick, besides its constant somersaulting clichés, is the repetition of the two films' casts, George C. Scott (as the fight promoter and the theater impresario), Barbara Harris, Trish Van Devere, Eli Wallach, Art Carney, and Red Buttons. Harry Hamlin plays the John Garfield-esque boxing hero in the drama, and Barry Bostwick the Dick Powell character in the musical; the requirements of the roles would have made for incongruity. "Barry Bostwick as a fighter with his shirt off?" said Donen.

Michael Kidd choreographed the picture and played the Hamlin character's Hungarian father (there is in fact a slight facial resemblance). "It was like coming up with dances for *Seven Brides for Seven Brothers,*" Kidd said. "It was something I didn't want to do at all, but again Stanley wouldn't let me say no."*

"Stanley and Michael Kidd rehearsed the musical numbers as if we were doing a Broadway show," said the dancer Ann Reinking, who played *Dynamite Hands*'s nightclub-singer moll, "Troubles" Moran. "There was no 'Hurry up and wait' atmosphere that you usually have on a movie set. Everything went smoothly, just as planned, because Stanley knew what he wanted, he had cast it as he wanted, and his experience told him that the littlest thing was the best thing.

"Even though *Movie Movie* was a silly movie," said Reinking, "the atmosphere that Stanley maintained on the set was very sophisticated. It wasn't a blind sophistication. It was a humorous and worldly sophistication."

---

* It was also Donen who prudently decided to alter the title to *Movie Movie*—"otherwise," he said, "I was afraid if people saw 'George C. Scott in Double Feature' on a marquee, they'd have thought they were seeing *Patton* on a double bill with *Islands in the Stream.*"

Part 5

Doctor

Donen produced the fifty-eighth annual Academy Awards presentation; Larry Gelbart stands to his right, surrounded by cohosts Alan Alda, Jane Fonda, and Robin Williams.

Curtain Call

"The Artist's Struggle"

THE WORST day of my life," said Donen, "was the day I turned sixty. It came as such a shock. I was always the baby. At fifty you're a grown man. But sixty is up there. I had a birthday party. I didn't want it, but I had it. It was pretty shocking. Suddenly I was sitting there surrounded by my friends. I had been sixteen. Then I was twenty. Now I was sixty."

On April 13, 1994, Stanley Donen turned seventy. "Christ," he said. "Now I'm into fucking middle age."

"They stopped making his kind of pictures," pronounced the town sage, Billy Wilder, himself no stranger to the subject of survival in Hollywood. Remarking on the underuse of Donen, Wilder said, "It's as if during the time of the Postimpressionist painters someone passed a law saying, 'You can no longer use the color yellow.' Think of how frustrated you would be if you were Van Gogh.' "

"Stanley had his career when he was a young man," stated Audrey Hepburn as she began to build a case for herself as well as for her friend Donen. "Perhaps careers really can only last a certain amount of time. But Stanley did start when he was very young."

When he was sixteen years old, during the summer of 1940, in the remaining weeks before autumn and his starting a new life in New York, Stanley Donen acceded to his father's wish that he attend college. The boy enrolled in some psychology courses at the University of South Carolina, in Columbia. The summer semester would mark the full extent of Donen's formal education.

On May 7, 1989,* the institution he had briefly attended forty-nine years earlier presented Donen with an honorary doctorate in fine arts. "I

---

* Helen Donen died that year, at the age of eighty-four. Stanley Donen delivered his mother's eulogy at the funeral.

think I'm unique," Donen said upon accepting. "The first tap dancer to be called doctor."

Donen did backtrack slightly in his otherwise inspirational commencement address to the graduates. He ventured that honorary degrees were "a little bit like hemorrhoids. Sooner or later every asshole gets one."

"I could have crawled into a hole when he said that over the loud-speaker," said his sister.

The honoree had some advice for the new graduates, especially, he told them, if they were considering a career in the arts, which, he lamented, "these days is beginning to look more and more like an extension of the advertising business." Should they embark upon lives as artists, Donen told the young people, "Don't have a safety net. If you have something to fall back on in case you don't succeed, you'll fall back on it."

Donen went on to thank six men who he said were instrumental in his life: Fred Astaire, who inspired him; Roger Edens and Arthur Freed, who had afforded him the opportunity to direct movies; Bob Fosse, who was a friend and collaborator; Cary Grant, who shared his life and talent with Donen; and, finally, Mordie Donen, whose "values and character," said his son, "have guided me over rough waters and smooth."

Donen, in his cap and gown, properly thanked his fellow dignitaries for the honor they bestowed upon him. Then he did something for the crowd that he had seen Fred Astaire do in a Columbia, South Carolina, movie house one day after school in 1933.

Stanley Donen tap-danced.

"WHEN HE GOT divorced from the French lady," said Billy Wilder, "he became 'Lonely Stanley Donen.' That was good for me, because we had a lot of lunches together."

Donen and Yvette Mimieux divorced in 1982. She had become friendly with the Las Vegas financier Kirk Kerkorian—he was the money-man responsible for buying and dismantling what was left of M-G-M—before she married California real estate magnate Howard Ruby.

"Stanley and Yvette remained extremely close," noted Peter Stone. "They would talk all day long on their car phones, go out to lunch with each other, and at one point they even exchanged houses, when Yvette remarried."

"Stanley tends to become better friends with his wives after he gets divorced from them," said his sister.

Donen, who had lived in Malibu and Beverly Hills with Mimieux, settled into the hilltop estate, on Bel Air's Stone Canyon Road, that had once belonged to the prominent entertainment attorney Greg Bautzer. Donen was out shopping with his former wife one day in 1990, when he met his future fifth ex-wife, Pam Braden, who was working in a boutique on Rodeo Drive. Following a ten-day courtship—Donen proposed over dinner four days after the two had met—Donen and Braden married at the Beverly Hills home of Yvette Mimieux and Howard Ruby.

"I don't know why," ventured Billy Wilder, "but I don't think Donen was ever a quick, one-night-stand kind of guy. So then one day, out of the blue, he calls me up and says, 'I'm getting married on Tuesday, and you are to be at Yvette Mimieux's house.' Well, that's a charming little story that should be set to music and dancing, because that sort of thing is not done every day. I told him, 'But you've only known this girl three days. Don't buy the car. Rent it first.' And he said, 'I know what I'm doing.' And he did. Pam's absolutely charming, a sweet girl, who just brightens his life immeasurably."

As for the thirty-six-year age difference between Pam and Stanley Donen, Wilder called it "a generation gap without a generation gap, although there are problems. She would like to have children. He wouldn't, although he has proven he can make them. He has kids all over the place. Some of them are executive producers."

Pam Donen said that the age difference did lead to a few awkward moments in her relationship with her husband. "When some friends of mine first came to the house and met Stanley," she said, "one of them stuck out his hand and said, 'It's nice to meet you, sir.' " She also felt a bit stifled in the company of some of Donen's crowd, although, she said, Billy and Audrey Wilder were cordial from the start. By Pam's own admission, she was never a film buff ("Stanley once tried to show me *Charade,* only I fell asleep"), and she said, "I think when I write my book about these times, I'll call it '*All They Ever Talked About Was Dead Movie Stars.*' "

In 1994, Stanley and Pam Donen divorced, on friendly terms. The previous summer, Donen left California to work on Broadway, and the following year, after the January 17 earthquake and its recurrent aftershocks, Donen sold his Bel Air house and took up residence again in the metropolis that represented to his sixteen-year-old self "the absolute best of the best" and that he celebrated so joyfully in the first movie he directed.

* * *

THE ACADEMY OF MOTION PICTURE ARTS AND SCIENCES board
of governors bestowed an honor upon Donen in 1986. It offered him a
job, to produce that year's Oscar broadcast. The show turned out to be
one of the few entertaining ones that body has ever been known to offer,
or, as *New York Times* television critic John J. O'Connor claimed, to be "the
best Oscar show in years, perhaps ever."

"It was to have been written fifty percent by Larry Gelbart and fifty
percent by Neil Simon," Donen said. "A week before they were both set to
start writing, Neil told me he didn't want to do it, it would take him away
from other things, and he bowed out. I'll never forgive him." In Simon's
place, Donen hired Glenn Gordon Caron, who had created the television
show *Moonlighting*. "Very nice of him," said Donen. (Later in the season,
Donen returned the favor for Caron, by supervising—without credit—a
Cyd Charisse–style dream ballet for *Moonlighting*'s two stars, Cybill Shepherd and Bruce Willis.*)

"When I said I'd produce the Oscar show," said Donen, "the Academy people told me that every year the show has to have a theme. I said,
'That's bull.'" The show did, however, carry an unmistakable personal
touch. Gene Kelly, Debbie Reynolds, and Donald O'Connor joined to
present the music awards. Larry Gelbart presented the writing awards.
Audrey Hepburn presented the costume award. Billy Wilder, John Huston, and Akira Kurosawa presented the Best Picture award. Irene Cara
sang a specialty number called "Here's to the Losers," highlighting nominated films that in their respective years had missed grabbing the crown,
among them, *Sunset Boulevard, E.T.,* and *Seven Brides for Seven Brothers*. To
open the show, Donen chose a montage of vintage film clips containing
great moments from the movies.

The first shot, in black and white, showed several chorus girls standing on the wings of antique aeroplanes.

They were flying down to Rio.

"YOU SAID you always wanted to direct a Broadway musical."

"I have always wanted to direct a Broadway musical."

* Another aftereffect of Donen's producing the Oscarcast was his directing a music video
for the year's music winner, Lionel Richie. The video was for Richie's best-selling single,
"Dancing on the Ceiling."

Rehearsing the Oscarcast: directors of note Donen, Wilder, Kurosawa, Huston

The two men speaking over lunch in Los Angeles were Martin Starger, who produced *Movie Movie,* and Donen. It was Starger who spoke first.

"You want to do one?" the producer proposed.

"When?" asked Donen.

"Tomorrow."

"Well, okay," said Donen. "I'm not doing anything tomorrow."

That's how Stanley Donen came to find himself standing in the middle of a rehearsal studio at the corner of Nineteenth and Broadway in New York at ten o'clock on a Monday morning in August 1993.* The show he was stepping into had been in the works, under a director named Susan Schulman, and was set to open to the public at the Minskoff Theater six weeks later.

"I have one word to say to Stanley," offered Kay Thompson, who heard news of his hiring a few days before it hit the papers. "Don't."

---

* Only the week before, plans had unraveled for a movie musical Donen was to produce and direct, based on Robert Louis Stevenson's *Dr. Jekyll and Mr. Hyde,* to star Michael Jackson. The pop singer's scandal involving alleged sexual relations with a young boy brought the project to a halt.

Ironically, the show Donen was coming in to doctor—and did, only not enough, because there simply was not sufficient time—was a stage adaptation of *The Red Shoes,* with music by Jule Styne, based on Michael Powell and Emeric Pressburger's artsy, often parodied fantasy that legions of balletomanes and schoolgirls considered the absolute last word on dance, the screaming-Technicolor picture that inspired countless balletic dream sequences in overproduced Hollywood musicals of the fifties, and the movie that in 1949 Arthur Freed thought had already been topped by Donen and Kelly's fresh dispatch of New York rushes for *On the Town.*

"The spine of the show is very powerful," said Donen, explaining why he was drawn to the property. "A man says that an artist can't have two loves. She can't have personal attachments of any kind and still find room in her life for her art. Then he finds himself filled with emotion about her, and he's caught in a trap, and once he's caught in it, he destroys her. That's a wonderful concept for a musical, the artist's struggle, and I'll do everything humanly possible to pull it off."

As for the difference between directing a film and directing a stage show, the "legendary director" (as he was referred to by all four New York dailies, including the broadsheet) said, "In the theater, everyone is around you the whole time and you have the entire show to deal with at once rather than having one tiny piece of the mosaic, the way you do in a movie. In the case of this show, there are tremendous pressures and you have to deal with personalities who are always in conflict.* Change one line, and three different people yell at you. In a movie I just do what I want and everybody finds out about it later."

IN THE LATE EIGHTIES, Robert Redford asked Donen to lead a seminar on the film musical at the actor's Sundance Institute in Utah, and a hesitant Donen accepted. "What could I possibly tell a group of film students?" he asked. Donen's solution was to begin compiling clips of his own musical numbers. To his surprise, he discovered that he had been responsible for more than 150 of them. Working on his Moviola, he whittled down to 49 the total he planned to show at Sundance, to be presented over a series of evenings. First, though, he decided to preview for friends what he had edited together, and they assembled inside Donen's screening room in the Bel Air house. He found the audience attentive, and himself intrigued by the material, "but when we got to Fred Astaire doing 'He

* The book of *The Red Shoes* was by Marsha Norman.

Loves and She Loves' with Audrey," said Donen, "I burst into tears. I told my friends, 'I have to leave you.' I had to be by myself for a while, because it's gone. It's not just that time is gone and Fred is gone, but the whole world has changed so dramatically. Humanity is so different today. And it's a tragedy."

UPON REFLECTION, the directorial career of Stanley Donen can be divided into three distinct phases, and, when taken either separately or cumulatively, "should encapsulate," according to one of his favorite colleagues, Frederic Raphael, "the Hollywood phenomenon in all its diversity."

What Raphael was referring to was that in his prolific forty-year-plus career span Donen had it all, the good and the bad and the vagaries of what exists between. He rode out the glory period of the studio system and reveled in its protection. He latched onto independent production in an international playground at a time when audiences and American tax laws richly rewarded such efforts. And after he had suffered through some well-meaning but low-performing misfires, Donen endured the chill so often experienced by a former boy wonder in Hollywood.

"When the talkies happened," said Donen, providing his own overview, "the studios hired all that talent I admired so much—Hecht and MacArthur, Kaufman and Hart, and all the songwriters: Gershwin, Porter, Kern. That's what I grew up on and wanted to be a part of. Hollywood had a very simple idea then. Take the guys who make noise, and put them to work for the movies. Today that's gone. We don't have a sense of theatricality and a literary background in movies anymore. And that's a great loss for the entire world."

Fortunately, the golden era is, for the most part, preserved. The movie musicals that Stanley Donen started directing at Metro-Goldwyn-Mayer in 1949 set a new standard and helped define and perfect that particular genre from its Eisenhower-era peak, when the world desperately needed color, dance, and clever voices, to its virtual extinction after some very expensive funerals in the sixties and seventies (the film musical having lived a fragile existence from the start). Capping a youthful developmental period in which Donen oversaw some brilliant individual sequences in *Cover Girl* and Gene Kelly's dance competition with the cartoon Jerry the Mouse in *Anchors Aweigh,* the formidable Donen musical canon consists of *On the Town,* with its powerful use of location, youthful innocence, and exuberance; *Royal Wedding,* with its tender moods and effective camera techniques (coupled with the awesome Jack-be-nimble individuality of

Fred Astaire); *Singin' in the Rain,* with its sharp irreverence toward its own medium; *Seven Brides for Seven Brothers,* with its keen command of body movement and inventive compositions for the otherwise cumbersome wide screen; *It's Always Fair Weather,* with its stab at depicting the real-life nature of former friendships and the harsh actualities of career turns; *Funny Face,* with its feast-for-the-eyes fusion of two dream worlds, that of a modern Cinderella story with the lives of fashion people; and *The Pajama Game,* with its imaginative use of settings and the ease with which it adapts an obviously stage-bound property to the vivid demands of the movie screen—as was also true, albeit to a lesser extent, of *Damn Yankees.*

By the late 1950s, Donen saw little reason to continue with Broadway musical adaptations, despite the practice becoming, with varying results, the growing trend among even such notable nonmusical film masters as Robert Wise, William Wyler, and Sir Carol Reed.* Putting aside musical playbacks, Donen turned his attention to well-dressed, European-flavored romances. The best of these were *Indiscreet, Charade,* and *Two for the Road,* respectively sly, witty, and bittersweet, and, in toto, distinctively graceful.†

In the late sixties and again a decade later, Donen exercised delightful creative stretches atypical of the mainstream and produced two side-splitting, cultish send-ups, *Bedazzled,* which took on Faust, and the more gentle *Movie Movie,* which took on two equally formidable influences, Clifford Odets and Busby Berkeley. The former, a deadpan comedy with depth, displayed the director's versatility (in content and tone, *Bedazzled* was seemingly as far afield from *Singin' in the Rain* as *Hamlet* is from *As You Like It*), while the second summed up his knowledge of and affection for the medium upon which he was weaned, the medium that gave him—and the world—Fred Astaire.

---

* Wise's 1960 *West Side Story* (codirected with Jerome Robbins), as well as his 1965 *The Sound of Music,* did not so much advance the art of the screen musical as monumentalize it. Both generated a Fort Knox in Oscars and ticket sales. Wyler's 1968 *Funny Girl* boasted some marvelous musical numbers (staged by Herbert Ross) but unraveled dramatically after intermission. Still, Barbra Streisand's renditions of "I'm the Greatest Star," "Don't Rain on My Parade," and "My Man" remain a triumph of performer power. Sir Carol's meticulously mounted 1968 Best Picture, *Oliver!,* while a substantial improvement over its stage-show progenitor, owes a substantial debt to the original blueprint from which it was borrowed, David Lean's 1947 *Oliver Twist.*

† Shortly after the death of Jacqueline Kennedy Onassis, Emily Prager wrote an essay in the *New York Times* in which she expressed a yearning for a return to the era of accessible elegance that was virtually embodied by the late Mrs. Onassis and two of her equally revered contemporaries, Grace Kelly and Audrey Hepburn. "I'm going to miss that combination of style and substance," wrote Prager in wistful admiration. Her observation could be equally applied to the world of elegance and grace Donen captured on film.

In between, or rather patched among the latter part of this multipartite third phase, Donen engineered what are best classified as disappointments, such strange bedfellows as *Staircase, The Little Prince,* and *Lucky Lady;* yet even when the by then veteran filmmaker hit a sour note—which as time went by required greater time from which to recover—the pictures themselves still bore his unmistakable personal polish and ever youthful eagerness to explore new themes.

"Movies," Donen insists, "should not pretend to be more important than the people watching them. It's not human, it's not nice. I think of myself as a 'meat and potatoes' kind of director and the characters in my movies as struggling. The actors in *Singin' in the Rain* are struggling. *Seven Brides for Seven Brothers* is very earthy stuff. I know that *Charade* is thought to be 'stylish,' whatever that means, but it has grisly murders in it, guys with their throats being cut. But 'stylish'? All right, so it's played in Paris, but it's a very rough-spirited movie."

As final proof of his egalitarian spirit, Donen notes that the heroes of his movies "danced on pavement, never on point."

Sometimes, too, they were so momentarily love drunk that they took to singing in the rain, or else, confined indoors, they magically danced on the ceiling.

Chronology

1924 Stanley Donen born April 13, in Columbia, South Carolina, to Helen and Mordie Donen. Metro-Goldwyn-Mayer, a division of Loew's Incorporated, is formed by merger of three film companies; Louis B. Mayer oversees California studio while Nicholas Schenck runs business operations in New York. Columbia Pictures is begun, under name C.B.C./Film Sales Company, by brothers Harry and Jack Cohn and exhibitor Joe Brandt.

1927 Charles Lindbergh crosses the Atlantic. Premiere of Warner Bros.'s *The Jazz Singer;* the movies talk and sing. On Broadway, Florenz Ziegfeld presents *Show Boat,* based on novel by Edna Ferber, with music and lyrics by Jerome Kern and Oscar Hammerstein II, incorporating dramatic themes of miscegenation, alcoholism, and gambling.

1928 *Amos 'n' Andy,* radio's first regularly scheduled entertainment series, takes to airwaves. Walt Disney's Mickey Mouse enjoys first box office success, in the cartoon short *Steamboat Willie.*

1929 Stock market crashes. Initial wave of Hollywood escapist movie musicals finds wide audience.

1932 Franklin D. Roosevelt elected President. Radio City Music Hall, "The Showplace of the Nation," opens in New York City.

1933 Fred Astaire and Ginger Rogers first partnered, playing secondary roles in RKO Christmas musical, *Flying Down to Rio.* Adolf Hitler rises to power in Germany.

1934 Motion Picture Production Code put into effect to stem rising tide of sensationalism on-screen, in particular the sexual innuendos of Paramount star Mae West (whose first leading man is Cary Grant).

1939 M-G-M releases *The Wizard of Oz.* Hollywood experiences its golden year of movie production. War breaks out in Europe.

1940 Stanley Donen graduates high school and moves to New York. Watershed musical *Pal Joey* opens at Ethel Barrymore Theater, December 25, with Gene Kelly as star and Donen in chorus.

1941   Collegiate musical *Best Foot Forward,* choreographed by Gene Kelly, with Donen as assistant (and in chorus), opens on Broadway. Japan attacks Pearl Harbor, December 7.

1942   Donen relocates to California, becomes M-G-M contract dancer and assistant to choreographer Charles Walters.

1943   Richard Rodgers and Oscar Hammerstein II's first collaborative effort, *Oklahoma!,* opens on Broadway, ushering in new tradition of plot-and-dance-driven musicals (choreographed by Agnes de Mille). M-G-M's *Best Foot Forward* premieres, with Donen in chorus. Studio also loans out Gene Kelly to Columbia for Rita Hayworth musical *Cover Girl;* Donen assists on Kelly's numbers; conceives and directs "Alter Ego" dance.

1944   *Cover Girl* makes Gene Kelly a star. *On the Town,* based on Jerome Robbins's ballet *Fancy Free,* opens on Broadway, with music by Leonard Bernstein and lyrics and book by Betty Comden and Adolph Green.

1945   Walt Disney combines live action with animation in *The Three Caballeros.* M-G-M presents Gene Kelly in *Anchors Aweigh,* containing sequence conceived, written, and directed by Donen, in which live-action Kelly dances with cartoon Jerry the Mouse. End of World War II.

1946   Donen signs new contract with M-G-M; cowrites scenario to *Take Me Out to the Ball Game,* with Gene Kelly, and sells to Arthur Freed. Irving Berlin's *Annie Get Your Gun* opens on Broadway. Donen doctors stage musical *Call Me Mister* during pre-Broadway tryout.

1947 –52   The House Committee on Un-American Activities investigates Hollywood for possible Communist activities.

1948   Donen marries Jeanne Coyne, a New York dancer, in Santa Monica, California (they divorce in 1951). Paramount "consent decree" case forces Hollywood studios to divest themselves of their movie theater chains. Dore Schary replaces Louis B. Mayer as M-G-M production chief.

1949   *On the Town,* codirected by Gene Kelly and Donen, opens at Radio City Music Hall.

1951   Donen directs first solo effort, *Royal Wedding,* with Fred Astaire. Louis B. Mayer loses power struggle with Dore Schary and resigns from M-G-M.

1952   Donen marries the actress Marion Marshall, in Los Angeles (two sons: Peter, born 1953, and Joshua, 1955; marriage dissolves in 1959). *Singin' in the Rain* premieres.

1953   Twentieth Century–Fox releases first picture in CinemaScope, *The Robe.* Donen directs his first musical in the wide-screen process, *Seven Brides for Seven Brothers.*

1954 Paramount introduces VistaVision.

1956 *My Fair Lady* opens on Broadway. Elvis Presley's movie debut, *Love Me Tender*. Dore Schary dismissed from M-G-M.

1957 Donen, on loan-out from M-G-M, directs *Funny Face* for Paramount, *The Pajama Game* for Warner Bros., and *Kiss Them for Me* for Twentieth Century–Fox. M-G-M contract expires; Donen moves to London, forms Grandon Productions with Cary Grant.

1958 French New Wave arrives on American shores; Jean-Luc Godard, one of its chief proponents, writes: "Stanley Donen is surely the master of the musical. *The Pajama Game* exists to prove it."

1960 Donen marries Lady Adelle Beatty (née Dillingham, of Oklahoma), in Henley, England (one son, Mark, born 1962; marriage ends in 1970). Donen begins production deal with Columbia, then transfers to Universal. John F. Kennedy elected President. Pop Art movement begins in America.

1963 Kennedy fatally shot in Dallas. Donen's *Charade* opens, with two references to "assassination" edited out. Arthur Freed, "the spark plug of the M-G-M musical," retires from studio (dies in 1973).

1964 The Beatles star in their first movie, a musical, *A Hard Day's Night,* directed by Richard Lester. *My Fair Lady,* directed by George Cukor, produced by Warner Bros.

1965 Twentieth Century–Fox's version of Rodgers and Hammerstein's *The Sound of Music,* directed by Robert Wise, becomes highest-grossing picture in history, motivating all studios to make musicals.

1967 Donen leaves Universal for Twentieth Century–Fox. Motion Picture Association of America institutes new ratings system to replace antiquated Production Code.

1968 Assassinations of Martin Luther King, Jr., and Robert F. Kennedy. Tet offensive in Vietnam. Richard M. Nixon elected President. Students strike in Paris. On Broadway, *Hair,* "The American Tribal Love-Rock Musical," opens.

1969 Twentieth Century–Fox's $24.5 million *Hello, Dolly!,* directed by Gene Kelly, is most expensive musical ever produced; its failure effectively kills off production of big-budget musicals.

1970 Las Vegas investor Kirk Kerkorian purchases M-G-M and begins slow process of dismantling company.

1972 Donen marries the actress Yvette Mimieux in Columbia, South Carolina (they divorce in 1982).

1974   Donen returns to live in Los Angeles and makes his first American movie in seventeen years, *Lucky Lady*.

1978   *Grease,* a fifties-style pop musical directed by Randal Kleiser, surpasses box office record of *The Sound of Music*.

1981   MTV launched, providing twenty-four hours a day of music videos on American television.

1985   Atlanta-based media baron Ted Turner purchases M-G-M film library for $1 billion.

1986   Donen produces Academy Awards television presentation, directs Lionel Richie "Dancing on the Ceiling" music video, and supervises a dance number on *Moonlighting* television show, with Cybill Shepherd and Bruce Willis. Cary Grant dies in Davenport, Iowa, while on speaking tour.

1987   Fred Astaire dies in Beverly Hills.

1990   Donen marries Pam Braden at the home of Yvette Mimieux and her husband, Howard Ruby, in Beverly Hills. (They divorce in 1994.)

1993   Audrey Hepburn dies in Tolochenaz, Switzerland. Donen assumes direction of Broadway musical *The Red Shoes*.

1994   Donen resumes residence in New York.

Filmography

As Assistant Choreographer

1. *Best Foot Forward.* 1943. M-G-M. Director: Edward Buzzell. Producer: Arthur Freed. Screenplay: Irving Brecher and Fred Finklehoff, based on the 1940 Broadway show of the same name produced by George Abbott, book by John Cecil Holm, music and lyrics by Hugh Martin and Ralph Blane. Choreographers: Charles Walters and Jack Donohue, assisted by Stanley Donen (uncredited). (Says Donen: "I was only an assistant to Jack Donohue, although I may have helped Chuck Walters too. And I was in the chorus.") Musical numbers: "Buckle Down, Winsocki," "You're Lucky," "Wish I May," "Three Men on a Date," "Ev'ry Time," "The Three B's," "Alive and Kicking," "The Flight of the Bumble Bee" (Rimsky-Korsakov), "Two O'Clock Jump" (Count Basie, Harry James, Benny Goodman). Cast: Lucille Ball, Harry James and His Music Makers, William Gaxton, Virginia Weidler, Tommy Dix, Nancy Walker, June Allyson, Kenny Bowers, Gloria DeHaven, Jack Jordan, Stanley Donen (uncredited). Technicolor. 95 minutes.

2. *Cover Girl.* 1944. Columbia. Director: Charles Vidor. Producer: Arthur Schwartz. Screenplay: Virginia Van Upp, adapted by Marion Parsonnet and Paul Gangelin from a play by Erwin Gelsey. Music: Jerome Kern. Lyrics: Ira Gershwin ("Make Way for Tomorrow" lyrics by E. Y. "Yip" Harburg, and "Poor John" by Fred W. Leigh and Harry E. Pether). Choreographers: Val Raset, Seymour Felix, Gene Kelly (uncredited), Stanley Donen (uncredited). Musical numbers: "The Show Must Go On," "Put Me to the Test," "Sure Thing," "That's the Best of All," "Make Way for Tomorrow," "Who's Complaining?," "Long Ago and Far Away," "Alter Ego" dance, "Poor John." Cast: Rita Hayworth (singing voice dubbed by Martha Mears), Gene Kelly, Lee Bowman, Phil Silvers, Eve Arden, Otto Kruger, Jinx Falkenburg, Leslie Brooks, Jess Barker, Anita Colby, Curt Bois, Ed Brophy, Thurston Hall, The Cover Girls. Technicolor. 105 minutes.

3. *Hey, Rookie.* 1944. Columbia. Director: Charles Barton. Producer: Irving Briskin. Screenplay: Harry Myers, Edward Eliescu, Jay Gorney, based on the play by K. B. Colvan and Doris Colvan. Choreographer: Val Raset,

with Stanley Donen (uncredited). Musical numbers: "There Goes Taps," "When the Yardbirds Come to Town," "So What Serenade," "Hey, Rookie," "Take a Chance," "You're Good for My Morale," "It's Great to Be in Uniform," "Streamlined Sheik," "It's a Swelluva Life in the Army." Cast: Ann Miller, Larry Parks, Joe Besser, Jimmy Little, Joy Sawyer, Selmer Jackson, Larry Thompson, Barbara Brown, Charles Trowbridge, Charles Wilson, Jack Gilford, Hi Lo Jack and a Dame, The Condos Brothers, The Vagabonds, The Johnson Brothers, Judy Clark and the Solid Senders, Bob Evans. 71 minutes.

4. *Anchors Aweigh.* 1945. M-G-M. Director: George Sidney. Producer: Joe Pasternak. Screenplay: Isobel Lennart. Story: Natalie Marcin. Choreographers: Gene Kelly, Stanley Donen. Musical numbers: "Anchors Aweigh," "Jealousy," "Donkey Serenade," "(All of a Sudden) My Heart Sings," "If You Knew Susie" (parody lyrics by Donen, uncredited), "What Makes the Sunset?," "I Begged Her," "We Hate to Leave," "The Charm of You," "I Fall in Love Too Easily," "Cradle Song," Waltz from Serenade in C (Tchaikovsky), "Largo Al Factotum" from *The Barber of Seville,* "La Cumparsita." Cast: Frank Sinatra, Kathryn Grayson, Gene Kelly, José Iturbi, Dean Stockwell, Pamela Britton, "Rags" Ragland, Billy Gilbert, Henry O'Neill, Carlos Ramirez, Edgar Kennedy, Grady Sutton, Leon Ames, Sharon McManus, Henry Armetta, James Flavin, Jerry the Mouse (uncredited). Technicolor. 141 minutes.

As Choreographer

1. *Jam Session.* 1944. Columbia. Director: Charles Barton. Producer: Irving Briskin. Screenplay: Manny Seff, from a story by Harlan Ware and Patterson McNutt. Musical numbers: "Cherokee," "I Can't Give You Anything but Love," "Murder He Says," "No Name Jive," "I Lost My Sugar in Salt Lake City," "Brazil," "It Started All Over Again," "Victory Polka," "Teddy Bear Boogie," "St. Louis Blues," "Jive Bomber," "C-Jam Blues." (Says Donen: "I don't know what the hell I did on this one, probably something with Ann Miller.") Cast: Ann Miller, Jess Barker, Louis Armstrong, Charles D. Brown, Eddie Kane, George Eldredge, Bill Shawn, Renie Riano, Clarence Muse, Pauline Drake, Charlie Barnet, Jan Garber, Teddy Powell, Alvino Rey, Glen Gray, The Pied Pipers, Nan Wynn. 78 minutes.

2. *Kansas City Kitty.* 1944. Columbia. Director: Del Lord. Producer: Ted Richmond. Screenplay: Manny Seff. Musical numbers: "Kansas City Kitty," "Tico Tico," "Nothing Boogie from Nowhere," "Pretty Kitty Blue Eyes." (Donen: "This one is so minor it's hardly worth mentioning.") Cast: Joan Davis, Bob Crosby, Matt Willis, Jane Frazee, Erik Rolf, Tim Ryan, Robert Emmett Keane. 63 minutes.

3. *Holiday in Mexico.* 1946. M-G-M. Director: George Sidney. Producer: Joe Pasternak. Screenplay: Isobel Lennart, from a story by William Kozlenko. Musical numbers: "I Think of You," "Walter Winchell Rumba," "Yo Te Amo Mucho (And That's That)," "You, So It's You," "And Dreams Remain," "Holiday in Mexico," "Ave Maria," "Les Filles de Cadiz," "Italian Street Song," Piano Concerto No. 2 in C Minor (Rachmaninoff), Polonaise in A Flat Major (Chopin), "Good Night, Sweetheart," "Three Blind Mice" (arranged by André Previn), "The Music Goes 'Round and Around," "Liebestod" from *Tristan and Isolde.* Cast: Jane Powell, Walter Pidgeon, José Iturbi, Roddy McDowall, Ilona Massey, Xavier Cugat, Tonia and Teresa Hero, Hugo Haas, Mikhail Rasumny, Helene Stanley, William (Bill) Phillips, Linda Christian. Technicolor. 127 minutes.

4. *No Leave, No Love.* 1946. M-G-M. Director: Charles Martin. Producer: Joe Pasternak. Screenplay: Charles Martin and Leslie Kardos. Musical numbers: "All the Time," "Love on a Greyhound Bus," "Isn't It Wonderful?," "It's Great to Be Back Home," "Old Sad Eyes," "When It's Love." Cast: Van Johnson, Keenan Wynn, Pat Kirkwood, Guy Lombardo, Edward Arnold, Marie Wilson, Leon Ames, Selena Royle. 119 minutes.

5. *Living in a Big Way.* 1947. M-G-M. Director: Gregory La Cava. Producer: Pandro S. Berman. Screenplay: Gregory La Cava and Irving Ravetch. Musical score: Lennie Hayton. Choreographers: Gene Kelly, Stanley Donen. Musical numbers: "It Had to Be You," "Fido and Me," Building Project Ballet (interpolation of "Ring Around the Rosy," "In and Out the Windows," "Loo by Loo," "Yankee Doodle"). Cast: Gene Kelly, Marie McDonald, Charles Winniger, Phyllis Thaxter, Spring Byington, Jean Adair, Clinton Sundberg, John Warburton, William (Bill) Phillips, John Alexander, Phyllis Kennedy, Bernadine Hayes. 103 minutes.

6. *This Time for Keeps.* 1947. M-G-M. Director: Richard Thorpe. Producer: Joe Pasternak. Screenplay: Gladys Lehman, from a story by Erwin Gelsey and Lorraine Fielding. Musical numbers: "Easy to Love," "Inka Dinka Doo," "Chiquita Banana," "No Wonder They Fall in Love," "Ten Per Cent Off," "The Man Who Found the Last Chord," "A Little Bit of This and a Little Bit of That," "Why Don't They Let Me Sing a Love Song?," "Little Big Shot," "I Love to Dance," "When It's Lilac Time on Mackinaw Island," "M'appari" from *Martha,* "La Donna è Mobile" from *Rigoletto.* Cast: Esther Williams, Lauritz Melchior, Jimmy Durante, Johnnie Johnston, Dame Mae Whitty, Sharon McManus, Dick Simmons, Ludwig Stossel, Xavier Cugat and His Orchestra. Technicolor. 105 minutes.

7. *Killer McCoy.* 1947. M-G-M. Director: Roy Rowland. Producer: Sam Zimbalist. Screenplay: Frederick Hazlitt Brennan, Thomas Lennon, George Bruce, George Oppenheimer. Musical number: "When-You-and-I-Were-Young-

Maggie Blues." Cast: Mickey Rooney, James Dunne, Sam Levene, Brian Donleavy, Ann Blyth, David Clarke, Tom Tully, Mickey Knox, James Bell, Gloria Holden. 104 minutes.

8. *The Big City.* 1948. M-G-M. Director: Norman Taurog. Producer: Joe Pasternak. Screenplay: Whitfield Cook and Anne Morrison, with additional dialogue by Aben Kandel, from a story by Miklos Laszlo, as adapted by Nanette Kutner. Musical numbers: "God Bless America," "Lullaby" (Brahms), "The Kerry Dance," "What'll I Do?," "Ok'l Baby Dok'l," "Shoo Baby," "I'm Gonna See a Lot of You," "Don't Blame Me," "Yippee-O-Yippee-Ay Ay." Cast: Margaret O'Brien (singing voice dubbed by Marni Nixon), Robert Preston, Danny Thomas, George Murphy, Betty Garrett, Lotte Lehmann, Karin Booth, Edward Arnold, Butch Jenkins, Connie Gilchrist, Page Cavanaugh Trio. 103 minutes.

9. *A Date with Judy.* 1948. M-G-M. Director: Richard Thorpe. Producer: Joe Pasternak. Screenplay: Dorothy Cooper and Dorothy Kingsley, based on radio characters created by Aleen Leslie. Musical numbers: "It's a Most Unusual Day," "Judaline," "I've Got a Date with Judy," "I'm Gonna Meet My Mary," "Strictly on the Corny Side," "Cuanto la Gusto," "Temptation," "Mulligatawny." Cast: Wallace Beery, Jane Powell, Elizabeth Taylor, Carmen Miranda, Xavier Cugat and His Orchestra, Robert Stack, Selena Royle, Leon Ames, Clinton Sundberg, George Cleveland, Lloyd Corrigan, Jerry Hunter, Jean McLaren. Technicolor. 114 minutes.

10. *The Kissing Bandit.* 1948. M-G-M. Director: Laszlo Benedek. Producer: Joe Pasternak. Screenplay: Isobel Lennart and John Briard Harding. Music and lyrics: Earl Brent and Edward Heyman ("Love Is Where You Find It" by Brent and Nacio Herb Brown). Musical numbers: "Love Is Where You Find It," "If I Steal a Kiss," "Señorita," "Siesta," "What's Wrong with Me?," "Tomorrow Means Romance," "I Like You," "Dance of Fury." Cast: Frank Sinatra, Kathryn Grayson, Ann Miller, Ricardo Montalban, Cyd Charisse, J. Carrol Naish, Mildred Natwick, Mikhail Rasumny, Billy Gilbert, Clinton Sundberg, Carleton E. Young, Sono Osato. Technicolor. 102 minutes.

11. *Take Me Out to the Ball Game* (British title: *Everybody's Cheering*). 1949. M-G-M. Director: Busby Berkeley. Producer: Joe Pasternak. Screenplay: Harry Tugend and George Wells. Story: Gene Kelly and Stanley Donen. Music: Roger Edens. Lyrics: Betty Comden and Adolph Green ("Take Me Out to the Ball Game" by Albert von Tilzer and Jack Norworth, and "The Hat My Father Wore on St. Patrick's Day" by William Jerome and Jean Schwartz). Choreographers: Gene Kelly and Stanley Donen. Musical numbers: "Take Me Out to the Ball Game," "O'Brien to Ryan to Goldberg," "The Right Girl for Me," "It's Fate, Baby, It's Fate," "Yes Indeedy," "The Hat My Father Wore on St. Patrick's Day," "Strictly U.S.A." Cast: Frank Sinatra, Esther

Williams, Gene Kelly, Betty Garrett, Edward Arnold, Jules Munshin, Richard Lane, Tom Dugan, Murray Alper, William Graf. Technicolor. 90 minutes.

12. *Double Dynamite.* 1951. RKO. Director: Irving Cummings. Producer: Irving Cummings, Jr. Screenplay: Melville Shavelson, with additional dialogue by Harry Crane, from an original story by Leo Rosten, based on a character created by Mannie Manheim. Music: Jule Styne. Lyrics: Sammy Cahn. Musical numbers: "Kisses and Tears," "It's Only Money." Cast: Jane Russell, Groucho Marx, Frank Sinatra, Don McGuire, Howard Freeman, Nestor Paiva, Frank Orth, Harry Hayden, William Edmunds, Russell Thorson, Joe Devlin, Lou Nova, Charles Coleman, Ida Moore, Hal K. Dawson, George Chandler, Jean de Briac. 80 minutes.

13. *Sombrero.* 1953. M-G-M. Director: Norman Foster. Producer: Jack Cummings. Screenplay: Norman Foster, Josefina Niggli, from Niggli's novel, *Mexican Village.* Music and lyrics: Ruben Fuentas, Ruben Mendez, Saul Chaplin, Agustín Lara, Ray Gilbert, Alfonso Esparza Orteo, A. Fernández Bustamente. Choreographer: Hermes Pan. Cast: Victorio Gassman, Nina Foch, Pier Angeli, Yvonne De Carlo, José Greco, Kurt Kasznar, Cyd Charisse, Walter Hampden, Rick Jason, Thomas Gomez. Note: Donen directed José Greco's specialty flamenco number. Technicolor. 103 minutes.

As Director (and, beginning in 1957, frequently as Producer)

1. *On the Town.* 1949. M-G-M. Directors: Gene Kelly and Stanley Donen. Producer: Arthur Freed. Associate producer: Roger Edens. Screenplay: Betty Comden and Adolph Green, from their 1944 musical play of the same name, based on the ballet *Fancy Free* by Jerome Robbins. Music: Leonard Bernstein ("New York, New York," "Come Up to My Place," "Miss Turnstiles Ballet," " 'A Day in New York' Ballet") and Roger Edens. Lyrics: Betty Comden and Adolph Green. Director of photography: Harold Rossen. Special effects: Warren Newcomb. Editor: Ralph E. Winters. Art directors: Cedric Gibbons, Jack Martin Smith. Set decorators: Edwin B. Willis, Jack D. Moore (associate). Costumes: Helen Rose. Choreographers: Gene Kelly and Stanley Donen. Musical director and conductor: Lennie Hayton. Orchestrations: Conrad Salinger. Sound recordists: Douglas Shearer, John A. Williams.

Musical numbers: "New York, New York," "Miss Turnstiles Ballet," "Prehistoric Man," "Come Up to My Place," "Main Street," "You're Awful," "On the Town," "Count on Me," " 'A Day in New York' Ballet," "Pearl of the Persian Sea."

Cast: Gene Kelly (Gabey), Frank Sinatra (Chip), Betty Garrett (Brunhilde Esterhazy), Ann Miller (Claire Huddesen), Jules Munshin (Ozzie), Vera-Ellen (Ivy Smith), Florence Bates (Mme. Dilyovska), Alice Pearce

(Lucy Shmeeler), George Meader (Professor), Bea Benaderet (Brooklyn girl), Eugene Borden (Walter), Hans Conried (François). Note: The voice of a sailor's girlfriend in a nightclub was dubbed by Judy Holliday.

Technicolor. 90 minutes. Radio City Music Hall engagement:* December 8, 1949–January 18, 1950.

2. *Royal Wedding* (British title: *Wedding Bells*). 1951. M-G-M. Director: Stanley Donen. Producer: Arthur Freed. Screenplay: Alan Jay Lerner, based on his story. Music: Burton Lane. Lyrics: Alan Jay Lerner. Director of photography: Robert Plack. Special effects: Warren Newcomb. Editor: Albert Akst. Art directors: Cedric Gibbons, Jack Martin Smith. Set decorators: Edwin B. Wallis, Alfred E. Spencer. Choreographer: Nick Castle. Dance assistants: Marilyn Christine, Dave Robel. Musical director: Johnny Green. Orchestrations: Conrad Salinger, Skip Martin. Sound recordist: Douglas Shearer.

Musical numbers: "Every Night at Seven," "Sunday Jumps," "Open Your Eyes," "You're All the World to Me," "The Happiest Day of My Life," "How Could You Believe Me When I Said I Loved You When You Know I've Been a Liar All My Life?," "Too Late Now," "I Left My Hat in Haiti," "What a Lovely Day for a Wedding."

Cast: Fred Astaire (Tom Bowen), Jane Powell (Ellen Bowen), Peter Lawford (Lord John Brindale), Sarah Churchill (Anne Ashmond), Keenan Wynn (Irving Klinger/Edgar Klinger), Albert Sharpe (James Ashmond), Viola Roache (Sarah Ashmond), Henri Letondal (purser), James Finlayson (cabbie), Alex Frazer (Chester), Jack Reilly (Pete Cumberly), William Cabanne (Dick), John Hedloe (Billy), Francis Bethancourt (Charles Gordon), André Charisse (steward).

Technicolor. 93 minutes. Radio City Music Hall engagement: March 8–April 11, 1951.

3. *Love Is Better Than Ever* (British title: *The Light Fantastic*). 1952 (filmed in 1950). M-G-M. Director: Stanley Donen. Producer: William H. Wright. Screenplay: Ruth Brooks Flippen. Director of photography: Harold Rosson. Editor: George Boemler. Art directors: Cedric Gibbons, Gabriel Scognamillo. Set decorators: Edwin B. Willis, Keogh Gleason. Costumes: Helen Rose. Musical director: Lennie Hayton. Sound recordist: Douglas Shearer.

Cast: Larry Parks (Jud Parker), Elizabeth Taylor (Anastacia "Stacy" Macaboy), Josephine Hutchinson (Mrs. Macaboy), Tom Tully (Mr. Macaboy), Ann Doran (Mrs. Levoy), Elinor Donahue (Patty Marie Levoy),

* Donen holds an impressive distinction when it comes to New York's six-thousand-seat "Showplace of the Nation." Fourteen of his movies have premiered there—fifteen if one includes the 1975 revival of *Singin' in the Rain*. The only filmmakers to top this record, each with eighteen pictures, were Mervyn LeRoy, whose first movie, *No Place to Go*, was in 1927 (Radio City Music Hall opened in 1932), and Vincente Minnelli, whose directorial bow, *Cabin in the Sky*, occurred in 1943.

Kathleen Freeman (Mrs. Kahrney), Doreen McCann (Albertina Kahrney), Alex Gerry ("Hamlet"), Dick Wessel (Smittie), Gene Kelly (himself). Note: Stanley Donen may be briefly spotted at Gene Kelly's restaurant table before Kelly hops over to greet Larry Parks and Elizabeth Taylor.

   81 minutes.

4. *Singin' in the Rain.* 1952. M-G-M. Directors: Gene Kelly and Stanley Donen. Producer: Arthur Freed. Screenplay: Betty Comden and Adolph Green. Music: Nacio Herb Brown. Lyrics: Arthur Freed. ("Fit as a Fiddle" music by Al Goodhart and Al Hartman, lyrics by Freed; "Make 'Em Laugh" music arguably by Cole Porter; "Moses Supposes" lyrics by Comden and Green, music by Roger Edens; introductory "vamp" to "Singin' in the Rain" by Edens.) Director of photography: Harold Rosson. Special effects: Warren Newcombe, Irving G. Reis. Editor: Adrienne Fazan. Art directors: Cedric Gibbons, Randall Duell. Set decorators: Edwin B. Wallis, Jacques Mapes. Costumes: Walter Plunkett. Choreographers: Gene Kelly and Stanley Donen. Musical director: Lennie Hayton. Sound recordist: Douglas Shearer.

   Musical numbers: "Singin' in the Rain," "Fit as a Fiddle," "All I Do Is Dream of You," "All I Do Is Dream of You" reprise and dance (cut), "Make 'Em Laugh," "I've Got a Feelin' You're Foolin'," "The Wedding of the Painted Doll," "Should I?," "Beautiful Girl," "You Were Meant for Me," "You Are My Lucky Star" (cut), "Moses Supposes," "Good Morning," "Would You?," "Broadway Melody" Ballet/"Broadway Rhythm," "You Are My Lucky Star"/Finale.

   Cast: Gene Kelly (Don Lockwood), Donald O'Connor (Cosmo Brown), Debbie Reynolds (Kathy Selden), Jean Hagen (Lina Lamont), Millard Mitchell (R. F. Simpson), Rita Moreno (Zelda Zanders), Douglas Fowley (Roscoe Dexter), Cyd Charisse (dancer in "Dream" Ballet), Madge Blake (Dora Bailey), King Donovan (Rod), Kathleen Freeman (Phoebe Dinsmore), Jimmie Thompson (lead chorus singer), Patricia Denise and Jeanne Coyne (dancers), Bill Chatham, Ernest Flatt, Don Hulbert, Robert Dayo (dance quartet), David Kasday (kid), Julius Tannen (man in experimental talkie). Note: Debbie Reynolds's "dubbing" of Jean Hagen's speaking voice in *The Dancing Cavalier* was, in fact, spoken by Jean Hagen and sung by Betty Noyes.

   Technicolor. 104 minutes. Radio City Music Hall engagement: March 27–May 7, 1952. Revival: May 5–May 18, 1975.

5. *Fearless Fagan.* 1952. M-G-M. Director: Stanley Donen. Producer: Edwin H. Knopf. Associate producer: Sidney Franklin, Jr. Screenplay: Charles Lederer, from an adaptation by Frederick Hazlitt Brennan, based on a story by Sidney Franklin, Jr., and Eldon W. Griffiths. Director of photography: Harold Lipstein. Special effects: A. Arnold Gillespie. Editor: George White. Art directors: Cedric Gibbons, Leonard Vasian. Set decorators: Edwin B. Wallis, Fred

MacLean. Musical director: Rudolph G. Kopp. Sound recordist: Douglas Shearer.

Musical number: "What Do You Think I Am?" (music by Hugh Martin, lyrics by Ralph Blane).

Cast: Janet Leigh (Abby Ames), Carleton Carpenter (Pvt. Floyd Hilson), Keenan Wynn (Sgt. Kelwin), Richard Anderson (Capt. Daniels), Ellen Corby (Mrs. Ardley), Barbara Ruick (nurse), John Call (Mr. Ardley), Robert Burton (Owen Gillman), Wilton Graff (Col. Horne), Parley Baer (Emil Tauchnitz), Jonathan Cott (Cpl. Geft).

78 minutes.

6. *Give a Girl a Break*. 1953. M-G-M. Director: Stanley Donen. Producer: Jack Cummings. Screenplay: Albert Hackett and Frances Goodrich, from a story by Vera Caspary. Music: Burton Lane. Lyrics: Ira Gershwin. ("Challenge Dance" music by André Previn and Saul Chaplin.) Director of photography: William C. Mellor. Special effects: Warren Newcombe, Irving G. Reis. Editor: Adrienne Fazan. Art directors: Cedric Gibbons, Paul Groesse. Set decorators: Edwin B. Wallis, Arthur Krams. Women's costumes: Helen Rose. Men's costumes: Herschel. Choreographers: Stanley Donen and Gower Champion. Musical directors: André Previn, Saul Chaplin. Sound recordist: Douglas Shearer.

Musical numbers: "Give a Girl a Break," "Nothing Is Impossible," "In Our United State," "Challenge Dance," "Give a Girl A Break" Instrumental Dance, "It Happens Every Time," "Applause, Applause."

Cast: Marge Champion (Madelyn Corlane), Gower Champion (Ted Sturgis), Debbie Reynolds (Suzy Doolittle), Helen Wood (Joanna Moss), Bob Fosse (Bob Dowdy), Kurt Kasznar (Leo Belney), Richard Anderson (Burton Bradshaw), William Ching (Anson Pritchett), Lurene Tuttle (Mrs. Doolittle), Larry Keating (Felix Jordan), Donna Martel (Janet Hallson).

Technicolor. 82 minutes.

7. *Seven Brides for Seven Brothers*. 1954. M-G-M. Director: Stanley Donen. Producer: Jack Cummings. Screenplay: Dorothy Kingsley, Frances Goodrich, and Albert Hackett, based on the 1943 story "The Sobbin' Women" by Stephen Vincent Benét. Music: Gene de Paul. Lyrics: Johnny Mercer. Director of photography: George Folsey. Special effects: A. Arnold Gillespie, Warren Newcombe. Editor: Ralph E. Winters. Art directors: Cedric Gibbons, Urie McCleary. Set decorators: Edwin B. Willis, Hugh Hunt. Costumes: Walter Plunkett. Choreographer: Michael Kidd. Musical directors: Adolph Deutsch, Saul Chaplin. Orchestrations: Alexander Courage, Conrad Salinger, Leo Arnaud. Sound recordist: Douglas Shearer.

Musical numbers: "Bless Yore Beautiful Hide," "Wonderful Day," "When You're in Love," "Goin' Co'tin'," "Barn-Raising" Dance ("Bless Yore Beautiful Hide"), "When You're in Love" reprise, "Lonesome Polecat," "Sobbin' Women," "June Bride," "Spring! Spring! Spring!"

Cast: Howard Keel (Adam Pontipee), Jane Powell (Milly), Jeff Richards (Benjamin), Russ Tamblyn (Gideon), Tommy Rall (Frank), Marc Platt (Daniel), Matt Mattox (Caleb), Jacques D'Amboise (Ephraim), Julie Newmeyer (Dorcas), Nancy Kilgas (Alice), Betty Carr (Sarah), Virginia Gibson (Liza), Ruta Kilmonis (Ruth), Norma Dogett (Martha), Ian Wolfe (Rev. Elcot), Howard Petrie (Peter Perkins), Earl Barton (Harry), Dante Di Paolo (Matt), Kelly Brown (Carl), Matt Moore (Ruth's uncle), Dick Rick (Dorcas's father), Marjorie Wood (Mrs. Bixby), Russell Simpson (Mr. Bixby).

Ansco color. CinemaScope. 103 minutes. Radio City Music Hall engagement: July 22–September 15, 1954.

8. *Deep in My Heart.* 1954. M-G-M. Director: Stanley Donen. Producer: Roger Edens. Screenplay: Leonard Spiegelgass, from the 1949 novel by Elliot Arnold, *Deep in My Heart: A Story Based on the Life of Sigmund Romberg.* Music: Sigmund Romberg. Lyrics: Harold Atteridge, Dorothy Donnelly, Oscar Hammerstein II, Otto Harbach, Herbert Reynolds, Cyrus Wood, Rida Johnson Young. Director of photography: George Folsey. Special effects: Warren Newcombe. Editor: Adrienne Fazan. Art directors: Cedric Gibbons, Edward Carfargo. Set decorators: Edwin B. Willis, Arthur Krams. Women's costumes: Helen Rose. Men's costumes: Walter Plunkett. Choreographer: Eugene Loring. Musical director: Adolph Deutsch. Orchestrations: Hugo Friedhofer, Alexander Courage. Sound recordist: Wesley C. Miller.

Music numbers: "The Riff Song"/Overture, "You Will Remember Vienna," "Leg of Mutton," "Softly, As in a Morning Sunrise," "Mr. and Mrs.," "I Love to Go Swimmin' with Wimmen," "The Road to Paradise," "Will You Remember?"/"Sweetheart," *Bombo* Audition ("Girls Good-bye," "The Very Next Girl I See," "Fat, Fat Fatima," "Zazza-Zazza-Doo-Doo"), "It," "Serenade," "One Alone," "Your Land and My Land," "Auf Wiedersehen," "Lover Come Back to Me," "Stouthearted Men," "When I Grow Too Old to Dream."

Cast: José Ferrer (Sigmund Romberg), Merle Oberon (Dorothy Donnelly), Helen Traubel (Anna Mueller), Doe Avedon (Lillian Romberg), Walter Pidgeon (J. J. Shubert), Paul Henreid (Florenz Ziegfeld), Tamara Toumanova (Gaby Deslys), Paul Stewart (Bert Townsend), David Burns (Lazar Berrison, Sr.), Isobel Elsom (Mrs. Harris), Jim Backus (Ben Judson), Douglas Fowley (Harold Butterfield), Russ Tamblyn (Lazar Berrison, Jr.), Cyd Charisse, Rosemary Clooney, Jane Powell, Vic Damone, Howard Keel, Tony Martin, Gene Kelly, Fred Kelly, Ann Miller, Joan Weldon, William Olvis, James Mitchell.

Eastman color. 132 minutes. Radio City Music Hall engagement: December 9, 1954–January 19, 1955.

9. *It's Always Fair Weather.* 1955. M-G-M. Directors: Gene Kelly and Stanley Donen. Producer: Arthur Freed. Screenplay: Betty Comden and Adolph

Green. Music: André Previn ("Music Is Better Than Words" by Roger Edens, "The Blue Danube" by Johann Strauss). Lyrics: Betty Comden and Adolph Green. Director of photography: Robert Bonner. Special effects: Warren Newcombe, Irving G. Reis. Editor: Adrienne Fazan. Art directors: Cedric Gibbons, Arthur Lonergan. Set decorators: Edwin B. Willis, Hugh Hunt. Costumes: Helen Rose. Choreographers: Gene Kelly and Stanley Donen. Musical director: André Previn. Orchestrations: André Previn. Sound recordist: Wesley C. Miller.

Musical numbers: "March! March!," "The Binge" Dance, "Time for Parting," "Ten-Year Montage," "The Blue Danube," "Music Is Better Than Words," "Midnight with Madeline," "Stillman's Gym," "Baby, You Knock Me Out!," "Once Upon a Time," "Situation-Wise," "I Like Myself," "Midnight with Madeline" reprise, "Thanks a Lot, but No Thanks," "The Throb of Manhattan," "Time for Parting" reprise.

Cast: Gene Kelly (Ted Riley), Dan Dailey (Doug Hallerton), Cyd Charisse (Jackie Leighton), Dolores Grey (Madeline Bradville), Michael Kidd (Angie Valentine), David Burns (Tim), Jay C. Flippen (Charles Z. Culloran), Steve Mitchell (Kid Mariacchi), Hal March (Rocky Heldon), Paul Moxie (Mr. Fielding), Peter Leeds (Mr. Trasker), Alex Gerry (Mr. Stamper), Madge Blake (Mrs. Stamper), Wilson Wood (Roy), Richard Simmons (Mr. Grigman), Almira Sessions (lady), Eugene Borden (chef). Note: Michael Kidd's singing voice was dubbed by Clark Burroughs, of the vocal group The Hi-Los.

Eastman color. CinemaScope. 129 minutes. Radio City Music Hall engagement: September 15–October 12, 1955.

10. *Funny Face.* 1957. Paramount. Director: Stanley Donen. Producer: Roger Edens. Screenplay: Leonard Gershe, from his unproduced musical play *Wedding Day.* Music and lyrics: George and Ira Gershwin. Additional music and lyrics: Roger Edens and Leonard Gershe ("Basal Metabolism," "Bonjour, Paris!," "On How to Be Lovely," "Think Pink!," "Marche Funebre"). Director of photography: Ray June. Special effects: John P. Fulton. Editor: Frank Bracht. Art directors: Hal Pereira, George W. Davis. Costumes: Edith Head. Audrey Hepburn's Paris wardrobe: Hubert de Givenchy. Visual consultant and main titles designer: Richard Avedon. Choreographers: Eugene Loring, Fred Astaire. Songs staged by Stanley Donen. Musical director: Adolph Deutsch. Orchestrations: Conrad Salinger, Van Cleave, Alexander Courage, Skip Martin. Sound recordists: George and Winston Leverett.

Musical numbers: "Think Pink!," "How Long Has This Been Going On?," "Funny Face," "Bonjour, Paris!," "Basal Metabolism," "Let's Kiss and Make Up," Paris Fashion Montage, "He Loves and She Loves," "On How to Be Lovely," "Marche Funebre," "Clap Yo' Hands," "'S Wonderful."

Cast: Audrey Hepburn (Jo Stockton), Fred Astaire (Dick Avery), Kay Thompson (Maggie Prescott), Michael Auclair (Prof. Emile Flostre), Robert

Flemyng (Paul Duval), Dovima (Marion), Virginia Gibson (Babs), Suzy Parker (special dancer), Sunny Harnett (special dancer), Sue England (Laura), Ruta Lee (Lettie), Jean Del Vel (hairdresser), Alex Gerry (Dovitch), Iphigenie Castiglioni (Armande). Note: Roger Edens may be spotted with the Baroness Ella van Heemstra at a café table during the "Bonjour, Paris!" number.

Technicolor. VistaVision. 103 minutes. Radio City Music Hall engagement: March 28–May 15, 1957.

11. *The Pajama Game.* 1957. Warner Bros. Directors: George Abbott and Stanley Donen. Producers: George Abbott and Stanley Donen. Associate producers: Frederick Brisson, Robert E. Griffith, Harold S. Prince. Screenplay: George Abbott and Richard Bissell, from their 1954 musical play of the same name, based on the 1953 novel *Seven-and-a-Half Cents,* by Richard Bissell. Music and lyrics: Richard Adler and Jerry Ross. Director of photography: Harry Stradling. Editor: William Ziegler. Art director: Malcolm Bert. Assistant art director: Frank Thompson. Set decorator: William Kuehl. Costumes: William and Jean Eckart. Choreographer: Bob Fosse. Musical director: Ray Heindorf. Orchestrations: Nelson Riddle, Buddy Bregman.

Musical numbers: "The Pajama Game," "Racing with the Clock," "I'm Not at All in Love" "I'll Never Be Jealous Again," "Hey There," "Once-a-Year Day," "Small Talk," "There Once Was a Man," "Steam Heat," "Hey There" reprise, "Hernando's Hideaway," "Seven-and-a-Half Cents."

Warner color. 101 minutes. Radio City Music Hall engagement: August 29–October 2, 1957.

12. *Kiss Them for Me.* 1957. Twentieth Century–Fox. Director: Stanley Donen. Producer: Jerry Wald. Screenplay: Julius Epstein, from the 1945 play of the same name by Luther Davis, based on the 1944 novel *Shore Leave,* by Frederic Wakeman. Director of photography: Milton Krasner. Special effects: L. B. Abbott. Editor: Robert Simpson. Art directors: Lyle R. Wheeler, Maurice Rumsford. Set decorators: Walter M. Scott, Stuart A. Reiss. Costumes: Charles Lemaire. Musical director: Lionel Newman. Orchestrations: Pete King, Skip Martin. Title song: Lionel Newman (music), Carroll Coates (lyrics), sung by the McGuire Sisters. Sound recordists: Charles Peck, Frank Moran.

Cast: Cary Grant (Andy Crewson), Jayne Mansfield (Alice Kratchna), Suzy Parker (Gwynneth Livingston), Leif Erickson (Eddie Turnbill), Ray Walston (J. G. "Mac" McCann), Larry Blyden (Mississipp' Hardy), Nathaniel Frey (Chief Petty Officer Ruddle), Werner Klemperer (Commander Wallec), Jack Mullaney (Ensign Lewis), Harry Carey, Jr. (Roundtree), Frank Nelson (Nielson), Caprice Yordan (Debbie), Ann McCrea (Lucille), Bill Phipps (Lt. Hendricks), Richard Deacon (Hotchkiss), Kathleen Freeman (Nurse Willinski), Maude Prickett (chief nurse), Rachel Stevens (Wave), Nancy Kulp (Wave at switchboard).

De Luxe color. CinemaScope. 103 minutes.

13. *Indiscreet.* 1958. A Grandon Production/Warner Bros. Director and producer: Stanley Donen. Associate producer: Sydney Streeter. Screenplay: Norman Krasna, from his 1953 play, *Kind Sir.* Director of photography: Frederick A. Young. Editor: Jack Harris. Art director: Don Ashton. Ingrid Bergman's costumes: Christian Dior, Pierre Balmain, and Lanvin-Castillo. Cary Grant's costumes: Quintino. Main titles designer: Maurice Binder. Musical directors: Richard Bennett, Ken Jones. Title song: James Van Heusen (music), Sammy Cahn (lyrics). Sound recordists: Richard Bird, Len Shilton. Sound editor: Winston Ryder.

 Cast: Cary Grant (Philip Adams), Ingrid Bergman (Anna Kalman), Cecil Parker (Alfred Munson), Phyllis Calvert (Margaret Munson), David Kossoff (Carl Banks), Megs Jenkins (Doris Banks), Oliver Johnston (Finleigh), Middleton Woods (Finleigh's clerk).

 Technicolor. 100 minutes. Radio City Music Hall engagement: June 26–August 13, 1958.

14. *Damn Yankees* (British title: *Whatever Lola Wants*). 1958. Warner Bros. Directors: George Abbott and Stanley Donen. Producers: George Abbott and Stanley Donen. Associate producers: Frederick Brisson, Richard Griffith, Harold S. Prince. Screenplay: George Abbott, from his and Douglass Wallop's 1955 musical play of the same name, based on the 1954 novel by Wallop, *The Year the Yankees Lost the Pennant.* Music and lyrics: Richard Adler and Jerry Ross. Director of photography: Harold Lipstein. Editor: Frank Bracht. Art director: Stanley Fleischer. Set decorator: John P. Austin. Costumes: William and Jean Eckart. Main titles design: Maurice Binder. Choreographer: Bob Fosse. Musical director: Ray Heindorf. Sound recordists: Stanley Jones, Dolph Thomas.

 Musical numbers: "Six Months Out of Every Year," "Good-bye, Old Girl," "Heart," "Shoeless Joe from Hannibal, Mo," "There's Something About an Empty Chair," "A Little Brains, a Little Talent," "Whatever Lola Wants," "Those Were the Good Old Days," "Who's Got the Pain?," "Heart" reprise, "Two Lost Souls," "There's Something About an Empty Chair" reprise.

 Cast: Tab Hunter (Joe Hardy), Gwen Verdon (Lola), Ray Walston (Applegate), Russ Brown (Van Buren), Shannon Bolin (Meg), Nathaniel Frey (Smokey), Jimmy Komack (Rocky), Rae Allen (Gloria), Robert Shafer (Joe Boyd), Jean Stapleton (Sister), Albert Linville (Vernon), Elizabeth Howell (Doris).

 Warner color. 111 minutes.

15. *Once More, With Feeling.* 1960. A Stanley Donen Production/Columbia. Director and producer: Stanley Donen. Associate producer: Paul B. Radin. Screenplay: Harry Kurnitz, based on his 1958 play of the same name. Director of photography: Georges Périnal. Editor: Jack Harris. Art director: Alex Trauner.

Costumes: Hubert de Givenchy. Main titles designer: Maurice Binder. Musical director: Muir Mathieson. Sound recordist: Joseph De Bretagne.

Cast: Yul Brynner (Victor Fabian), Kay Kendall (Dolly Fabian), Geoffrey Toone (Dr. Hilliard), Maxwell Shaw (Grisha Gendel), Mervyn Johns (Mr. Wilbur, Jr.), Martin Benson (Bardini), Harry Lockhart (Chester), Gregory Ratoff (Maxwell Archer), Shirley Ann Field (Angela Hopper), Grace Newcomb (Mrs. Wilbur), C. S. Stuart (Manning), Colin Drake (doctor), Andrew Paulds (interviewer), C. E. Joy (Sir Austin Flapp), Barbara Hall (secretary).

Technicolor. 92 minutes. Radio City Music Hall engagement: February 11–March 2, 1960.

16. *Surprise Package.* 1960. A Stanley Donen Production/Columbia. Director and producer: Stanley Donen. Screenplay: Harry Kurnitz, based on the 1958 novel by Art Buchwald, *A Gift from the Boys.* Director of photography: Christopher Challis. Editor: James Clark. Art director: Don Ashton. Costumes: Mattli. Main titles designer: Maurice Binder. Musical director: Benjamin Frankel. Title song: James Van Heusen (music), Sammy Cahn (lyrics). Sound recordist: John Cox.

Cast: Yul Brynner (Nico March), Mitzi Gaynor (Gabby Rogers), Noël Coward (King Pavel II), Eric Pohlmann (Stefan Miralis), George Coulouris (Dr. Hugo Panzer), Guy Deghy (Tibor Smolny), Warren Mitchell (Klimatis), Lyndon Brook (Stavrin), Man Mountain Dean (Igor Trofin), Bill Nagy (Johnny Stettina), Lionel Murtin and Barry Foster (U.S. marshals).

99 minutes.

17. *The Grass Is Greener.* 1960. Grandon Productions, Ltd./Universal-International. Director and producer: Stanley Donen. Associate producer: James Ware. Screenplay: Hugh and Margaret Williams, from their 1959 play of the same name. Director of photography: Christopher Challis. Editor: James Clark. Art director: Paul Sheriff. Set decorator: Vernon Dixon. Deborah Kerr's costumes: Hardy Amies. Jean Simmons's costumes: Christian Dior. Main titles designer: Maurice Binder. Musical directors: Douglas Gamley, Len Stevens. Music and lyrics: Noël Coward. Sound recordist: John Cox.

Cast: Cary Grant (Victor Rhyall), Deborah Kerr (Hilary Rhyall), Robert Mitchum (Charles Delacro), Jean Simmons (Hattie), Moray Wilson (Sellers).

Technicolor. Technirama. 104 minutes.

18. *Charade.* A Stanley Donen Production/Universal. Director and producer: Stanley Donen. Associate producer: James Ware. Screenplay: Peter Stone, from the short story by Stone and Marc Behm, "The Unsuspecting Wife." Director of photography: Charles Lang, Jr. Art director: Jean d'Eaubonne. Audrey Hepburn's costumes: Hubert de Givenchy. Main titles designer: Maurice Binder. Musical composer and director: Henry Mancini. Title song:

Henry Mancini (music), Johnny Mercer (lyrics). Sound recordists: Jacques Carrère, Bob Jones.

Cast: Cary Grant (Peter Joshua), Audrey Hepburn (Regina "Reggie" Lambert), Walter Matthau (Hamilton Batholomew), James Coburn (Tex Penthollow), George Kennedy (Herman Scobie), Ned Glass (Leopold Gideon), Jacques Marin (Inspector Édouard Grandpierre), Paul Bonifas (Felix), Dominque Minot (Sylvia Gaudet), Thomas Chelimsky (Jean-Louis Gaudet).

Technicolor. 113 minutes. Radio City Music Hall engagement: December 5, 1963–January 22, 1964.

19. *Arabesque.* 1966. A Stanley Donen Enterprises Production/Universal. Director and producer: Stanley Donen. Assistant producer: Denis Holt. Screenplay: Julian Mitchell, Stanley Price, Pierre Marton (pseudonym for Peter Stone), based on the novel by Alex Gordon, *The Cipher.* Director of photography: Christopher Challis. Editor: Frederick Wilson. Art director: Reece Pemberton. Sophia Loren's costumes: Christian Dior. Main titles designer: Maurice Binder. Musical arranger and director: Henry Mancini. Sound recordists: John W. Mitchell, Colin Le Mesurier.

Cast: Gregory Peck (David Pollock), Sophia Loren (Yasmin Azir), Alan Badel (Beshravi), Kieron Moore (Yussef), Carl Duering (Hassan Jena), John Merivale (Sloane), Duncan Lamont (Webster), George Coulouris (Ragheeb), Ernest Clark (Beauchamp), Harold Kasket (Mohammed Lufti).

Technicolor. Panavision. 105 minutes. Radio City Music Hall engagement: May 5–June 8, 1966.

20. *Two for the Road.* 1967. A Stanley Donen Films, Inc. Production/Twentieth Century–Fox. Director and producer: Stanley Donen. Assistant producer: James Ware. Screenplay: Frederic Raphael. Director of photography: Christopher Challis. Special effects: Gilbert Manzow. Editors: Richard Marden, Madeleine Gug. Art director: Willy Holt. Assistant art director: Marc Frederix. Set decorator: Roger Volper. Audrey Hepburn's costumes: Sophie Rochas, Ken Scott, Michele Rosier, Paco Rabanne, Mary Quant, Foale Tuffin. Albert Finney's costumes: Hardy Amies. Main titles designer: Maurice Binder. Musical composer and director: Henry Mancini. (Lyrics to title song by Leslie Bricusse appear only on sound-track album.) Sound recordist: Jo De Bretagne.

Cast: Audrey Hepburn (Joanna Wallace), Albert Finney (Mark Wallace), William Daniels (Howard Maxwell Manchester), Eleanor Bron (Cathy Maxwell Manchester), Claude Dauphin (Maurice Dalbret), Nadia Grey (Françoise Dalbret), George Descrieres (David), Gabrielle Middleton (Ruthie), Kathy Chelimsky (Caroline), Carol Van Dyke (Michelle), Karyn Balm (Simone), Jacqueline Bisset (Jackie).

Technicolor. Panavision. 112 minutes. Radio City Music Hall engagement: April 27–May 24, 1967.

21. *Bedazzled.* 1968. A Stanley Donen Enterprises Production/Twentieth Century–Fox. Director and producer: Stanley Donen. Screenplay: Peter Cook, from a story by Peter Cook and Dudley Moore. Director of photography: Austin Dempster. Editor: Richard Marden. Art director: Terence Knight. Assistant art director: Ted Tester. Costumes: Yvonne Caffin, Clare Rendlesham. Eleanor Bron's costumes: Jean Muir. Peter Cook's costumes: Cue at Austin Reed. Dudley Moore's costumes: Mr. Risk. Main titles designer: Maurice Binder. Animation: Bailey Pettengel Design, Ltd. Musical composer and director: Dudley Moore. Sound recordists: John Purchese, Doug Turner.

    Cast: Peter Cook (George Spiggot), Dudley Moore (Stanley Moon), Eleanor Bron (Margaret Spencer), Raquel Welch (Lillian Lust), Michael Bates (Inspector Clarke), Bernard Spear (Irving Moses), Parnell McGarry (Gluttony), Howard Goorney (Sloth), Alba (Vanity), Barry Humphries (Envy), Daniele Noel (Avarice), Robert Russell (Anger), Peter Hutchins (P. C. Roberts), Max Faulkner (priest), Martin Boddy (cardinal), John Steiner (TV announcer), Robin Hawdon (Randolph), Eric Chitty (Seed), Michael Trubshawe (Lord Dowdy), Evelyn Moore (Mrs. Wisby), Lockwood West (St. Peter).

    De Luxe color. Panavision. 107 minutes.

22. *Staircase.* 1969. A Stanley Donen Films, Inc., Production/Twentieth Century–Fox. Director and producer: Stanley Donen. Screenplay: Charles Dyer, from his 1969 play of the same name presented by the Royal Shakespeare Company. Director of photography: Christopher Challis. Editor: Richard Marden. Art director: Willy Holt. Costumes: Clare Rendlesham. Main titles designer: Maurice Binder. Musical composer and director: Dudley Moore. Sound recordists: Alex Pront, Jean-Louis Ducarmé.

    Cast: Richard Burton (Harry C. Leeds), Rex Harrison (Charlie Dyer), Cathleen Nesbitt (Harry's mother), Beatrix Lehmann (Charlie's mother), Gordon Heath (postman), Stephen Lewis (Jack), Jake Kavanagh (choirboy), Dermot Kelly (gravedigger), Avril Angers (Miss Richard), Neil Wilson (policeman), Shelagh Fraser (cub mistress), Gwen Nelson (mistress), Pat Heywood (nurse), Rogers and Starr (singers in drag).

    De Luxe color. Panavision. 96 minutes.

23. *The Little Prince.* 1974. A Stanley Donen Films, Inc., Production/Paramount. Director and producer: Stanley Donen. Associate producer: A. Joseph Tandet. Screenplay: Alan Jay Lerner, based on the 1943 novel of the same name by Antoine de Saint-Exupéry. Music: Frederick Loewe. Lyrics: Alan Jay Lerner. Director of photography: Christopher Challis. Special effects: John Richardson. Editors: Peter Boita, John Guthridge. Art director: Norman Reynolds. Production designer: John Barry. Costumes: Shirley Russell, Tim Goodchild. "Be Happy" choreographer: Ronn Forella. "Snake in the Grass" choreographer: Bob Fosse. Main titles designer: Maurice Binder. Musical

director: Angela Morley. Sound recordists: Jim Willis, John Richardson, Bill Rowe.

Musical numbers: "It's a Hat"/"I Need Air," "I'm on Your Side," "Be Happy," "You're a Child," "I Never Met a Rose," "Why Is the Desert?," "A Snake in the Grass," "Closer and Closer and Closer," "The Little Prince."

Cast: Richard Kiley (The Pilot), Steven Warner (The Little Prince), Bob Fosse (The Snake), Gene Wilder (The Fox), Joss Ackland (The King), Clive Revill (The Businessman), Victor Spinetti (The Historian), Graham Crowden (The General), Donna McKechnie (The Rose).

Technicolor. 88 minutes. Radio City Music Hall engagement: November 7, 1974–January 15, 1975.

24. *Lucky Lady.* 1975. Twentieth Century–Fox. Director: Stanley Donen. Producer: Michael Gruskoff. Screenplay: Willard Huyck, Gloria Katz. Director of photography: Geoffrey Unsworth (battle sequence photographed by Rico Browning). Editors: Peter Boita, George Hively (battle sequence edited by Tom Rolfe). Production designer: John Barry. Art director: Norman Reynolds. Costumes: Lilly Fenichel. Main titles designer: Dan Perri. Musical director: Ralph Burns. Title song and "Get While the Gettin's Good": John Kander (lyrics), Fred Ebb (music). Sound recordist: Theodore Soderberg.

Cast: Gene Hackman (Kibby), Liza Minnelli (Claire), Burt Reynolds (Walker), Geoffrey Lewis (Captain Aaron Mosely), John Hillerman (Christy McTeague), Robby Benson (Billy Weber), Michael Hordern (Captain Rockwell), Anthony Holland (Mr. Tully), John McLiam (Rass Huggins), Val Avery (Dolph), Louis Guss (Bernie), William H. Bassett (Charley), Emilio Fernández (Ybarra), Raymond Guth (Brother Bob), Duncan McLeod (auctioneer), Milt Kogan (Supercargo), Suzanne Zenor (brunette), Richard Caine (young bootlegger), Richard Armbruster (Hanson), Doyle Baker (Gene), Michael Greene (Turley).

De Luxe color. 117 minutes.

25. *Movie Movie.* 1978. A Lord Lew Grade Production/Warner Bros. Director and producer: Stanley Donen. Executive producer: Martin Starger. Screenplay: Larry Gelbart, Sheldon Kellor. "Dynamite Hands" director of photography: Charles Rosher, Jr. "Baxter's Beauties of 1933" director of photography: Bruce Surtees. Special effects: Cinema Research Corp. Editor: George Hively. Art director: Jack Fisk. Set decorator: Jerry Winderlich. Costumes: Patty Norris. Choreographer: Michael Kidd. "Torchin' for Bill" choreographer: Stanley Donen. Main titles design: Dan Perri. Music: Ralph Burns. Additional music for "Baxter's Beauties of 1933": Buster Davis. Lyrics: Larry Gelbart, Sheldon Keller. Musical arranger: Buster Davis. Sound recordist: James Webb, Jr.

"Baxter's Beauties of 1933" musical numbers: "Torchin' for Bill," "I Just Need the Girl," "Just Shows to Go Ya," "Lucky Day."

Introductory host: George Burns.

"Dynamite Hands" cast: George C. Scott (Gloves Molloy), Trish Van Devere (Betsy McGuire), Red Buttons (Peanuts), Eli Wallach (Vince Marlow), Harry Hamlin (Joey Popchick), Ann Reinking (Troubles Moran), Jocelyn Brando (Mama Popchick), Michael Kidd ("Pop" Popchick), Kathleen Beller (Angie Popchick), Barry Bostwick (Johnny Danko), Art Carney (Dr. Blaine), Clay Hodges (Sailor Lawson), George P. Wilbur (Tony Norton), Peter T. Stader (Barney Keegle), James Lennon (fight announcer). Note: Stanley Donen may be spotted briefly as the nightclub emcee who introduces Troubles Moran, "now in her eighth month."

"Baxter's Beauties of 1933" cast: George C. Scott (Spats Baxter), Barbara Harris (Trixie Lane), Barry Bostwick (Dick Cummings), Trish Van Devere (Isobel Stuart), Red Buttons (Jinx Murphy), Eli Wallach (Pop), Rebecca York (Kitty), Art Carney (Dr. Bowers), Maidie Norman (Gussie), Jocelyn Brando (Mrs. Updike), Charles Lane (Mr. Pennington), Barney Martin (motorcycle cop), Dick Winslow (Tinkle Johnson), Sebastian Brook (Fritz). Note: An unshaven Stanley Donen may be spotted briefly behind the wheel of a taxi.

Black and white ("Dynamite Hands") and color ("Baxter's Beauties of 1933"). 105 minutes.

26. *Saturn 3*. 1980. Lord Lew Grade in association with Elliot Kastner/Associated Film Distribution. Director and producer: Stanley Donen (replacing John Barry as director). Executive producer: Martin Starger. Screenplay: Martin Amis (and Frederic Raphael, uncredited), from a story by John Barry. Director of photography: Billy Williams. Special effects: Colin Chilvers. Editor: Richard Marden. Production designer: Stuart Craig. Art director: Norman Dorme. Costumes: Anthony Mendleson. Musical composer and director: Elmer Bernstein. Orchestrations: Christopher Palmer.

Cast: Farrah Fawcett (Alex), Kirk Douglas (Adam), Harvey Keitel (Benson/James), Douglas Lambert (Real Captain James), Ed Bishop (Harding), Christopher Muncke (second crewman).

Color. 95 minutes.

27. *Blame It on Rio*. 1984. A Sherwood Production and Sidney Kimmel Presentation/Twentieth Century–Fox. Director and producer: Stanley Donen. Executive producer: Larry Gelbart. Associate producer and production manager: Roberta Relyea. Screenplay: Charlie Peters and Larry Gelbart, based on Claude Berri's 1977 film *Un Moment d'Egarement* (*One Wild Moment*). Director of photography: Reynalda Vilalobos. Editors: George Hively, Richard Marden. Music: Ken Wannberg, Oscar Castro Neves. Art director: Marcos Flaksman. Set decorator: Yeda De Mello Lewinsohn. Sound: Jim Willis.

Cast: Michael Caine (Matthew Hollis), Joseph Bologna (Victor Lyons), Valerie Harper (Karen Hollis), Michelle Johnson (Jennifer Lyons), Demi

Moore (Nicole Hollis), José Lewgoy (Eduardo), Lupe Gigliotti (Signora Botega), Michael Menaugh (Peter), Ana Luci Lima and Maria Helena Velasco (macumba ladies), Zeni Pereira (mother of the bride), Eduardo Conde (singer in club), Betty Von Wien (Isabella), Nelson Dantas (doctor), Thomas Lee Mahon (Lorenzo), Victor Aim (Bernardo), Jane Duboc (singer in café), Romulo Arantes (Diego), Giovanna Sodre (Astrid), Grupo Senzala (Capoeirista), Angelo Mattos (dancer).

Metrocolor. 110 minutes.

Selected Bibliography

Abbott, George. *Mister Abbott.* New York: Random House, 1963.

Altman, Rick. *The American Film Musical.* Bloomington and Indianapolis: Indiana University Press, 1989.

Arden, Eve. *Three Phases of Eve.* New York: St. Martin's Press, 1985.

Armes, Roy. *A Critical History of British Cinema.* New York: Oxford University Press, 1978.

Astaire, Fred. *Steps in Time.* New York: Harper, 1959.

Basinger, Jeanine. *A Woman's View: How Hollywood Spoke to Women, 1930–1960.* New York: Alfred A. Knopf, 1993.

Beckerman, Bernard, and Howard Siegman, eds. *On Stage: Selected Theatre Reviews from* The New York Times, *1920–1970.* New York: Arno Press, 1973.

Bell, Joseph N. "On Location in Mexico with Liza and Friends," *The New York Times,* Arts and Leisure, June 29, 1975.

Bellmer, Rudy. *Behind the Scenes: The Making of. . .* Hollywood: Samuel French Trade, 1990.

Benson, Sheila. "In the Big Apple for 'Movie Movie,'" *Pacific Sun,* January 5–11, 1979.

Bergman, Ingrid, and Alan Burgess. *Ingrid Bergman: My Story.* New York: Delacorte Press, 1980.

Blum, Daniel. *The Pictorial History of the American Theatre.* New York: Greenberg Publishers, 1950.

Bogdanovich, Peter. *Pieces of Time.* New York: Arbor House, 1973.

Bookspan, Martin, and Ross Yockey. *André Previn: A Biography.* Garden City, N.Y.: Doubleday, 1981.

Brady, John. *The Craft of the Screenwriter.* New York: Simon & Schuster, 1981.

Bragg, Melvyn. *Richard Burton: A Life.* Boston: Little, Brown, 1988.

Braun, Eric. *Deborah Kerr.* New York: St. Martin's Press, 1977.

Bruccoli, Matthew J. *John O'Hara: A Descriptive Bibliography.* Pittsburgh: University of Pittsburgh Press, 1978.

————. *The O'Hara Concern: A Biography of John O'Hara.* New York: Random House, 1975.

Burton, Humphrey. *Leonard Bernstein.* New York: Bantam Books, 1994.

Casper, Joseph Andrew. *Stanley Donen.* Metuchen, N.J.: The Scarecrow Press, 1983.

Chaplin, Saul. *The Golden Age of the Movie Musical and Me.* Norman: University of Oklahoma Press, 1994.

Comden, Betty, and Adolph Green. *Singin' in the Rain.* London: Lorrimer Publishing, 1972.

Connor, Jim. *Ann Miller: Tops in Taps*. New York: Franklin Watts, 1981.

Crist, Judith. *Take 22: Moviemakers on Moviemaking*. New York: Continuum, 1991.

Croce, Arlene. *The Fred Astaire and Ginger Rogers Book*. New York: Dutton, 1987.

Deschner, Donald. *The Complete Films of Cary Grant*. New York: Citadel Press, 1991.

Donen, Stanley. "Remembering Audrey." *Vogue,* April 1993, 390–91, 465–67.

Dunn, Don. *The Making of "No, No Nanette."* Secaucus, N.J.: Citadel Press, 1972.

Eames, John Douglas. *The M-G-M Story*. New York: Portland House, 1989.

Engel, Lehman. *Their Words Are Music: The Great Theater Lyricists and Their Lyrics*. New York: Crown Publishers, 1975.

Farber, Stephen. "Why Couldn't This 'Lady' Have an Unhappy Ending?" *The New York Times,* December 14, 1975.

Finler, Joel W. *The Hollywood Story*. New York: Crown Publishers, 1988.

Fordin, Hugh. *Getting to Know Him: A Biography of Oscar Hammerstein*. New York: Random House, 1977.

————. *The World of Entertainment: Hollywood's Greatest Musicals*. New York: Doubleday, 1975.

Frugone, Juan Carlos (prologue and epilogue, in collaboration with John Russell Taylor). *Stanley Donen . . . y no fueron tan felices*. Valladolid, Spain: Semana Internacional de Cine, 1989.

Fuller, Graham. "Gene Kelly," *Interview,* May 1994, 110–12.

Garrett, George P., O. B. Hardison, Jr., and Jane R. Gelfman, eds. *Film Scripts Three: Charade, The Apartment, The Misfits*. New York: Irvington Publishers, 1989.

Givray, Claude de. "Beau fixe sur la comédie musical," *Cahiers du Cinema,* August–September 1956, 43–45.

Godard, Jean-Luc. *Godard on Godard*. Edited by Jean Narboni and Tom Milne. New York: Viking Press, 1972.

Goldman, Herbert G. *Jolson: The Legend Comes to Life*. New York: Oxford University Press, 1988.

Gottfried, Martin. *All His Jazz: The Life and Death of Bob Fosse*. New York: Bantam Books, 1990.

Green, Benny, ed. *A Hymn to Him: The Lyrics of Alan Jay Lerner*. New York: Limelight Editions, 1987.

Green, Stanley. *Broadway Musicals Show by Show*. Milwaukee: Hal Leonard Publishing, 1987.

————. *Hollywood Musicals Year by Year*. Milwaukee: Hal Leonard Publishing, 1990.

Greenberg, James. "The Sound of Money." *Connoisseur,* February 1992, 22–24, 94–96.

Gross, Michael. "War of the Poses." *New York,* April 27, 1992, 24–33.

Halliwell, Leslie. *Halliwell's Filmgoer's Companion*. New York: Charles Scribner's Sons, 1988.

Harris, Warren G. *Natalie & R.J.* New York: Doubleday, 1988.

Harrison, Rex. *A Damned Serious Business: My Life in Comedy*. New York: Bantam Books, 1991.

Harvey, Stephen. *Directed by Vincente Minnelli*. New York: The Museum of Modern Art and Harper & Row, Publishers, 1989.

Havoc, June. *More Havoc*. New York: Harper & Row, 1980.

Hirsch, Foster. *Acting Hollywood Style*. New York: Harry N. Abrams, 1991.

Hirschhorn, Clive. *Gene Kelly: A Biography.* London: W. H. Allen, 1974.

―――. *The Hollywood Musical.* London: Pyramid Books, 1991.

Holtzman, Will. *Judy Holliday.* New York: G. P. Putnam's Sons, 1982.

Hotchner, A. E. *Doris Day: Her Own Story.* New York: William Morrow, 1975.

Johnson, Dorris, and Ellen Leventhal, eds. *The Letters of Nunnally Johnson.* New York: Alfred A. Knopf, 1981.

Kael, Pauline. *5001 Nights at the Movies.* New York: Henry Holt, 1991.

―――. *I Lost It at the Movies.* Boston and Toronto: Little, Brown, 1965.

―――. *When the Lights Go Down.* New York: Holt, Rinehart, and Winston, 1980.

Katz, Ephraim. *The Film Encyclopedia.* New York: Perigee Books, 1979.

Kelly, Gretchen. "Cyd Charisse Then and Now." *Dance Pages,* Spring 1992, 22–27.

Kimball, Robert, ed. *The Lyrics of Cole Porter.* New York: Alfred A. Knopf, 1983.

―――. *The Lyrics of Ira Gershwin.* New York: Alfred A. Knopf, 1993.

―――. *The Lyrics of Lorenz Hart.* New York: Alfred A. Knopf, 1986.

Kissel, Howard. *David Merrick: The Abominable Showman.* New York: Applause Books, 1993.

Kobal, John. *People Will Talk.* New York: Alfred A. Knopf, 1984.

Kotsilibas-Davis, James, and Myrna Loy. *Myrna Loy: Being and Becoming.* New York: Alfred A. Knopf, 1987.

Lambert, Gavin. *Norma Shearer.* New York: Alfred A. Knopf, 1990.

Latham, Caroline, and Jeannie Sakol. *All About Elizabeth.* New York: Onyx Books, 1991.

Lazar, Irving, with Annette Tapert. *Swifty: My Life and Good Times.* New York: Simon and Schuster, 1995.

Lees, Gene. *Inventing Champagne: The Worlds of Lerner and Loewe.* New York: St. Martin's Press, 1990.

Lerner, Alan Jay. *The Street Where I Live.* New York: W. W. Norton, 1978.

Lesley, Cole. *Remembered Laughter.* New York: Alfred A. Knopf, 1977.

Logan, Joshua. *Josh.* London: W. H. Allen, 1977.

Lurie, Diana. "Beautiful Pacesetter of London Whirl." *Life,* February 10, 1967, 50–56.

MacShane, Frank, ed. *Collected Stories of John O'Hara.* New York: Random House, 1984.

Malcolm, Derek. *Robert Mitchum.* New York: Hippocreen Books, 1987.

Mancini, Henry, with Gene Lees. *Did They Mention the Music?* New York: Contemporary Books, 1989.

Mariani, John. "Come on with the Rain." *Film Comment,* May/June 1978, 7–12.

Mast, Gerald. *Can't Help Singin': The American Musical on Stage and Screen.* Woodstock, N.Y.: The Overlook Press, 1987.

Moseley, Roy, with Philip and Martin Masheter. *Rex Harrison.* New York: St. Martin's Press, 1987.

Mueller, John. *Astaire Dancing: The Musical Films.* New York: Alfred A. Knopf, 1985.

Naremore, James. *The Films of Vincente Minnelli.* Cambridge, Eng.: Cambridge University Press, 1993.

Osato, Sono. *Distant Dances.* New York: Alfred A. Knopf, 1980.

Parish, James Robert, and Ronald L. Bowers. *The M-G-M Stock Company: The Golden Era.* New York: Bonanza Books, 1972.

Payn, Graham, and Sheridan Morley, eds. *The Noël Coward Diaries.* Boston: Little, Brown, 1982.

Peyser, Joan. *Bernstein: A Biography.* New York: Beechtree Books, William Morrow, 1987.

Powell, Jane. *The Girl Next Door . . . And How She Grew.* New York: William Morrow, 1987.

Prager, Emily. "Elegance for All." *The New York Times,* Styles, June 12, 1994.

Previn, André. *No Minor Chords: My Days in Hollywood.* New York: Doubleday, 1991.

Reynolds, Debbie, and David Patrick Columbia. *Debbie: My Life.* New York: William Morrow, 1988.

Rodgers, Richard. *Musical Stages.* New York: Random House, 1975.

Rosenberg, Deena. *Fascinating Rhythm: The Collaboration of George and Ira Gershwin.* New York: Dutton, 1991.

Rosenfield, Paul. *The Club.* New York: Warner Books, 1993.

Rother, Larry. "At 106, George Abbott Is Still Batting for 'Damn Yankees.' " *The New York Times,* Arts and Leisure, Feb. 27, 1994.

Rubin, Martin. *Showstoppers: Busby Berkeley and the Tradition of Spectacle.* New York: Columbia University Press, 1993.

Saint-Exupéry, Antoine de. *The Little Prince.* Translated by Katherine Woods. New York: Harcourt, Brace, 1943.

Saltzman, Barbara. " 'Two for the Road' Is Back in All Its Wide-Screen Glory." *Los Angeles Times,* August 23, 1991.

Sarris, Andrew. *The American Cinema.* New York: E. P. Dutton, 1968.

Schary, Dore. *Heyday.* Boston: Little, Brown, 1979.

Secrest, Meryle. *Leonard Bernstein.* New York: Alfred A. Knopf, 1994.

Sennett, Ted. *The Art of Hanna-Barbera.* New York: Viking Books, 1989.

Shipman, David. *The Great Movie Stars.* New York: Bonanza Books, 1970.

Silvers, Phil, with Robert Saffron. *The Laugh Is on Me.* Englewood Cliffs, N.J.: Prentice-Hall, 1973.

Sinatra, Nancy. *Frank Sinatra, My Father.* Garden City, N.Y.: Doubleday, 1985.

Sklar, Robert. *Film: An International History of the Medium.* New York: Harry N. Abrams, 1993.

Smith, Liz. "Richard Burton: 'Well, Don't Look So Surprised.' " *The New York Times,* January 26, 1969.

Soloman, Aubrey. *Twentieth Century–Fox: A Corporate and Financial History.* Metuchen, N.J.: The Scarecrow Press, 1988.

Suskind, Steven. *Opening Night on Broadway.* New York: Schirmer Books, 1990.

Thomas, Kevin. "Stanley Donen: After 'Singin' in the Rain,' a Flood of Elegant Films." *Los Angeles Times,* March 10, 1968.

Thomas, Tony. *Music for the Movies.* London: Tantivy Press, 1973.

Tibbetts, John. "Stanley Donen." *American Classic Screen,* March/April 1984, 24–28.

Tomkies, Mike. *The Robert Mitchum Story: "It Sure Beats Working."* Chicago: Henry Regnery, 1972.

Vermilye, Jerry, and Mark Ricci. *The Films of Elizabeth Taylor.* New York: Citadel Press, 1989.

Walker, Alexander. *Elizabeth: The Life of Elizabeth Taylor.* New York: Grove Weidenfeld, 1990.

Wilson, Nancy. *Evenings with Cary Grant.* New York: William Morrow, 1991.

Woodward, Ian. *Audrey Hepburn.* London: W. H. Allen, 1984.

Yaffe, James. *The American Jews: Portrait of a Split Personality.* New York: Random House, 1968.

Acknowledgments

FOR THEIR UNSTINTING GENEROSITY with their resources, recollections, and Rolodexes, the author wishes to express his appreciation to the following individuals, many of whom also lent their percipient voices to the text:

The late Mr. George Abbott, Lethe Adams, June Allyson, the late Lindsay Anderson, Susan Heller Anderson, Richard Avedon, the late Lucille Ball, Mary Lea Bandy, William Barbera, David Begelman, Sheila Benson, Bruce Birkenhead, Barry Bostwick, Kathleen Brady, Ralph Burns, Lee Buttala, the late Sammy Cahn, Carleton Carpenter, Christopher Challis, Cyd Charisse, Judy Clarke, Cy Coleman, Betty Comden, Ned Comstock, Mary Corliss, Richard Corliss, Bob Cosenza, Steve Cuozzo, Ruda Dauphin, Carla Davis, Gwen Davis, Luther Davis, Gloria DeHaven, the late Agnes de Mille, B. G. Dilworth IV, Mark Donen, Pam Donen, the late José Ferrer, the late Bob Fosse, Larry Gelbart, Leonard Gershe, Adolph Green, Claire Grimes, Lee Gross, Joseph Hanna, Rob Harris, Robert A. Harris, the late Stephen Harvey, Harry Haun, the late Audrey Hepburn, Katharine Hepburn, Dr. James Holderman, Marvine Howe, Betty Lee Hunt, Willard Huyck, Judy Jacksina, Diane Jaust, Van Johnson, Gloria Katz, Brent Kearns, Gene Kelly, William S. Kenly III, Wendy Keys, Michael Kidd, Howard Kissel, William Koshland, Burton Lane, Janet Leigh, Robert Mackintosh, the late Henry Mancini, Howard Mandelbaum, Ron Mandelbaum, Andy Marx, Walter Matthau, Dennis Millay, Dudley Moore, Laura Morris, Kevin Murphy, Bill Murray, Joan Myers, Phyllis Newman, Joanna Ney, Stuart Ng, Marsha Norman, Stephen Paley, Jerry Pam, Gregory Peck, Johnnie Planco, Harold S. Prince, Maria Pucci, Saint Clair Pugh, Frederic Raphael, Roger Rees, Ann Reinking, Debbie Reynolds, Frank Rowley, Julie Salamon, Gerald Siegal, Joel Siegel, Jackie Sigmund, Aviva Slesin, Liz Smith, John Springer, William E. Spruill, Martin Starger, Thomas L. Stepp, Peter Stone, the late Jule Styne, Bertrand Tavernier, Clyde Taylor, Marc Thibodeau, Kay Thompson, Doris

Toumarkine, Gwen Verdon, Deborah Kerr Viertel, Betty K. Walker, the late Nancy Walker, William Lucas Walker, Ray Walston, Nicholas Wapshott, Deanna Wenble, Billy Wilder, Esther Williams, and Robert Wolders.

Special thanks to the patient editor Victoria Wilson. Out of an all-star chorus of voices heard in connection with this book over the past four years, hers remained the truest and clearest.

Another influential voice belonged to the critic, teacher, and friend Judith Crist. Thirty years ago, on the *Today* show, she demonstrated for America that there was far more to expressing critical thought than sticking one's thumb in the air. And while she and I continue to disagree on movies, often and loudly, the respect and affection I feel for her only increases each year.

IN ADDITION TO the interviews with several of the primary sources listed above, further research for this book was conducted in the United States Library of Congress, Washington, D.C.; the Margaret Herrick Library of the Academy of Motion Picture Arts and Sciences, Beverly Hills; The New York Public Library for the Performing Arts, Lincoln Center, New York City; the main library of the University of Southern California, Los Angeles (Arthur Freed, Roger Edens, Jerry Wald, and Warner Bros. private collections); Cinémathèque Ontario, Toronto; the Department of History, Southern Methodist University, Dallas; the Instructional Services Center of the University of South Carolina; and the Institut Lumière, Lyon, France.

To serve as reference points, the films of Stanley Donen were for the most part viewed on commercial videocassette and, when available, laser disc. In only a few instances was it necessary to track down existing sixteen-millimeter prints. To that end, Douglas J. Lemza of Films, Inc., served as an invaluable source.

The most valuable, it turned out, proved to be my family and closest friends: Alice B. Acheson, Vernel Bagneris, Alfred and Phyllis Balk, Ben Barenholtz, Irene Bignardi, Patti Cadby-Birch, Kay Carlson, Kathleen Carroll, Shaun Considine, Jonathan Davis, Margaret Denk, Susan Dweck, Gertrude and Sanford Gerber, Peggy Glance, Lorraine Gordon, Adele Herz, Chris Hill, Gail and Paul Jacobs, Dorothy Loudon, Francia Mendoza, Pucci Meyer, Carol Morgan, Barbara and David Morowitz, Judy and Terry Mowschenson, Nina Pinsky, Gladys Poll, Constance Regnier, Diane Reid, Evelyn Renold, Dorit Reznek, Beatrice Rich, Dana Ross, Edythe and

Robert Ross, Dorothy Sanson, Warren Schomaker, Pippa Scott, Richard and Teresa Silverman, Helga Stephenson, Alice K. Turner, and Raymond L. Vandenberg.

Finally, it may appear gratuitous to thank the subject of this book, Stanley Donen. So be it.

STEPHEN M. SILVERMAN
New York City
May 1995

Index

Note: Page references to photographs or their captions are in *italics*.

A NOTE ON THE TYPE

This book was set in Garamond, a type named for the famous Parisian type cutter Claude Garamond (ca. 1480–1561). Garamond, a pupil of Geoffroy Tory, based his letters on the types of the Aldine Press in Venice, but he introduced a number of important differences, and it is to him that we owe the letter now known as "old style."

The version of Garamond used for this book was first introduced by the Monotype Corporation of London in 1922. It is not a true copy of any of the designs of Claude Garamond, but can be attributed to Jean Jannon, a Protestant printer working in Sedan in the early seventeenth century, who had worked with Garamond's romans earlier but who was denied their use because of Catholic censorship. Jannon's matrices came into the possession of the Imprimerie nationale, where they were thought to be by Garamond himself, and were so described when the Imprimerie revived the type in 1900. The italic is based on the types of Robert Granjon, a type cutter and printer active in Antwerp, Lyons, Paris, and Rome from 1523 to 1590.

Composed by North Market Street Graphics,
Lancaster, Pennsylvania

Printed and bound by Quebecor Printing, Martinsburg,
Martinsburg, West Virginia

Designed by Cassandra J. Pappas

B
Donen
S

Silverman, Stephen
M.

Dancing on the
ceiling.

$35.00

DATE			

4/9/96

BAKER & TAYLOR